Fundamentals of Software Architecture

Practical guide to building resilient software and high-performance systems

Craig Risi

bpb

www.bpbonline.com

First Edition 2025

Copyright © BPB Publications, India

ISBN: 978-93-65898-118

To View Complete
BPB Publications Catalogue
Scan the QR Code:

Dedicated to

My wife, **Jacqui Risi**

About the Author

A man of many talents, but no sense of how to use them. **Craig Risi** could be out changing the world but would prefer to make software instead. Probably the reason why Nick Fury refused to take his calls. He possesses a passion for software design, but more importantly software quality and designing systems that can achieve this in a technically diverse and constantly evolving tech world.

Craig has over 20 years of experience across the development, testing, and management disciplines in various software industries, but he still feels he learns something new every day. It is the continued change and evolution of the software industry that motivates him to keep learning and finding ways to improve. More than just playing with tech though, it's people that make software come together – and so Craig believes in developing people and empowering them to make a success out of the software they build.

When not playing with software he can often be found spending time with family, writing, designing board games, or running long distances for no apparent reason. He is also a massive fan of comic books and Star Wars, so if you see him concentrating intensely, he is probably just trying to use the force.

Craig is also the writer of several books and writes regular articles on his blog sites and various other tech sites around the world. He is also an international speaker on a wide range of different software development topics, though these experiences only make him even more excited about the future of the industry in South Africa.

About the Reviewer

Kartoue Mady Demdah, Ph.D., is a data scientist at Olameter Inc. with seven years of experience in data science, machine learning, and statistics. He earned his Ph.D. in Mathematics from the *University of Rennes I and the University of Pisa*.

Over the years, he has developed expertise in computer vision, graph neural networks, time series analysis, and **natural language processing (NLP)**. In addition to his Ph.D., he holds a Professional Certificate in Digital Transformation from MIT, covering AI, IoT, cloud computing, blockchain, and cybersecurity. His technical proficiency spans Python, SQL, TensorFlow, PyTorch, AWS, and Azure.

Beyond his technical skills, Kartoue is deeply committed to mentorship and community engagement. He actively participates in AI hackathons, promotes data philanthropy, and shares his expertise to support the growth of the AI community.

Acknowledgement

Thank you for taking the time to purchase this book and hopefully it will give you as much enjoyment into reading it as it did for me in writing it. The role of a software architect is one of continued learning, so no doubt even after reading this one, you will continue reading even more insightful books on different topics and continue to grow on these topics. But, for giving me so much of your time to read this – I do appreciate it.

Special thanks also go out to BPB Publications for the support and incredible editing that makes my writing come across a lot better than it really is.

This book would not have been possible without the many people in my career who have helped me understand many of the concepts in this book more clearly. So, I want to thank those many unnamed mentors, managers and colleagues who have worked with me over the years and helped me to learn many different aspects of software architecture and software development.

However, most importantly - to my loving wife – who has sacrificed the time with me in helping me put this book together. Without her support, writing this book would not have been possible and she has been the backbone in my career that has helped me to thrive. I am incredibly grateful to have someone who supports me the way she does.

Preface

This book is for all people in the software space keen to know a little bit more about what software architects do, and their importance in the software development life-cycle. The book looks at both the technical aspects of software architecture and the softer side of skills to present a well-rounded view of all the crucial skills required for people to become software architects.

The book does not require in-depth technical knowledge to be of value, though there will be some technical models and patterns discussed and why they are effective, so a basic understanding of software principles is required.

This book lays out the fundamentals of what software architecture is, what skills are required to be a skilled software architect, and some of the best practices to follow for companies to leverage software architecture the most in their companies. Too many companies place too little emphasis on the importance of proper architectural design in their software processes and through this book, we hope to teach the reader about its importance and how proper software design can have a marked improvement on the resultant developed software.

Below is an outline of all the chapters:

Chapter 1: Defining Software Architecture - This foundational chapter lays the groundwork for understanding the significance of software architecture. In this chapter, we explain why software architecture is so important to the overall development process of the software, look at the different high-level attributes of design that matter, and briefly explain the consequence of poor software architecture to further explain the importance of the practice.

Chapter 2: The Role of a Software Architect - In this chapter, we delve into the multifaceted role of a software architect, outlining key responsibilities and expectations. We explore the pivotal relationship between architects and development teams, emphasizing effective communication and collaboration for successful project outcomes. The chapter delves into the architect's crucial role in aligning technical decisions with overarching business goals, and how their choices can significantly impact the organization.

Chapter 3: Architectural Properties - This chapter looks at the different properties that form the foundation of good architectural design and represent all the things architects need to consider in order to design effective applications that meet the needs of performance, maintainability and long-term resilience.

Chapter 4: The Importance of Modularity - Before we look at the different architectural styles and patterns, we will take some time to look at modularity in software design and why it is important to be aware of these different principles and to build modularity into all aspects of software design. This means ensuring each module has well-defined responsibilities and interacts with other modules through well-defined interfaces.

Chapter 5: Architectural Styles - In this chapter we talk about what makes an architectural style versus the different patterns that exist. For each style, we will break down how it works, look at the different benefits it offers, and what type of applications it would be best for.

Chapter 6: Architectural Patterns - In this chapter we dive into more detail of the different architectural patterns that can be considered, shedding light on their distinct characteristics and applications. The chapter navigates through practical examples to illustrate the decision-making process when choosing patterns, looking at the different pros and cons of each pattern and when they might be best applied in different situations.

Chapter 7: Component Architecture - After looking at architectural patterns, it is important to now delve into software components and how they also play a role in software architecture, but at a smaller level. This includes component identification and the breaking down of a system into modular and reusable elements. We will also have a look at concepts of coupling and cohesion and look at the interdependence and internal unity of components that impact system design.

Chapter 8: Architecting for Performance - This chapter provides an insightful examination of assessing software patterns for performance and designing components to operate optimally. It begins by exploring methodologies for measuring the performance of code, offering a comprehensive overview of tools and techniques used to gauge efficiency and identify potential bottlenecks.

Chapter 9: Architecting for Security - This chapter underscores the paramount importance of security in software architecture, unraveling its critical role in safeguarding systems from evolving threats. Delving into secure design patterns, the chapter explores tried-and-true methodologies for integrating security into the very fabric of software architecture. Moreover, the chapter emphasizes the significance of secure coding practices, guiding developers in crafting robust, resilient code. Through an exploration of secure coding principles, readers learn to implement defensive coding techniques that stand as a formidable line of defense against malicious exploits.

Chapter 10: Design and Presentation - This chapter looks at design principles that create robust and scalable software systems. It delves into the foundations of design thinking in software architecture, emphasizing a holistic approach that aligns technological decisions with user needs and business objectives. Readers are guided through a spectrum of design principles, exploring concepts such as modularity, reusability, and scalability, essential for crafting architectures that stand the test of time.

The chapter takes a closer look at best practices for the presentation layer, focusing on creating user interfaces that are intuitive, responsive, and user-friendly. Through real-world examples, readers gain practical insights into optimizing the user experience while adhering to design principles.

Chapter 11: Evolutionary Architecture - This chapter delves into the core principles of Evolutionary Architecture, emphasizing the importance of flexibility and adaptability. This chapter will be split up into sections of why change is necessary, some architectural strategies for dealing with change, and how teams can best update and evolve their design without interfering with system operation or incurring high levels of redevelopment costs.

Technically, this will look at designing for independence and isolation, a look at modular design principles but then also how best to navigate and handle tech debt in teams and apply them technically. A significant portion of the chapter is dedicated to continuous integration in supporting evolving architectures. Readers learn how automated integration processes can streamline development workflows, enabling architects to implement changes smoothly while maintaining system integrity.

Chapter 12: Soft Skills for Software Architects - No architect can thrive no their technical skills alone and needs to work with development teams, various product stakeholders, clients and other architects to build an effective software solution. That is why there is a chapter set aside to look at soft skills that are critical for architects to master to be able to effectively lead others and teams toward executing a successful strategy.

In this chapter, we will start looking at the core principles of an architect's role which require them to take a leadership role in companies, and then unpacking specific skills that will help them to fulfil this leadership need effectively.

Chapter 13: Writing Technical Requirements - Writing technical requirements for architects is a critical aspect of the project planning process. By carefully defining the functional, performance, and design criteria, architects can ensure that their designs meet the needs of stakeholders while adhering to industry standards and regulations. Effective communication and documentation are essential for maintaining clarity and facilitating collaboration throughout the project lifecycle.

Chapter 14: Development Practices - Software is built by development teams and so it is important in this book that we make an effort to discuss development practices and have a detailed understanding of the different development practices across the software industry and the impact they have on delivery in different ways, This is vital so that software architects can work with the various engineering teams on the correct methodologies and practices that will suit their vision for the software.

Through this chapter, we will look at different at how different Agile, DevOps, and CI/CD methodologies influence architectural decisions, and provide strategies for architects to thrive in this dynamic environment.

Chapter 15: Architecture as Engineering - This chapter explores the invaluable contributions of architecture to the broader field of software engineering. In this chapter, readers will gain a holistic understanding of architecture's role in shaping software engineering practices in a company and ensuring the success of complex projects.

This chapter is important because architects need to align in how software design and ensure they design software that allows for the software engineering processes discussed in the previous chapter. This includes looking at different design techniques that can help teams achieve repeatable results and lasting success - largely built on the foundation of a design that works effectively across the team and its skillsets

Importantly this chapter will also discuss metrics. Metrics provides architects with the ability to quantitatively assess and improve the quality of their designs. Readers learn how to leverage metrics to evaluate performance, maintainability, and other crucial aspects, enabling informed decision-making throughout the software development lifecycle.

Chapter 16: Testing in Software Architecture - This chapter focuses on the critical aspect of ensuring testability in software architecture, illuminating the importance of building systems that are robustly and effectively testable. The chapter delves into unit testing for architectural components, providing architects with a nuanced understanding of how to design and implement tests for individual components.

This chapter serves as a comprehensive guide for architects, offering practical strategies and insights to embed testability into software architecture, ensuring the reliability and quality of the final product.

Chapter 17: Current and Future Trends in Software - The chapter focuses on emerging technologies in software architecture, from blockchain to edge computing, AI and ML and providing architects with a forward-looking perspective on how these innovations might influence architectural decision-making. We will also discuss how AI/ML can inform and enhance architectural choices, from automated decision support to predictive analytics, through data-driven design techniques.

Anticipating and adapting to industry changes is a critical aspect of software architecture and so thus cater will also have a look at tips that architects can leverage to be better prepared for these industry changes and how to identify and adapt to them quicker.

Chapter 18: Synthesizing Architectural Principles - In this chapter we revisit the core themes that have underscored each chapter, emphasizing the interconnectedness of architectural decisions with project success, business impact, and user satisfaction. The importance of adaptability and agility in the face of evolving technologies and industry landscapes becomes evident, as architects are not just designers but strategic navigators steering organizations toward success.

The concluding chapter serves as a call to action, encouraging architects to continually refine their craft and embrace lifelong learning as the speed of software innovation continues to rapidly escalate and makes the role of software architecture and design increasingly more critical.

Code Bundle and Coloured Images

Please follow the link to download the
Code Bundle and the *Coloured Images* of the book:

https://rebrand.ly/tzhaooe

The code bundle for the book is also hosted on GitHub at
https://github.com/bpbpublications/Fundamentals-of-Software-Architecture.
In case there's an update to the code, it will be updated on the existing GitHub repository.

We have code bundles from our rich catalogue of books and videos available at
https://github.com/bpbpublications. Check them out!

Errata

We take immense pride in our work at BPB Publications and follow best practices to ensure the accuracy of our content to provide with an indulging reading experience to our subscribers. Our readers are our mirrors, and we use their inputs to reflect and improve upon human errors, if any, that may have occurred during the publishing processes involved. To let us maintain the quality and help us reach out to any readers who might be having difficulties due to any unforeseen errors, please write to us at :

errata@bpbonline.com

Your support, suggestions and feedbacks are highly appreciated by the BPB Publications' Family.

Did you know that BPB offers eBook versions of every book published, with PDF and ePub files available? You can upgrade to the eBook version at www.bpbonline. com and as a print book customer, you are entitled to a discount on the eBook copy. Get in touch with us at :

business@bpbonline.com for more details.

At **www.bpbonline.com**, you can also read a collection of free technical articles, sign up for a range of free newsletters, and receive exclusive discounts and offers on BPB books and eBooks.

Piracy

If you come across any illegal copies of our works in any form on the internet, we would be grateful if you would provide us with the location address or website name. Please contact us at **business@bpbonline.com** with a link to the material.

If you are interested in becoming an author

If there is a topic that you have expertise in, and you are interested in either writing or contributing to a book, please visit **www.bpbonline.com**. We have worked with thousands of developers and tech professionals, just like you, to help them share their insights with the global tech community. You can make a general application, apply for a specific hot topic that we are recruiting an author for, or submit your own idea.

Reviews

Please leave a review. Once you have read and used this book, why not leave a review on the site that you purchased it from? Potential readers can then see and use your unbiased opinion to make purchase decisions. We at BPB can understand what you think about our products, and our authors can see your feedback on their book. Thank you!

For more information about BPB, please visit **www.bpbonline.com**.

Join our book's Discord space

Join the book's Discord Workspace for Latest updates, Offers, Tech happenings around the world, New Release and Sessions with the Authors:

https://discord.bpbonline.com

Table of Contents

Prologue

Once upon a time, in the bustling kingdom of Codeburg, there lived a group of talented engineers and developers who toiled day and night to build magnificent software structures that would stand the test of time. Amidst the lines of code and the hum of servers, there emerged a figure known as the Software Architect, a wise and visionary leader with the ability to shape the very foundations of the digital realm.

In the heart of Codeburg, there was a great castle known as The Repository, where the kingdom's most critical software projects were guarded. The Software Architect, a seasoned guardian of The Repository, was tasked with designing the blueprint for these projects, ensuring they were robust, scalable, and adaptable to the ever-changing winds of technology.

As the sun rose over Codeburg, casting its light upon the kingdom, the Software Architect embarked on a quest to understand the needs of the kingdom's citizens: developers, project managers, and even the elusive users. With a map of requirements in hand, the architect set out to build structures that not only met the immediate demands but also anticipated the challenges that lay ahead.

On this journey, the Software Architect encountered various challenges: dragons of technical debt, treacherous swamps of conflicting requirements, and the labyrinthine maze of legacy code. Yet, armed with the sword of architectural patterns and the shield of modular design, our protagonist persevered.

Architectural patterns were like spells in the architect's magical repertoire, enabling the creation of robust fortresses against bugs and vulnerabilities. Each line of code was carefully woven into the fabric of the architecture, forming a tapestry that told the story of both the present and the future.

In the kingdom of Codeburg, collaboration was key, and the Software Architect became a maestro orchestrating the symphony of developers. Meetings were not mere gatherings but strategic councils, where decisions were made with foresight, and everyone had a role to play in the grand design.

As the Software Architect's influence spread, so did the understanding of the importance of testability. Testing became an integral part of the architecture, ensuring that every component could withstand the fires of scrutiny. The architect, like a vigilant sentinel, introduced continuous integration and continuous delivery, forging a path where changes were seamless, and the kingdom's software evolved with grace.

The tale of the Software Architect in Codeburg became legendary. The kingdom prospered, and the architects who followed in the footsteps of their predecessors continued to build upon the legacy, adapting to new technologies and challenges.

And so, the story goes on in Codeburg, where the Software Architect remains a guardian of innovation, a weaver of digital dreams, and a beacon of wisdom in the ever-expanding landscape of software architecture.

Okay, this story above sounds more like a childhood fairy tale than an explanation of what software architecture entails, but I felt it was a fitting introduction because I think that software architecture is often not given the right importance in the software world. As a result, the idea of what a software architect does can oftentimes feel like the stuff of fantasy than what actually occurs in the average company.

I have seen it many times when companies end up suffering under the weight of incorrectly architected applications, either stuck with software that is not performant, is buggy, or is expensive to operate and maintain. These companies will then put pressure on engineering teams to try and fix the issues and turn things around while trying to deliver more features at an increasing pace, rather than revisiting their design. This leads to frustrated teams and excessive maintenance that makes the software delivery more expensive than it needs to be. Something which can be fine for many large organizations, but has killed off far too many start-ups.

Which is one of the reasons why I feel this book is so important. While most companies have software architects and rely heavily on their software architecture roadmap for their development delivery, their role is often not prioritized. Architects are often not empowered enough. Giving decision-making to managers and CTOs, who may not be skilled enough in this department, leads to them making decisions on the strategy of the company. These decisions are based on what they feel is best for the business and not necessarily based on what is right for the software solution, leaving the software and its resultant delivery in a mess. All because proper software architectural procedures were not followed, and the company likely did not listen.

The hope is that by empowering more people to understand the critical role that software architecture plays in the software delivery process, we can increase awareness across engineering teams. As more engineers grasp its importance, we can begin to see teams and companies place greater emphasis on proper software design. This, in turn, will empower architects to take the lead in driving technical decision-making within companies.

During this book, we will frequently revisit our world of *Codeburg* to explain aspects of software architecture more plainly, but we will also spend many chapters delving into technical topics that explain some architectural terms in more detail.

So, whether you come from a technical background or are new to the world of software architecture, you will hopefully be able to take something away from this book.

CHAPTER 1

Defining Software Architecture

Introduction

Upon reading the prologue of the book, you must have understood that software architecture is important and should not exist in the world of fairy tales—what is software architecture, and what does it entail?

Software architecture refers to the high-level structuring of a software system, which involves making key design decisions to ensure that the system's components work cohesively to meet the specified requirements. It encompasses various elements, such as the organization of software components, the interaction patterns among them, and the guidelines governing their design and evolution.

While other roles in the software development process are involved in the creation of specific functions, algorithms, and executable code that make the software work, the software architect is more concerned with how everything will fit together and focuses on the bigger structure of the software applications. They are also concerned about how the various components should fit together, and not just the code that will achieve the end result.

This does not mean that the software architect is not concerned with the code or involved in the coding process. A successful software architect needs to be very familiar with the coding patterns and style. They need to achieve their overall vision for the software in development and be capable enough to review and take accountability that the delivered code meets their purposes. At a high level, a software architect is focused on the various aspects of software design, which we will be discussing in the chapter ahead.

Structure

In this chapter, we will discuss the following topics:

- Structural elements
- Architectural patterns and styles
- Architectural decision making
- Architecture in software development lifecycle

Objectives

By the end of this chapter, you will be able to understand the role of software architecture in the software development landscape and how it fits across all other processes. This chapter sets the basis for topics that we will discuss in later chapters.

Structural elements

These are different types of software components that are required to work together to create a final cohesive application or user experience. We will look at each of these aspects in more detail in *Chapter 7, Architectural Components*:

- **Components:** The modular building blocks of a system that encapsulate specific functionalities.
- **Connectors**: The mechanisms that enable communication and interaction between components (for example, APIs, messaging protocols).
- **Data**: The way information is stored, accessed, and managed within the system.

Architectural patterns and styles

Patterns represent bigger design processes that are followed across an application's design. They help us understand how certain structural elements fit together and provide a cohesive flow of data and information between the different structural elements. The following are some important attributes that need to be considered in software architecture:

- **Design patterns**: Reusable solutions for common design problems that help in creating flexible and maintainable software.
- **Architectural styles**: High-level patterns that define the overall organization and structure of a system (for example, client-server, microservices, monolithic).

- **Quality attributes**: Software architecture focuses not just on trying to solve for the existing functional purposes of an application, but also needs to keep in mind various quality aspects to ensure the software meets the long-term needs.

  We will unpack some of these important quality attributes in *Chapter 3, Architectural Properties*.

  Some high-level considerations in this area are outlined as follows:

  - **Performance**: How well the system responds to user inputs and handles load.

  - **Scalability**: The system's ability to grow and handle increased demand.

  - **Reliability**: The system's ability to consistently perform as expected under various conditions.

  - **Maintainability**: How easily the system can be updated, extended, or modified.

  - **Security**: Measures taken to protect the system against unauthorized access and data breaches.

- **Design principles**: Along with building the bigger patterns in how applications work, it is also important for software architecture to focus on important design principles that ensure the software can meet the quality attributes design.

  The following is an example of two different design principles, though we will unpack these in more detail in later chapters on architectural styles and architectural patterns:

  - **SOLID principles**: A set of five design principles for writing maintainable and scalable software.

  - **Separation of Concerns**: Dividing a software system into distinct sections, each addressing a different concern. This is something we will unpack further in *Chapter 4, The Importance of Modularity*, when we speak about design modularity.

- **Service-oriented architecture (SOA)**: Designing software as a set of loosely coupled, independently deployable services.

- **Microservices**: Breaking down a system into small, independent services that can be developed, deployed, and scaled independently.

Architectural decision making

Often when designing software, you will come across times when there is no one best approach to design your application or part of an application. Architects will then be required to make trade-offs and identify the best way forward. Also, they need to ensure that their reasons are properly documented so that they are understood and defended should concerns arise later in the application lifecycle.

The following are some critical things in architecture that need to be considered in the decision-making process:

- **Purpose of the architected decisions**:

  The role of the chosen software architecture should be clear. It should support the core functional purpose of the application and system. If a software architecture cannot support the business reason for a system functioning, then it is likely not going to work as a viable solution.

- **Balancing innovation and functionality with budgetary requirements**:

  Software architecture does not just solve a technical problem but also needs to work within the budgetary constraints of the business and how it can enable a software system to be designed in a way that meets the budgetary requirements of a business. Where possible, the constraints are factored into the decision-making process.

- **Selection criteria**:

  Identify the key factors that form a part of the assessment and the eventual reasons behind the chosen selection.

- **Trade-offs**:

  Choosing between conflicting architectural goals based on project constraints. The architect will often need to play a critical role in balancing different delivery and technical needs and be a key decision maker in identifying the way forward for the software development team.

- **What needs to be built versus what needs to be integrated**:

  Not all solutions might require development, and often, there may be other third-party solutions that can solve a problem. Software architecture will need to define the strategy behind which parts of a business a company can look to outsource versus what should be built itself.

- **Standards and compliance factors**:

  The compliance and software standards that directed the final outcome of the architectural decision, along with the development standards that may be required to ensure its successful deployment.

- **Ownership**:

  Software architecture defines both the technical structure of how an application should be built, but also a clearly defined structure of who owns it within an organization so that future decisions on its design, operation and, maintenance can be easily conducted.

- **Decision documentation**:

  Recording and communicating the rationale behind architectural decisions. It might be a role that is natural for many architects, but being able to document and clearly envision the software design and the reason for certain decisions plays an important role in ensuring it can be executed correctly.

- **Testing and continuous integration/continuous deployment (CI/CD)**:

  Software does not just need to be designed according to how it will function, but also how it should be tested. It is important for software architects to consider this important aspect in their design and ensure that the software produced can allow for quick and easy testing, can be effectively mocked and automated, and takes into consideration the CI needs of the software delivery process.

  We will look at various aspects of software testability throughout this book, wherever it applies, and unpack the software testing required in *Chapter 15, Architecture as Engineering*, where we have devoted an entire chapter to software testing.

- **Testability**:

  Designing the system in a way that makes it easy to test its components in isolation and as a whole.

- **CI/CD practices**:

  Implementing processes for automated testing and CI/CD to ensure a streamlined and reliable software delivery pipeline.

- **Success criteria**:

  How do we know a chosen system design is successful and meets the long-term needs of an application? Software architecture should define this metric and how it should be measured to allow for continued evaluation.

In essence, software architecture provides a blueprint for creating software systems that are not only functional but also scalable, maintainable, and adaptable to change. It involves making strategic decisions that guide the development process and influence the system's overall behavior and characteristics.

Through this book, we will unpack these different facets and how they fit into the software delivery process.

Architecture in software development lifecycle

It is difficult to explain software architecture without also explaining where it fits into the software development process. While we can herald the software architect as a lone figure who is designing the overall structure of any given set of software components and applications, the reality is that the software architect forms a part of a bigger team required to deliver a software system. As such, it is important to understand how and where the process of architecture fits into the broader life cycle of a software system.

Let us revisit our story of Codeburg:

Now in Codeburg, there was a software architect named Serena who found herself at the heart of a grand **software development life cycle (SDLC)** adventure. Codeburg was known for its vibrant coding communities, where developers, testers, and project managers collaborated to bring digital dreams to life. But they were not so sure how architecture will play a role in all this.

Serena, a seasoned architect with a keen eye for design and a knack for balancing technical prowess with soft skills, embarked on a journey to shepherd a revolutionary project through the intricate SDLC process.

Act 1: The visionary blueprint

In the initiation phase, Serena donned her visionary hat. She met with stakeholders, listened to their aspirations, and deciphered the intricate tapestry of requirements. With a stroke of creativity, she crafted the architectural vision, outlining the system's structure, components, and the seamless flow of user experiences. This vision would be the guiding star for the entire project.

Act 2: Foundation of design

As the project moved into the design phase, Serena's architectural acumen took center stage. She collaborated with development teams, sketching out the blueprint into detailed design documents. Her role resembled that of an orchestra conductor, harmonizing various components and ensuring that the design aligned with the project's goals. The team looked up to Serena for guidance, and her designs became the solid foundation upon which the code would dance.

Act 3: Agile collaboration

When the coding phase unfolded, Serena transitioned into an Agile maestro. She embraced iterative development, working closely with developers, addressing concerns, and adapting the architecture to evolving requirements. Serena's leadership and collaboration skills shone as she facilitated daily stand-ups, sprint planning, and provided valuable insights that guided the development orchestra towards the project's crescendo.

Act 4: Guardianship of quality

Quality assurance was paramount in Serena's role during the testing phase. She championed automated testing practices, ensuring that the architecture's integrity remained intact. Serena worked hand-in-hand with the testing team, validating that each component fit seamlessly into the grand design. Her attention to detail prevented architectural regressions and guaranteed a robust final product.

Act 5: Deployment choreography

When the time for deployment arrived, Serena's role transformed into that of a choreographer. She orchestrated the deployment process, ensuring a smooth transition from development to production. Serena collaborated with operations teams to set up infrastructure, implemented CI/CD pipelines, and mitigated any deployment hiccups, ensuring the grand finale was flawless.

Act 6: Post-launch symphony

Even after the project's release, Serena's involvement persisted. She monitored the system's performance, gathering insights from real-world usage. Feedback from users and stakeholders was invaluable, guiding Serena in fine-tuning the architecture for future enhancements. Her post-launch reflections contributed to a continuous improvement cycle, ensuring that Codeburg's digital kingdom remained cutting-edge.

Serena's leadership, technical expertise, and ability to navigate the intricacies of the software development journey set a standard for aspiring architects in the realm. In the end, the project's success was not just a triumph for Serena but a testament to the crucial role played by a software architect in the magical world of Codeburg's SDLC.

Now we can learn from Serena's story that Software architecture plays a crucial role throughout the entire SDLC, influencing decisions and outcomes at every stage.

Regardless of the SDLC in operation at an organization, whether Waterfall, Agile, or DevOps, architecture should be included in every facet to bring the full software design to realization.

It is not just about laying a blueprint for how applications should be designed but also keeping an eye on the development process to identify if it is maintainable and testable enough. It is also important to review the implementation to ensure it is done correctly. Also, look into the deployment and post-implementation support to ensure the design meets the required expectations.

Essentially, software architecture is not just *design once and the job is done* but rather a process of continual improvement and refinement to better align software to the needs of both its technical operation and business purpose.

Here is a breakdown of the role architecture plays in the different phases of the SDLC:

- **Requirements analysis and planning**:
  - o **Identification of architectural requirements**: Understanding the high-level needs of the system and mapping them to architectural considerations.
  - o **Risk mitigation**: Identifying potential risks early and proposing architectural strategies to mitigate them.

- **Design and specification**:
  - o **High-level design**: Defining the overall structure, components, and their interactions to meet the functional and non-functional requirements.
  - o **Guidance for developers**: Providing a roadmap for development teams, ensuring consistency and alignment with the overall system architecture.
  - o **Modifiability and scalability**: Designing for ease of modification and scalability based on anticipated future needs.

- **Development**:
  - o **Coding guidelines**: Enforcing coding standards and best practices to ensure that the implemented code aligns with the architectural design.
  - o **Communication and collaboration**: Facilitating communication among development teams by providing a shared understanding of the system's architecture.

- **Testing**:
  - o **Functional testing**: Ensuring that the architecture supports effective testing strategies, including unit testing, integration testing, and system testing.
  - o **Non-functional testing**: Evaluating the system's security, scalability, and performance against architectural expectations and requirements.

- **Deployment**:
  - o **Scalability and reliability**: Ensuring that the architecture supports the deployment of the system to various environments while maintaining scalability and reliability.
  - o **Deployment planning**: Guiding the deployment process to minimize downtime and ensure a smooth transition from development to production.

- **Operations and maintenance**:
  - o **Ease of maintenance**: Designing for maintainability, making it easier for teams to troubleshoot, fix bugs, and implement updates.

- o **Monitoring and optimization**: Supporting the implementation of monitoring tools and practices to optimize the system's performance and address issues proactively.

- **Evolution and adaptation**:

  - o **Flexibility for change**: Providing a foundation that allows the system to evolve and adapt to changing requirements and technologies.

  - o **Architectural decision records**: Documenting architectural decisions to guide future updates and modifications.

- **Communication and documentation**:

  - o **Communication tool**: Acting as a communication tool for stakeholders, ensuring a shared understanding of the system's structure and behavior.

  - o **Documentation**: Providing a reference point for developers, architects, and other stakeholders to understand the rationale behind architectural decisions.

- **Cost-efficiency**:

  - o **Efficient design**: When evaluating architectural patterns, it is the architect's job to be aware of different costing factors and design a solution that is cost effective on operation, while meeting the needs of scale. This is especially relevant in the cloud space, where costs can grow rapidly when software is not correctly designed.

  - o **Resource allocation**: Helping in optimal resource allocation by identifying critical areas that require more attention and resources.

Conclusion

In summary, software architecture is not a one-time activity but an ongoing process that permeates the entire software development lifecycle. Its importance lies in providing a strategic framework, aligning development efforts, and ensuring the creation of software systems that meet both current and future needs efficiently and effectively.

The architect plays a role throughout the life cycle of an application, from conceptualizing how the software should be built. As part of the delivery, providing guidance and ensuring the expected design can be achieved (or issues are successfully mitigated). And in monitoring the operation of the application and making updates and improvements along the way, along with ensuring it is successfully maintained so that it can continue to perform its required functions.

In the next chapter, we will understand the role of a software architect in more detail, along with the technical details of software architecture in the following chapters.

Join our book's Discord space

Join the book's Discord Workspace for Latest updates, Offers, Tech happenings around the world, New Release and Sessions with the Authors:

https://discord.bpbonline.com

## CHAPTER 2

The Role of a Software Architect

Introduction

To begin our journey of understanding software architecture, it is important to understand the role that a software architect plays in an organization. In this chapter, we will explain the vital tasks and responsibilities that an architect will play in an organization and how they should interact with development teams in fulfilling these responsibilities. Further, we will look at the different types of software architects often found in many large organizations.

Structure

In this chapter, we will discuss the following topics:

- Re-visiting Codeburg
- Epilogue: Architect's triumph
- Key aspects of the software architect's role
- Relationship with development teams
- Types of software architects in an enterprise

Objectives

By the end of this chapter, you will understand the tasks and responsibilities of a software architect, learn how they interact with different members of a development team, and become familiar with the various types of software architects within an organization.

Re-visiting Codeburg

Now that we know what software architecture is, we need to understand what exactly software architects do and what role they should fulfill in an organization. Let us revisit *Codeburg* to get a better idea of this, returning once again to our heroic *Serena*.

Act 7: The quest for scalability

A new project emerged on the horizon, one that demanded unprecedented scalability. Serena, with her architectural foresight, jumped into the challenge. She became a scaling sorceress, crafting an architecture that could gracefully grow with the kingdom's expanding digital populace. Her meticulous design ensured that the system could handle the influx of users without crumbling under the weight of its success.

Act 8: Battling complexity monsters

As the project's complexity grew, Serena faced formidable complexity monsters that lurked in the shadows of intricate requirements. Undeterred, she wielded the sword of simplicity, slaying these monsters with elegant and streamlined architectural patterns. Serena's ability to untangle the most intricate webs of complexity earned her the title of Codeburg's Complexity Slayer.

Act 9: Security enchantment

A dark cloud of cybersecurity threats loomed over Codeburg. Serena, donning the armor of security consciousness, embarked on a quest to fortify the kingdom's digital walls. She implemented encryption spells, safeguarded sensitive data, and established secure communication channels.

Serena's dedication to cybersecurity turned her into Codeburg's Guardian against the forces of digital darkness.

Act 10: Resilience in the face of bugs

In the midst of the development battles, an army of bugs threatened to disrupt the peace. *Serena, the Bug Battler,* led her team with resilience. She implemented robust error-handling mechanisms, conducted thorough debugging campaigns, and instilled a culture of quality throughout Codeburg. Serena's commitment to bug-slaying became a legend, inspiring developers across the kingdom.

Act 11: Time-traveling architect

A unique project called for a visionary approach. Serena, the time-traveling architect, gazed into the future of technology. She envisioned upcoming trends and prepared Codeburg's architecture for the challenges that lay ahead. Serena's time-traveling insights transformed her into a beacon of innovation, ensuring that Codeburg's digital realm remained ahead of its time.

Act 12: Architectural wisdom

As Serena's heroic journey continued, her wisdom became legendary. She shared her architectural knowledge through mentorship, guiding the next generation of architects in Codeburg. Serena's legacy extended beyond the lines of code; it became a tapestry of architectural wisdom woven into the very fabric of the kingdom's digital legacy.

Epilogue: Architect's triumph

Serena's heroic saga culminated in a triumph that echoed across Codeburg. The projects she touched flourished, and the kingdom's digital landscape thrived under the influence of her architectural prowess. Serena's attributes—foresight, simplicity, security, resilience, and innovation had not only shaped the destiny of Codeburg's software but also elevated the role of software architect to new heights.

In the end, Serena stood as a revered figure in the digital annals of Codeburg, a symbol of how a software architect, armed with the right attributes, could turn every line of code into a magical enchantment, weaving dreams into the very fabric of the kingdom's digital destiny. Thus, the heroic tale of Serena, the software architect, became a timeless legend in the ever-evolving kingdom of Codeburg.

The aforementioned story might be incredibly embellished and fantastical in terms of what an architect actually does, but it does explain some of the important attributes required to be an architect—strong technical skills, the ability to break down complexity, resilience, and vision to design software for future needs and not just current demands.

The intention here is not to portray a software architect as the sole hero in this story because the reality is that it takes many people to make any software project a success.

The role of a software architect in a company is multifaceted and involves a combination of technical expertise, strategic thinking, and effective communication.

Key aspects of the software architect's role

The following are some key aspects of the software architect's role:

- **System design and planning:**
  - o **Architectural design**: Define the high-level structure and organization of software systems, making decisions on components, modules, and their interactions.
  - o **Scalability and performance planning**: Plan for system scalability and performance to meet the current and future demands.

- **Technology selection:**
  - o **Evaluate technologies**: Stay updated on emerging technologies and assess their suitability for the company's projects.
  - o **Tool and framework selection**: Choose appropriate tools and frameworks that align with the architectural vision.

- **Guidance to development teams:**
  - o **Provide technical leadership**: Offer guidance to development teams on architectural best practices and principles.
  - o **Code review**: Participate in, or lead code reviews to ensure that the implemented code adheres to the architectural design and coding standards.

- **Risk management:**
  - o **Identify and mitigate risks**: Anticipate potential risks related to the software architecture and develop strategies to mitigate them.
  - o **Trade-off analysis**: Make informed decisions on trade-offs between conflicting requirements. An architect should focus just as much on why certain approaches should not be followed as on why certain design approaches should be considered. Understanding the trade-offs between different design approaches helps to make an informed decision, while also allowing certain deficiencies with a chosen design model to be better mitigated.

- **Communication with stakeholders:**
  - o **Collaborate with stakeholders**: Work closely with product and project managers and other stakeholders to understand requirements and constraints.
  - o **Presentations and documentation**: Communicate the architectural vision through presentations, documentation, and other means to ensure a shared understanding among stakeholders.

- **Quality assurance:**
  - o **Ensure quality attributes**: Focus on non-functional requirements such as reliability, maintainability, and security.
  - o **Testing strategies**: Collaborate with testing teams to ensure that the architecture supports effective testing strategies.

- **Continuous improvement:**
  - o **Adaptation to industry trends**: Stay abreast of industry trends and evolving best practices and adapt the architectural approach accordingly.

- o **Feedback loop**: Establish a feedback loop to learn from past projects and continuously improve architectural practices.

- **Project management support:**

  - o **Estimation**: Provide insights into the complexity and technical challenges associated with the proposed architecture to assist in project estimation.

  - o **Milestone planning**: Contribute to project planning by defining architectural milestones and deliverables.

- **Security considerations:**

  - o **Security architecture**: Integrate security considerations into the architectural design to safeguard against potential threats.

  - o **Compliance**: Ensure that the software architecture complies with industry standards and regulations.

- **Capacity planning:**

  - o Architects collaborate with infrastructure and operations teams to plan resource allocation and capacity based on the architectural design. While this is not something they should take responsibility for, it is important that the skills required to execute the architectural design are considered and managed from a people perspective.

- **Mentorship and training:**

  - o **Knowledge transfer**: Mentor junior developers and share architectural knowledge within the team.

  - o **Training programs**: Contribute to training programs to enhance the team's understanding of architectural concepts and principles.

In essence, the software architect serves as a bridge between business needs and technical solutions, contributing to the success of projects by providing a solid and adaptable architectural foundation. This role requires a blend of technical acumen, leadership skills, and the ability to navigate complex challenges in the ever-evolving landscape of software development.

Relationship with development teams

We understand the role that architects play in the SDLC process, but how does that translate when they need to work directly with teams? The following list explores how architects can ensure a good relationship with development teams:

- **Interaction with other teams:** A successful interaction between software architects and development teams involves effective communication, guidance, and collaboration throughout the software development lifecycle. Architects should engage with development teams from the early stages of a project, working closely with developers to understand their perspectives and challenges.

- **Effective communication:** Clear and open communication channels ensure developers comprehend the architectural vision, design decisions, and overall goals. Architects should provide guidance on best practices, coding standards, and the rationale behind architectural choices.

- **Regular code reviews:** Regular code reviews, led or participated in by the architect, offer opportunities to align the implemented code with the architectural design, fostering consistency and quality. Moreover, architects should empower developers by involving them in decision-making processes, encouraging a sense of ownership and responsibility for the software's success. An architect should ensure there is continuous collaboration with the team, regular knowledge-sharing sessions, and mentoring between different members in place. All of these activities contribute to a dynamic and innovative development environment where the architect serves as a facilitator of learning and growth.

- **Feedback and collaboration:** Architects should be receptive to feedback from developers, adapting architectural strategies based on real-world implementation challenges and experiences. This collaborative and inclusive approach ensures that the software architecture is not only well-conceived but also successfully translated into robust and maintainable code by the development team.

- **Business impact**: Software architects have a profound impact on the overall business by aligning technical decisions with strategic goals, contributing to organizational success, and ensuring that technology solutions meet business objectives.

- **Strategic alignment**: Software architects work closely with business stakeholders to understand organizational objectives and align technical strategies with these goals. This ensures that technology investments directly contribute to business success.

- **Cost-efficiency and resource optimization**: Architects contribute to efficient resource allocation by making informed decisions about technology choices, minimizing unnecessary expenses, and optimizing infrastructure and development efforts.

- **Risk management**: By identifying and mitigating technical risks early in the software development process, architects contribute to project success and reduce the likelihood of costly issues later.

- **Efficient development**: Well-designed architectures, guided by software architects, facilitate faster development cycles and shorter time-to-market, allowing the business to respond quickly to market demands and changes in customer preferences. A successful architect does not design a system without considering the development impact on the implementation teams.

- **Business agility**: Architects design systems that are scalable and adaptable, enabling the business to grow and respond to changing market conditions without the need for extensive redesign or redevelopment. It is important for architects to align closely with their business counterparts to understand how the software can help achieve this agility.

- **Innovative solutions**: Software architects contribute to innovation by evaluating emerging technologies and proposing solutions that can give the business a competitive advantage. They ensure that the technology foundation supports the organization's unique selling propositions while also exploring new solutions to ensure the software can deliver on future demands.

- **Reliability and performance**: Architects focus on non-functional requirements, such as reliability and performance, ensuring that software systems meet or exceed customer expectations. This contributes to customer satisfaction and loyalty.

- **Regulatory compliance**: Architects address security and regulatory compliance concerns, safeguarding the business against legal and financial risks associated with data breaches or non-compliance. It is important to be aware of the different legal and compliance needs that a system needs to adhere to (especially around various global data and privacy laws) and ensure a system design conforms to these.

- **Maintenance and support**: Architects design systems with maintainability in mind, reducing the total cost of ownership by making it easier and more cost-effective to maintain, troubleshoot, and support applications over time.

- **Technology roadmap**: Architects contribute to the development of a strategic technology roadmap, ensuring that the business invests in technologies that are aligned with long-term objectives and industry trends.

- **Team collaboration**: Collaboration with cross-functional teams is essential for architects. By working closely with various departments, architects ensure that technology solutions support not only development needs but also those of operations, marketing, sales, and other business units.

Types of software architects in an enterprise

We have discussed everything that a software architect does, but in the enterprise landscape, there may be various forms of software architects who specialize in specific things within the organization. With complexity in the software space only growing, the list of architects focuses on specific aspects of design, and business only continues to grow. So, while not exhaustive, the following are some of the roles that you may typically find in a large organization that requires architects to focus on a wide variety of different things.

- **Enterprise architect**: Enterprise architects focus on the overall architecture of an organization's IT systems and how they align with business objectives. They develop strategies, standards, and guidelines for the organization's technology infrastructure, applications, and data management. Enterprise architects often work closely with business stakeholders to ensure IT initiatives support business goals.

- **Solution architect**: Solution architects design and oversee the implementation of specific solutions or systems within an organization. They analyze business requirements, assess technology options, and develop architectural designs that meet the needs of the project. Solution architects often work with development teams to ensure the architecture is implemented correctly and meets quality standards.

- **Software architect**: Software architects focus on the architecture of individual software applications or systems. They design the overall structure of the software, including components, modules, interfaces, and interactions. Software architects make decisions about technologies, frameworks, and patterns to use, and they often provide technical guidance and leadership to development teams.

- **Infrastructure architect**: Infrastructure architects focus on designing the underlying infrastructure and systems that support software applications. They design and plan networks, servers, storage, and other IT infrastructure components to ensure scalability, reliability, and performance. Infrastructure architects may also be involved in cloud computing, virtualization, and disaster recovery planning.

- **Data architect**: Data architects focus on the design and management of an organization's data assets. They develop data models, database schemas, and data integration strategies to ensure that data is organized, accessible, and secure. Data architects may work closely with business analysts, data scientists, and developers to implement data-driven solutions.

- **Security architect**: Security architects focus on designing and implementing security measures to protect an organization's IT systems, data, and assets. They assess security risks, develop security policies and procedures, and design security controls to mitigate threats and vulnerabilities. Security architects may specialize in areas such as network security, application security, or cloud security.

- **Integration architect**: Integration architects focus on designing and implementing solutions to integrate disparate systems, applications, and data sources within an organization. They develop integration architectures, message formats, and protocols to ensure seamless communication and data exchange between systems. Integration architects may also work with external partners or vendors to integrate third-party systems.

- **Quality/Automation architect**: Quality and automation architects tend to focus on looking at software design from a testability perspective. They ensure that software meets the needs of the various testing teams and design the automation frameworks that will be used to execute the automated tests that check the system.

- **Performance architect**: Performance architects specialize in optimizing the solution design and ensuring the software design meets the various performance, load, soak, and stress needs of the environment. The performance architect designs both the frameworks that help to test these different aspects of performance and is an expert in identifying the bottlenecks in the design that may inhibit the software from achieving these targets, and helping teams to optimize code efficiencies in the system.

- **UI/UX architect**: UI/UX architects focus on the design and user experience of software applications. They develop user interface designs, interaction patterns, and usability guidelines to ensure that software applications are intuitive, efficient, and user-friendly. UI/UX architects may also conduct user research, usability testing, and prototyping to validate design decisions.

Although each of these roles may have a specific focus, the nature of the role and the design principles they need to consider remain the same. So, even though each aspect of software architecture can become quite specialized, the principles shared in this book will remain relevant to all of them, and so this book serves as a strong foundation regardless of specialization.

Conclusion

In summary, software architects serve as strategic enablers, influencing the overall success of the business by providing technical leadership, mitigating risks, optimizing resources, and ensuring that technology solutions align with and contribute to the broader business objectives. Their impact extends beyond the codebase to shape the organization's ability to innovate, adapt, and thrive in a competitive landscape.

A successful architect can engage with respective business and development teams to build alignment in achieving the delivery of design systems.

We will discuss some of the soft skills that software architects can develop to help achieve this in a later chapter. However, understanding the role architects play in the development process will prepare them for the technical discussions in the next chapters.

Join our book's Discord space

Join the book's Discord Workspace for Latest updates, Offers, Tech happenings around the world, New Release and Sessions with the Authors:

https://discord.bpbonline.com

CHAPTER 3
Architectural Properties

Introduction

Software architecture requires designing often extremely complex systems that help achieve a specific outcome. While it can be easy to focus primarily on the functional objective that needs to be achieved, it is important that software architects also consider various properties in their designs to ensure that the software delivers beyond this scope.

In this chapter, we will unpack important properties of software development that software architects need to be aware of to achieve the best level of architectural design.

It is important to note that in this chapter, we will mostly describe the different properties that architects need to be aware of. In later chapters, we will unpack how we use some of these properties to decide the correct architectural approach.

Structure

In this chapter, we will discuss the following topics:

- Performance
- Reliability
- Security
- Maintainability

- Flexibility
- Accessibility
- Interoperability
- Portability

Objectives

The purpose of this chapter is to guide the reader through the various properties that must be considered in architectural design. A clear understanding of these properties equips a software architect to effectively design solutions that address a broad range of requirements. Crucially, it is essential for architects to comprehend the potential trade-offs between these properties and understand how focusing on one aspect can impact others.

With a comprehensive grasp of these properties, a software architect should be able to identify which are most critical for their specific project and make informed decisions about the necessary trade-offs. This ensures a balanced approach, aiming to satisfy as many architectural requirements as possible.

Performance

The following section explores performance, encompassing throughput, latency, and scalability, which determine the overall responsiveness, capacity, and adaptability of the system.

Throughput

Throughput represents the amount of data or information that passes through a software system. It can be further divided into four categories, as follows:

- **Data processing rate**: Throughput often refers to how quickly a system can process data. This could be measured in various units, such as bytes per second, transactions per second, requests per minute, etc. For example, in a database system, throughput might refer to the number of queries it can execute per second.

- **Network throughput**: In networking, throughput typically describes the amount of data transferred successfully over a network in a given time period. It is often measured in **bits per second (bps)**, **kilobits per second (kbps)**, or **megabits per second (Mbps)**. Higher throughput indicates faster data transfer rates.

- **Parallel processing**: Throughput can also refer to the amount of work done by a parallel processing system in a given time. This includes systems that utilize parallelism to execute tasks concurrently, such as multi-threaded applications or distributed computing systems. This is also especially relevant in many data streaming or cloud functions that require operation at the same time.

- **Input/output (I/O) throughput:** I/O throughput measures the rate at which a system can read from or write to storage devices, such as hard drives, **solid-state drives (SSDs)**, or in modern cloud terms, the speed at which data can also transfer to the chosen form of cloud storage. It is critical for assessing the performance of storage systems and ensuring efficient data access.

Latency

Latency refers to the time it takes for a system to respond to a request or to complete a task. Unlike throughput, which measures the rate of processing, latency focuses on the delay or lag experienced during task execution. Latency can significantly impact a system's responsiveness and perceived performance.

The following is a breakdown of latency in software terms:

- **Response time:** Latency is often synonymous with response time, which is the time it takes for a system to respond to a user's request. This could include the time taken for a web server to generate and return a web page in response to an HTTP request or the time taken for a database to process a query and return results.

- **Network latency:** In networking, latency refers to the time it takes for data to travel from the source to the destination over a network. It includes factors such as propagation delay (time taken for signals to travel through the medium) and transmission delay (time taken to transmit data over the network).

- **I/O latency:** Similar to I/O throughput, I/O latency focuses on the delay experienced during input/output operations, such as reading from or writing to storage devices. High I/O latency can result in slow data access and affect the overall performance of applications that rely heavily on disk I/O.

- **Processing latency:** This refers to the time it takes for a system to process a task or operation internally. It includes the time taken for CPU processing, memory access, and any other computational tasks. Optimizing processing latency often involves improving algorithm efficiency and system architecture.

Scalability

Scalability is a system's ability to handle increasing workloads or resource growth while maintaining or improving performance. It is a critical consideration for designing and building software systems that can adapt to changing demands efficiently.

Scalability can come in the following forms:

- **Vertical scalability:** This involves increasing the capacity of a single resource within a system, such as upgrading the CPU, memory, or storage of a server. However, vertical scalability often has limits and can become expensive or impractical beyond a certain point.

- **Horizontal scalability**: Also known as scale-out scalability, this involves adding more instances of resources, such as servers or nodes, to distribute the workload across multiple machines. Horizontal scalability typically offers better scalability potential and can handle larger workloads by adding more resources in a distributed manner.

- **Load balancing**: In horizontally scalable systems, load balancing techniques are used to distribute incoming requests or tasks evenly across multiple resources to prevent overload on any single node and utilize resources efficiently.

- **Database scalability**: Scaling databases can be particularly challenging due to their central role in many applications. Techniques such as sharding (partitioning data across multiple database instances), replication (creating copies of data across multiple nodes), and caching are commonly used to improve database scalability.

- **Elasticity**: Elasticity refers to the ability of a system to automatically provision and de-provision resources based on demand. Cloud computing platforms often provide elasticity features, allowing applications to scale up or down dynamically in response to workload changes.

Reliability

The following properties relate to software reliability and are important architectural properties to consider when making software more reliable:

- **Fault tolerance**: Fault tolerance refers to a system's ability to continue operating properly in the event of a failure or fault within one or more of its components. It involves designing systems to withstand and recover from failures gracefully, ensuring continuous operation and minimal disruption to users.

- **Redundancy**: Fault-tolerant systems often incorporate redundancy at various levels to mitigate the impact of failures. This could include hardware redundancy (for example, using RAID arrays for disk redundancy), software redundancy (for example, deploying redundant services or components), or data redundancy (for example, replicating data across multiple nodes).

- **Failover**: Failover mechanisms are used to automatically switch to backup resources or components when a failure is detected. This could involve redirecting traffic to redundant servers, activating standby database instances, or promoting replica nodes to primary status in distributed systems.

- **Replication**: Replicating data, services, or components across multiple nodes or locations helps ensure availability and resilience against failures. Replication can be synchronous (where updates are propagated immediately to all replicas) or asynchronous (where updates are propagated periodically).

- **Health monitoring**: Fault-tolerant systems continuously monitor the health and status of components to detect failures or anomalies early. Health monitoring mechanisms can include heartbeat signals, health checks, and performance metrics monitoring.

- **Isolation**: Isolating components or services from each other can prevent failures from propagating across the system. Techniques such as containerization (for example, Docker and Kubernetes), serverless functions, and microservices architecture help isolate services and minimize the blast radius of failures.

- **Graceful degradation**: Systems should degrade gracefully under high load or failure conditions rather than experiencing catastrophic failures. This could involve shedding non-critical workloads, throttling requests, or providing degraded functionality to maintain essential services.

Availability

Availability refers to the proportion of time that a system is operational and accessible for use. It measures reliability and indicates how consistently a system can deliver its services to users without interruption or downtime.

Basic aspects of availability include the following:

- **Uptime**: Availability is often expressed as a percentage representing the ratio of time a system is operational (up) to the total time (up + downtime). For example, a system with 99.9% availability is operational for 99.9% of the time and may experience only a few hours of downtime per year.

- **Redundancy and failover**: Redundancy and failover mechanisms are crucial for improving availability by providing backup resources or components to take over when primary resources fail. This could involve deploying redundant servers, using load balancers to distribute traffic across multiple instances, or implementing automatic failover mechanisms.

- **Fault tolerance**: Fault-tolerant systems are designed to minimize downtime and ensure continuous operation in the face of failures or faults. By incorporating redundancy, failover mechanisms, and other fault tolerance techniques, systems can maintain high availability even when individual components fail.

- **Monitoring and alerting**: Continuous monitoring of system health, performance, and availability is essential for detecting issues early and responding promptly to prevent or minimize downtime. Monitoring tools and alerting mechanisms can notify administrators of potential problems, allowing them to take corrective actions proactively.

- **Performance optimization**: Performance optimization plays a role in availability by ensuring that systems can handle expected workloads efficiently without becoming overwhelmed. Scaling resources, optimizing code, and tuning configurations can help maintain high availability under varying load conditions.

- **Disaster recovery**: Implementing disaster recovery strategies, such as data backups, offsite replication, and recovery procedures, is essential for ensuring availability in the event of catastrophic failures or disasters. These measures help restore operations quickly and minimize the impact of downtime.

Security

Software security involves safeguarding software systems and applications from malicious attacks, vulnerabilities, and data breaches. It encompasses a range of strategies such as secure coding practices, encryption, access controls, vulnerability testing, and regular security updates. The goal is to ensure the confidentiality, integrity, and availability of software by protecting it against unauthorized access, misuse, and modification, ultimately minimizing risks and potential damages to both the system and its users.

Authentication

Authentication is the process of verifying the identity of a user or system entity, typically before granting access to resources or services. It is a fundamental aspect of security and access control in software systems, ensuring that only authorized individuals or entities can perform specific actions or access protected information.

The following are aspects that software architects use to build authentication into their different software systems:

- **Credentials**: Authentication typically involves validating the credentials provided by a user, such as a username and password, digital certificate, API token, or biometric data (for example, fingerprint or facial recognition). The system compares these credentials against stored records to verify the user's identity.

  o **Authentication factors**: Authentication can be based on one or more factors, including:

    ▪ **Knowledge factors**: Something the user knows (for example, password, PIN).

    ▪ **Possession factors**: Something the user has (for example, smart card, mobile device).

    ▪ **Inherence factors**: Something inherent to the user (for example, fingerprint, retina).

    ▪ **Location factors**: Where the user is accessing the system from (for example, IP address, geolocation).

- **Multi-factor authentication (MFA)**: MFA enhances security by requiring users to provide multiple authentication factors to access a system or service. For example, combining a password (knowledge factor) with a one-time code sent to the user's mobile device (possession factor) significantly reduces the risk of unauthorized access.

- **Authentication protocols and standards**: Various authentication protocols and standards are used in software systems to facilitate secure authentication, including:

  - **OAuth**: A widely used authorization framework for granting access to resources. It is important to research and look into if you are considering developing or integrating an authentication system.

  - **OpenID connect**: An identity layer built on OAuth 2.0 provides authentication and user identity information.

  - **Lightweight Directory Access Protocol (LDAP)**: A protocol used for accessing and managing directory information services, often used for centralized authentication in organizations.

  - **Security Assertion Markup Language (SAML)**: An XML-based framework for exchanging authentication and authorization data between parties.

  - **JSON web tokens (JWT)**: A compact, URL-safe means of representing claims to be transferred between two parties, often used for authentication and authorization.

- **Session management**: Once a user is authenticated, the system typically creates a session to maintain the user's authenticated state. Session management involves securely managing session tokens, expiring inactive sessions, and protecting against session hijacking or fixation attacks.

- **Authorization**: While authentication verifies users' identities, authorization determines what actions or resources they are allowed to access after being authenticated. Authentication and authorization work together to control access to system resources based on user identity and permissions.

Authorization

Authorization is the process of determining and controlling what a user or system can do once their identity has been authenticated. It involves setting rules and permissions that dictate the actions users are permitted to perform, the resources they can access, and the data they are allowed to modify. Authorization ensures that users only have access to the data and functionality they need, preventing unauthorized activities and helping maintain system security.

- **Authentication vs. authorization:**

  While authorization is related to authentication, it differs in the following ways:

  - *Authentication* confirms the user's identity (e.g., using passwords or biometrics).

  - *Authorization* defines what actions or resources the authenticated user is allowed to access.

- **Types of authorization models:**

  - **Role-based access control (RBAC):**

    - Users are assigned roles, and each role has a set of predefined permissions.

    - **Example**: A *Manager* role may have access to employee records, while a *Staff* role may have limited access.

  - **Attribute-based access control (ABAC):**

    - Access is granted based on a combination of user attributes (e.g., department, job title), resource attributes, and environmental factors (e.g., time of day, device used).

    - **Example**: A user might be allowed access to sensitive data only during working hours from a company device.

  - **Discretionary access control (DAC):**

    - Resource owners have the discretion to set access permissions for their resources.

    - **Example**: A file owner may decide who can read or write the file.

  - **Mandatory access control (MAC):**

    - Access is regulated by a central authority based on security labels and policies, often used in highly secure systems like government agencies.

- **Authorization techniques:**

  - **Access control lists (ACLs)**: Lists specifying what actions individual users or groups can perform on a particular resource (e.g., read, write, execute).

  - **Policy-based authorization**: Access control policies define rules for granting permissions, typically used in complex environments where rules are based on various factors (e.g., ABAC).

  - **OAuth and OpenID Connect**: Protocols used in modern web applications to manage third-party access without exposing credentials, allowing limited access to certain resources.

- **Importance of authorization:**
  - Prevents data breaches by limiting access to sensitive information.
  - Reduces the risk of privilege escalation, where users might gain unauthorized access to restricted resources.
  - Ensures compliance with data protection laws and industry standards (e.g., GDPR, HIPAA).
  - Enhances overall system security by enforcing the principle of least privilege, ensuring users have only the permissions they need to perform their jobs.

Data encryption

Data encryption refers to transforming plaintext (unencrypted) data into ciphertext (encrypted) data using cryptographic algorithms. Encryption is a fundamental technique for protecting sensitive information from unauthorized access or interception by unauthorized parties.

The following are some of the different forms of encryption that it is important for architects to know about:

- **Encryption algorithms**: Encryption algorithms are mathematical functions used to transform plaintext data into ciphertext and vice versa. Common encryption algorithms include:
  - **Symmetric encryption**: Uses a single key for both encryption and decryption. Examples include **Advanced Encryption Standard (AES)** and **Data Encryption Standard (DES)**.
  - **Asymmetric encryption**: Uses a pair of public and private keys, where data encrypted with one key can only be decrypted with the other key. Examples include **Rivest-Shamir-Adleman (RSA)** and **Elliptic Curve Cryptography (ECC)**.
- **Key management**: Effective encryption requires secure management of encryption keys, including generation, storage, distribution, rotation, and revocation. Key management systems help ensure the confidentiality and integrity of encryption keys, protecting them from unauthorized access or disclosure.
- **Data at rest encryption**: Encrypting data at rest involves encrypting data stored on storage devices, such as hard drives, databases, or cloud storage. This protects data from unauthorized access if the storage device is stolen or compromised.
- **Data in transit encryption**: Encrypting data in transit involves encrypting data as it travels over networks, such as the Internet or internal networks. **Transport Layer Security (TLS)** and its predecessor, **Secure Sockets Layer (SSL)**, are commonly used protocols for securing communication channels and encrypting data in transit.

- **End-to-end encryption (E2EE)**: E2EE ensures that data is encrypted from the sender's device all the way to the recipient's device, with decryption only possible by the intended recipient. This prevents intermediaries, including service providers, from accessing plaintext data.

- **Data integrity**: Encryption not only protects data confidentiality but also ensures data integrity by detecting unauthorized modifications or tampering. Cryptographic hash functions, such as **Secure Hash Algorithm-256 (SHA-256)**, are used to generate fixed-size hash values that uniquely represent the contents of data.

- **Compliance and regulations**: Many industries and jurisdictions have specific compliance requirements and regulations governing data encryption practices, such as the **Health Insurance Portability and Accountability Act (HIPAA)** in healthcare and the **General Data Protection Regulation (GDPR)** in the European Union or the **Protection of Personal Identification Act (POPIA)** from South Africa.

Maintainability

A software solution should not be designed to solve a problem and be built right, but also needs to factor in maintainability. Unlike most physical structures, software is constantly changing. This requires a software architect to consider the following properties to ensure the final designed solution can be easily modified and improved upon without requiring significant effort or rework.

Modularity

Modularity is the design principle of breaking down a software system into smaller, independent, and interchangeable modules or components. Each module encapsulates a set of related functionalities with well-defined interfaces for interaction with other modules. Modularity promotes reusability, maintainability, and scalability by allowing developers to build, test, and modify individual components without affecting the entire system.

Modularity can be enforced in software through the following ways:

- **Encapsulation**: Modules encapsulate their internal details, hiding implementation details from other modules and providing well-defined interfaces for interaction. This helps reduce complexity and dependencies, allowing modules to be developed, tested, and maintained independently.

- **Abstraction**: Modularity encourages abstraction, where complex functionalities are abstracted into simpler, higher-level interfaces. Abstraction hides unnecessary details and exposes only relevant information, making modules easier to understand and use.

- **Reusability**: Modular design promotes code reuse by allowing modules to be reused in different parts of the system or other projects. Reusable modules save development time and effort and help maintain consistency across projects.

- **Scalability**: Modular architectures facilitate scalability by allowing systems to be easily extended or modified to accommodate changing requirements or increased workloads. New functionalities can be added by developing and integrating new modules without redesigning the entire system.

- **Dependency management**: Modularity helps manage dependencies between different parts of the system by explicitly defining dependencies between modules. This allows developers to understand and control the dependencies, making it easier to maintain and update the system.

Testability

Testability refers to the ease with which software components, systems, or applications can be tested to verify their correctness, functionality, and performance. A highly testable software design facilitates the creation and execution of tests, enabling developers to identify and fix defects, validate requirements, and ensure software quality throughout the development lifecycle.

While we unpack this in more detail in *Chapter 10, Design and Presentation,* the following are some high-level aspects of testable software design:

- **Modularity and separation of concerns**: Testable software designs often embrace modularity and separation of concerns, breaking down complex systems into smaller, independent units or modules. Modularity isolates functionality within modules, making it easier to write focused tests and validate individual components in isolation.

- **Clear and well-defined interfaces**: Testable software exposes clear and well-defined interfaces for interacting with its components, allowing developers to write tests that simulate inputs, outputs, and interactions with the system. Well-designed interfaces promote encapsulation, abstraction, and decoupling, facilitating test creation and maintenance.

- **Dependency injection and inversion of control: Dependency injection (DI)** and **inversion of control (IoC)** patterns promote testability by decoupling components and their dependencies, making it easier to substitute dependencies with mock objects or test doubles during testing. DI and IoC enable developers to control dependencies, isolate components, and write unit tests with minimal external dependencies.

- **Mocking and stubbing**: Testable software often leverages mocking and stubbing frameworks to create lightweight, controllable substitutes for dependencies, such as external services, databases, or APIs. Mock objects simulate the behavior of real dependencies, enabling developers to isolate and test components independently of external systems.

- **Automated testing support**: Testable software is designed with automated testing in mind, providing support for writing, executing, and managing automated tests efficiently. This includes integration with testing frameworks, assertion libraries, and **continuous integration (CI)** pipelines, enabling automated regression testing, code coverage analysis, and test result reporting.

- **Isolation and determinism**: Testable software ensures that tests are isolated and deterministic, meaning they produce consistent and predictable results across different test runs and environments. Isolation prevents tests from interfering with each other, while determinism ensures reproducibility and reliability of test outcomes.

- **Instrumentation and debugging support**: Testable software may include instrumentation and debugging features to assist developers in diagnosing and troubleshooting issues during testing. Logging, tracing, and profiling capabilities provide visibility into test execution and help identify performance bottlenecks, resource leaks, or unexpected behaviors.

Documentation

Documentation is the practice of creating and maintaining comprehensive records of a software system's design, implementation, and usage. Effective documentation serves as a guide for developers, testers, and other stakeholders, promoting easier understanding, collaboration, and maintenance of the system. It reduces complexity by capturing essential details and ensuring that team members can follow and extend the work over time. Proper documentation plays a critical role in improving software maintainability, helping teams reduce technical debt, and enhancing overall productivity.

Documentation can enhance software maintainability through the following ways:

- **Clarity and transparency**: Good documentation makes the system's architecture, components, and processes clear to all team members. It provides a roadmap for understanding how different parts of the system work, reducing confusion and minimizing the learning curve for new team members. Clear documentation also helps developers quickly grasp the intent and scope of various features and modules.

- **Standardization**: By documenting code style, design patterns, and best practices, teams can ensure consistency across the project. This makes it easier for multiple developers to contribute to the system without introducing disjointed coding styles or architectural practices. Standardized documentation ensures alignment across different teams working on the same project.

- **Knowledge transfer**: Documentation captures institutional knowledge that may otherwise be lost when team members leave or move to other projects. Well-maintained documentation allows knowledge to be easily passed between team members, reducing reliance on individuals and ensuring continuity of understanding even when staff turnover occurs.

- **Error prevention and debugging**: Comprehensive documentation helps developers avoid repeating mistakes by clearly outlining past decisions, design rationales, and known issues. During debugging or enhancement, developers can refer to documentation to understand previous problem-solving approaches, facilitating quicker issue resolution.

- **Version control and updates**: Continuous updating of documentation ensures that it remains aligned with the current system. As the software evolves, so should the documentation. This ensures that developers always work with up-to-date information, preventing the confusion that outdated or incomplete documentation can cause.

- **Accessibility and collaboration**: Documentation provides a shared resource for teams, promoting collaboration by making knowledge easily accessible to everyone. This facilitates better communication across departments, such as development, quality assurance, and product management. Having documentation central to the process helps break down silos and encourages cross-functional teamwork.

Flexibility

Flexibility is the ability of a software system or component to adapt and evolve in response to changing requirements, environments, or user needs. A flexible software design enables developers to make modifications, enhancements, or extensions to the software without significant effort or disruption to existing functionality. Flexibility is essential for accommodating evolving business needs, technology advancements, and user preferences over time.

The following is a breakdown of ways flexibility can be achieved in software design, many of which we will go through in the next chapter:

- **Modularity and loose coupling**: Flexible software designs embrace modularity and loose coupling, breaking down complex systems into smaller, independent modules or components. Modularity isolates functionality within modules, allowing developers to modify or replace individual components without affecting the entire system. Loose coupling reduces dependencies between components, making it easier to extend or replace parts of the system without impacting others.

- **Abstraction and encapsulation**: Flexibility is promoted through abstraction and encapsulation, where complex implementation details are hidden behind well-defined interfaces and abstractions. Abstraction allows developers to interact with components at a higher level of granularity, while encapsulation protects internal details from external manipulation, enabling changes to be made without affecting other parts of the system.

- **Configuration and parameterization**: Flexible software systems often provide configuration options or parameters that allow users or administrators to customize behavior, settings, or preferences without modifying the underlying code. Configuration files, settings dialogs, or API parameters enable users to tailor the software to their specific needs without requiring code changes.

- **Extension points and hooks**: Flexible software architectures incorporate extension points or hooks that enable developers to add custom functionality or plugins to the system. Extension points define well-defined interfaces or integration points where additional features can be seamlessly integrated without modifying the core codebase. Plugins or extensions enhance the functionality of the software and allow users to extend its capabilities according to their requirements.

- **Dynamic behavior and runtime adaptability**: Flexible software designs support dynamic behavior and runtime adaptability, allowing systems to adjust their behavior or configurations dynamically based on changing conditions or user interactions. Runtime configuration changes, feature toggles, or runtime polymorphism enable software to adapt to evolving requirements or environments without downtime or recompilation.

- **Open standards and interoperability**: Flexible software solutions adhere to open standards and interoperability protocols, enabling seamless integration with external systems, tools, or services. Open standards promote compatibility, interoperability, and vendor neutrality, allowing software to work effectively in diverse environments and ecosystems.

Accessibility

Accessibility refers to the design and implementation of software systems and user interfaces that can be easily accessed and used by individuals with disabilities. This includes considerations for users with visual, auditory, motor, cognitive, or other impairments, ensuring they can perceive, understand, navigate, and interact with software applications effectively.

This is often primarily part of a software's UI design, which users will primarily interact with, but many other backend interactions can also help to provide accessibility to a software system, which are listed as follows:

- **User interface (UI) design**: Accessible UI design involves creating user interfaces that are perceivable, operable, understandable, and robust for users with disabilities. This includes considerations, such as:

  o Providing alternative text for images to assist users with visual impairments.

- o Ensuring sufficient color contrast for users with low vision.

- o Offering keyboard navigation options for users who cannot use a mouse.

- o Using descriptive labels and instructions to aid users in understanding interface elements.

- o Avoiding reliance on time-based interactions that may be challenging for some users.

- **Screen reader compatibility**: Screen readers are assistive technologies used by individuals with visual impairments to navigate and interact with software applications. Ensuring compatibility with screen readers involves:

  - o Using semantic HTML markup to provide meaningful structure and context.

  - o Adding **Accessible Rich Internet Applications (ARIA)** attributes to enhance accessibility for dynamic web content.

  - o Testing applications with screen readers to identify and address accessibility issues.

- **Captioning and transcripts**: Providing captions for audio content and transcripts for video content ensures accessibility for users who are deaf or hard of hearing. This includes:

  - o Adding closed captions to videos to provide synchronized text descriptions of spoken dialogue and sound effects.

  - o Offering transcripts for audio content to provide a text-based alternative for users who cannot hear audio.

- **Accessible documentation and help resources**: Documentation and help resources should be accessible to users with disabilities. This includes:

  - o Providing documentation in multiple formats, such as HTML, PDF, and plain text.

  - o Ensuring that documentation is well-organized, searchable, and navigable using assistive technologies.

  - o Offering alternative formats or assistance for users who cannot access documentation independently.

Interoperability

Interoperability refers to the ability of different systems, applications, or components to seamlessly exchange and use data or services with each other. It enables disparate systems to work together effectively, facilitating communication, data sharing, and collaboration across heterogeneous environments.

The following form of interoperability should be considered in the design of a software system:

- **Data interoperability**: This involves the ability of systems to exchange and interpret data formats and structures in a consistent and meaningful way. Data interoperability ensures that information can be shared and understood across different systems, regardless of the underlying technologies or platforms.

- **Service interoperability**: **Service-oriented architectures** (**SOA**) and web services enable interoperability by providing standardized protocols and interfaces for accessing and invoking services. This allows systems to communicate and interact with each other over networks, enabling seamless integration and collaboration.

- **Protocol interoperability**: Interoperability often relies on standardized communication protocols and **application programming interfaces** (**APIs**) that define how systems can interact with each other. Common protocols and APIs facilitate interoperability by providing a common language and set of rules for communication.

- **Platform interoperability**: Platform interoperability refers to the ability of systems running on different platforms or operating systems to work together seamlessly. This includes cross-platform compatibility, where applications developed for one platform can run on another platform without modification.

- **Standards compliance**: Interoperability is often achieved through adherence to industry standards and specifications. Standards bodies, such as the **World Wide Web Consortium** (**W3C**) and the **Internet Engineering Task Force** (**IETF**), define standards for data formats, communication protocols, and APIs to promote interoperability across systems and technologies.

- **Middleware and integration technologies**: Middleware and integration technologies play a crucial role in achieving interoperability by providing tools and frameworks for connecting disparate systems. Examples include message brokers, **enterprise service buses** (**ESBs**), and integration platforms facilitating data transformation, routing, and orchestration.

- **Semantic interoperability**: Semantic interoperability ensures that systems can understand and interpret the meaning of exchanged data consistently and unambiguously. This often requires using ontologies, vocabularies, and semantic standards to establish shared meaning and semantics across systems.

Portability

Portability refers to the ability of software applications, components, or systems to be easily transferred or adapted for use in different environments, platforms, or operating systems without modification or with minimal effort. A portable software solution can run effectively across diverse computing environments, offering flexibility, ease of deployment, and reduced dependency on specific hardware or software configurations.

Portability comes in the following forms:

- **Cross-platform compatibility**: Portable software is designed to be compatible with multiple platforms, including different operating systems (for example, Windows, macOS, Linux), hardware architectures (for example, x86, ARM), and runtime environments (for example, Java Virtual Machine, .NET Common Language Runtime). Cross-platform compatibility enables software to reach a broader audience and increases its usability across different devices and environments.

- **Platform-independent dependencies**: Portable software minimizes dependencies on platform-specific libraries, APIs, or hardware features that could limit its compatibility with other platforms. Instead, it relies on standard, platform-independent libraries, programming languages, or runtime environments to ensure consistent behavior across different environments.

- **Standardized file formats and protocols**: Portable software often uses standardized file formats, data interchange formats, or communication protocols to facilitate interoperability and data exchange with other systems. Standardization ensures that software can communicate and exchange data effectively with external systems or tools, regardless of their underlying technologies or implementations.

- **Dynamic linking and runtime environments**: Portable software may use dynamic linking or runtime environments to manage dependencies and runtime configurations dynamically. Dynamic linking allows software to link to required libraries at runtime, reducing the need for static compilation and enabling flexibility in deployment. Runtime environments, such as **Java Runtime Environment** (JRE) or .NET Framework, provide a consistent execution environment for software across different platforms.

- **Virtualization and containerization**: Virtualization and containerization technologies, such as **virtual machines** (**VMs**) and container platforms (for example, Docker), can enhance portability by encapsulating software and its dependencies into isolated, self-contained units. Virtualized or containerized applications can run consistently across different host systems without modification, simplifying deployment and management.

- **Adherence to standards and best practices**: Portable software adheres to industry standards, best practices, and design principles for achieving cross-platform compatibility and portability. This includes following established coding conventions, avoiding platform-specific APIs or features, and using portable programming languages or frameworks.

Conclusion

Software architects must become very familiar with all these different properties and how they can be achieved and implemented in their software designs. When these basic tenets are followed through the software design process, it will ensure that the system can deliver successfully for any organization, both in achieving its purpose and in being able to operate, maintain, and update efficiently.

Now, understanding these different properties and how to implement them effectively is not an easy task. In the following chapters, we will look at various patterns, components, and styles in software architecture and how they can help architects achieve these properties in their designs.

In the next chapter, we will look at software modularity and the importance that this plays in good software design.

Join our book's Discord space

Join the book's Discord Workspace for Latest updates, Offers, Tech happenings around the world, New Release and Sessions with the Authors:

https://discord.bpbonline.com

CHAPTER 4
The Importance of Modularity

Introduction

As much as software architecture is about designing systems that need to interconnect with each other, it is also critical that software architects understand the importance of modularity and all software components working in isolation.

The purpose of modularity is essentially about bringing simplicity into the overall software design. The more complex a system is, the more difficult it becomes to achieve the different architectural properties defined in the previous chapter.

And whereas a software system might need to remain complex in its entirety to perform its required operation (especially big financial systems), the design can be simplified by introducing modularity into all aspects of the software design.

Structure

In this chapter, we will discuss the following topics:

- Importance of modularity
- Testing
- Removing the legacy factor

- Error isolation
- Interoperability

Objectives

Given the critical role of modularity in contemporary software design, it is essential for software architects to master the strategies that enable it. This chapter will elucidate the significance of modularity in the design process and guide the reader through the key design principles that facilitate achieving it effectively.

Importance of modularity

Let us start by explaining modularity's importance to the world of software architecture by once again revisiting the world of Codeburg and shining the light on another talented architect named *Elara*:

In Codeburg, many people believed software architecture was not just a profession; it was an art form. One of those was Elara, and like any artist, Elara understood the importance of modularity, a concept she had learned from her mentor, the wise old coder named *Master Byte*.

One day, as Elara was working on a new project, she encountered a fellow programmer named Jax who scoffed at the idea of modularity. *Why waste time breaking things down into tiny pieces?* Jax argued. *Just write it all in one massive block of code. It's faster that way!*

But Elara shook her head, gently explaining, *Modularity is not about speed, Jax. It's about clarity, flexibility, and scalability. By breaking our code into modular components, we can easily debug, maintain, and expand our programs.*

Jax shrugged, dismissing her words, and went on his way, leaving Elara to her work. Undeterred, she continued to build her project with meticulous attention to modularity, crafting each module with care and precision.

As weeks passed, both Elara and Jax completed their projects. Elara's code was elegant and easy to understand, while Jax's code was a tangled mess of complexity. When the time came to make updates and fixes, Elara's modular design allowed her to make changes swiftly and without error. But Jax struggled to untangle the web of his own making, spending countless hours trying to decipher his own code.

In the end, Elara's project was praised for its efficiency and reliability, earning her the respect of her peers and the admiration of Master Byte. Jax, on the other hand, learned a valuable lesson about the importance of modularity the hard way, vowing to approach his future projects with a newfound appreciation for clarity and organization.

Modularity might be one of the principal properties of software architecture discussed in the previous chapter. Still, it is so important to modern software design that the author decided to give it an entire chapter that leaves it as part of a bigger chapter.

With software systems only growing in size and complexity over the years and likely to become increasingly more complicated in the future, modularity is one of the most critical design elements allowing software longevity.

Our technological world is constantly evolving, and all this evolution, innovation, and new ideas means that our software needs to be updated, improved, and supported constantly. The ease of making these changes allows teams to keep up with these evolving requirements and ensure the software can not only meet its current functional needs, but future ones too.

The following are some benefits that modularity brings to the software world:

- **Ease of understanding**: Modular code is easier to understand because it is broken down into smaller, more manageable components. Developers can focus on understanding and working with one module at a time rather than trying to comprehend the entire system at once.

- **Ease of maintenance**: When a software system is modular, making changes and updates becomes more straightforward. Developers can modify or replace individual modules without affecting other parts of the system, reducing the risk of introducing bugs and making maintenance tasks more efficient.

- **Reusability**: Modular code is inherently more reusable. Once a module has been developed and tested, it can be reused in other projects with minimal modifications. This saves time and effort, promotes consistency across projects, and reduces the likelihood of errors.

- **Scalability**: Modular systems are easier to scale. As requirements change or the system needs to accommodate larger workloads, additional modules can be added, or existing modules can be modified or replaced, allowing the system to grow flexibly and adaptively.

- **Collaboration**: Modularity facilitates collaboration among developers. Different teams or individuals can work on separate modules simultaneously, reducing dependencies and the likelihood of conflicts. This allows for more efficient development processes, especially in larger projects with distributed teams.

- **Testing**: Modular code is easier to test because modules can be tested independently of each other. This makes identifying and isolating bugs easier, leading to more reliable and robust software.

- **Encapsulation**: Modules encapsulate functionality, hiding implementation details and exposing only the necessary interfaces to interact with other modules. This improves code maintainability, as changes to one module are less likely to have unintended consequences on other system parts.

- **Cost**: Building and running software is expensive. While putting in the extra effort to make software modular might seem like a lot of work and a costly exercise, it makes the software cheaper to operate, and the extra longevity it brings to the overall design of the system makes it far cheaper overall.

Modularity is essential, and any software system that is not modular will likely run into significant issues as its life expands. In fact, a lack of modularity is one of the core reasons why so many big applications are considered legacy today.

Aspects of modularity

The following sub-section discusses some key attributes that architects will need to consider and how they play a part in achieving modularity in the software.

Maintainability

Maintainability is one of the most critical attributes of a well-designed software system. It refers to the ease with which software can be modified, fixed, or enhanced over time. Two essential factors that enhance maintainability are **localized changes** and **clear interfaces**, which are described as follows:

- **Localized changes**

    Localized changes mean that when a change is made to the software, its impact is limited to a specific area or component of the system. The goal is to avoid cascading changes that spread across multiple components, which can make modifications complex and error-prone.

    o **Modular design**: The system is divided into self-contained, independent modules or components. Changes in one module should not affect others unless absolutely necessary.

    o **Separation of concerns**: Each part of the system should handle a distinct responsibility, allowing for changes to be focused on specific areas without unintended side effects.

    o **Encapsulation**: Details of how things work internally in a module are hidden, ensuring that modifications to its internals do not affect the rest of the system as long as the external behavior remains the same.

    o **Benefits**: By ensuring changes are localized, it becomes easier to maintain and evolve the system, which leads to less risk of introducing bugs and reducing overall complexity.

- **Clear interfaces**

    Clear interfaces refer to the design of well-defined, consistent, and easily understandable points of interaction between different components or modules in the software system.

o **Defining contracts**: An interface should act as a contract between components, specifying what is required (inputs) and what is provided (outputs) without revealing the internal workings. This ensures consistency and clarity.

o **Low coupling**: Interfaces should be designed to minimize dependencies between components. The more decoupled the system is, the easier it is to change or replace parts without breaking others.

o **Documentation**: Clear interfaces also mean well-documented public methods and APIs, ensuring that developers understand how to interact with the system. This helps prevent misuse and simplifies future development or maintenance.

o **Consistency**: Maintaining consistent naming conventions, behavior, and structure in the interfaces makes it easier for developers to understand and extend the system without confusion.

Combined impact on maintainability

When **changes are localized** and **interfaces are clear**, maintainability is greatly improved. Developers can work on different parts of the system without worrying about unintended side effects, while clear interfaces help them understand the system better, making future changes easier to implement and less prone to error.

Scalability

Scalability refers to a system's ability to handle increased load, whether it is more data, users, or requests, without compromising performance or stability. The two main approaches to scaling a system are **horizontal scalability** and **vertical scalability**, which are described as follows:

- **Horizontal scalability**

  Horizontal scalability (scaling out) refers to adding more machines or nodes to distribute the workload. Instead of upgrading a single machine, you add additional systems to share the load.

  o **How it works**: In a horizontally scalable architecture, multiple servers work together as part of a distributed system. Each new server takes on a portion of the workload, which can be either user requests, data processing, or storage.

  o **Key characteristics**:

    ▪ **Load balancing**: A load balancer is often used to distribute requests evenly across multiple servers.

- **Stateless architecture**: Often requires the system to be stateless or able to replicate data across different nodes to avoid dependencies on a single server.

- **Fault tolerance**: If one server fails, others can take over, increasing system resilience.

- **Cloud adoption**: Cloud platforms like AWS, Azure, and Google Cloud make horizontal scaling straightforward, with services like auto-scaling that dynamically add or remove instances based on demand.

○ **Examples**:

- Web applications that add more web servers as traffic grows.

- Distributed databases like Cassandra or MongoDB, where data is spread across multiple nodes.

○ **Benefits**:

- Unlimited scalability in theory (as long as you can add more machines).

- Fault tolerance and high availability.

○ **Challenges**:

- Complex system management.

- Network latency as the system grows larger.

- **Vertical scalability (scaling up):**

Vertical scalability means increasing the capacity of a single machine by adding more resources, such as CPU, RAM, or storage. Refer to the following list for the key concepts related to vertical scalability:

○ **How it works**: When a system is vertically scalable, it can handle more workload by upgrading the hardware. This might involve moving to a more powerful server with faster processors, more memory, or larger storage.

○ **Key characteristics**:

- **Single machine**: You enhance a single machine's power rather than adding new ones.

- **Memory-bound and CPU-bound tasks**: Systems with heavy computational tasks or large memory requirements benefit from vertical scaling.

- **Database scaling**: Traditional relational databases (like MySQL or PostgreSQL) are often easier to scale vertically than horizontally.

- o **Examples**:
  - Upgrading a web server to handle more concurrent connections.
  - Adding more RAM to a database server to improve performance.
- o **Benefits**:
  - Simple to implement compared to horizontal scaling.
  - No need for complex distributed systems, making it easier to manage.
- o **Challenges**:
  - Limited by the maximum hardware capacity of the machine.
  - It has a single point of failure, so if the machine fails, the entire system goes down.
  - High-performance hardware can become expensive.

Choosing between horizontal and vertical scalability

The choice between horizontal and vertical scalability depends on several of the following factors:

- **Workload characteristics**: If your system can be distributed (e.g., web applications), horizontal scaling is often preferable. For computationally heavy or database-bound tasks, vertical scaling might be simpler.
- **Growth projections**: Horizontal scaling is more future-proof, especially when considering the potential for massive growth.
- **Cost**: Vertical scaling can be cheaper initially, but it has hard limits, while horizontal scaling offers more flexibility and cost-efficiency at scale.

When to use horizontal scaling:

- Large, distributed systems with a need for high availability.
- Systems that must handle massive amounts of traffic or data (like social media platforms or e-commerce websites).

When to use vertical scaling:

- Systems that require high computational power but are constrained to a single machine, such as specific database or analytics applications.
- Scenarios where simplicity and ease of management are more important than limitless growth.

Reusability

Reusability is a core principle in software design that focuses on developing components or modules that can be used in multiple contexts or applications without modification. The goal is to reduce redundancy, minimize development time, and improve maintainability. Two key aspects that enable reusability are **encapsulation** and **library or component reuse**, described as follows:

- **Encapsulation:**

  Encapsulation is the practice of hiding the internal details and implementation of a module, exposing only what is necessary through well-defined interfaces. It is a fundamental principle of object-oriented programming but also applies to modular and component-based architectures. Refer to the following list for the key concepts related to encapsulation:

  o **How encapsulation enables reusability**:

  - **Abstraction**: Encapsulation allows you to create an abstract view of the module, focusing only on what it does rather than how it does it. By abstracting away implementation details, you can reuse the module in various contexts without needing to understand or modify its internal workings.

  - **Loose coupling**: When modules are encapsulated, dependencies are minimized. This means that changes in one part of the system (e.g., the internals of a module) do not affect other parts, making the module more adaptable to different use cases.

  - **Defined interfaces**: With a clear and stable interface, other components can interact with the module without needing to know its inner workings. This reduces integration complexity and enhances the module's applicability.

  o **Examples**:

  - An encapsulated class for handling database connections that only exposes `connect()`, `disconnect()`, and `executeQuery()` methods. The internal logic of handling the connection pool is hidden, making it easy to use in multiple applications.

  - A UI component library where individual components, like buttons or dropdown menus, are encapsulated and provide consistent behavior and styling across different projects.

  o **Benefits**:

  - Encourages reuse by making components adaptable to various scenarios.

- Reduces the risk of errors during modification since the internal details are hidden.

- **Library or component reuse**

Library or component reuse is the practice of developing generic libraries, components, or modules that can be used across different applications or systems. It involves creating reusable building blocks that serve common functionalities. Refer to the following list for the key concepts related to library or component use:

- **How library or component reuse works**:

    - **Modular design**: Create components with single responsibilities and clear boundaries. Each component should do one thing well and be usable independently.

    - **Parameterization and configurability**: Make components configurable through parameters or options. This way, the same component can be adapted to different requirements without altering the core logic.

    - **Creating reusable libraries**: Libraries (collections of reusable functions, classes, or modules) serve as a centralized point for common utilities like logging, authentication, or data processing, making it easy to integrate these features across projects.

- **Examples**:

    - **Utility libraries**: Libraries like *lodash* for JavaScript or the Apache Commons library for Java provide utility functions that can be reused across various projects to handle string manipulation, collections, or concurrency.

    - **Reusable UI components**: Design systems like *Material UI* or *Bootstrap* offer a set of reusable UI components that can be used to build consistent interfaces across applications.

    - **Microservices or API-based reuse**: A microservice designed to handle payments can be reused across multiple applications in an organization without changes.

- **Benefits**:

    - **Reduced development time**: By reusing existing components, developers can focus on building new features rather than reinventing the wheel.

    - **Consistency**: Reusing components ensures that the same logic or functionality behaves consistently across different parts of the system.

    - **Centralized updates**: When a library or reusable component is updated, all applications using it benefit from improvements or bug fixes.

Best practices for achieving reusability

To make the most of encapsulation and library or component reuse, consider the following:

- **Design with reusability in mind**: During the design phase, identify functionalities that could be reused across different projects and build them as separate components or modules.

- **Document interfaces and usage**: Clearly document how to use each reusable component or library. Good documentation improves adoption and helps other developers understand how to integrate it into their systems.

- **Follow SOLID principles**: The SOLID principles (especially the **Single Responsibility Principle** and **Interface Segregation Principle**) help create more reusable, modular components.

- **Keep components decoupled**: Avoid tight coupling between components to ensure that each can be used independently.

- **Use design patterns**: Patterns like *Factory*, *Adapter*, and *Decorator* are useful for designing reusable components that can adapt to different contexts without changing their core functionality.

By focusing on encapsulation and creating well-defined, reusable libraries or components, software engineers can build more modular, maintainable, and adaptable systems that save time and effort across different projects.

Flexibility and adaptability

In software design, flexibility and adaptability are essential to ensure systems can evolve, integrate new technologies, and respond to changing business needs with minimal disruption. Two crucial concepts that contribute to flexible and adaptable software are **replaceability** and **plug-and-play architecture**, which are described as follows:

- **Replaceability**

    Replaceability refers to the ability to substitute one component, module, or service with another without significantly impacting the rest of the system. Replaceable components are designed to be independent, adhering to a well-defined contract or interface that any alternative implementation can conform to. The following are some key concepts of replaceability:

    o **How replaceability enhances flexibility**:

        ▪ **Loose coupling**: Replaceable components are loosely coupled to the rest of the system. This means that one part can be removed or replaced without necessitating changes in other parts.

        ▪ **Well-defined interfaces**: By defining clear and stable interfaces, you create a contract that allows multiple implementations. As long as the interface contract is maintained, any component adhering to it can be swapped in or out.

- **Version upgrades and substitutions**: Replaceability allows you to upgrade to newer versions or replace parts of the system with improved or more modern alternatives, such as swapping out a relational database with a NoSQL database if it better suits future needs.

- **Technology independence**: You can use different technologies or frameworks for different parts of the system without locking yourself into one particular stack.

○ **Examples**:

- **Database replaceability**: Using a **data access layer** (**DAL**) that abstracts database interactions enables you to switch from MySQL to PostgreSQL, for example, without affecting the rest of the system.

- **Service replaceability**: A payment processing service could have a standard API interface, allowing you to switch between PayPal, Stripe, or other payment providers with minimal change to the overall application.

- **Logging framework**: You can design a logging framework that allows you to easily swap between different logging libraries (e.g., Log4j, Serilog, or a custom solution) based on the system's needs or updates.

○ **Benefits**:

- Allows for easy replacement of outdated or underperforming components.

- Facilitates technology upgrades without needing to refactor the entire system.

- Minimizes risks when experimenting with new technologies or services, as components can easily be replaced.

- **Plug-and-play architecture**

Plug-and-play architecture refers to a system design where components can be added, removed, or replaced seamlessly, without extensive configuration or rework. The idea is that new components can be plugged in to extend or modify functionality without disrupting existing parts of the system.

○ **How plug-and-play enhances adaptability**:

- **Modular design**: Components are designed to be independent and self-contained. New modules can be added to the system with minimal configuration.

- **Standardized interfaces**: In a plug-and-play architecture, all components interact through standardized interfaces or protocols. As long as a new component adheres to the expected interface, it can be integrated seamlessly.

- **Dynamic extension**: The system can dynamically load and unload components, making it adaptable to new functionalities or changes without downtime.

- **Configuration-driven**: Components can be added or removed via configuration rather than code changes, allowing for flexibility at runtime.

o **Examples**:

- **Plugin systems**: Many software applications, such as web browsers (e.g., Chrome or Firefox) or **content management systems** (**CMS**) like WordPress, follow a plug-and-play architecture by allowing third-party plugins to be added for extended functionality without modifying the core system.

- **Microservices architecture**: A microservices-based system is inherently plug-and-play, where new services can be added to the architecture, and existing ones can be replaced independently, as long as they comply with the defined API contracts.

- **Modular frameworks**: Systems like **Open Service Gateway Initiative** (**OSGi**) for Java allow developers to plug in modules or services at runtime, supporting dynamic module management without restarting the system.

o **Benefits**:

- Facilitates rapid innovation and experimentation by allowing new components to be tested without altering core functionality.

- Encourages the development of reusable, modular components.

- Makes systems future-proof and able to adapt to new business requirements or technologies.

- Simplifies system upgrades and maintenance by allowing components to be added or replaced without downtime.

Best practices

The best practices for implementing replaceability and plug-and-play architecture are as follows:

- **Design for interfaces, not implementations**: Ensure components communicate through well-defined interfaces or APIs, allowing multiple implementations to be swapped in and out as needed.

- **Modularize the system**: Break down the system into smaller, self-contained modules that handle specific responsibilities, making it easier to replace or plug in new modules.

- **Use dependency injection**: Dependency injection allows for easier replacement of components, as dependencies can be dynamically swapped based on configuration, without hard-coding the component's implementation.

- **Adopt design patterns for flexibility**: Patterns like *Strategy*, *Adapter*, and *Factory* promote flexibility by abstracting away implementation details, allowing different components or algorithms to be plugged in dynamically.

- **Ensure backward compatibility**: When upgrading or replacing components, maintain backward compatibility with existing interfaces to ensure seamless transitions.

- **Leverage configuration files**: Use configuration files to specify which components or services should be used, allowing changes to be made without modifying code.

- **Focus on modular testing**: To support replaceability, ensure each module is independently tested. This makes it easier to verify that replacing one component would not introduce regressions or new bugs.

Combined impact on flexibility and adaptability

The combined impact of replaceability and plug-and-play architecture on flexibility and adaptability is as follows:

- **Replaceability** and **plug-and-play architecture** contribute to the flexibility and adaptability of a system by allowing for continuous evolution without disrupting existing functionality.

- These principles ensure that a system is future-proof, enabling it to adapt to new business demands, integrate new technologies, or recover from failure more easily. By designing with these concepts in mind, software becomes more robust, maintainable, and easier to scale over time.

Understandability

Understandability is key to building software that is easy to read, comprehend, and maintain. It directly affects how easily new developers can join a project, how quickly bugs can be identified, and how effectively features can be added or changed. Two fundamental principles that enhance understandability are **separation of concerns** and **abstraction**, defined as follows:

- **Separation of concerns**

  Separation of concerns (SoC) refers to the principle of dividing a system into distinct sections, each of which addresses a specific concern or responsibility. This ensures that each part of the system has a well-defined purpose and that unrelated functionalities do not mix. The following list outlines some key concepts of SoC:

  - **How SoC enhances understandability**:

    - **Modular code**: By separating different concerns, you create a modular codebase where each module or component focuses on a specific functionality. This makes it easier for developers to understand each part in isolation without getting overwhelmed by complexity.

    - **Isolation of logic**: When concerns are separated, different types of logic (e.g., business logic, data access logic, and presentation logic) are isolated into their own components or layers. This makes it easier to reason about the system as a whole, and to find and fix issues.

    - **Reduces complexity**: Each module or class only deals with its designated responsibility, preventing the intermingling of unrelated functionalities. This reduces cognitive load for developers trying to understand how a piece of code works.

  - **Examples**:

    - **Model-View-Controller (MVC) pattern**: A classic example of separation of concerns in action, where the application is divided into three layers:

      - ❖ **Model**: Manages the data and business logic.

      - ❖ **View**: Handles the presentation of data to the user.

      - ❖ **Controller**: Manages user inputs and updates the model or view as necessary.

    - **Microservices architecture**: Each microservice is responsible for a specific business capability. This makes it easier to develop, maintain, and scale individual services independently.

    - **Layered architecture**: Separating concerns into different layers, such as presentation, application, business logic, and data layers, makes each layer more understandable by limiting the responsibilities of each part.

  - **Benefits**:

    - **Clarity**: Each part of the system has a clearly defined role, making it easier to understand what each component does.

- **Maintainability**: Changes to one concern do not affect others, making it easier to modify, enhance, or fix a part of the system.

- **Collaboration**: Different teams can work on separate concerns (e.g., front-end developers can work on the view, while back-end developers work on the business logic) without stepping on each other's toes.

- **Abstraction:** Abstraction is the process of hiding complex implementation details and exposing only the essential features needed to interact with a system or component. It allows developers to focus on higher-level concepts without needing to worry about the underlying complexity. Refer to the following list for the key concepts related to abstraction:

  - **How abstraction enhances understandability**:

    - **Simplifies complexity**: Abstraction hides the intricate details of how things work, presenting a simplified interface to interact with. This reduces the amount of information developers need to process at any given time.

    - **Improves focus**: Developers can focus on solving problems at a high level, working with abstract representations of data or behavior, rather than being bogged down by low-level details.

    - **Encourages reuse**: Abstract components can be reused across different parts of the system, providing a consistent interface that hides the complexity of implementation.

  - **Examples**:

    - **Class hierarchies in object-oriented programming (OOP)**: In OOP, abstract classes or interfaces define common behaviors or attributes that are shared across different concrete implementations. Developers interact with the abstraction (e.g., an interface for a PaymentProcessor) without needing to understand the specific implementation details (e.g., whether it's Stripe, PayPal, etc.).

    - **APIs**: An API is an abstraction layer that provides a set of functionalities or services while hiding the underlying implementation. For instance, developers interact with a REST API to fetch user data without knowing the internal workings of the database.

    - **File systems**: The concept of a file is an abstraction that hides the complexity of how data is stored on disk. Developers can open, read, and write files without needing to know about the underlying file structure or hardware details.

    ○ **Benefits**:

- **Simplifies interactions**: Abstraction presents a simplified interface, making the system easier to use and understand.

- **Enhances modularity**: By abstracting away complexity, you can build systems where parts are easily swappable without affecting the rest of the system, as long as they adhere to the abstraction.

- **Improves maintainability**: When you need to change the implementation, abstraction ensures that these changes are confined to one place without affecting other parts of the system.

Combined impact on understandability

The combined impact of SoC and abstraction on understandability is as follows:

- **SoC** ensures that different aspects of the system are isolated, making it easier for developers to understand each part individually without needing to know the whole system.

- **Abstraction** further simplifies the system by hiding unnecessary details and exposing only the necessary features, making interactions with the system more intuitive and easier to reason about.

Together, these principles significantly reduce the complexity of large systems, enabling developers to focus on specific tasks without being overwhelmed by the system's intricacies.

Best practices

The following are the best practices for improving understandability through SoC and abstraction:

- **Divide responsibilities clearly**: Ensure that different parts of the system (e.g., data access, business logic, user interface) are clearly separated into distinct layers or components.

- **Use interfaces and abstract classes**: Define common behaviors through interfaces or abstract classes to hide specific implementation details while allowing flexibility in how those behaviors are realized.

- **Encapsulate implementation details**: Ensure that the internal workings of a component or module are hidden, exposing only the necessary public methods or APIs for interacting with it.

- **Document abstractions**: Provide clear documentation for interfaces and abstract components to make it easier for developers to understand how to interact with them.

- **Follow well-known design patterns**: Design patterns such as *Facade*, *Adapter*, and *Decorator* can help introduce levels of abstraction, simplifying interactions and improving SoC.

By leveraging SoC and abstraction, you create a codebase that is easier to understand, maintain, and evolve, especially as the system grows in complexity.

Parallel development

Parallel development is an essential practice in modern software development that allows multiple teams or developers to work on different parts of a system at the same time. To make this possible, it is important to enable **concurrent development** while minimizing issues like **merge conflicts**, which can occur when multiple developers work on the same codebase. Refer to the following list for the key concepts related to concurrent development and reduced merge conflicts:

- **Concurrent development**

  Concurrent development refers to the ability of multiple developers or teams to work on different parts or features of a software project simultaneously without disrupting each other's work. This is especially important for large projects with tight deadlines or where multiple features are being developed in parallel.

  - **How concurrent development supports parallel development**:
    - **Branching strategies**: Effective branching strategies, such as feature branching, enable developers to work on isolated copies of the codebase. This allows teams to build new features, fix bugs, or refactor code concurrently without immediately affecting the main codebase.
    - **Task and module separation**: Tasks should be clearly defined and assigned to different teams or developers, ensuring that work is done on separate, non-overlapping modules or features.
    - **Continuous integration (CI)**: A CI pipeline allows code changes to be regularly integrated into the main branch, ensuring that the software remains in a working state while allowing teams to test their work early and often.
  - **Examples**:
    - **Feature branching**: In Git or similar version control systems, developers create separate branches for each feature. For example, Team A works on the user login feature, and Team B works on the shopping cart feature in separate branches, allowing them to develop in parallel.
    - **Microservices architecture**: Different teams can work on individual microservices simultaneously. Because services are loosely coupled and communicate via APIs, work can proceed independently.

- **Agile development**: In Agile methodologies like *Scrum*, teams can break down the system into smaller increments (sprints) and assign different parts of the project to different teams or individuals, supporting concurrent progress.

o **Benefits**:

- Increases development speed by allowing multiple teams to contribute to the project at the same time.

- Reduces bottlenecks, as teams are not waiting for others to finish their work.

- Enables flexibility, as different parts of the system can be developed and tested in parallel.

- **Reduced merge conflicts**

Merge conflicts occur when multiple developers modify the same files or code sections in different branches, leading to conflicting changes when they try to merge their work back into the main branch. To support parallel development effectively, it is critical to minimize the occurrence of these conflicts.

o **How reduced merge conflicts support parallel development**:

- **Branching hygiene**: Keeping branches small and focused on specific tasks (e.g., a single feature or bug fix) helps reduce the likelihood of merge conflicts. Regularly merging changes from the main branch into feature branches also ensures that teams are working with the latest version of the code.

- **Clear module ownership**: By clearly defining which teams or developers own certain parts of the codebase, you reduce the chance of multiple people making changes to the same files.

- **Modular architecture**: By designing the system in a modular way, teams can work on independent modules or components, which reduces the risk of conflicts. Each module can be worked on in isolation and merged back into the main codebase with minimal overlap.

- **Automated testing and CI**: Running automated tests on every commit helps catch issues early. This minimizes the number of conflicts that arise during merges, as automated tests will fail if changes break existing functionality.

o **Examples**:

- **Frequent integration**: Merging feature branches into the main branch regularly helps teams detect and resolve conflicts early, before they escalate. This also ensures that no branch deviates too far from the mainline code.

- **Code reviews**: Conducting code reviews before merging helps catch potential conflicts or overlapping work early, as reviewers can flag changes that may cause issues in other parts of the system.

- **Gitflow**: Gitflow is a branching model where feature branches are merged into a development branch first, before moving into production. This provides an additional layer of conflict resolution, as changes are reviewed and tested before they reach the main branch.

- **Code linters and formatters**: Using tools like linters or code formatters ensures that all developers follow the same coding style. This helps reduce conflicts that arise from formatting differences.

- **Benefits**:

  - **Faster resolution**: When merge conflicts are minimized, the overall process of merging branches becomes smoother and faster.

  - **Less rework**: Reducing conflicts helps avoid costly rework, where developers might have to go back and rewrite parts of their code to resolve conflicts.

  - **More stable code**: Regular merging with minimal conflicts keeps the main branch in a working state, reducing the risk of introducing bugs during the integration process.

Best practices for enabling parallel development

The following are the best practices for enabling parallel development:

- **Adopt a robust branching strategy**: Use version control systems like Git and follow branching models like *Gitflow, feature branching,* or *trunk-based development* to support concurrent development.

  - Feature branches isolate development work from the main branch, enabling developers to work in parallel without affecting each other's progress.

  - Trunk-based development encourages frequent integration with the main branch, reducing the size of changes and the chance of conflicts.

- **Define clear ownership of modules or components**: Assign different teams or developers clear ownership of specific parts of the codebase. This prevents overlapping changes to the same files, reducing conflicts.

- **Encourage small, incremental changes**: Developers should avoid making large, sweeping changes to the codebase. Instead, focus on small, manageable changes that can be reviewed and merged quickly. This minimizes the risk of conflicts and makes it easier to resolve them when they do occur.

- **Leverage CI/CD pipelines**: Automated pipelines help detect integration issues early and frequently, allowing teams to address conflicts before they become more complex and harder to resolve.

- **Use code reviews and pull requests**: Code reviews not only help maintain quality but also catch potential conflicts early. Reviewers can identify areas of overlap and suggest changes to prevent merge conflicts.

- **Frequent integration**: Regularly merge changes from feature branches back into the main branch. This reduces the likelihood of long-lived branches, which are more prone to conflicts when eventually merged.

- **Apply modular design principles**: By designing the system in a modular or microservices architecture, teams can work on independent parts of the system. This limits the impact of changes to individual modules, reducing the potential for conflicts.

Combined impact on parallel development

The combined impact of concurrent development and reduced merge conflicts are as follows:

- **Concurrent development** enables teams to work simultaneously on different parts of the system, increasing productivity and development speed.

- **Reducing merge conflicts** ensures that the process of integrating different teams' work back into the main branch is smooth, preventing costly delays and rework.

Together, these principles allow organizations to scale development efforts, maintain a stable codebase, and deliver features faster, even in large, complex projects.

Encapsulation of complexity

Encapsulation is a fundamental principle in software design that promotes **hiding complexity** to make systems easier to use and maintain. It ensures that users or other parts of the system do not need to understand the intricate workings of a component, focusing instead on its interfaces and the services it provides. Two important aspects of encapsulating complexity are **hidden implementation details** and **black-box abstraction**, which are described as follows:

- **Hidden implementation details**

  Hidden implementation details refer to the practice of concealing the internal workings of a system or component while exposing only the necessary functionality through a public interface. The consumer of the component interacts with the system based on what it does, not how it does it. This encapsulation shields users from unnecessary complexity.

- How hidden implementation details help encapsulate complexity:
  - **Simplifies usage**: By hiding the internal logic, developers using the component only need to know how to interact with it, not how it works. This reduces the cognitive load and allows them to focus on high-level tasks.

  - **Encourages modularity**: Each component or class manages its internal complexity and provides a simple, well-defined interface. This modular approach allows developers to build and understand systems in pieces.

  - **Promotes flexibility**: When implementation details are hidden, the internal workings of a component can be changed or optimized without affecting other parts of the system, as long as the public interface remains consistent.

- **Examples**:
  - **Class methods and fields**: In **object-oriented programming (OOP)**, internal fields (data) of a class are kept private, while public methods are used to access or modify them. For example, the user of a `Car` class might call a method `startEngine()`, but they do not need to know how the engine starts internally.

  - **Database abstraction layers**: Developers interact with databases through abstract methods or libraries (e.g., using an ORM like Hibernate), without needing to understand how SQL queries are generated or optimized.

  - **API services**: When developers interact with APIs, they only need to know the input parameters and the expected output. How the API internally processes the request (e.g., retrieving data from multiple sources, caching, error handling) is abstracted away.

- **Benefits**:
  - **Reduces complexity for users**: Consumers only interact with what is necessary, without getting bogged down by internal details.

  - **Improves maintainability**: Since the internal logic is hidden, changes to the implementation can be made without affecting other parts of the system.

  - **Enforces consistency**: The interface becomes a stable contract, allowing the underlying implementation to evolve as needed while maintaining consistent functionality.

- **Black-box abstraction**

  A black-box abstraction refers to a design where the internal workings of a system or component are completely hidden, and users only interact with the inputs and outputs. In a black-box abstraction, the system is treated as a black box, meaning you do not need to understand how it works internally to use it effectively. The focus is purely on what it does, not how it does it.

  - **How black-box abstraction encapsulates complexity**:
    - **Focuses on functionality**: Users of a black-box system only need to know what inputs to provide and what outputs to expect. This hides all the internal processes and logic that lead to the result.
    - **Isolates change**: Since the internal details are abstracted away, changes to the implementation can be made without users needing to adjust how they interact with the system.
    - **Encourages reuse**: Black-box components are highly reusable because they expose a consistent interface, allowing them to be used in different parts of the system or even across different projects.

  - **Examples**:
    - **Software libraries**: A math library that provides functions like **add(x, y)** or **sqrt(x)** is a black-box abstraction. Users only care about providing the correct inputs and receiving the correct outputs, without needing to understand how the math operations are implemented.
    - **APIs**: When using a web API (e.g., Google Maps API), the consumer sends a request with inputs (e.g., location data), and the API returns a response (e.g., map data or directions). The user has no need to know how the data is processed behind the scenes.
    - **Cloud services**: Cloud platforms like AWS provide services such as object storage (S3) or databases (RDS), which users interact with through simple interfaces. They do not need to know how these services manage physical servers, replication, or data persistence.

  - **Benefits**:
    - **Simplifies interaction**: Users can work with a complex system without understanding its internals, reducing the learning curve.
    - **Increases modularity**: Since a black-box abstraction provides a consistent interface, it can be used interchangeably with other components as long as they meet the same input-output requirements.

- **Enables encapsulated change**: The internal logic can evolve or be optimized over time, without forcing users to change how they interact with the component.

Impact of hidden implementation details and black-box abstraction

Together, hidden implementation details and black-box abstraction ensure that complex systems are broken down into smaller, understandable components. By limiting what users see and need to understand, these principles simplify the process of interacting with the system, making the software easier to develop, maintain, and scale. The combined impact of hidden implementation details and black-box abstraction on encapsulation is as follows:

- **Simplified interactions**: Users of the system only need to understand the public interface, not the internal mechanics. This reduces complexity for both developers and users.

- **Modular design**: Components are easier to replace, test, and reuse because their internal workings are encapsulated, and interaction is based solely on their exposed interfaces.

- **Flexibility**: Changes to a component's implementation can be made without affecting other parts of the system, as long as the interface contract remains unchanged.

- **Consistency**: The stable interfaces provided by black-box abstractions ensure that different teams or services can interact without needing to know how the other side works internally.

Best practices

The best practices for achieving encapsulation through hidden details and black-box abstraction are as follows:

- **Use access modifiers effectively**: In OOP, use private, protected, or public access modifiers to control access to class internals. Only expose what is necessary, and keep everything else hidden.

- **Design clear interfaces**: Create well-defined interfaces for components that describe what the component does, without exposing how it does it. This provides a consistent point of interaction, regardless of changes in implementation.

- **Apply abstraction consistently**: In cases like APIs, libraries, or services, provide a clear contract (e.g., REST API documentation) that specifies inputs, outputs, and expected behaviors, while hiding all processing behind the scenes.

- **Promote modularity**: Ensure that each module or component in the system has a single responsibility. This allows it to be developed, tested, and maintained independently, reducing overall complexity.

- **Utilize design patterns**: Design patterns such as *Facade*, *Proxy*, and *Adapter* can help encapsulate complexity by providing simplified interfaces to more complex systems.

- **Document interfaces, not internals**: Focus on documenting how users should interact with a component (its public methods and expected behaviors), rather than documenting how it works internally. This helps reinforce the encapsulation of complexity.

By adopting these practices, systems become easier to understand and maintain, while also becoming more robust to change.

Achieving modularity in code design

We have looked at the importance of having modularity in your code design, but it is also important to practically show how this can be achieved in several ways through the design of your code, code organization, documentation, testing, version control, and error handling.

We will start with the most common form of modularity, breaking down code into smaller functions.

The following is a basic example of how modularity can be used in a coding solution:

Unmodularized code:

```
def factorial(n):
    if n == 0:
        return 1
    else:
        return n * factorial(n - 1)
print(factorial(5))
```

This unmodularized version has everything within a single function. While it works fine for small tasks like calculating a factorial, it becomes less manageable as the codebase grows. The reason is as follows:

- **Readability and maintainability**: As the code grows, it becomes harder to read and maintain. All the logic is cramped into one function, making it challenging to understand its purpose at a glance.

- **Reusability**: The factorial calculation logic is tightly coupled with the function itself. If you wanted to use the factorial calculation in another part of your code, you would need to copy the entire factorial function.

Modularized code: Now, let us modularize the code as follows:

```
def factorial(n):
    if n == 0:
```

```
        return 1
    else:
        return n * factorial(n - 1)
def main():
    print(factorial(5))

if __name__ == "__main__":
    main()
```

In this modularized version, the following software properties are better addressed:

- **Readability and maintainability**: The logic for calculating the factorial is still there, but it is now separated into its own function. This separation makes the code easier to read and maintain. To understand how the factorial is calculated, you only need to look at the factorial function.

- **Reusability**: Since factorial logic is its own function, it can be easily reused in other parts of the codebase. If you need to calculate the factorial of a number elsewhere, you can call the factorial function without duplicating code.

- **Testing and debugging**: Modularized code is easier to test and debug. Each function can be tested independently, making it easier to identify and fix issues.

- **Scalability**: As your codebase grows, modularization allows for easier scaling and management. You can organize related functions into modules, making navigating and working with large codebases easier.

Modularity might take longer and look more complex in design, but it brings a lot of benefits to the lifespan of the code when done correctly.

Code organization

Another important way to bring modularization into your code design is through code organization. Maintain a clear and consistent code structure. Use meaningful names for variables, functions, and modules. Follow established coding conventions and style guides. The following is an example of well-organized code:

```
def calculate_area(length, width):
    return length * width

def calculate_perimeter(length, width):
    return 2 * (length + width)
```

In the preceding example, we offer two functions that can take the same variables and use them to either calculate area or perimeter. It is very clear what everything does simply by looking at the meaningful names of both functions and variables, and even if a person is not a skilled programmer, they should be able to identify what is being done on the code simply just in how well defined everything is.

Documentation

While code should be well structured and readable, commenting what it does also helps to make future maintenance easier. Provide thorough documentation for the code, including comments within the code and external documentation where necessary. Things like the function of the code, requirements linked to it, how it is tested, and the reason for certain code choices should also be included.

Let us look at the first function written by the author, but this time, add proper comments to explain the logic:

```
def factorial(n):
    """
    Calculate the factorial of a given number.
    Args:
        n (int): The number for which factorial is to be calculated.

    Returns:
        int: The factorial of the given number.
    """
    if n == 0:
        return 1
    else:
        return n * factorial(n - 1)

def main():
    """
    The main function of the program.
    """
    # Calculate the factorial of 5 and print the result
    print(factorial(5))

if __name__ == "__main__":
    # If this script is executed directly, run the main function
    main()
```

Even though the code was uncomplicated, it is significantly easier to understand the logic behind everything and what each module does by providing detailed comments in the code.

This may seem like something that architects should not concern themselves with, but by providing proper guidelines and structure on how code should be commented on and enforcing this in the review process, you can greatly increase the ease with which code can be maintained in the future.

Testing

We will discuss testing in more detail in *Chapter 15, Architecture as Engineering*, but it has been added here because modularized code can also be easily tested with basic unit tests. To fully benefit from code modularization, it is critical to also write unit tests to ensure that each broken-down part of the code operates correctly.

Let us look at an example using the aforementioned factorial code:

```python
import unittest
from factorial import factorial
class TestFactorialFunction(unittest.TestCase):
    def test_factorial_with_zero(self):
        # Test factorial of 0
        self.assertEqual(factorial(0), 1)

    def test_factorial_with_positive_number(self):
        # Test factorial of a positive number
        self.assertEqual(factorial(5), 120)

    def test_factorial_with_negative_number(self):
        # Test factorial of a negative number (expecting ValueError)
        with self.assertRaises(ValueError):
            factorial(-1)

if __name__ == '__main__':
    unittest.main()
```

If you cannot follow the preceding script, the following is a brief explanation of what it is doing:

- **import unittest**: Importing the **unittest** module for creating and running unit tests.

- **from factorial import factorial**: Importing the factorial function from the factorial module to test.

- **class TestFactorialFunction(unittest.TestCase)**: Creating a test case class that inherits from **unittest.TestCase**.

- **test_factorial_with_zero, test_factorial_with_positive_number, test_factorial_with_negative_number**: These are test methods that check different scenarios of the factorial function.

- **unittest.main()**: This line runs the tests when the script is executed directly.

Now, when you run this test script, it will execute each test method and report whether they pass or fail. This way, you can ensure that each module of your code behaves as expected under various conditions.

Any future work done on this module can now be easily tested. Since we have covered a wide number of conditions in the testing itself, our integration testing with the modules becomes far simpler, as we will not need to explore some of the negative conditions that we are already checking for here.

Version control

Use version control systems like Git to track changes to the codebase. Commit small, atomic changes with descriptive commit messages. This makes it easier to trace the history of changes and revert to previous versions if necessary.

Error-handling

Implement robust error-handling mechanisms to handle unexpected situations and failures gracefully. Use try-except blocks and raise meaningful exceptions with informative error messages. The following example, while simple, shows how, when an error occurs, either through the fault of the users, the software, or an external factor, an appropriate and easy-to-understand error message is displayed. In this code example, it is simply raising an error on a division by zero:

```python
def divide(a, b):
    try:
        result = a / b
    except ZeroDivisionError:
        raise ValueError("Cannot divide by zero")
    return result
```

By incorporating these practices into the software development process, you can significantly improve its maintainability, making it easier to understand, modify, and extend over time.

Removing the legacy factor

Legacy does not mean the software design is poor, in fact, many of the core financial systems of today that keep the world running are considered legacy and contain some exceptional code and design that makes them so useful.

However, by not being modular, it will become incredibly difficult for companies to maintain these applications from a cost, security, performance, and overall operational perspective. Since they were so critical and touched core systems, the risk of updates became too high, and companies left them for too long. If they had been designed in a modular fashion, this pain could have been avoided. Companies would have been able to make significant updates to keep these systems more up-to-date with modern processing, security, and technology needs without risking causing catastrophic outages. Hundreds of millions of dollars could have been saved in the interim as well.

So, the benefits of modularity are clear, and we can even see from a coding perspective how it can be easily done.

However, achieving it requires far more than just the simple coding solution mentioned previously. Hence, the following section discusses some other important things at a higher architectural level that form a part of software design to make it more modular.

Localized changes

When a software system is designed with localized changes in mind, changes made to one module should ideally have minimal or no impact on other modules. This is achieved by ensuring that modules are loosely coupled, meaning they have minimal dependencies on each other, and that each module has a well-defined interface through which it interacts with other modules.

Let us consider a simple example of a software system for managing a library. In this system, we have modules for managing books, patrons, and loans. Now, let us say we want to add a new feature that allows librarians to track the status of overdue books. This would involve making localized changes to the **loans** module.

The following points explain how we might implement this feature with localized changes:

- **Modify the loans module**: We would make changes to the loans module to include functionality for identifying overdue books. This might involve adding a new method or updating an existing one to check the due date of each loan and compare it to the current date.

    o **loans.py**:

```python
class Loan:
    def __init__(self, book, patron, due_date):
        self.book = book
        self.patron = patron
        self.due_date = due_date

    def is_overdue(self):
        return self.due_date < datetime.now().date()
```

    o **New method to check if a loan is overdue**:

```python
def get_overdue_loans(loans):
    overdue_loans = []
    for loan in loans:
        if loan.is_overdue():
            overdue_loans.append(loan)
    return overdue_loans
```

- **Update the user interface**: We would also need to update the user interface to display information about overdue books. This might involve modifying existing screens or adding new ones specifically for managing overdue books.

  - # **ui.py**:

    ```
    def display_overdue_books(overdue_books):
        print("Overdue Books:")
        for book in overdue_books:
            print(f"- {book.title} (Due Date: {book.due_date})")
    ```

By making changes only to the loans module and the user interface related to managing overdue books, we keep the modifications localized. Other modules, such as books and patrons, remain unchanged, minimizing the risk of introducing bugs or unintended consequences in those areas of the system.

This example demonstrates how localized changes allow us to introduce new features or modify existing functionality in a specific part of the software system without impacting the rest of the system.

Clear interfaces

Clear interfaces in software design refer to well-defined boundaries between different modules, components, or layers of a system. These interfaces serve as contracts that specify how different parts of the system can interact with each other.

Let us consider a simple example of clear interfaces in the context of a messaging application. In this application, we have separate modules for sending messages, receiving messages, and displaying messages in the user interface.

The following is how we might define clear interfaces between these modules:

- **Sending messages interface**:

```
# send_message.py
class MessageSender:
    def send_message(self, recipient, message):
        """

        Sends a message to the specified recipient.
        Parameters:
        recipient (str): The recipient of the message.
        message (str): The content of the message.
        Returns:
        bool: True if the message was sent successfully, False
otherwise.
        """

        pass  # Implementation of sending message
```

- **Receiving messages interface**:

```
# receive_message.py
class MessageReceiver:
    def receive_message(self):
        """

        Receives a message from the message queue.
        Returns:
        tuple: A tuple containing the sender and content of the
received message.
        """

        pass  # Implementation of receiving message
```

- **User interface**:

```
# display_message.py
class MessageDisplay:
    def display_message(self, sender, message):
        """

        Displays a message in the user interface.
        Parameters:
        sender (str): The sender of the message.
        message (str): The content of the message.
        """

        pass  # Implementation of displaying message
```

In this example, each module defines a clear interface that specifies the methods or functions it provides and the parameters it expects. For sending messages, the interface specifies a **send_message** method that takes a recipient and a message as arguments. Similarly, the receiving messages interface defines a **receive_message** method that returns a tuple containing the sender and content of the received message. Finally, the user interface defines a **display_message** method that takes a sender and a message as arguments to display the message in the user interface.

By defining clear interfaces like these, developers working on different parts of the messaging application can independently implement their modules without knowing the details of the other modules. This promotes modularity, encapsulation, and flexibility in the design, making the system easier to maintain, extend, and evolve. Additionally, clear interfaces facilitate testing, as modules can be tested independently using mock implementations of the interfaces.

Encapsulation

Encapsulation is one of the fundamental principles of OOP, and it refers to the bundling of data and methods that operate on that data into a single unit, called a class. Encapsulation hides the internal state of an object from the outside world and only exposes a controlled interface for interacting with the object.

There are several key aspects to encapsulation, which are as follows:

- **Data hiding**: Encapsulation allows data to be hidden within a class, preventing direct access from outside the class. This protects the integrity of the data and prevents unintended modification or misuse.

- **Abstraction**: Encapsulation provides an abstraction layer that separates the implementation details of an object from its external interface. Users of the class interact with the object through its public methods, without needing to know how those methods are implemented internally.

- **Access control**: Encapsulation allows the class to control access to its data and methods through access modifiers such as public, private, and protected. Public methods can be accessed by external code, while private methods and data are only accessible within the class itself, ensuring that the internal state of the object remains consistent.

- **Information hiding**: Encapsulation hides the complexity of the implementation details from the users of the class, providing a clear and simplified interface for interacting with the object. This helps to reduce complexity and improve code readability.

- **Security**: Encapsulation helps to improve security by restricting access to sensitive data and operations. By encapsulating data within a class and providing controlled access through methods, you can prevent unauthorized manipulation of the data.

The following is a simple example in Python demonstrating encapsulation:

- **Class Car**:
```
def __init__(self, make, model):
    self._make = make   # Encapsulation: make is a private
attribute
    self._model = model # Encapsulation: model is a private
attribute

def get_make(self):
    return self._make

def get_model(self):
    return self._model
def set_make(self, make):
    self._make = make
def set_model(self, model):
    self._model = model
```

- **# Usage**:
```
car = Car("Toyota", "Corolla")
print(car.get_make())  # Accessing make using a public method
print(car.get_model()) # Accessing model using a public method
```

In this example, the **attributes** **_make** and **_model** are encapsulated within the **Car** class, and access to them is controlled through getter and setter methods. This hides the internal state of the **Car** object and provides a clear interface for interacting with it.

Library or component reuse

Library or component reuse refers to the practice of leveraging existing software libraries, modules, or components in the development of new software systems rather than reinventing the wheel. It involves identifying and integrating reusable assets into new projects to accelerate development, improve quality, and reduce costs.

The following are some key aspects of library or component reuse:

- **Abstraction**: Reusable libraries or components abstract away implementation details, providing a clean interface for interacting with their functionality. This abstraction allows developers to focus on using the component without needing to understand its internal workings.

- **Standardization**: Reusable libraries or components often adhere to established standards and best practices, ensuring consistency and interoperability across different projects. This standardization simplifies integration and reduces the risk of compatibility issues.

- **Quality**: Reusable libraries or components are typically well-tested and maintained, leading to higher quality and reliability compared to custom-built solutions. By leveraging existing assets with a proven track record, developers can reduce the risk of introducing bugs or vulnerabilities into their software.

- **Time-to-market**: Library or component reuse can significantly reduce the time-to-market for new software projects by providing pre-built solutions for common tasks or functionalities. Developers can focus on building the unique aspects of their application while relying on existing components for standard or generic functionality.

- **Cost savings**: Reusing existing libraries or components can lead to cost savings by reducing development effort, minimizing the need for specialized expertise, and avoiding the overhead of maintaining custom-built solutions. This allows organizations to allocate resources more efficiently and focus on delivering value to their customers.

Examples of reusable libraries or components include the following:

- UI frameworks (for example, React, Angular, SwiftUI)
- Database libraries (for example, SQLAlchemy, Hibernate)
- Networking libraries (for example, Retrofit, Alamofire)
- Logging and error handling libraries (for example, log4j, Sentry)

- Data processing libraries (for example, pandas, Apache Spark)
- Encryption and security libraries (for example, OpenSSL, Bouncy Castle)

Organizations can streamline development, improve quality, and deliver more robust and feature-rich software solutions by incorporating library or component reuse into the software development process.

Isolation

Isolation in software development refers to the principle of keeping different parts of a system separate from each other, often to prevent unintended interactions or to manage complexity effectively. Isolation can be applied at various levels, including within modules, between modules, or even between different layers of the software architecture.

The following are some key aspects of isolation in software development:

- **Module-level isolation**: Within a software module, isolation involves encapsulating data and functionality so that changes to one part of the module do not affect other parts. This promotes modularity and allows for easier maintenance and debugging. For example, in OOP, classes provide a way to encapsulate data and methods, effectively isolating the implementation details from the rest of the system.

- **Dependency management**: Isolation helps manage dependencies between different modules or components of a software system. By minimizing dependencies and ensuring loose coupling between modules, changes to one module are less likely to have ripple effects on other parts of the system. Dependency injection is a common technique used to achieve this kind of isolation, where dependencies are passed into a component from the outside rather than being hard-coded.

- **Testing isolation**: Isolation is crucial in testing to ensure that each unit of code can be tested independently of other units. Unit tests should be isolated from external dependencies, such as databases or network services, to ensure reliable and repeatable results. Techniques such as mocking and stubbing are used to isolate the unit under test from its dependencies during testing.

- **Fault isolation**: Isolation helps contain errors or faults within a specific part of the system, preventing them from spreading and affecting other parts. For example, in microservices architecture, each service is isolated from others, so a failure in one service does not bring down the entire system. Similarly, in operating systems, processes are isolated from each other to prevent a crash in one process from affecting others.

- **Concurrency isolation**: In concurrent or multi-threaded applications, isolation is important to prevent race conditions and ensure data consistency. Techniques such as locks, mutexes, and transactions are used to isolate critical sections of code and coordinate access to shared resources among multiple threads or processes.

Overall, isolation is a key principle in software development that promotes modularity, maintainability, reliability, and scalability. By keeping different parts of a system isolated from each other, developers can manage complexity more effectively and build robust and resilient software solutions.

Abstraction

Abstraction in software development simplifies complex systems by focusing on essential properties while ignoring irrelevant details. It involves representing the relevant aspects of a system while hiding unnecessary complexity, thus making the system easier to understand, use, and maintain.

The following are some key aspects of abstraction in software development:

- **Conceptualization**: Abstraction allows developers to conceptualize complex systems by breaking them down into manageable, high-level concepts. This helps in understanding the system's structure and behavior without getting bogged down by implementation details.

- **Generalization**: Abstraction involves identifying common patterns and generalizing them to create reusable solutions. This allows developers to encapsulate common functionality into abstract classes, interfaces, or design patterns, making it easier to reuse and extend in different contexts.

- **Information hiding**: Abstraction involves hiding the internal details of a component or module and exposing only the essential features through a well-defined interface. This promotes encapsulation and reduces the complexity of interacting with the component, making it easier to use and maintain.

- **Modeling**: Abstraction is essential for creating models that represent real-world entities or systems in a simplified form. These models help developers reason about the behavior of the system, analyze its properties, and make informed design decisions.

- **Layering**: Abstraction often involves layering different levels of functionality to create a hierarchical structure. Each layer provides a level of abstraction that hides the complexity of the layers below it, allowing developers to work at different levels of granularity.

- **Encapsulation**: Abstraction and encapsulation are closely related concepts. Encapsulation involves bundling data and behavior into a single unit, while abstraction involves hiding unnecessary details and exposing only the essential features through a well-defined interface.

Examples of abstraction in software development include the following:

- **Object-oriented programming**: Classes and objects provide a mechanism for abstraction by encapsulating data and behavior into reusable components.

- **Application programming interfaces (APIs)**: APIs abstract the underlying implementation of software components and provide a simplified interface for interacting with them.

- **Design patterns**: Design patterns, such as *Factory, Strategy,* and *Observer,* abstract common design solutions into reusable templates.

- **Domain-specific languages (DSLs):** DSLs provide a high-level abstraction for expressing domain-specific concepts and operations, making it easier to work with complex systems in specific domains.

Overall, abstraction is a powerful concept in software development that helps manage complexity, promote reuse, and improve maintainability. By abstracting away unnecessary details and focusing on essential properties, developers can create more understandable, flexible, and scalable software solutions.

Error isolation

Error isolation is a software engineering principle that aims to contain and minimize the impact of errors or failures within a system. It involves designing systems so that when an error occurs, its effects are confined to a specific component, module, or layer and do not propagate to other parts of the system. Error isolation is crucial for maintaining system stability, reliability, and availability.

We looked at an example of error handling in code earlier in this chapter, helping to break down code at a modular level, but there is a lot more to error handling that needs to be considered by the software architect. It is not just about highlighting that an error exists, but also ensuring that an error in parts of an application or software system does not cause errors elsewhere, and allows for faster issue fixing and resolution.

The following are some key aspects of error isolation:

- **Error handling**: Effective error handling mechanisms are essential for isolating errors within a system. By handling errors at the appropriate level of abstraction, such as within individual modules or components, developers can prevent them from propagating to higher levels of the system or affecting other components.

- **Fault tolerance**: Error isolation can be enhanced through the use of fault tolerance techniques, such as redundancy, replication, and graceful degradation. These techniques allow the system to continue functioning even in the presence of errors or failures, limiting their impact on overall system performance.

- **Testing and monitoring**: Comprehensive testing and monitoring strategies are essential for identifying and isolating errors within a system. By regularly testing individual modules and monitoring system behavior in real-time, developers can quickly detect and isolate errors before they escalate and affect other parts of the system.

- **Containment mechanisms**: Error isolation can be further reinforced through the use of containment mechanisms, such as sandboxes, containers, or virtualization. These mechanisms provide a controlled environment for executing code, limiting the potential damage caused by errors or malicious behavior.

- **Logging and auditing**: Logging and auditing mechanisms are essential for tracking the occurrence of errors within a system and diagnosing their root causes. By logging relevant information, such as error messages, stack traces, and system events, developers can identify and isolate errors more effectively.

- **Failure containment**: Failure containment is a crucial concept in software architecture that focuses on minimizing the impact of a failure within a specific component or module, preventing it from spreading to other parts of the system. By designing software with clear boundaries and dependencies, architects ensure that issues can be isolated quickly and do not compromise the entire application's stability. This approach not only enhances system reliability but also simplifies maintenance and troubleshooting, enabling developers to address problems more efficiently and with minimal disruption to the overall system functionality.

- **Graceful degradation**: Graceful degradation is a design strategy used in software engineering to ensure that when certain functionalities become unavailable, the system continues to operate with reduced functionality rather than failing completely. This approach improves user experience and system reliability by allowing users to access core features even under suboptimal conditions. Implementing graceful degradation involves designing fallback options that kick in when specific components fail or when the system is under stress, ensuring continuity of service and preserving the integrity of the user experience even in the face of partial system failures.

Overall, error isolation is a critical aspect of software engineering that helps ensure the reliability, availability, and resilience of systems. By designing systems with error isolation in mind and implementing appropriate error handling and containment mechanisms, developers can minimize the impact of errors and failures, resulting in more robust and stable software solutions.

Interoperability

Software interoperability refers to the ability of different systems, applications, or components to communicate and work together effectively, often across diverse platforms, languages, or technologies. It ensures that various systems can exchange data, share resources, and operate seamlessly and coordinately.

The following are some key aspects of interoperability in software:

- **Standards compliance**: Interoperability often relies on adherence to industry standards and protocols for data exchange, communication, and integration.

Standards such as HTTP, TCP/IP, XML, JSON, and REST provide common formats and conventions for interoperability between different systems.

- **API design**: APIs define the interfaces through which different software components can interact with each other. By providing well-defined APIs, software developers can enable interoperability between their systems and external applications, services, or platforms.

- **Standardized interfaces**: All interfaces that need to communicate with each other need to follow a consistent pattern to allow development teams to easily create systems that can speak to each other. Think of it as. placing rules that allow them to all speak the same language and understand each other without any need for complex translation.

- **Data formats and protocols**: Interoperability requires agreement on data formats and communication protocols to ensure that systems can understand and process information exchanged between them. Standardized data formats such as XML, JSON, and CSV, as well as communication protocols like *HTTP, MQTT*, and *AMQP*, facilitate interoperability between systems.

- **Middleware and integration platforms**: Middleware and integration platforms provide tools and services for connecting disparate systems and enabling data exchange between them. These platforms often include features such as message brokering, data transformation, and protocol mediation to facilitate interoperability.

- **Service-oriented architecture (SOA)**: SOA is an architectural approach that promotes interoperability by organizing software systems into loosely coupled, interoperable services. Each service exposes well-defined interfaces and can be accessed independently, enabling systems to communicate and collaborate effectively.

- **Web services and microservices**: Web services and microservices are architectural styles that emphasize interoperability by encapsulating functionality into modular, independently deployable components. These components communicate through well-defined APIs and protocols, enabling systems to interact and collaborate at a granular level.

- **Cross-platform compatibility**: Interoperability often requires support for multiple platforms, operating systems, and programming languages. Cross-platform compatibility ensures that software systems can run and communicate seamlessly across diverse environments, enabling interoperability in heterogeneous computing environments.

- **Interoperability testing**: Interoperability testing is essential for ensuring that systems can communicate and work together effectively. It involves validating the compatibility of different systems, APIs, and protocols to ensure seamless integration and interoperability.

Overall, interoperability is a critical aspect of modern software development, enabling systems to collaborate, share resources, and deliver value in interconnected and heterogeneous computing environments. By adopting standards-based approaches, designing well-defined APIs, and leveraging middleware and integration platforms, developers can achieve seamless interoperability between diverse systems and technologies.

Conclusion

The different aspects mentioned in this chapter can be quite extensive, but if combined, they can help in achieving the successful modularity of your application design and ensure that your software system can withstand the needs of the future.

Breaking down software and becoming more modular is a technically complex issue, and given all the factors considered in this chapter, it is surprising that many companies continue to struggle with it today.

However, a software architect can balance these aspects by understanding the principles. And just like the story we shared in *Codeburg* at the start of this chapter, the extra effort will pay off and lead to software that is highly functional, is of high quality, can be easily updated and maintained without disrupting the rest of the system, and most importantly, from a developer perspective, fun to work with.

In the next chapter, we will look at different architectural styles to include in your software design.

Join our book's Discord space

Join the book's Discord Workspace for Latest updates, Offers, Tech happenings around the world, New Release and Sessions with the Authors:

https://discord.bpbonline.com

CHAPTER 5
Architectural Styles

Introduction

We already discussed various architectural properties in *Chapter 3, Architectural Properties,*. and in this chapter, we will be discussing architectural styles. So, let us find out what a pattern is and how it differs from an architectural property in this chapter.

Structure

In this chapter, we will discuss the following topics:

- The difference between styles and patterns
- Layered architecture
- Client-server architecture
- Microservices architecture
- Service-oriented architecture
- Event-driven architecture
- Component-based architecture
- Space-based architecture
- Repository or data-centric architecture

- Hexagonal or ports and adapters architecture
- Event-driven microservices architecture
- Pipeline-based architecture
- Clean Architecture

Objectives

By the end of this chapter, you will understand the different types of architectural styles that exist, how they impact the function and performance of the systems and applications being design and how to make the correct practical trade-offs in selecting the right styles for a particular solution.

The difference between styles and patterns

Architectural styles refer to a set of characteristic design elements, principles, and motifs that define the overall appearance and form of a building or structure. These styles often emerge within specific historical periods or cultural contexts and reflect the prevailing architectural trends, technologies, and social values of their time. Architectural styles encompass various aspects of design, including the arrangement of space, materials used, decorative elements, and structural features.

Architectural properties, on the other hand, encompass a broader range of characteristics that contribute to the overall functionality, aesthetics, and performance of a building or structure. These properties may include factors such as building materials, structural integrity, energy efficiency, sustainability, accessibility, and technological innovations.

While architectural styles focus primarily on the visual and stylistic aspects of design, architectural properties encompass a wider range of considerations that affect the functionality, durability, and environmental impact of a building. In essence, architectural styles define the appearance and character of a structure, while architectural properties address its practicality, performance, and suitability for its intended use.

Differences between architectural styles and other architectural properties can be summarized as follows:

- **Focus**: Architectural styles focus on aesthetic and stylistic elements, while architectural properties encompass functional, structural, and performance-related considerations.

- **Scope**: Architectural styles define the overall visual appearance and design motifs of a building, while architectural properties encompass a broader range of factors, such as materials, structural integrity, energy efficiency, and sustainability.

- **Historical context**: Architectural styles often emerge within specific historical periods or cultural contexts, reflecting the prevailing architectural trends and societal values of their time. Architectural properties, however, are concerned with contemporary issues such as sustainability, technological advancements, and building regulations.

- **Design elements vs. performance factors**: Architectural styles primarily deal with design elements such as form, ornamentation, and spatial arrangement, whereas architectural properties address practical concerns, such as structural stability, thermal performance, and environmental impact.

While architectural styles define the visual and stylistic characteristics of a building, architectural properties encompass a broader range of factors that contribute to its functionality, performance, and sustainability. Both aspects are crucial in the design and construction of buildings, reflecting a balance between aesthetic expression and practical considerations.

However, to define architectural style more correctly, we also need to consider how it differs from an architectural pattern, which we will be going through in the next chapter.

The terms *architectural style* and *architectural pattern* are related but refer to different aspects of architectural design, shown as follows:

- **Architectural style**: An architectural style refers to a distinctive set of design principles, motifs, and characteristics that define the visual appearance and form of a building or structure.

  Architectural styles emerge within specific historical periods or cultural contexts and reflect the prevailing architectural trends, technologies, and social values of their time.

  Examples of architectural styles include Gothic, Renaissance, Baroque, Modernism, Postmodernism, and Contemporary.

  Architectural styles are primarily concerned with the overall aesthetic expression and design language of a building.

- **Architectural pattern:** An architectural pattern refers to a general reusable solution to a commonly occurring problem in architectural design.

  Architectural patterns provide abstract templates for organizing the structure and behavior of software systems or building designs.

  These patterns capture best practices and design principles that address various concerns such as scalability, maintainability, flexibility, and performance.

  Examples of architectural patterns include layered architecture, client-server architecture, **Model-View-Controller** (**MVC**), microservices, and event-driven architecture.

Architectural patterns are more concerned with the organization and arrangement of components or modules within a system, focusing on functional and structural aspects rather than stylistic considerations.

In summary, while architectural styles define the visual appearance and form of buildings within specific historical or cultural contexts, architectural patterns provide reusable solutions to common design problems in architecture, software engineering, or other fields. Architectural styles emphasize aesthetic expression and design language, whereas architectural patterns focus on functional organization and structural arrangements.

Now that we have a clear identification of what an architectural style is, we will now look at the different styles in more detail, the different benefits they offer, and what type of applications they would be best for.

Layered architecture

Layered architecture, also known as multitier architecture or n-tier architecture, is a design pattern commonly used in software engineering and system architecture. It divides a software application into distinct layers or tiers, each responsible for handling specific aspects of functionality. These layers are typically organized hierarchically, with each layer building upon the services provided by the layer beneath it. Layered architecture promotes modularity, scalability, and maintainability by separating concerns and enforcing clear boundaries between different parts of the system.

Refer to the following figure:

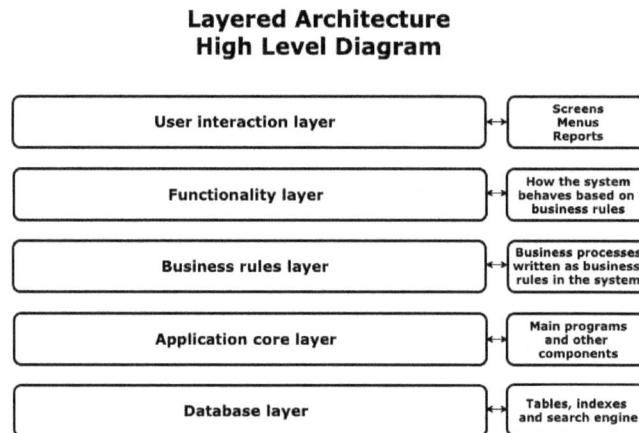

Figure 5.1: Layered architecture high level diagram

The typical layers in a layered architecture include:

- **Presentation layer (UI layer)**: This is the topmost layer of the architecture, responsible for presenting the user interface to the end-users. It handles user input, displays information, and interacts with the users. This layer often includes components such as web pages, user interfaces, and presentation logic.

- **Application layer (business logic layer)**: The application layer sits beneath the presentation layer and contains the business logic or application-specific logic of the software. It orchestrates the application's functionality by processing requests from the presentation layer, executing business rules, and coordinating interactions between different parts of the system. This layer encapsulates the core logic of the application independently of the user interface or data access mechanisms.

- **Domain layer (business objects layer)**: The domain layer represents the core domain objects, entities, and business rules of the application. It encapsulates the domain logic and data models that define the essential concepts and behaviors within the problem domain. The domain layer focuses on modeling real-world entities and their interactions, providing a clear abstraction of the application's business domain.

- **Data access layer (persistence layer)**: The data access layer is responsible for accessing and manipulating data stored in persistent storage systems such as databases, files, or external services. It abstracts the details of data storage and retrieval, providing a unified interface for accessing data regardless of the underlying data sources. This layer often includes components such as **data access objects (DAOs)**, repositories, or **Object-Relational Mapping (ORMs)**.

By separating concerns into distinct layers, layered architecture enables developers to achieve better modularity, maintainability, and scalability in software systems. It also facilitates parallel development and allows for easier integration of new features or changes in the future. However, it is essential to carefully design the communication and dependencies between layers to prevent tight coupling and ensure that each layer remains cohesive and independent.

Here is when you might consider using it:

- **Complex applications**: Layered architecture is particularly suitable for complex applications with multiple functional components and layers of abstraction. It provides a clear separation of concerns, making it easier to manage and maintain the codebase.

- **Scalability**: Layered architecture promotes scalability by allowing different layers of the application to scale independently. This scalability is essential for applications experiencing varying levels of load or undergoing future growth.

- **Modifiability and maintainability**: The modular structure of layered architecture facilitates easier maintenance and modifications. Developers can make changes to one layer without affecting the other layers, reducing the risk of unintended consequences and simplifying the debugging process.

- **Parallel development**: Layered architecture enables parallel development by dividing the application into distinct layers. Different teams or developers can work on separate layers concurrently, speeding up the development process and reducing dependencies.

- **Reusability**: Components within each layer can be designed for reusability, allowing developers to leverage existing functionality across different parts of the application. This promotes code reuse and helps avoid duplication of effort.

Here are some situations where you might consider alternative architectural patterns:

- **Simple applications:** For small or straightforward applications with minimal complexity, the overhead of implementing a layered architecture may outweigh the benefits. In such cases, a simpler architectural approach or a monolithic design may be more appropriate.

- **Performance-critical systems**: Layered architecture introduces overhead in terms of communication and data passing between layers. In performance-critical systems where every millisecond counts, minimizing these overheads may be a higher priority, and alternative architectures such as microservices or event-driven architecture may be preferred.

- **Tightly coupled systems**: If the components within your system are tightly coupled and interdependent, enforcing strict layer boundaries in a layered architecture may be challenging. In such cases, a more flexible or decentralized architecture may be better suited to accommodate the system's requirements.

- **Legacy systems**: Retrofitting a layered architecture onto an existing legacy system can be challenging and may not always be feasible. Legacy systems with complex dependencies or architectural constraints may benefit more from incremental improvements or modernization efforts rather than a complete architectural overhaul.

Client-server architecture

Client-server architecture is a computing model that divides tasks or processes between clients and servers in a networked environment. In this architecture, clients are the end-user devices or applications that request services or resources from servers, which are centralized systems responsible for processing and fulfilling these requests. Client-server architecture enables distributed computing, where tasks are distributed among multiple interconnected devices or systems, allowing for scalability, resource sharing, and centralized management.

Refer to the following figure:

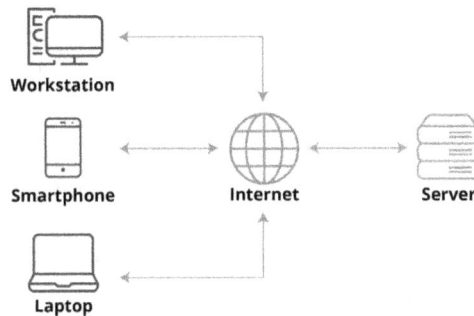

Figure 5.2: *Client-server architecture*

Client-server architecture is a computing model that divides tasks or processes between clients and servers in a networked environment. In this architecture, clients are the end-user devices or applications that request services or resources from servers, which are centralized systems responsible for processing and fulfilling these requests. Client-server architecture enables distributed computing, where tasks are distributed among multiple interconnected devices or systems, allowing for scalability, resource sharing, and centralized management.

Key components of client-server architecture include:

- **Client**: A client is a device, application, or software component that initiates requests for services or resources from servers. Clients can be desktop computers, laptops, smartphones, tablets, or other devices capable of accessing a network and interacting with server-based applications. Clients send requests to servers over a network, typically using protocols such as HTTP, FTP, or TCP/IP.

- **Server**: A server is a centralized system or software application that responds to client requests by providing services, processing data, or delivering resources. Servers are responsible for executing tasks, managing resources, and fulfilling client requests in a timely manner. Servers can be dedicated hardware devices or virtualized instances running on physical servers or cloud platforms.

Client-server architecture can be further classified into different types based on the nature of communication between clients and servers:

- **Two-tier architecture**: Also known as **client-server architecture**, this model consists of two primary layers: the client layer and the server layer. Clients communicate directly with a centralized server to request and receive services or resources. This architecture is suitable for small-scale applications with a limited number of clients and relatively simple client-server interactions.

- **Three-tier architecture**: In this model, the client-server architecture is divided into three layers: the presentation layer, the application layer, and the data layer.

The presentation layer handles user interface interactions, the application layer executes business logic and processes client requests, and the data layer manages data storage and retrieval. Three-tier architecture provides better scalability, modularity, and separation of concerns compared to two-tier architecture.

- **N-tier architecture**: This architecture extends the three-tier model by adding additional layers or tiers to accommodate more complex systems or distributed environments. N-tier architecture separates different aspects of functionality into multiple layers, allowing for better scalability, flexibility, and maintainability. Each tier may perform specific functions such as caching, load balancing, security, or integration with external systems.

Client-server architecture is commonly used in various types of applications and systems, including:

- Web applications and websites

- Enterprise software systems

- Database management systems

- File servers and storage systems

- Email servers and messaging systems

- Network infrastructure and services

Factors to consider for client-server deployment

When to use client-server architecture:

- **When scalability and resource sharing are required**: Client-server architecture allows for scalable systems where multiple clients can access centralized resources or services.

- **When centralized management is necessary**: Centralized servers enable administrators to manage and control access to resources, data, and services from a single point.

- **When reliability and fault tolerance are important**: Redundant servers and load balancing mechanisms can enhance system reliability and fault tolerance in client-server architectures.

When not to use client-server architecture:

- **For simple standalone applications**: Client-server architecture may introduce unnecessary complexity for small-scale applications with few users or limited functionality.

- **When real-time communication is critical**: Client-server architectures may introduce latency or performance issues in real-time applications that require immediate response times.

- **When offline operation is essential**: Client-server architectures rely on network connectivity, which may not be suitable for applications that need to operate offline or in disconnected environments.

Microservices architecture

Microservices architecture is a software development approach that structures an application as a collection of loosely coupled, independently deployable services. Each service is designed to perform a specific business function and communicates with other services through lightweight mechanisms such as *APIs* or message brokers. Microservices promote modularity, scalability, and agility by breaking down complex applications into smaller, manageable components that can be developed, deployed, and scaled independently.

Refer to the following figure:

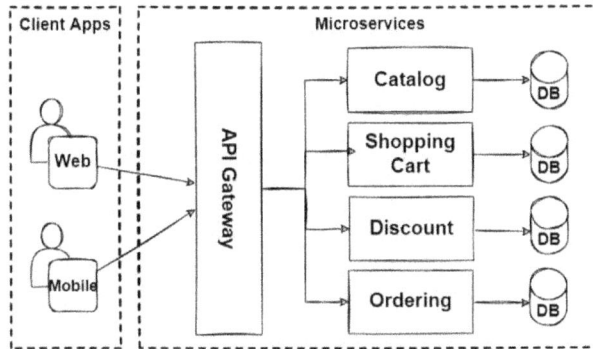

Figure 5.3: *Microservices architecture*

Key characteristics of microservices architecture include:

- **Service decomposition:** Applications are decomposed into small, focused services, each responsible for a specific business capability or domain. Each microservice encapsulates a set of related functionalities, such as user authentication, order processing, or product catalog management.

- **Loose coupling**: Microservices communicate with each other through well-defined APIs or protocols, such as RESTful APIs or messaging queues. Services are loosely coupled, meaning they can be developed, deployed, and maintained independently without impacting other services. This allows teams to work autonomously and evolve their services without disrupting the entire system.

- **Independently deployable**: Each microservice is independently deployable, allowing teams to release updates or new features without affecting the entire application. This enables faster release cycles, continuous delivery, and easier rollback in case of issues or failures.

- **Scalability**: Microservices architecture supports horizontal scalability by allowing individual services to be scaled independently based on demand. Services can be deployed across multiple servers or containers, and load balancers can distribute incoming requests to maintain performance and availability.

- **Polyglot persistence**: Microservices allow for the use of different data storage technologies suited to the specific requirements of each service. This flexibility, known as polyglot persistence, enables teams to select the most appropriate databases or data storage solutions for their individual services.

- **Fault isolation**: Microservices architecture promotes fault isolation, meaning that failures in one service do not cascade to other services or the entire system. This enhances system resilience and fault tolerance, as failures are contained within the affected service and do not impact the overall application.

- **Organizational alignment**: Microservices architecture aligns with modern agile and DevOps practices, allowing organizations to structure development teams around small, cross-functional teams responsible for individual services. This enables teams to take ownership of their services throughout the entire software development lifecycle.

Microservices architecture is well-suited for complex, large-scale applications with evolving requirements and diverse technology stacks. It offers several benefits, including improved agility, scalability, and resilience. However, adopting microservices also introduces challenges such as distributed system complexity, service communication overhead, and operational overhead associated with managing multiple services. Organizations should carefully consider their requirements, team capabilities, and operational maturity before adopting microservices architecture.

Considerations to deploy microservices architecture

When to use microservices architecture:

- **Complex applications**: Microservices architecture is beneficial for complex applications with multiple business domains or functionalities. Breaking down such applications into smaller, independent services can simplify development, deployment, and maintenance.

- **Scalability requirements**: If your application needs to handle varying levels of load or traffic, microservices architecture allows you to scale individual services independently. This scalability flexibility can help in optimizing resource usage and improving overall system performance.

- **Technology diversity**: Microservices architecture supports polyglot programming, allowing different services to use technologies and programming languages best suited for their specific requirements. This flexibility enables teams to leverage the strengths of various technologies and tools within the same application.

- **Agile development**: Microservices align well with agile development methodologies, enabling teams to work independently, iterate quickly, and release updates frequently. Each service can be developed, tested, and deployed autonomously, facilitating a faster time-to-market for new features and improvements.

- **Organizational structure**: Microservices architecture facilitates organizational alignment with small, cross-functional teams responsible for individual services. This decentralized approach empowers teams to take ownership of their services, fostering innovation, accountability, and collaboration within the organization.

When not to use microservices architecture:

- **Simple applications**: For small, straightforward applications with limited functionality and low complexity, microservices architecture may introduce unnecessary overhead in terms of development, deployment, and maintenance. A monolithic architecture might be more suitable in such cases.

- **Resource constraints**: Building and managing multiple services in a microservices architecture can require additional resources, both in terms of infrastructure and development effort. If your organization has limited resources or expertise in distributed systems, microservices might not be the best choice.

- **Communication overhead**: Microservices architecture relies on inter-service communication, which can introduce latency and complexity compared to monolithic architectures. If your application requires high-performance, real-time communication between components, microservices might not be the optimal solution.

- **Operational complexity**: Microservices introduce operational overhead in terms of service discovery, monitoring, logging, and deployment automation. If your organization lacks the necessary tooling or expertise to manage distributed systems effectively, the complexity of microservices may outweigh the benefits.

- **Legacy systems**: Retrofitting legacy applications into a microservices architecture can be challenging and may not always yield significant benefits. It is essential to assess the existing architecture, technology stack, and business requirements before deciding to migrate to microservices.

Service-oriented architecture

Service-oriented architecture (SOA) is a software design approach that structures applications as a collection of loosely coupled services. These services are designed to be self-contained, modular, and reusable components that perform specific business functions or tasks. SOA promotes interoperability, flexibility, and scalability by enabling services to be accessed and orchestrated across heterogeneous environments, platforms, and technologies.

Refer to the following figure:

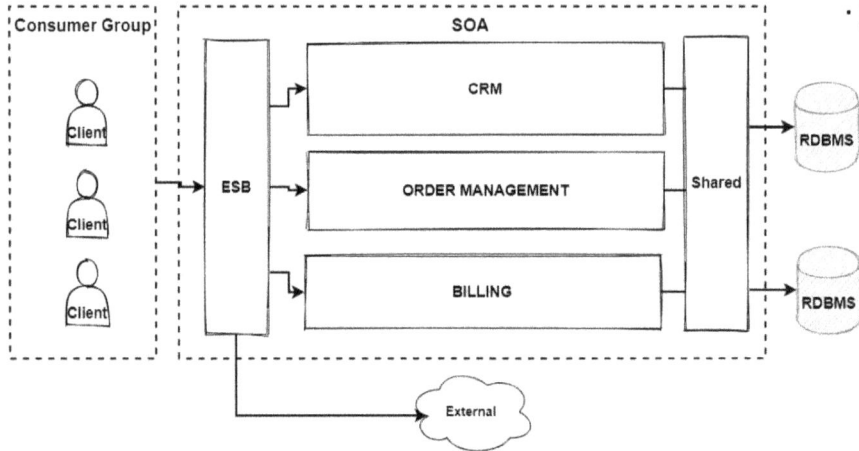

Figure 5.4: Service-oriented architecture

The key principles and characteristics of SOA include:

- **Service abstraction**: Services in SOA are abstracted from their underlying implementation details, allowing consumers to interact with them based on standardized interfaces and protocols. This abstraction promotes service reusability and decouples service consumers from service providers.

- **Service autonomy**: Services in SOA are autonomous entities that operate independently of each other. They have control over their own data, behavior, and lifecycle, enabling them to be developed, deployed, and managed independently.

- **Service reusability**: SOA encourages the creation of reusable services that can be leveraged across multiple applications and business processes. By encapsulating specific functionalities into services, organizations can avoid redundant development efforts and promote code reuse.

- **Service interoperability**: SOA promotes interoperability between services by standardizing communication protocols, data formats, and service contracts. This enables services to communicate and exchange data seamlessly, even if they are implemented using different technologies or platforms.

- **Service composability**: SOA enables the composition of services into larger, composite applications or business processes. Services can be orchestrated and combined to fulfill complex business requirements, allowing organizations to adapt and evolve their systems more effectively.

- **Service discoverability**: SOA provides mechanisms for service discovery, allowing service consumers to dynamically locate and invoke services based on their capabilities and interfaces. Service registries, directories, or discovery protocols facilitate the discovery of available services within the SOA ecosystem.

- **Service governance**: SOA emphasizes the importance of service governance to ensure consistency, quality, and compliance across the services within an organization. Service governance involves defining policies, standards, and guidelines for service development, deployment, and management.

SOA can be implemented using various architectural styles and technologies, including web services (e.g., SOAP, REST), message-oriented middleware (e.g., JMS, AMQP), and service-oriented integration platforms (e.g., ESB, EAI). It is widely used in enterprise IT environments to build scalable, interoperable, and flexible systems that can adapt to changing business requirements and technology landscapes.

Overall, SOA provides a modular, decentralized approach to software design, enabling organizations to build distributed systems that are more agile, resilient, and responsive to business needs.

When to use SOA:

- **Complex applications**: SOA is well-suited for building complex applications with multiple interdependent components and business processes. It allows organizations to break down large, monolithic systems into smaller, modular services that can be developed, deployed, and maintained independently.

- **Integration requirements**: SOA is beneficial when integrating disparate systems, applications, or data sources within an organization. It provides a flexible and interoperable framework for connecting heterogeneous environments and enabling seamless communication and data exchange between different systems.

- **Scalability and flexibility**: SOA enables organizations to scale their systems horizontally by deploying and orchestrating services across distributed environments. This scalability flexibility allows for better resource utilization and supports dynamic scaling to handle varying levels of demand.

- **Service reusability**: SOA promotes service reusability by encapsulating specific functionalities into reusable services that can be leveraged across multiple applications and business processes. This reduces redundancy, promotes code reuse, and accelerates development efforts.

- **Business agility**: SOA facilitates business agility by allowing organizations to quickly adapt and respond to changing market conditions, customer requirements, or regulatory changes. Services can be easily composed, recomposed, or replaced to support evolving business needs and priorities.

When not to use SOA:

- **Simple applications**: For small, straightforward applications with limited complexity and functionality, SOA may introduce unnecessary overhead in terms of development, deployment, and management. A simpler architectural approach, such as a monolithic architecture, might be more appropriate in such cases.

- **Performance-critical applications**: SOA introduces overhead in terms of service communication, serialization, and deserialization, which can impact the performance of real-time or high-throughput applications. If low latency or high performance is a critical requirement, other architectural styles, such as microservices or event-driven architecture, might be more suitable.

- **Resource constraints**: Building and managing a service-oriented architecture can require additional resources, both in terms of infrastructure and development effort. If your organization has limited resources or expertise in distributed systems, SOA might not be the best fit for your project.

- **Legacy systems**: Retrofitting legacy applications into an SOA can be challenging and may not always yield significant benefits. It is essential to assess the existing architecture, technology stack, and business requirements before deciding to adopt SOA for legacy modernization efforts.

- **Organizational maturity**: Successfully implementing SOA requires a mature understanding of service-oriented principles, governance, and best practices within the organization. If your organization lacks the necessary expertise or organizational maturity to adopt and sustain SOA, it may lead to challenges in implementation and adoption.

Event-driven architecture

Event-driven architecture (EDA) is a software design pattern in which the production, detection, consumption, and reaction to events are central to the architecture of applications and systems. In an EDA, components within the system communicate asynchronously by producing or consuming events, allowing for loose coupling, scalability, and flexibility.

Refer to the following figure:

Event-Driven Architecture (EDA)

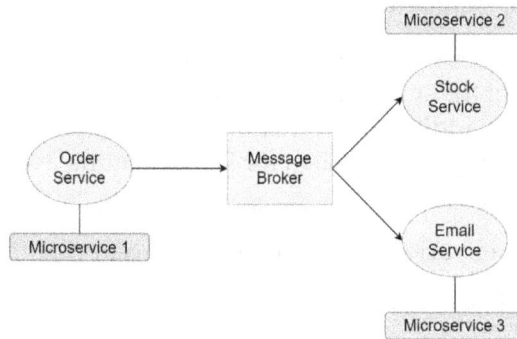

***Figure 5.5**: Event-driven architecture*

Key concepts and characteristics of EDA include:

- **Events**: Events are occurrences or notifications of significant changes or actions within a system. Examples of events include user actions, system state changes, sensor readings, messages received from external systems, or business transactions. Events are typically represented as structured data and are emitted by event sources or publishers.

- **Event sources or publishers**: Event sources are components within the system that generate and emit events. These can be user interfaces, applications, services, sensors, databases, or external systems. Event sources publish events to an event bus or message broker for distribution to interested subscribers.

- **Event bus or message broker**: The event bus or message broker serves as a communication infrastructure that facilitates the distribution of events within the system. It acts as a centralized or decentralized intermediary that routes events from publishers to subscribers. Event buses can be implemented using various technologies, such as message queues, publish-subscribe systems, or streaming platforms.

- **Event subscribers or consumers**: Event subscribers are components within the system that register interest in specific types of events and consume them as they are received. Subscribers react to events by executing predefined actions, updating their internal state, triggering further processing, or producing new events. Event subscribers can be applications, services, functions, or business processes.

- **Asynchronous communication**: EDA promotes asynchronous communication between components, allowing them to operate independently of each other. Components react to events in a decoupled manner, enabling better scalability, fault tolerance, and responsiveness.

- **Event-driven processing**: In an EDA, systems are designed to respond to events as they occur, rather than being driven by predefined control flows or request-response interactions. This enables systems to be more reactive, adaptive, and event-triggered, facilitating real-time processing and decision-making.

- **Event sourcing**: EDA often employs event sourcing as a data modeling pattern, where the state of the system is derived from a sequence of immutable events. This approach enables auditability, versioning, and temporal querying of system state, as well as providing a mechanism for implementing event-driven workflows and business processes.

EDA is commonly used in various domains and applications, including:

- Real-time analytics and monitoring systems
- **Internet of Things** (**IoT**) applications
- Microservices-based architectures
- Reactive and streaming data processing platforms
- Business process management and workflow automation systems
- Event-driven integrations and **enterprise service buses** (**ESBs**)

Overall, EDA provides a flexible and scalable approach to building modern, reactive systems that can efficiently handle asynchronous events, adapt to changing conditions, and support real-time interactions and processing.

When to use EDA:

- **Real-time processing**: EDA is ideal for systems that require real-time processing of events and asynchronous communication between components. It enables systems to react to events as they occur, facilitating timely decision-making and responsiveness.

- **Loose coupling**: EDA promotes loose coupling between components by decoupling event producers from event consumers. This allows components to operate independently, making the system more modular, scalable, and resilient to changes.

- **Scalability**: EDA supports scalable architectures by allowing components to be distributed and scaled independently based on workload and demand. It enables systems to handle large volumes of events and scale horizontally to accommodate growing workloads.

- **Flexibility and agility**: EDA enables systems to be more flexible and adaptable to changing requirements and business needs. Components can be easily added, removed, or modified without disrupting the overall system, making it easier to evolve and maintain over time.

- **Complex event processing**: EDA is well-suited for systems that require complex event processing, such as pattern matching, filtering, aggregation, or correlation of events. It provides a framework for implementing event-driven workflows, business rules, and decision-making logic.

- **Event-driven integrations:** EDA is beneficial for integrating heterogeneous systems, applications, and data sources that communicate via events. It provides a unified event bus or message broker that facilitates seamless communication and interoperability between disparate components.

When not to use EDA:

- **Simple applications**: For small, straightforward applications with limited complexity and interaction between components, EDA may introduce unnecessary overhead in terms of development and maintenance. A simpler architectural approach, such as a monolithic or request-response architecture, might be more appropriate.

- **Synchronous communication**: If your application primarily relies on synchronous communication patterns, where components interact via direct request-response interactions, EDA may not be the best fit. Request-response architectures may be more suitable for tightly coupled systems with synchronous communication requirements.

- **Low event volume:** If your application deals with a low volume of events or primarily operates in a batch processing mode, EDA may not provide significant benefits. The overhead associated with event-driven processing and communication may outweigh the advantages in such scenarios.

- **Lack of expertise**: Implementing and managing an EDA requires expertise in event-driven design patterns, distributed systems, and message-driven architectures. If your organization lacks the necessary skills or experience, adopting EDA may lead to implementation challenges and operational complexities.

- **Legacy systems**: Retrofitting legacy applications into an event-driven architecture can be challenging and may not always yield significant benefits. It is essential to assess the existing architecture, technology stack, and business requirements before deciding to adopt EDA for legacy modernization efforts.

Component-based architecture

Component-based architecture (**CBA**) is a software design approach that emphasizes the construction of software systems from reusable, self-contained components. In this architecture, software components encapsulate specific functionality or features and can be assembled and integrated to build larger systems. Components communicate with each other through well-defined interfaces, promoting modularity, reusability, and maintainability. Refer to the following figure:

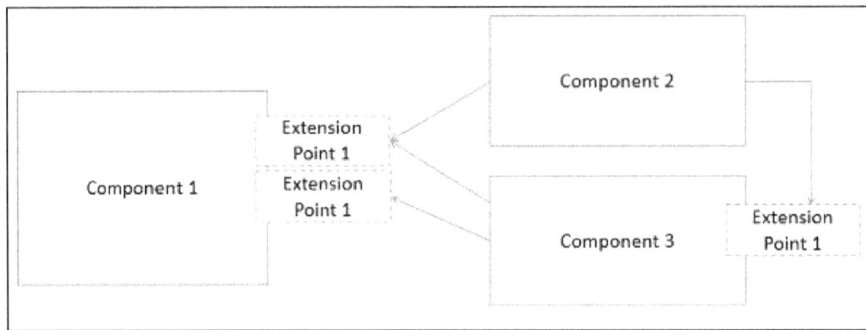

Figure 5.6: Component-based architecture

Key concepts and characteristics of CBA include:

- **Components**: Components are modular units of software that encapsulate specific functionality or features. Components are self-contained, meaning they can be developed, deployed, and maintained independently of other components. Examples of components include user interface elements (UI components), business logic components, data access components, and middleware components.

- **Interface-based communication**: Components communicate with each other through well-defined interfaces, specifying the methods, properties, and events that can be accessed or invoked by other components. Interface-based communication promotes loose coupling between components, enabling them to interact without relying on implementation details.

- **Reusability**: CBA promotes component reusability by enabling components to be developed once and reused in multiple contexts or applications. Reusable components reduce redundancy, accelerate development, and improve consistency across software systems.

- **Modularity**: CBA encourages the decomposition of software systems into smaller, modular components, each responsible for a specific aspect of functionality. Modularity enhances maintainability, as components can be individually modified, replaced, or extended without affecting other parts of the system.

- **Interoperability**: Components in CBA can be developed using different technologies, programming languages, or platforms, as long as they adhere to common interface standards. This promotes interoperability between components and enables integration with existing systems or third-party libraries.

- **Dynamic composition**: CBA supports dynamic composition, allowing components to be dynamically instantiated, assembled, and interconnected at runtime. This dynamic composition enables flexibility in system configuration and adaptation to changing requirements or environments.

- **Component lifecycle management**: CBA includes mechanisms for managing the lifecycle of components, including instantiation, initialization, activation, deactivation, and disposal. Component lifecycle management ensures proper initialization and cleanup of resources and helps maintain system stability and reliability.

CBA is commonly used in various software development contexts, including:

- **Graphical user interface (GUI)** development frameworks, where UI components are assembled to build user interfaces.

- Enterprise application development, where business logic components are integrated to implement complex business processes.

- Middleware platforms, where reusable components provide infrastructure services such as messaging, transaction management, and security.

- Component-based development frameworks and libraries, such as JavaBeans, .NET Framework, and AngularJS.

Overall, CBA provides a flexible and scalable approach to software design, enabling the construction of modular, reusable, and interoperable software systems. It promotes best practices such as separation of concerns, modularity, and reusability, contributing to improved productivity, maintainability, and software quality.

When to use CBA:

- **Large and complex systems**: CBA is well-suited for building large-scale and complex software systems where modularity, reusability, and maintainability are essential. Breaking down such systems into reusable components can simplify development, promote code reuse, and facilitate collaboration among development teams.

- **Reusable components**: If your project involves developing software components that can be reused across multiple applications or projects, CBA provides a framework for creating, managing, and integrating reusable components. This can accelerate development, reduce redundancy, and improve consistency across software systems.

- **GUI development**: CBA is commonly used in GUI development frameworks, where UI components (such as buttons, menus, and dialogs) are assembled to build user interfaces. GUI frameworks based on CBA principles enable developers to create modular, customizable, and responsive user interfaces.

- **Enterprise application development**: In enterprise application development, CBA can help manage the complexity of implementing complex business processes and workflows. By decomposing business logic into reusable components, organizations can build flexible, scalable, and maintainable enterprise systems.

- **Middleware and infrastructure services**: CBA is suitable for developing middleware platforms and infrastructure services that provide common functionality, such as messaging, transaction management, security, and caching. Reusable components in these domains enable organizations to build scalable, interoperable, and extensible middleware solutions.

When not to use CBA:

- **Simple applications**: For small, straightforward applications with limited complexity and functionality, CBA may introduce unnecessary overhead in terms of development and maintenance. A simpler architectural approach, such as a monolithic architecture or script-based development, might be more appropriate.

- **Performance-critical systems**: In performance-critical systems where low latency and high throughput are essential requirements, the overhead associated with component-based communication and runtime instantiation may negatively impact performance. In such cases, more lightweight and optimized architectural styles may be preferable.

- **Legacy systems**: Retrofitting legacy applications into a component-based architecture can be challenging and may not always yield significant benefits. It is essential to assess the existing architecture, technology stack, and business requirements before deciding to adopt CBA for legacy modernization efforts.

- **Resource constraints**: Building and managing a component-based architecture can require additional resources, both in terms of infrastructure and development effort. If your organization has limited resources or expertise in component-based development, CBA may not be the best fit for your project.

- **Lack of reusability**: If your project does not involve developing reusable components or if the components are highly specialized and unlikely to be reused in other contexts, the benefits of CBA may be limited. In such cases, other architectural styles focused on specific requirements or constraints may be more suitable.

Space-based architecture

Refer to the following figure showcasing space-based architecture:

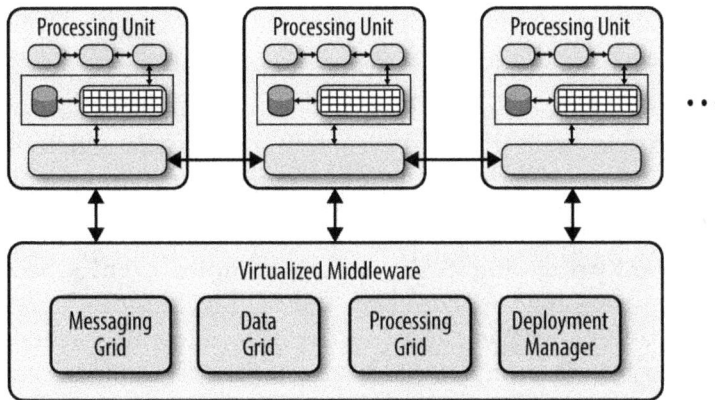

Figure 5.7: Space-based architecture

Space-based architecture (SBA), also known as **tuple space** or **data grid architecture**, is a distributed computing model designed to address scalability, fault tolerance, and responsiveness requirements of large-scale, real-time applications. SBA is based on the concept of a shared memory space, or *space*, where data and processing units (often called *agents*) interact asynchronously through the exchange of data tuples.

Key concepts and characteristics of SBA include:

- **Shared memory space**: In SBA, the shared memory space serves as a distributed data store where information is stored and accessed by multiple processing units (agents). The space is typically partitioned and distributed across multiple nodes in a distributed system, enabling horizontal scalability and fault tolerance.

- **Data tuples**: Data in SBA is represented as tuples, which are lightweight, self-contained data structures consisting of named fields or attributes. Tuples can encapsulate various types of data, such as application state, events, messages, or commands. Tuples are stored in the shared memory space and can be accessed and manipulated by agents.

- **Asynchronous communication**: SBA promotes asynchronous communication between agents through the exchange of data tuples in the shared memory space. Agents produce and consume tuples independently of each other, enabling loose coupling and parallel processing of data.

- **Event-driven processing**: SBA enables event-driven processing, where agents react to the presence or absence of specific tuples in the shared memory space. Agents can register interest in certain types of tuples and perform actions based on incoming tuples or changes in the state of the space.

- **Scalability and elasticity**: SBA provides scalability and elasticity by distributing data and processing across multiple nodes in a distributed system. The shared memory space can dynamically scale up or down to accommodate changes in workload or demand, allowing the system to handle varying levels of throughput and concurrency.

- **Fault tolerance**: SBA enhances fault tolerance by replicating data tuples across multiple nodes in the distributed system. If a node fails or becomes unavailable, other nodes can continue to serve requests and maintain system availability by replicating or redistributing data as needed.

- **Complex event processing**: SBA supports **complex event processing (CEP)** by enabling agents to analyze, correlate, and aggregate tuples in real-time. Agents can detect patterns, trigger alerts, or perform automated actions based on the occurrence of specific events or conditions in the shared memory space.

SBA is commonly used in various domains and applications, including:

- Real-time analytics and monitoring systems

- Financial trading and risk management platforms

- Online gaming and virtual worlds

- IoT applications

- High-frequency trading and algorithmic trading systems

Overall, SBA provides a flexible and scalable approach to building large-scale, real-time applications that require high throughput, low latency, and fault tolerance. By leveraging the shared memory space and asynchronous communication, SBA enables systems to be more responsive, adaptive, and resilient to changes in workload and environment.

When to use SBA:

- **Real-time processing**: SBA is well-suited for applications that require real-time processing and analysis of large volumes of data. It enables asynchronous communication and parallel processing of data tuples, allowing systems to react quickly to events and changes in the environment.

- **Scalability and elasticity**: If your application needs to scale horizontally to handle increasing workload or demand, SBA provides a scalable architecture by distributing data and processing across multiple nodes in a distributed system. The shared memory space can dynamically scale up or down to accommodate changes in workload, ensuring system availability and performance.

- **Fault tolerance**: SBA enhances fault tolerance by replicating data tuples across multiple nodes in the distributed system. If a node fails or becomes unavailable, other nodes can continue to serve requests and maintain system availability by replicating or redistributing data as needed.

- **Complex event processing**: SBA supports **complex event processing (CEP)** by enabling agents to analyze, correlate, and aggregate tuples in real-time. It allows systems to detect patterns, trigger alerts, or perform automated actions based on the occurrence of specific events or conditions in the shared memory space.

- **Asynchronous communication**: SBA promotes loose coupling and asynchronous communication between components, enabling components to interact independently of each other. This decoupling facilitates parallel processing, improves system responsiveness, and simplifies system integration and maintenance.

When not to use SBA:

- **Simple applications**: For small, straightforward applications with limited complexity and interaction between components, SBA may introduce unnecessary overhead in terms of development and maintenance. A simpler architectural approach, such as a monolithic architecture or microservices architecture, might be more appropriate.

- **Low data volume**: If your application deals with a low volume of data or primarily operates in a batch processing mode, SBA may not provide significant benefits. The overhead associated with distributed data storage and processing may outweigh the advantages in such scenarios.

- **Resource constraints**: Building and managing a distributed system based on SBA can require additional resources, both in terms of infrastructure and development effort. If your organization has limited resources or expertise in distributed systems, SBA may not be the best fit for your project.

- **Legacy systems**: Retrofitting legacy applications into a space-based architecture can be challenging and may not always yield significant benefits. It is essential to assess the existing architecture, technology stack, and business requirements before deciding to adopt SBA for legacy modernization efforts.

- **Synchronous communication requirements**: If your application primarily relies on synchronous communication patterns, where components interact via direct request-response interactions, SBA may not be the best fit. Request-response architectures may be more suitable for tightly coupled systems with synchronous communication requirements.

Repository or data-centric architecture

Repository or data-centric architecture is a software architecture pattern that focuses on managing and accessing data in a centralized repository. In this architecture, data is treated as a first-class citizen, and the primary goal is to provide efficient storage, retrieval, and manipulation of data for applications and users.

Refer to the following figure:

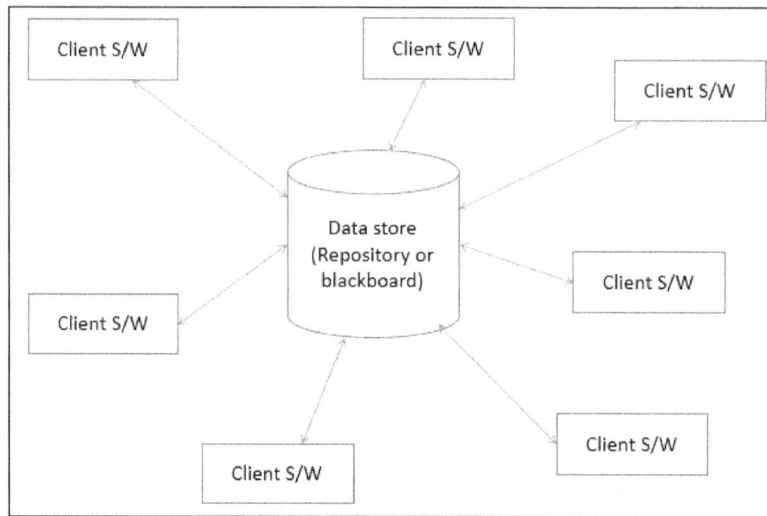

Figure 5.8: Data-centric architecture

Key concepts and characteristics of repository or data-centric architecture include:

- **Centralized data repository**: In this architecture, a centralized data repository serves as the primary storage for all application data. The repository can be implemented using a **database management system (DBMS)** or a data storage technology appropriate for the specific requirements of the application.

- **Data abstraction layer**: Repository architecture typically includes a data abstraction layer that encapsulates the interaction with the underlying data repository. This layer provides a set of standardized interfaces and methods for accessing and manipulating data, shielding application components from the complexities of data storage and retrieval.

- **Separation of concerns**: Repository architecture promotes the separation of concerns by isolating data access and manipulation logic from other application components, such as user interfaces, business logic, and presentation layers. This separation enables better maintainability, reusability, and testability of the application codebase.

- **Data integrity and consistency**: Centralizing data in a repository allows for enforcing data integrity constraints and ensuring data consistency across the application. By defining and enforcing data validation rules, constraints, and relationships within the repository, applications can maintain the integrity and reliability of their data.

- **Data access optimization**: Repository architecture enables optimization of data access and retrieval by implementing efficient data storage and indexing strategies.

By organizing data in a structured manner and utilizing indexing and caching mechanisms, applications can improve data access performance and reduce latency.

- **Security and access control**: Centralizing data in a repository facilitates implementing security measures and access control mechanisms to protect sensitive data from unauthorized access or manipulation. Access to data can be restricted based on user roles, permissions, or other authentication mechanisms.

- **Data integration and interoperability**: Repository architecture supports data integration and interoperability by providing a unified data access layer that abstracts the underlying data sources and formats. Applications can seamlessly access and integrate data from multiple sources, including databases, file systems, web services, and external APIs.

Repository or data-centric architecture is commonly used in various types of applications, including:

- **Enterprise resource planning (ERP)** systems
- **Customer relationship management (CRM)** systems
- **Content management systems (CMS)**
- Data-driven web applications
- Business intelligence and reporting applications

Overall, repository or data-centric architecture provides a structured and efficient approach to managing and accessing data in software applications. By centralizing data storage and providing a standardized data access layer, this architecture pattern facilitates scalability, maintainability, and security of data-driven applications.

When to use repository or data-centric architecture:

- **Data-intensive applications**: Repository or data-centric architecture is well-suited for applications that deal with large volumes of data or require complex data management operations. Centralizing data management simplifies data access, manipulation, and maintenance.

- **Applications with complex data relationships**: If your application has complex data relationships or requires frequent access to related data entities, centralizing data management in a repository can simplify data querying and retrieval operations.

- **Applications requiring data consistency**: Repository or data-centric architecture is beneficial for applications that require strong data consistency and integrity guarantees. Centralized data management helps ensure that changes to data are made in a controlled and consistent manner.

- **Applications with security requirements**: If your application has strict security requirements, such as data encryption, access control, and audit trails, centralizing data management in a repository can facilitate centralized security enforcement and compliance.

When not to use repository or data-centric architecture:

- **Simple applications**: For small, straightforward applications with limited data management requirements, repository or data-centric architecture may introduce unnecessary complexity and overhead. A simpler architectural approach, such as file-based or lightweight database storage, might be more appropriate.

- **Applications with high concurrency requirements**: If your application requires high levels of concurrency and performance, centralizing data management in a single repository may become a bottleneck. In such cases, distributed data storage and caching mechanisms may be more suitable.

- **Applications requiring high availability**: If your application requires high availability and fault tolerance, centralizing data management in a single repository may pose a single point of failure. Distributed data storage and replication strategies may be needed to ensure continuous availability and resilience.

- **Applications with diverse data needs**: If your application needs to support diverse data types, structures, or access patterns, centralizing data management in a single repository may not provide the flexibility needed to accommodate these requirements. A more flexible data storage approach, such as polyglot persistence, may be preferable.

Hexagonal or ports and adapters architecture

Hexagonal architecture, also known as **ports** and **adapters architecture**, is a software design pattern that emphasizes the separation of concerns and the independence of the application's core logic from its external dependencies and infrastructure. This architectural style was introduced by *Alistair Cockburn* in 2005 and is often associated with the principles of **domain-driven design (DDD)**.

Refer to the following figure:

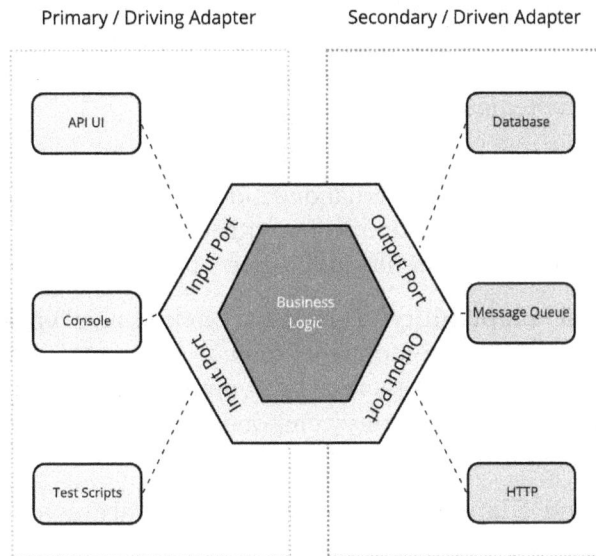

Figure 5.9: *Ports and adapters architecture*

Key concepts and characteristics of hexagonal or ports and adapters architecture include:

- **Hexagonal shape**: The architecture is named after its hexagonal shape, which represents the core of the application surrounded by ports and adapters. The core contains the business logic and domain model of the application, while the ports and adapters handle input/output interactions with external systems and dependencies.

- **Ports**: Ports represent interfaces through which the application interacts with external systems or components. Ports define the contract or API for communication, allowing the core logic to remain agnostic of specific implementation details. Ports can include input ports (for receiving external requests or events) and output ports (for sending responses or notifications).

- **Adapters**: Adapters are responsible for implementing the ports and connecting the core logic to external systems or dependencies. Adapters translate requests and responses between the core and external systems, handle data formatting and serialization, and encapsulate interaction with infrastructure components such as databases, web services, or messaging systems.

- **Separation of concerns**: Hexagonal architecture promotes the separation of concerns by isolating the core application logic from its external dependencies. This separation makes the application more modular, testable, and maintainable, as changes to external systems or infrastructure do not affect the core business logic.

- **Dependency inversion principle (DIP)**: Hexagonal architecture adheres to the DIP, which states that high-level modules should not depend on low-level modules; both should depend on abstractions. In the context of hexagonal architecture, this principle ensures that the core logic depends on abstract interfaces (ports) rather than concrete implementations (adapters).

- **Testability**: The architecture facilitates testing by allowing the core logic to be tested independently of its external dependencies. Mock or stub implementations can be used to simulate interactions with external systems during unit tests, enabling thorough testing of the application's behavior and functionality.

- **Flexibility and adaptability**: Hexagonal architecture enables flexibility and adaptability by allowing components to be easily replaced or modified without affecting the core logic. Adapters can be swapped or extended to support different external systems or infrastructure components, facilitating system evolution and integration with new technologies.

Hexagonal or ports and adapters architecture is commonly used in various types of applications, including:

- Web applications and APIs

- Microservices architectures

- Command-line applications

- DDD applications

- Enterprise systems and business applications

When to use hexagonal or ports and adapters architecture:

- **Complex applications**: Hexagonal architecture is well-suited for complex applications with multiple external dependencies and interactions. It helps manage complexity by isolating the core logic from external concerns and promoting modularity and maintainability.

- **Testability**: If your application requires extensive testing, especially unit testing of core business logic, hexagonal architecture facilitates testing by allowing components to be easily isolated and mocked during testing.

- **Flexibility and adaptability**: If your application needs to evolve over time and integrate with diverse external systems or technologies, hexagonal architecture provides flexibility and adaptability by decoupling the core logic from its dependencies.

- **DDD**: Hexagonal architecture aligns well with the principles of DDD, which emphasize modeling the application's domain and business logic separately from infrastructure concerns. It supports the development of domain-centric architectures that focus on the core business domain.

When not to use hexagonal or ports and adapters architecture:

- **Simple applications**: For small, straightforward applications with minimal external dependencies and interactions, hexagonal architecture may introduce unnecessary complexity and overhead. A simpler architectural approach, such as layered architecture or monolithic design, might be more appropriate.

- **Performance-critical systems**: If your application requires high performance and low latency, especially for I/O-bound operations, hexagonal architecture may introduce overhead due to the additional layers of abstraction and indirection. In such cases, more optimized architectural styles may be preferable.

- **Resource constraints**: Building and managing a hexagonal architecture can require additional resources, both in terms of development effort and infrastructure. If your organization has limited resources or expertise, hexagonal architecture may not be the best fit for your project.

- **Applications with tight coupling to external systems**: If your application is tightly coupled to specific external systems or technologies, such as proprietary APIs or legacy systems, hexagonal architecture may not provide significant benefits. In such cases, it may be challenging to decouple the core logic from its dependencies.

In summary, hexagonal or ports and adapters architecture is a powerful architectural style for building flexible, maintainable, and testable applications, especially in complex and evolving domains. However, it is essential to carefully consider the specific requirements, constraints, and trade-offs before deciding to adopt this architecture for a project.

Event-driven microservices architecture

Event-driven microservices architecture is an architectural style that combines the principles of microservices with event-driven design patterns. In this architecture, microservices are loosely coupled, independently deployable, and communicate asynchronously through the exchange of events. This approach enables building scalable, resilient, and flexible systems that can efficiently handle complex interactions and workflows.

Refer to the following figure:

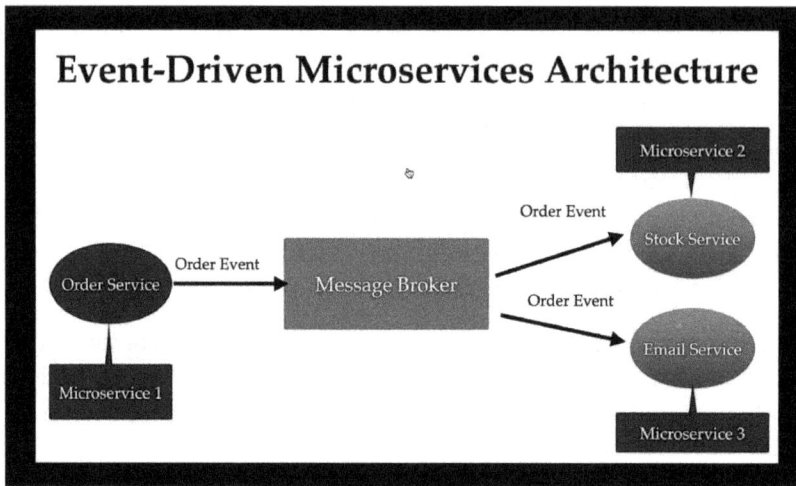

Figure 5.10: *Event-driven microservices architecture*

Key concepts and characteristics of event-driven microservices architecture include:

- **Microservices**: The architecture decomposes the application into a set of small, independently deployable services, each responsible for a specific domain or business capability. Microservices promote modularity, flexibility, and scalability by allowing teams to develop, deploy, and maintain services independently.

- **Event-driven communication**: Microservices communicate with each other asynchronously through the exchange of events. Events represent significant occurrences or changes within the system and can include actions, state changes, or notifications. Event-driven communication enables loose coupling between services, allowing them to operate independently and react to events in real-time.

- **Event bus or message broker**: The architecture typically includes an event bus or message broker that serves as a communication infrastructure for routing events between microservices. The event bus decouples producers of events (publishers) from consumers of events (subscribers), enabling scalable and flexible communication patterns.

- **Event sourcing**: Event-driven microservices often employ event sourcing as a data modeling pattern, where the state of the system is derived from a sequence of immutable events. Event sourcing enables auditability, versioning, and temporal querying of system state, as well as providing a mechanism for implementing event-driven workflows and business processes.

- **Event-driven processing**: Microservices in an event-driven architecture react to events by executing predefined actions, updating their internal state, triggering further processing, or producing new events. Event-driven processing enables systems to be more reactive, adaptive, and event-triggered, facilitating real-time processing and decision-making.

- **Saga pattern**: In scenarios involving distributed transactions and long-running business processes, event-driven microservices architecture often employs the saga pattern. Sagas are sequences of coordinated transactions that span multiple microservices and are initiated in response to events. Sagas help maintain consistency and integrity across distributed systems by orchestrating compensating actions in case of failures or errors.

- **Command query responsibility segregation (CQRS)**: Event-driven microservices architecture often aligns with the principles of CQRS, separating command-side (write) and query-side (read) responsibilities. Commands are represented as events that trigger state changes or side effects, while queries are optimized for read-only access and reporting.

Event-driven microservices architecture is commonly used in various domains and applications, including:

- E-commerce and retail systems

- Financial services and trading platforms

- Logistics and supply chain management

- IoT applications

- Real-time analytics and monitoring systems

When to use event-driven microservices architecture:

- **Complex interactions**: Event-driven microservices architecture is well-suited for applications with complex interactions, workflows, and integrations between components. It enables systems to react to events in real-time, facilitating dynamic and adaptive behavior.

- **Scalability requirements**: If your application needs to scale horizontally to handle varying levels of demand or workload, event-driven microservices architecture provides a scalable architecture by decoupling services and enabling asynchronous communication.

- **Real-time processing**: If your application requires real-time processing of events and data streams, event-driven microservices architecture enables systems to react quickly to changes and events, supporting real-time analytics, monitoring, and decision-making.

- **Flexibility and resilience**: Event-driven microservices architecture promotes flexibility and resilience by decoupling services and enabling them to operate independently. It allows systems to evolve over time, adapt to changing requirements, and recover from failures or errors gracefully.

- **Event-driven workflows**: If your application involves event-driven workflows, business processes, or integrations with external systems, event-driven microservices architecture provides a framework for implementing event-driven processing and orchestration of distributed transactions.

When not to use event-driven microservices architecture:

- **Simple applications**: For small, straightforward applications with limited complexity and interaction between components, event-driven microservices architecture may introduce unnecessary overhead in terms of development and maintenance. A simpler architectural approach, such as a monolithic architecture or microservices without event-driven communication, might be more appropriate.

- **Performance-critical systems**: In performance-critical systems where low latency and high throughput are essential requirements, the overhead associated with event-driven communication and processing may negatively impact performance. In such cases, more optimized architectural styles may be preferable.

- **Resource constraints**: Building and managing an event-driven microservices architecture can require additional resources, both in terms of infrastructure and development effort. If your organization has limited resources or expertise in distributed systems, event-driven microservices architecture may not be the best fit for your project.

- **Legacy systems integration:** Retrofitting legacy applications into an event-driven microservices architecture can be challenging and may not always yield significant benefits. It is essential to assess the existing architecture, technology stack, and business requirements before deciding to adopt event-driven microservices architecture for legacy modernization efforts.

In summary, event-driven microservices architecture is a powerful architectural approach for building scalable, resilient, and flexible systems that can efficiently handle complex interactions and workflows. However, it is essential to carefully evaluate the specific requirements, constraints, and trade-offs before deciding to adopt this architecture for a project.

Pipeline-based architecture

Pipeline-based architecture is a software design pattern where data processing tasks are organized into a sequence of processing stages, forming a pipeline. Each stage in the pipeline performs a specific operation or transformation on the input data and passes the processed data to the next stage. This architectural style is commonly used for stream processing, data transformation, and workflow automation tasks.

Refer to the following figure:

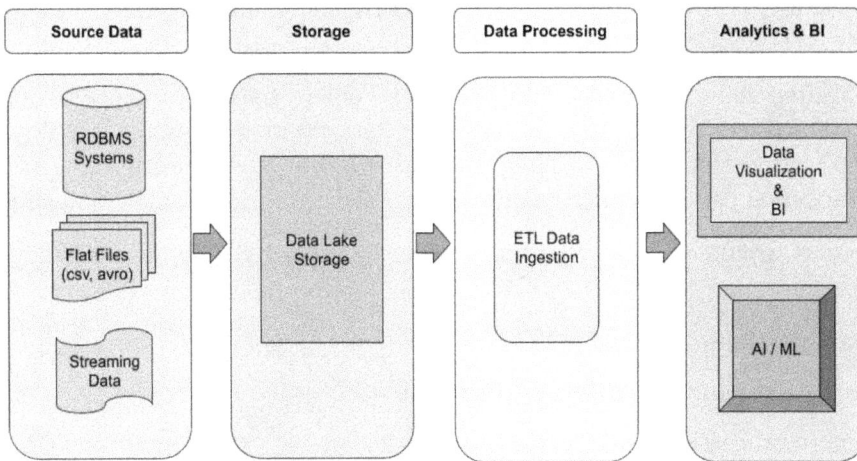

Figure 5.11: *Pipeline-based architecture*

Key concepts and characteristics of pipeline-based architecture include:

- **Sequential processing**: In pipeline-based architecture, data flows sequentially through a series of processing stages, with each stage performing a specific operation or transformation on the data. The output of one stage serves as the input to the next stage, forming a linear data processing flow.

- **Modularity**: Pipeline-based architecture promotes modularity by decomposing complex data processing tasks into smaller, reusable processing stages. Each stage encapsulates a specific functionality or processing step, making the pipeline easier to understand, maintain, and extend.

- **Parallelism**: Pipelines can exploit parallelism by processing multiple data items concurrently or distributing processing tasks across multiple processing nodes. Parallel processing can improve throughput, reduce latency, and optimize resource utilization, especially for compute-intensive or data-intensive tasks.

- **Flexibility**: Pipeline-based architecture provides flexibility in composing and configuring processing pipelines to meet specific requirements and use cases. Developers can easily customize pipelines by adding, removing, or rearranging processing stages to adapt to changing needs or optimize performance.

- **Fault tolerance**: Pipelines can incorporate fault tolerance mechanisms to handle errors, failures, or exceptions that may occur during data processing. Techniques such as error handling, retries, and checkpointing can help ensure robustness and reliability in the face of failures.

- **Data transformation**: Pipelines are commonly used for data transformation tasks, where input data undergoes a series of transformations or processing steps to produce desired output data. Examples of data transformations include data cleansing, normalization, aggregation, enrichment, and analysis.

- **Stream processing**: Pipeline-based architecture is often used for real-time or near-real-time stream processing applications, where data is processed continuously as it arrives, rather than in batch mode. Stream processing pipelines enable applications to analyze, transform, and respond to streaming data in real-time, supporting use cases such as monitoring, alerting, and anomaly detection.

Pipeline-based architecture is commonly used in various domains and applications, including:

- **Extract, transform, load (ETL)** pipelines
- Data processing and analytics platforms
- Stream processing frameworks
- Workflow automation systems
- **Continuous integration and deployment (CI/CD)** pipelines

When to use pipeline-based architecture:

- **Data processing pipelines**: Pipeline-based architecture is well-suited for applications that involve sequential data processing tasks, such as ETL pipelines, data transformation workflows, and stream processing applications.

- **Real-time processing**: If your application requires real-time or near-real-time processing of streaming data, pipeline-based architecture provides a framework for building stream processing pipelines that can analyze, transform, and respond to data in real-time.

- **Scalability and parallelism**: If your application needs to scale processing capacity or leverage parallelism to handle large volumes of data, pipeline-based architecture enables parallel execution of processing stages and distributed processing across multiple nodes.

- **Modularity and reusability:** If your application can be decomposed into reusable processing stages or components, pipeline-based architecture facilitates modularity and reusability by encapsulating functionality within individual stages and composing pipelines from reusable components.

When not to use pipeline-based architecture:

- **Simple processing tasks**: For small, straightforward processing tasks with minimal complexity and sequential processing requirements, pipeline-based architecture may introduce unnecessary overhead and complexity. A simpler approach, such as sequential programming or scripting, might be more appropriate.

- **Batch processing**: If your application primarily deals with batch processing of static data sets rather than real-time or streaming data, pipeline-based architecture may not provide significant benefits. Batch processing frameworks or tools may be more suitable for such use cases.

- **Complex workflow orchestration**: If your application involves complex workflow orchestration, where processing tasks depend on complex dependencies, conditions, or decision logic, pipeline-based architecture alone may not be sufficient. Workflow management systems or orchestration frameworks may be needed to manage complex workflows effectively.

- **Highly stateful processing**: If your application requires extensive state management or coordination between processing stages, pipeline-based architecture may introduce challenges in managing stateful processing and ensuring consistency across stages. Stateful stream processing frameworks or state management solutions may be more appropriate for such use cases.

In summary, pipeline-based architecture is a powerful architectural style for building data processing pipelines, stream processing applications, and workflow automation systems. However, it is essential to carefully evaluate the specific requirements, constraints, and trade-offs before deciding to adopt this architecture for a project.

Clean Architecture

This last architectural style is not really a style that serves a bigger functional purpose like the others, but is rather a style that consolidates different styles in a clean and modular fashion.

Clean Architecture is a software architectural style introduced by *Robert C. Martin*. It emphasizes the separation of concerns and the independence of the application's business logic from external dependencies and frameworks. The primary goal of Clean Architecture is to create systems that are flexible, maintainable, and easily testable by enforcing a clear separation of concerns and maintaining a strict dependency hierarchy.

It is a style that could be combined with some of the other functional designs to try and identify the best overall architectural style to use for a particular application. Refer to the following figure:

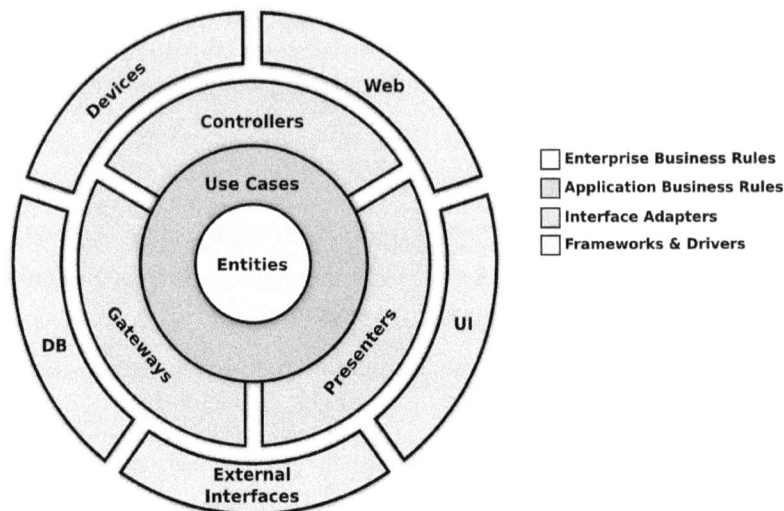

Figure 5.12: Clean Architecture

Key concepts and principles of Clean Architecture include:

- **Separation of concerns**: Clean Architecture divides the system into distinct layers, with each layer representing a different concern or responsibility. These layers are designed to be independent of each other, promoting modularity, maintainability, and flexibility.

- **Dependency rule**: The architecture adheres to the dependency rule, which states that dependencies should flow inward, toward higher-level policies and abstractions, and should not cross architectural boundaries. This rule ensures that the inner layers of the system are independent of external frameworks, databases, or UI components.

- **Layered architecture**: Clean Architecture typically consists of several layers, including the innermost domain layer containing the core business logic, followed by intermediate layers such as application, interface, and infrastructure layers. Each layer depends only on the layers beneath it, creating a clear separation of concerns and responsibilities.

- **Use cases and entities**: Clean Architecture distinguishes between use cases (or interactors) and entities. Use cases represent the application's business logic and encapsulate specific actions or operations that the system can perform. Entities represent domain objects or business entities and encapsulate the core business data and behavior.

- **Dependency Inversion Principle (DIP)**: Clean Architecture adheres to the DIP, which states that high-level modules should not depend on low-level modules; both should depend on abstractions. By relying on abstractions and interfaces, rather than concrete implementations, Clean Architecture promotes loose coupling and flexibility.

- **Testability**: Clean Architecture emphasizes testability by designing systems that are easily testable at various levels, including unit tests for individual components, integration tests for interactions between components, and end-to-end tests for system-wide behavior. The clear separation of concerns and the use of interfaces facilitate mocking and stubbing during testing.

- **Framework independence**: Clean Architecture advocates for framework independence by isolating framework-specific code within the outer layers of the system. This allows the core business logic to remain unaffected by changes to external frameworks, libraries, or technologies, promoting longevity and maintainability.

Clean Architecture is technology-agnostic and can be implemented in various programming languages and platforms. It provides a flexible and adaptable architectural framework for building a wide range of software systems, including web applications, mobile apps, desktop applications, and enterprise systems.

Benefits of Clean Architecture

Some benefits of Clean Architecture are as follows:

- **Modularity**: Clean Architecture promotes modularity by dividing the system into independent layers and components, making it easier to understand, maintain, and extend the codebase.

- **Testability**: The architecture facilitates testability by enabling components to be easily isolated and tested in isolation, improving the reliability and stability of the software.

- **Flexibility**: Clean Architecture allows for flexibility in adapting to changing requirements, technologies, and environments, as changes can be localized to specific layers or components without affecting the entire system.

- **Maintainability**: By enforcing clear separation of concerns and maintaining a strict dependency hierarchy, Clean Architecture improves the maintainability of software systems, reducing the risk of code entanglement and technical debt.

- **Scalability**: Clean Architecture supports scalability by enabling systems to scale horizontally and vertically, as changes and optimizations can be applied incrementally without disrupting the overall architecture.

Overall, Clean Architecture provides a robust and adaptable framework for building software systems that are maintainable, testable, and resilient to change. It encourages best practices such as separation of concerns, dependency inversion, and test-driven development, contributing to the creation of high-quality software.

Conclusion

There are a lot of different styles that a software architect needs to consider when designing an application. And these are only the ones that are perhaps most commonly used at the time of writing. Due to the nature of ever-evolving software design, there will always be newer styles that will be conceived to take advantage of the existing hardware and application needs at the time.

However, the principles that apply to these different styles will remain relevant regardless of the new styles introduced, and as long as a software architect understands the value that each style offers to their application, they will be able to combine and alter these styles to best meet the needs of the application.

The process of finding the right style to choose for a particular software application is an important one, but one which we will only go into at the end of the next chapter on Architectural Patterns as the process for selection for both will follow a similar approach and it is important, we have a good understanding of the different architectural patterns too in order to do this effectively.

Join our book's Discord space

Join the book's Discord Workspace for Latest updates, Offers, Tech happenings around the world, New Release and Sessions with the Authors:

https://discord.bpbonline.com

CHAPTER 6
Architectural Patterns

Introduction

In the previous chapter on architectural styles, we provided a definition of what a pattern is when trying to identify the difference between styles and patterns. In summary, an architectural pattern is a reusable solution to a commonly occurring problem in software architecture within a given context. It provides a structural framework for designing software systems by defining a set of rules, guidelines, and best practices for organizing code, components, and interactions. Architectural patterns help architects and developers make high-level design decisions that address concerns such as scalability, maintainability, flexibility, and performance.

Like different architectural styles though, architectural patterns are not strict templates but rather guidelines that can be adapted and combined based on the specific requirements and constraints of a project. Choosing the appropriate architectural pattern depends on factors such as system requirements, scalability needs, development team expertise, and the nature of the problem domain.

We will now unpack how the different patterns work and, in some cases, also provide some code examples to show more explicitly how these will look when applying them to your codebase.

Structure

In this chapter, we will discuss the following topics:

- Model-View-Controller pattern
- Repository Pattern
- Publish-Subscribe pattern
- Singleton pattern
- Adapter pattern
- Decorator pattern
- Observer pattern
- Testability of architectural patterns
- Choosing styles for different scenarios

Objectives

By the end of this chapter, you will understand the difference between an architectural pattern and architectural styles, what the different patterns are, and how to apply different architectural patterns to find the right solutions for your application and system design.

Model-View-Controller pattern

Model-View-Controller (**MVC**) is a software architectural pattern commonly used for developing user interfaces that separates the representation of information from the user's interaction with it. It divides an application into three interconnected components, each with specific responsibilities, shown as follows:

- **Model (M)**: The Model represents the application's data and business logic. It encapsulates the data structure and behavior of the application, including data validation, manipulation, and storage. The Model notifies the View of any changes in the data, allowing the View to update accordingly.

- **View (V)**: The View is responsible for presenting the data to the user and handling user interface interactions. It displays the Model's data to the user through a **graphical user interface** (**GUI**) or other presentation formats. The View receives user input and forwards it to the Controller for processing.

- **Controller (C)**: The Controller acts as an intermediary between the Model and the View, handling user input and updating the Model accordingly. It interprets user actions, such as button clicks or form submissions, and invokes appropriate operations on the Model. The Controller then updates the View with any changes in the Model's state.

Key principles and characteristics of the Model-View-Controller pattern include:

- **Separation of concerns**: MVC promotes separation of concerns by dividing the application into distinct components responsible for data management (Model), user interface presentation (View), and user interaction handling (Controller). This separation enhances modularity, maintainability, and testability of the application.

- **Flexibility and reusability**: MVC enables flexibility and reusability by decoupling the user interface from the underlying data and business logic. Changes to one component (e.g., the Model) can be made without affecting other components (e.g., the View or Controller), allowing for easier modifications and updates to the application.

- **Support for multiple Views**: MVC supports multiple Views of the same data, allowing developers to create different presentations or representations of the Model for different user interfaces or devices. For example, the same Model can be rendered as a web page, a mobile app, or a desktop application using different Views.

- **User interface independence**: MVC allows for user interface independence, enabling developers to modify or replace the user interface (View) without affecting the underlying data or business logic (Model). This flexibility facilitates the adaptation of the application to changing user interface requirements or technologies.

MVC is widely used in web development frameworks, desktop application frameworks, and mobile application development platforms. It provides a structured and modular approach to building user interfaces, promoting code organization, maintainability, and scalability. However, variations of MVC, such as **Model-View-Presenter** (**MVP**) and **Model-View-ViewModel** (**MVVM**), have emerged to address specific requirements and preferences in different application domains.

When to use MVC:

- **Web development**: MVC is well-suited for web development, particularly in frameworks like Ruby on Rails, Django, Laravel, and ASP.NET MVC. It provides a clear separation between the presentation layer (View), business logic (Model), and user input handling (Controller), making it easier to manage and maintain web applications.

- **Modular applications**: MVC promotes modular development by separating concerns into distinct components. This makes it suitable for building applications with complex functionality that can be divided into manageable modules, allowing for easier maintenance, testing, and collaboration among developers.

- **Large teams**: For projects involving large development teams, MVC provides a structured approach to software development, allowing developers to work on different components independently without stepping on each other's toes. The separation of concerns facilitates parallel development and reduces conflicts between team members.

- **Scalability**: MVC supports scalable application development by providing a clear separation of concerns, which allows for the easy addition of new features or changes without impacting other parts of the application. This makes it suitable for applications that need to scale to accommodate growing user bases or evolving requirements.

- **Multiple user interfaces**: MVC allows for the development of multiple user interfaces (Views) that interact with the same underlying data and business logic (Model). This flexibility makes it suitable for applications that need to support different platforms or devices with distinct user interface requirements.

When not to use MVC:

- **Simple applications**: For small, straightforward applications with minimal complexity and functionality, MVC may introduce unnecessary overhead in terms of architecture and code organization. In such cases, a simpler architectural approach or framework may be more appropriate to avoid unnecessary complexity.

- **Real-time applications**: MVC is not well-suited for real-time applications that require continuous updates or bidirectional communication between clients and servers, such as chat applications or online gaming platforms. Other architectural patterns, like WebSocket-based architectures or event-driven architectures, may be more suitable for real-time applications.

- **Tight coupling**: MVC can lead to tight coupling between the View and the Controller, especially in cases where the View relies heavily on the Controller to perform business logic or data manipulation. This tight coupling can make the application more difficult to maintain and test, especially as it grows in size and complexity.

- **Overhead in small teams**: For projects with small development teams or solo developers, MVC may introduce unnecessary complexity and overhead, particularly if the project does not require the level of modularity and separation of concerns provided by MVC. In such cases, simpler architectural patterns or frameworks may be more suitable for rapid development and prototyping.

- **Performance-critical applications**: In performance-critical applications where every millisecond counts, the overhead introduced by the MVC pattern, such as the additional layers of abstraction and indirection, may impact performance. In such cases, developers may opt for more lightweight architectural patterns or frameworks optimized for performance.

Model-View-ViewModel

MVVM is a software architectural pattern that facilitates the separation of concerns in user interface development, particularly in applications with **graphical user interfaces** (**GUIs**). MVVM is an evolution of the MVC pattern, tailored specifically for modern UI frameworks and technologies, such as **Windows Presentation Foundation** (**WPF**), Xamarin, and AngularJS.

In the MVVM pattern, the application is divided into three main components:

- **Model (M)**: The Model represents the data and business logic of the application. It encapsulates the application's data, state, and behavior, independent of the user interface. The Model notifies the ViewModel of any changes to its state.

- **View (V)**: The View is responsible for presenting the user interface to the user. It displays the data provided by the ViewModel and forwards user input events to the ViewModel for processing. Unlike traditional MVC, the View in MVVM is passive and does not contain any application logic.

- **ViewModel (VM)**: The ViewModel acts as an intermediary between the View and the Model. It exposes data and operations from the Model to the View, providing a presentation layer for the user interface. The ViewModel translates data from the Model into a format suitable for display in the View and responds to user interactions by invoking commands or operations on the Model.

Key principles and characteristics of the MVVM pattern include:

- **Separation of concerns**: MVVM promotes separation of concerns by separating the presentation logic (ViewModel) from the user interface (View) and the business logic (Model). This separation enhances modularity, maintainability, and testability of the application.

- **Data binding**: MVVM relies heavily on data binding to establish communication between the View and the ViewModel. Data binding mechanisms allow the View to automatically update its appearance in response to changes in the ViewModel, and vice versa, without the need for explicit event handling or manual synchronization.

- **Declarative programming**: MVVM encourages declarative programming paradigms, where the user interface is defined in a declarative markup language (e.g., XAML in WPF) and bound to the ViewModel using data binding expressions. This approach simplifies UI development and promotes code readability and maintainability.

- **Testability**: MVVM facilitates unit testing by decoupling the user interface logic (ViewModel) from the actual user interface (View). This allows developers to write automated tests for the ViewModel's behavior without requiring interaction with the graphical user interface, improving test coverage and reliability.

- **Platform independence**: MVVM is platform-independent and can be used with various UI frameworks and technologies, including desktop, web, and mobile applications. It provides a consistent architectural pattern for UI development across different platforms, promoting code reuse and portability.

MVVM is commonly used in modern UI development frameworks, such as WPF, Xamarin, AngularJS, and Vue.js, to build scalable, maintainable, and testable applications with rich user interfaces. It provides a structured approach to UI development, promoting code organization, separation of concerns, and maintainability.

When to use MVVM:

- **Rich user interfaces**: MVVM is well-suited for applications with rich, interactive user interfaces that require complex data bindings, validation, and behavior. It provides a structured approach to UI development, facilitating the creation of dynamic and responsive user interfaces.

- **Cross-platform development**: MVVM is platform-independent and can be used with various UI frameworks and technologies, making it suitable for cross-platform development. It provides a consistent architectural pattern for UI development across different platforms, promoting code reuse and portability.

- **Testability**: MVVM promotes testability by separating the user interface logic (ViewModel) from the actual user interface (View). This allows developers to write automated tests for the ViewModel's behavior without requiring interaction with the graphical user interface, improving test coverage and reliability.

- **Data-driven applications**: MVVM is ideal for data-driven applications where the user interface is heavily dependent on data from the underlying data model. It provides a structured approach to data binding and presentation logic, making it easier to manage and update the user interface in response to changes in the data model.

When not to use MVVM:

- **Simple user interfaces**: For applications with simple user interfaces and minimal interaction requirements, MVVM may introduce unnecessary overhead and complexity. In such cases, a simpler architectural pattern, such as MVC or MVP, may be more appropriate.

- **Performance-critical applications**: In performance-critical applications where every millisecond counts, the overhead introduced by data binding and ViewModel mediation may impact performance. In such cases, developers may opt for more lightweight architectural patterns or frameworks optimized for performance.

- **Limited data binding support**: Some UI frameworks or technologies may have limited support for data binding or lack features necessary for implementing the MVVM pattern effectively. In such cases, developers may need to consider alternative architectural patterns or frameworks better suited to the platform's capabilities.

Repository Pattern

The Repository Pattern is a design pattern commonly used in software development to separate the logic that retrieves data from a data source (such as a database, web service, or file system) from the rest of the application. It provides a centralized interface for accessing and managing data, hiding the details of data access logic from the higher layers of the application.

Key components and concepts of the Repository Pattern include:

- **Repository**: The repository is an abstraction layer that acts as a mediator between the application's business logic and the data source. It encapsulates the logic for querying, storing, updating, and deleting data, providing a uniform interface for data access operations.

- **Entities**: Entities represent the domain objects or data structures managed by the repository. Each entity typically corresponds to a table in a database or an object in an object-oriented programming language.

- **Data source**: The data source is the underlying storage mechanism from which the repository retrieves and persists data. This can include databases, web services, file systems, in-memory data structures, or any other form of persistent storage.

- **Data access logic**: The repository encapsulates the data access logic required to interact with the data source. This logic includes tasks such as executing queries, processing results, handling transactions, and mapping data between the application's domain model and the data source's schema.

- **Abstraction**: The repository provides an abstraction layer that shields the rest of the application from the details of the underlying data source. This promotes modularity, testability, and maintainability by decoupling the application's business logic from the specifics of data access.

- **Single Responsibility Principle (SRP)**: The Repository Pattern adheres to the SRP by separating concerns related to data access from other responsibilities within the application. This improves code organization and makes it easier to manage and extend the application over time.

Benefits of using the Repository Pattern include:

- **Modularity and encapsulation**: The Repository Pattern promotes modularity and encapsulation by encapsulating data access logic within a separate component. This allows the rest of the application to interact with the repository through a well-defined interface, without needing to know the details of how data is accessed and managed.

- **Testability**: The separation of concerns facilitated by the Repository Pattern makes it easier to unit test the application's business logic independently of the data access logic. Mock implementations of the repository can be used during testing to simulate interactions with the data source, enabling thorough testing of the application's behavior.

- **Flexibility and maintainability**: By abstracting data access logic behind a repository interface, the application becomes more flexible and maintainable. Changes to the underlying data source or data access logic can be implemented within the repository without affecting the higher layers of the application.

- **Centralized data access logic**: The Repository Pattern centralizes data access logic within a single component, making it easier to manage and refactor. This improves code organization and reduces duplication of data access logic across multiple parts of the application.

Overall, the Repository Pattern is a valuable tool for managing data access logic in software applications, promoting modularity, testability, and maintainability. It is particularly useful in applications with complex data access requirements or those that need to support multiple data sources or storage mechanisms.

When to use the Repository Pattern:

- **Complex data access logic:** Use the Repository Pattern when your application has complex data access requirements, such as querying data from multiple sources, performing data transformations, or implementing custom data retrieval strategies. The Repository Pattern can encapsulate this complexity, providing a unified interface for interacting with the data source.

- **Modular architecture**: Use the Repository Pattern when you want to promote modularity and separation of concerns in your application. By isolating data access logic within a separate component, the Repository Pattern helps maintain a clear separation between the business logic and the data access logic, making the application easier to understand, maintain, and extend.

- **Testability**: Use the Repository Pattern when you want to improve the testability of your application. By abstracting data access behind a repository interface, you can easily substitute mock implementations of the repository during unit testing, allowing you to test the application's business logic in isolation from the data access logic.

- **Flexibility and maintainability**: Use the Repository Pattern when you anticipate changes to the underlying data source or data access logic over time. By decoupling the application's business logic from the specifics of data access, the Repository Pattern makes it easier to adapt to changes in the data schema, database technology, or data access requirements without affecting other parts of the application.

- **Multiple data sources**: Use the Repository Pattern when your application needs to interact with multiple data sources or storage mechanisms. The Repository Pattern can abstract away the differences between these data sources, providing a uniform interface for accessing and managing data regardless of the underlying implementation.

When not to use the Repository Pattern:

- **Simple data access logic**: If your application has straightforward data access requirements and does not require complex querying, filtering, or transformation of data, the overhead introduced by the Repository Pattern may be unnecessary. In such cases, direct data access methods (e.g., using an ORM or database client) may be more appropriate and efficient.

- **Over-abstraction**: Avoid using the Repository Pattern when it leads to over-abstraction or unnecessary complexity in your application. If the repository interface becomes bloated with methods that are rarely used or overly generic, it can hinder code readability and maintainability. In such cases, consider simplifying the data access logic or using a simpler approach.

- **Tightly coupled data access**: If your application's data access logic is tightly coupled with specific database technologies or frameworks, the Repository Pattern may not provide significant benefits. Trying to abstract away such tight coupling may introduce unnecessary complexity without adding value. Instead, embrace the strengths of the underlying technology or framework and focus on encapsulating only the necessary complexity.

- **Performance-critical applications**: In performance-critical applications where every millisecond counts, the additional layers of abstraction introduced by the Repository Pattern may impact performance. If performance is a primary concern, consider optimizing data access logic using more direct and efficient methods, such as raw SQL queries or optimized database access libraries.

- **Small, throwaway projects**: For small, simple projects with limited scope and lifespan, the overhead of implementing the Repository Pattern may outweigh its benefits. In such cases, prioritize simplicity and rapid development over architectural elegance, and opt for straightforward data access methods that meet the project's immediate needs without unnecessary abstraction.

Publish-Subscribe Pattern

The Publish-Subscribe Pattern is a messaging pattern used in software architecture to facilitate communication between different components of an application or system in a loosely coupled manner. In this pattern, components are decoupled from each other and communicate indirectly through a message broker, also known as a pub-sub system.

Key components and concepts of the Publish-Subscribe Pattern include:

- **Publisher**: A Publisher is a component or entity that generates messages or events and publishes them to the message broker. Publishers are responsible for producing messages and broadcasting them to one or more subscribers interested in receiving them.

- **Subscriber**: A Subscriber is a component or entity that registers interest in receiving messages or events of a particular type or topic. Subscribers subscribe to specific topics or channels within the pub-sub system and receive messages published to those topics.

- **Message broker**: The message broker, also known as the pub-sub system, is responsible for routing messages from publishers to subscribers based on predefined topics or channels. It acts as an intermediary that facilitates communication between publishers and subscribers without direct coupling between them.

- **Topics or channels**: Topics or channels are named channels through which messages are published and subscribed to within the pub-sub system. Publishers publish messages to specific topics, and subscribers subscribe to topics of interest, allowing them to receive relevant messages.

- **Message payload**: The message payload contains the actual data or information being transmitted from the publisher to the subscriber. It can include any type of data, such as text, JSON, XML, binary data, or custom message formats.

- **Asynchronous communication**: The Publish-Subscribe Pattern facilitates asynchronous communication between components, allowing publishers and subscribers to operate independently of each other. Publishers can continue generating messages without waiting for subscribers to process them, and subscribers can receive messages as they become available.

- **Scalability and flexibility**: The Publish-Subscribe Pattern promotes scalability and flexibility by decoupling publishers and subscribers from each other. This allows for the dynamic addition or removal of publishers and subscribers without affecting the overall system architecture.

Benefits of using the Publish-Subscribe Pattern include:

- **Loose coupling**: The Publish-Subscribe Pattern promotes loose coupling between components by decoupling publishers and subscribers from each other. This allows for greater flexibility, maintainability, and scalability of the system.

- **Asynchronous communication**: Publish-Subscribe Pattern facilitates asynchronous communication between components, enabling better responsiveness, scalability, and fault tolerance in distributed systems.

- **Flexibility in message routing**: The use of topics or channels in the pub-sub system allows for flexible message routing, enabling messages to be selectively delivered to interested subscribers based on their subscription preferences.

- **Scalability**: The Publish-Subscribe Pattern supports scalable architectures by allowing multiple publishers and subscribers to operate concurrently. This makes it suitable for building distributed systems that need to handle a large volume of messages or events.

Common use cases for the Publish-Subscribe Pattern include:

- Event-driven architectures

- Real-time messaging systems

- Logging and monitoring systems

- IoT applications

- Distributed systems and microservices architectures

When to use the Publish-Subscribe Pattern:

- **Decoupled communication**: Use the Publish-Subscribe Pattern when you need to facilitate communication between components in a loosely coupled manner, allowing them to operate independently of each other.

- **Scalability requirements**: Use the Publish-Subscribe Pattern when you need to build scalable architectures that can handle a large volume of messages or events and support concurrent processing by multiple publishers and subscribers.

- **Asynchronous communication**: Use the Publish-Subscribe Pattern when you need to implement asynchronous communication between components, enabling better responsiveness, scalability, and fault tolerance in distributed systems.

- **Dynamic subscriptions**: Use the Publish-Subscribe Pattern when you need to support dynamic addition or removal of publishers and subscribers without impacting the overall system architecture. This allows for greater flexibility and adaptability in evolving systems.

When not to use the Publish-Subscribe Pattern:

- **Simple, synchronous communication**: If your application requires simple, synchronous communication between components with tightly coupled interactions, the overhead of implementing the Publish-Subscribe Pattern may not be justified. In such cases, direct method calls or synchronous messaging may be more appropriate.

- **Performance-critical applications**: In performance-critical applications where every microsecond counts, the additional overhead introduced by the Publish-Subscribe Pattern may impact performance. If performance is a primary concern, consider using more lightweight communication mechanisms optimized for low latency and high throughput.

- **Small, single-component applications**: For small, single-component applications with limited communication requirements, the complexity of implementing the Publish-Subscribe Pattern may outweigh its benefits. In such cases, simpler communication mechanisms, such as direct method calls or shared memory, may suffice.

Singleton Pattern

The Singleton Pattern is a creational design pattern that ensures a class has only one instance and provides a global point of access to that instance. It is commonly used when you need to control the instantiation of a class to ensure that only one instance exists throughout the lifetime of the application.

Key features and concepts of the Singleton Pattern include:

- **Private constructor**: The **Singleton** class typically has a **private** constructor to prevent external instantiation of the class.

- **Static instance**: The **Singleton** class contains a **static** member variable that holds the single instance of the class.

- **Static method for access**: The **Singleton** class provides a **static** method that allows other classes to access the single instance of the class.

- **Lazy initialization (optional)**: The **Singleton** instance can be lazily initialized, meaning it is created only when it is first accessed. This helps improve performance by deferring instantiation until it is actually needed.

- **Thread safety (optional)**: Depending on the threading model of the application, the **Singleton** instance may need to be made thread-safe to ensure that it is properly initialized and accessed in a multi-threaded environment.

Here is a basic example of a Singleton implementation in Java:

```java
public class Singleton {
    // Static member variable to hold the single instance of the class
    private static Singleton instance;

    // Private constructor to prevent external instantiation
    private Singleton() {
    }

    // Static method to provide access to the single instance
    public static Singleton getInstance() {
        // Lazy initialization: create the instance if it doesn't exist yet
        if (instance == null) {
```

```
            instance = new Singleton();
        }
        return instance;
    }
}
```

The **Singleton** class has a private constructor to prevent external instantiation. The static **getInstance()** method is used to access the single instance of the class. The instance is lazily initialized, meaning it is created only when **getInstance()** is first called and the instance variable is null.

While the Singleton Pattern provides a simple and effective way to ensure that only one instance of a class exists, it also has some drawbacks and considerations:

- **Global state**: The Singleton instance represents global state, which can lead to tight coupling between classes and make the code harder to test and maintain.

- **Thread safety**: In multi-threaded environments, special care must be taken to ensure that the Singleton instance is properly initialized and accessed in a thread-safe manner. This may involve using synchronization mechanisms or alternative approaches, like double-checked locking or initialization-on-demand.

- **Testability**: Due to its global state nature, classes that depend on the Singleton instance may be harder to test in isolation. Dependency injection and inversion of control techniques can help mitigate this issue by allowing Singleton dependencies to be injected or mocked during testing.

Overall, the Singleton Pattern should be used judiciously, considering its implications on code maintainability, testability, and thread safety. While it can be a useful tool in certain scenarios, it is important to weigh its benefits against its drawbacks and consider alternative approaches when appropriate.

When to use the Singleton Pattern:

- **Single instance requirement**: Use the Singleton Pattern when you need to ensure that a class has only one instance throughout the lifetime of the application. This is useful for managing global state or resources that should be shared across multiple parts of the application.

- **Resource management**: Use the Singleton Pattern when you need to centralize the management of a shared resource, such as a database connection pool, thread pool, configuration settings, or cache. By encapsulating the creation and access to the resource within a Singleton instance, you can ensure consistent and efficient usage.

- **Logging and auditing**: Use the Singleton Pattern for logging and auditing functionality, where you want to maintain a single log instance that aggregates messages from various parts of the application. This allows for centralized logging and ensures that log messages are written to a single destination in a consistent manner.

- **Stateful objects**: Use the Singleton Pattern for stateful objects that represent a unique entity in the application, such as a session manager, user preferences manager, or application context. By ensuring that these objects have only one instance, you can maintain consistency and avoid conflicts due to concurrent access.

- **Performance optimization**: Use the Singleton Pattern for performance optimization purposes, such as lazy initialization of expensive resources or objects. By lazily initializing the Singleton instance only when it is first accessed, you can defer the resource allocation until it is actually needed, improving application start-up time and memory usage.

When not to use the Singleton Pattern:

- **Dependency injection**: If your application uses dependency injection frameworks, like Spring or Guice, consider using dependency injection instead of the Singleton Pattern. Dependency injection allows for more flexible and testable code by decoupling components and providing better control over object instantiation and lifecycle management.

- **Global state management**: Avoid using the Singleton Pattern for managing global state that introduces tight coupling between components and makes the code harder to understand, maintain, and test. Consider alternative architectural patterns, such as dependency injection, event-driven architecture, or service-oriented architecture, to achieve better modularity and separation of concerns.

- **Multi-threaded environments**: Be cautious when using the Singleton Pattern in multi-threaded environments, as it may introduce thread-safety issues if not implemented carefully. Consider using thread-safe Singleton implementations or alternative concurrency patterns, such as dependency injection with scoped beans or thread-local storage, to ensure safe access to shared resources.

- **Overuse**: Avoid overusing the Singleton Pattern for every class or component in your application, as it can lead to excessive global state and tight coupling between components. Instead, use the Singleton Pattern judiciously for classes or components that truly require a single instance and benefit from centralized management.

- **Testing and mocking**: Be mindful of the impact of the Singleton Pattern on testability and mocking in your application. Classes that depend on Singleton instances may be harder to test in isolation due to their global state nature. Consider using dependency injection or inversion of control techniques to facilitate easier testing and mocking of dependencies.

Adapter Pattern

The Adapter Pattern is a structural design pattern that allows objects with incompatible interfaces to work together. It acts as a bridge between two incompatible interfaces by converting the interface of a class into another interface that a client expects. This pattern is particularly useful when integrating existing or third-party code into an application without modifying their source code.

Key components and concepts of the Adapter Pattern include:

- **Target**: The Target is the interface that the client expects to interact with. It defines the desired interface that the client uses to communicate with objects.

- **Adaptee**: The Adaptee is the existing class or component with an incompatible interface that needs to be integrated into the client's code. The Adaptee's interface is different from the interface expected by the client.

- **Adapter**: The Adapter is a wrapper class that bridges the gap between the Target interface and the Adaptee interface. It implements the Target interface and delegates calls to the Adaptee, translating them into a format that the Adaptee can understand.

- **Client**: The Client is the class or component that interacts with the Target interface. It is unaware of the existence of the Adapter and communicates directly with objects through the Target interface.

The Adapter Pattern can be implemented in two ways:

- **Class adapter**: In a class adapter, the Adapter class inherits from both the Target interface and the **Adaptee** class. It extends the **Adaptee** class and implements the **Target** interface, allowing it to act as a bridge between the two interfaces.

- **Object adapter**: In an object adapter, the **Adapter** class contains an instance of the **Adaptee** class as a private member variable. It implements the **Target** interface and delegates calls to the **Adaptee** instance, effectively acting as a wrapper around the **Adaptee** object.

Here is a basic example of the Adapter Pattern in Java code:

```java
// Target interface
interface Target {
    void request();
}

// Adaptee class with incompatible interface
class Adaptee {
    void specificRequest() {
        System.out.println("Adaptee's specificRequest method");
    }
}
// Adapter class implementing the Target interface
class Adapter implements Target {
```

```
    private Adaptee adaptee;

    Adapter(Adaptee adaptee) {
        this.adaptee = adaptee;
    }
    @Override
    public void request() {
        adaptee.specificRequest(); // Delegate call to Adaptee's
specificRequest method
    }
}
// Client class
public class Client {
    public static void main(String[] args) {
        Adaptee adaptee = new Adaptee();
        Target adapter = new Adapter(adaptee);
        adapter.request(); // Call the request method through the adapter
    }
}
```

In this example, the **Adaptee** class has a method **specificRequest()** with an incompatible interface. The **Adapter** class implements the **Target** interface and contains an instance of the **Adaptee** class. It delegates calls to the **specificRequest()** method of the **Adaptee** instance within its **request()** method, effectively adapting the Adaptee's interface to the **Target** interface.

The **Client** class interacts with the **Target** interface through the **Adapter** without needing to know about the existence of the **Adaptee** class or its incompatible interface.

When to use the Adapter Pattern:

- **Integration with third-party libraries**: Use the Adapter Pattern when integrating existing or third-party code into your application that has incompatible interfaces. Adapters allow you to adapt the interfaces of these components to match the interfaces expected by your application.

- **Legacy code migration**: Use the Adapter Pattern when migrating or refactoring legacy code with outdated interfaces to modern interfaces. Adapters can serve as a bridge between the old and new interfaces, allowing for a smoother transition.

- **Interface standardization:** Use the Adapter Pattern when standardizing interfaces across different subsystems or components within your application. Adapters can help unify interfaces and promote consistency and interoperability between components.

When not to use the Adapter Pattern:

- **Compatible interfaces**: Avoid using the Adapter Pattern when the interfaces of the objects you want to integrate are already compatible with each other. In such cases, direct communication between objects without adapters may be more straightforward and efficient.

- **Overuse**: Avoid overusing the Adapter Pattern for every interaction between objects with slightly different interfaces. Excessive use of adapters can lead to unnecessary complexity and overhead in the codebase. Instead, consider refactoring or redesigning interfaces where possible to minimize the need for adapters.

- **Misuse as a workaround**: Avoid using the Adapter Pattern as a workaround for poor design or architecture. While adapters can help integrate incompatible components, they should not be used to patch fundamental design flaws or architectural issues in the application. Instead, focus on addressing the root cause of the compatibility problems.

Decorator Pattern

The Decorator Pattern is a structural design pattern that allows behavior to be added to individual objects dynamically, without affecting the behavior of other objects from the same class. It is commonly used to extend or enhance the functionality of objects at runtime by wrapping them in one or more decorators.

Key components and concepts of the Decorator Pattern include:

- **Component**: The Component is the interface or abstract class defining the interface for objects that can be decorated. It defines the base functionality that decorators can extend.

- **Concrete Component**: The Concrete Component is the base class or implementation of the Component interface. It represents the core functionality that decorators enhance.

- **Decorator**: The Decorator is an abstract class that implements the Component interface and has a reference to an instance of the Component. It acts as a wrapper around the component, adding additional behavior or responsibilities.

- **Concrete Decorator**: The Concrete Decorator is a subclass of the Decorator class that adds specific functionality to the wrapped component. It overrides methods of the Component interface to extend or modify their behavior.

The Decorator Pattern allows behavior to be added to objects dynamically at runtime by composing them with multiple decorators. Each decorator adds its own functionality to the object, allowing for a flexible and modular approach to extending object behavior.

Here is a basic example of the Decorator Pattern in Java:

```java
// Component interface
interface Coffee {
    String getDescription();
    double getCost();
}
// Concrete Component
class SimpleCoffee implements Coffee {
    @Override
    public String getDescription() {
        return "Simple coffee";
    }
    @Override
    public double getCost() {
        return 1.0;
    }
}
// Decorator
abstract class CoffeeDecorator implements Coffee {
    protected Coffee decoratedCoffee;

    public CoffeeDecorator(Coffee decoratedCoffee) {
        this.decoratedCoffee = decoratedCoffee;
    }
    @Override
    public String getDescription() {
        return decoratedCoffee.getDescription();
    }
    @Override
    public double getCost() {
        return decoratedCoffee.getCost();
    }
}
// Concrete Decorator
class MilkDecorator extends CoffeeDecorator {
    public MilkDecorator(Coffee decoratedCoffee) {
        super(decoratedCoffee);
    }
    @Override
    public String getDescription() {
        return super.getDescription() + ", with milk";
    }
```

```java
    @Override
    public double getCost() {
        return super.getCost() + 0.5;
    }
}
// Concrete Decorator
class SugarDecorator extends CoffeeDecorator {
    public SugarDecorator(Coffee decoratedCoffee) {
        super(decoratedCoffee);
    }
    @Override
    public String getDescription() {
        return super.getDescription() + ", with sugar";
    }
    @Override
    public double getCost() {
        return super.getCost() + 0.2;
    }
}
// Client
public class Main {
    public static void main(String[] args) {
        Coffee coffee = new SimpleCoffee();
        System.out.println(coffee.getDescription() + ": $" + coffee.
getCost());

        Coffee milkCoffee = new MilkDecorator(coffee);
        System.out.println(milkCoffee.getDescription() + ": $" +
milkCoffee.getCost());

        Coffee sugarMilkCoffee = new SugarDecorator(milkCoffee);
        System.out.println(sugarMilkCoffee.getDescription() + ": $" +
sugarMilkCoffee.getCost());
    }
}
```

In this example, **Coffee** is the Component interface representing a **coffee** object. **SimpleCoffee** is the Concrete Component implementing the **Coffee** interface.

CoffeeDecorator is the abstract **Decorator** class that extends the **Coffee** interface and contains a reference to an instance of **Coffee**. **MilkDecorator** and **SugarDecorator** are Concrete Decorator classes that add **milk** and **sugar** to the **coffee**, respectively.

The **Main** class demonstrates how to create and use decorated **coffee** objects. Each decorator wraps the base **coffee** object and adds its own functionality (description and cost) to the output.

When to use the Decorator Pattern:

- **Dynamic behavior extension**: Use the Decorator Pattern when you need to add or modify the behavior of objects dynamically at runtime, without affecting other objects from the same class or introducing subclasses for each variation.

- **Flexible composition**: Use the Decorator Pattern when you want to achieve flexible and modular composition of objects by combining multiple decorators in different combinations. This allows for fine-grained control over object behavior and avoids the need for large numbers of subclasses.

- **Open-Closed Principle**: Use the Decorator Pattern to adhere to the Open-Closed Principle, which states that classes should be open for extension but closed for modification. Decorators can extend the behavior of objects without modifying their source code, making it easy to add new functionality without altering existing code.

When not to use the Decorator Pattern:

- **Simple or static behavior**: Avoid using the Decorator Pattern for objects with simple or static behavior that does not need to be extended or modified dynamically at runtime. In such cases, simpler approaches like subclassing may be more appropriate.

- **Performance considerations**: Be cautious when using the Decorator Pattern in performance-critical applications, as each decorator adds an additional layer of indirection and overhead. In scenarios where performance is a primary concern, consider alternative approaches that minimize overhead, such as direct method calls or caching.

Observer Pattern

The Observer Pattern is a behavioral design pattern that defines a one-to-many dependency between objects, so that when one object changes its state, all its dependents are notified and updated automatically. It is often used to implement distributed event handling systems or to implement MVC architectures.

Key components and concepts of the Observer Pattern include:

- **Subject (or observable)**: The Subject is the object that holds the state and sends notifications to observers when its state changes. It maintains a collection of observers and provides methods to add, remove, and notify observers.

- **Observer**: The Observer is the interface or abstract class that defines the contract for objects that should be notified of changes in the subject's state. Observers register themselves with the subject to receive notifications.

- **Concrete Subject**: The Concrete Subject is a concrete implementation of the Subject interface. It holds the actual state and triggers notifications to its observers when the state changes. It also provides methods to manage the collection of observers.

- **Concrete Observer**: The Concrete Observer is a concrete implementation of the Observer interface. It registers with a subject to receive notifications and defines how it should respond to changes in the subject's state.

Here is a basic example of the Observer Pattern in Java:

```java
import java.util.ArrayList;
import java.util.List;

// Subject (or Observable)
interface Subject {
    void addObserver(Observer observer);
    void removeObserver(Observer observer);
    void notifyObservers();
}
// Concrete Subject
class WeatherStation implements Subject {
    private int temperature;
    private List<Observer> observers = new ArrayList<>();

    public void setTemperature(int temperature) {
        this.temperature = temperature;
        notifyObservers();
    }
    @Override
    public void addObserver(Observer observer) {
        observers.add(observer);
    }
    @Override
    public void removeObserver(Observer observer) {
        observers.remove(observer);
    }
    @Override
    public void notifyObservers() {
        for (Observer observer : observers) {
            observer.update(temperature);
        }
    }
}
// Observer
interface Observer {
```

```
        void update(int temperature);
}
// Concrete Observer
class WeatherDisplay implements Observer {
    @Override
    public void update(int temperature) {
        System.out.println("Temperature updated: " + temperature);
    }
}
public class Main {
    public static void main(String[] args) {
        WeatherStation weatherStation = new WeatherStation();
        WeatherDisplay display1 = new WeatherDisplay();
        WeatherDisplay display2 = new WeatherDisplay();

        weatherStation.addObserver(display1);
        weatherStation.addObserver(display2);

        weatherStation.setTemperature(25);
    }
}
```

In this example:

- Subject is represented by the **WeatherStation** class, which holds the temperature state and maintains a list of observers.

- Observer is represented by the **Observer** interface, defining the **update()** method.

- Concrete Subject is the **WeatherStation** class, which implements the **Subject** interface and notifies observers when the temperature changes.

- Concrete Observer is the **WeatherDisplay** class, which implements the **Observer** interface and updates the temperature display when notified.

When to use the Observer Pattern:

- **Loose coupling**: Use the Observer Pattern when you want to achieve loose coupling between objects, allowing them to interact without having explicit knowledge of each other's implementation details.

- **Event handling**: Use the Observer Pattern when implementing event handling systems, where objects need to be notified of changes or events occurring in other objects without tight coupling.

- **Model-View-Controller**: Use the Observer Pattern to implement the Observer part of the MVC architecture, where the model notifies registered views of changes in its state.

When not to use the Observer Pattern:

- **Overhead in small systems**: Avoid using the Observer Pattern in small, simple systems where the overhead of maintaining a list of observers and notifying them of changes may outweigh the benefits of loose coupling.

- **Complexity in maintenance**: Avoid using the Observer Pattern in scenarios where maintaining the relationship between subjects and observers becomes overly complex or difficult to manage, especially in large-scale systems with many observers.

Testability of architectural patterns

Testability is a critical aspect of software development, and it is essential to consider how well architectural patterns support effective testing. How easily an application or module can be tested plays a massive role in the maintainability of the system, and so understanding the testability of different patterns is an important aspect to consider in the evaluation process of choosing which pattern to use.

While we will have an entire chapter devoted to software testing later in the book, it is useful to have an understanding at this point of how the different patterns can be leveraged to make the system more testable.

Here is a breakdown of the testability of some common architectural patterns:

- **Model-View-Controller:**
    - **Testability**: MVC promotes testability by separating concerns. Models can be unit-tested independently of views and controllers, enabling comprehensive testing of the application's components.
    - **Advantages**: Well-suited for unit testing and automated testing frameworks.

- **Repository Pattern:**
    - **Testability**: The Repository Pattern abstracts data access, making it testable through mocking or substitution of repositories during unit tests.
    - **Advantages**: Enables the isolation of data access logic for testing.

- **Publish-Subscribe Pattern:**
    - **Testability**: Publish-Subscribe allows decoupled communication, simplifying the testing of individual components. Publishers and subscribers can be tested independently.
    - **Advantages**: Supports isolated testing of components through event-based communication.

- **Singleton Pattern:**

  - **Testability**: While Singleton instances are globally accessible, their behavior can be tested similarly to other classes. Mocking frameworks can be employed for unit testing.

  - **Advantages**: Testability depends on how well dependencies are managed in Singleton instances.

- **Adapter Pattern:**

  - **Testability**: The Adapter Pattern helps in adapting interfaces, making it possible to test components independently by creating mock or stub adapters.

  - **Advantages**: Facilitates testing through interface adaptability.

- **Decorator Pattern:**

  - **Testability**: Decorators can be tested independently, as they add responsibilities to an object. Unit testing can be applied to the core object and each decorator.

  - **Advantages**: Enables modular testing of enhanced or decorated components.

- **Observer Pattern:**

  - **Testability**: The Observer Pattern supports testing of observers and subjects independently. Observers can be tested for their reaction to state changes.

  - **Advantages**: Allows isolated testing of components responding to state changes.

In general, the testability of architectural patterns relies on their ability to support modular testing, isolation of components, and the ease of setting up test scenarios. It is essential to implement patterns in a way that facilitates automated testing and enables the use of testing frameworks and tools to ensure the reliability and correctness of software systems.

Choosing styles for different scenarios

Deciding on the most appropriate architectural style for an application involves considering various factors, including the application's requirements, constraints, and context. Here is a step-by-step guide to help you make an informed decision:

- **Understand the requirements:**

  - Start by thoroughly understanding the functional and non-functional requirements of the application. Consider factors such as scalability, performance, maintainability, flexibility, security, and extensibility.

  - Identify the key features, use cases, and workflows that the application needs to support.

- **Analyze the domain and problem space:**

  - Analyze the domain or problem space in which the application operates. Consider the nature of the data, business logic, and interactions involved.

  - Identify any domain-specific patterns, constraints, or regulations that may influence the choice of architectural style.

- **Evaluate constraints and context:**

  - Take into account any constraints or limitations imposed by the project context, such as budget, timeline, available technology stack, team expertise, and organizational policies.

  - Consider the existing infrastructure, legacy systems, and integration requirements that the application needs to work with.

- **Consider trade-offs and priorities:**

  - Evaluate the trade-offs associated with different architectural styles in relation to the application's requirements and constraints. For example, consider the trade-offs between scalability and simplicity, or between performance and maintainability.

  - Prioritize the architectural qualities (e.g., scalability, maintainability, performance) that are most critical for the success of the application.

- **Review use cases and patterns:**

  - Review common use cases, architectural patterns, and best practices relevant to the application domain. Consider how well-known architectural styles, such as layered architecture, microservices, or event-driven architecture, align with the application's requirements and use cases.

  - Evaluate the suitability of specific architectural patterns for addressing the application's challenges and goals.

- **Prototype and experiment:**

  - Consider prototyping or experimenting with different architectural styles or patterns to assess their feasibility and effectiveness in addressing the application's requirements.

  - Build small proof-of-concept projects or conduct technical spikes to evaluate the practicality and suitability of different architectural approaches.

- **Involve stakeholders and collaborate:**

  - Involve stakeholders, including business owners, product managers, developers, architects, and other relevant parties, in the decision-making process.

- o Collaborate with team members to gather diverse perspectives, insights, and expertise that can inform the decision on the architectural style.

- **Document and communicate:**

  - o Document the rationale behind the chosen architectural style, including its alignment with the application's requirements, constraints, and context.

  - o Clearly communicate the chosen architectural approach to all stakeholders and team members to ensure alignment and understanding.

- **Iterate and adapt:**

  - o Recognize that architectural decisions are not set in stone and may need to be revisited and adjusted over time as the application evolves, new requirements emerge, or new insights are gained.

  - o Continuously monitor and evaluate the effectiveness of the chosen architectural style and be prepared to iterate and adapt as needed.

By following these steps and considering the specific requirements, constraints, and context of the application, you can make a well-informed decision about the most appropriate architectural style to use. Remember that there is no one-size-fits-all solution, and the best architectural approach will depend on the unique characteristics and goals of your application.

Conclusion

Patterns play a big role in structure the code together and provide all developers and engineers working on an application with a clear guideline of how they need to go about building an application.

Many patterns and styles may work well together and so it is important when considering the correct approach for an application design that you familiarize yourself with the last two chapters to better evaluate the right holistic approach for each part of an application.

There is no one perfect solution to solving any software problem, but by applying the benefits and drawbacks of all the different patterns and coupling this with proper evaluation against the required criteria and then it is possible for a suitable solution to be obtained that will meet all the relevant design criteria.

In the next chapter, we will look at different architectural components that you get and the impact and role they play in the overall design of your software.

## CHAPTER 7

Component Architecture

Introduction

Many of the architectural principles and structures discussed focus on design and looking at software from the ground up. However, seldom does an architect get to design something from scratch, and this is why it is so important to understand the individual role that different components have in a software application. It helps not just in breaking down software into smaller, modularized components, but more importantly, understanding the role that each component plays in an existing application makes it easy for an architect to makes sense of a system and identify how the existing design patterns may or may not be aiding them in achieving their given purpose.

To explain the point better, let us return to Codeburg and our *Architect Sir Alistair*:

Having successfully implemented a modular architecture in his previous project, he now turned his attention to a new endeavor: an ambitious undertaking to create a digital library to preserve the kingdom's rich history and knowledge.

As *Sir Alistair* embarked on this monumental task, he understood the importance of functional decomposition, a fundamental principle in software architecture. Functional decomposition involves breaking down the system's functionality into smaller, manageable components, each responsible for a specific task or operation.

With this in mind, *Sir Alistair* gathered his team of skilled developers and began the process of functional decomposition. They carefully analyzed the requirements of the digital library, identifying the key features and functionalities it needed to encompass. Then, they systematically decomposed these functionalities into smaller modules, ensuring clarity, cohesion, and maintainability.

One of the most critical aspects of the digital library was its search functionality. *Sir Alistair* recognized that efficient search capabilities were essential for users to access the vast repository of knowledge contained within the library. So, he and his team decomposed the search functionality into several distinct modules:

- **Indexing module**: Responsible for parsing and indexing the content of documents, allowing for fast and accurate retrieval.

- **Query processing module**: Handles user queries and translates them into search operations, optimizing search results based on relevance and user preferences.

- **Ranking module**: Evaluates the relevance of search results using various ranking algorithms, ensuring that the most pertinent information is presented to the user first.

- **User interface module**: Provides an intuitive interface for users to interact with the search functionality, displaying results in a user-friendly manner and facilitating navigation through the library's content.

As *Sir Alistair* and his team worked diligently on each module, they encountered challenges and obstacles along the way. However, through collaboration, creativity, and perseverance, they overcame these hurdles, refining their design and implementing robust solutions.

Finally, after months of dedicated effort, the digital library was ready to be unveiled to the kingdom. As *Sir Alistair* presented the completed project to the royal court, he spoke of the importance of functional decomposition in guiding the architectural design process. He emphasized how breaking down complex functionalities into manageable components had enabled them to build a scalable, extensible, and efficient system.

The digital library was met with resounding praise, hailed as a testament to *Sir Alistair's* vision and expertise as an architect. And in the kingdom of Codeburg, the tale of *Sir Alistair* and the importance of functional decomposition became yet another legend, a timeless reminder of the principles that guided the craft of software architecture.

So, the preceding might be one example of how an architect, like *Sir Alistair*, might go about trying to understand the different components in an application.

Now that we understand how looking into the different aspects of a system allows an architect to design a system better, let us look at how this can be applied practically.

Structure

In this chapter, we will discuss the following topics:

- Component identification
- Decomposing the system
- Establishing communication protocols
- Dependency management
- Cohesion
- Coupling
- Guidelines for coupling and cohesion
- High cohesion, low coupling
- Single Responsibility Principle
- Encapsulation

Objectives

By the end of this chapter, you will understand the different software components that exist within your bigger architectural styles and patterns and the role they play in your bigger software design.

Component identification

Identifying components can become a complex process to undertake, especially when looking at large, complex systems. So, it is important that we identify a systematic approach an architect can take to identify components effectively:

- **Define the scope**: Clearly define the scope of the project or the system you are working on. Understand its purpose, function, and the requirements it needs to fulfill. This will provide a framework for identifying relevant components.

- **Break down the system**: Break down the entire system or building into smaller, manageable parts. This could be done hierarchically, starting from the overall structure and then diving into subsystems and individual components.

- **Analyze functionality**: Understand the functions that the system or building needs to perform. Identify the key functional requirements and how they are distributed across different components.

- **Consider interactions**: Analyze how different components interact with each other within the system. Identify dependencies, inputs, outputs, and any feedback loops between components.

- **Refer to standards and regulations**: Consider relevant standards, regulations, and best practices applicable to the type of building or system you are designing. This can help ensure compliance and safety.

- **Utilize existing knowledge**: Draw from existing knowledge and precedents in similar projects or systems. This can provide insights into common components and solutions that have been successful in the past.

- **Utilize modeling tools**: Use architectural modeling tools to visualize the components within the system or building. This can help in organizing and categorizing components based on their properties and functions.

- **Document and review**: Document your component identification process thoroughly. Create diagrams, lists, or other documentation to clearly illustrate the identified components. Review this documentation regularly to ensure completeness and accuracy.

- **Seek feedback**: Collaborate with other stakeholders, such as clients, engineers, and builders, to validate your component identification. Their input can provide valuable perspectives and help identify any overlooked components or issues.

- **Iterate and refine**: Recognize that component identification is an iterative process. As the design evolves and more information becomes available, revisit your component identification to refine and improve it as needed.

By following these steps, architects can systematically identify components within a building or system, ensuring that all necessary elements are accounted for and properly integrated into the design.

Decomposing the system

Decomposing a system involves breaking it down into smaller, more manageable parts or subsystems. This process is essential for understanding the system's structure, function, and relationships between its components. Here is how an architect can approach decomposing a system effectively:

- **Identify system boundaries**: Begin by defining the boundaries of the system you are decomposing. Clearly delineate what is considered part of the system and what lies outside of it. This helps in establishing the scope of your decomposition.

- **Understand system functionality**: Gain a thorough understanding of the system's overall functionality and objectives. Identify the primary functions it needs to perform and the requirements it must satisfy.

- **Hierarchical decomposition**: Decompose the system hierarchically, starting from the top-level system and then breaking it down into progressively smaller subsystems and components. Each level of decomposition should represent a coherent and manageable unit.

- **Identify subsystems**: Identify major subsystems or modules within the system based on their distinct functionality or responsibilities. Subsystems should encapsulate related components and perform specific tasks within the overall system.

- **Define interfaces**: Clearly define interfaces between subsystems to specify how they interact and communicate with each other. Interfaces should describe the inputs, outputs, and interactions required for seamless integration between subsystems.

- **Consider abstraction levels**: Decide on the appropriate level of abstraction for each subsystem and component. Balance between too much detail, which can lead to complexity, and too little detail, which may obscure important information.

- **Use functional decomposition**: Break down the system based on its functional aspects. Identify the key functions that the system performs and decompose them into smaller, more manageable sub-functions and tasks.

- **Consider physical decomposition**: Alternatively, decompose the system based on its physical components or elements. Identify the physical parts of the system and how they are interconnected to perform the desired functions.

- **Iterate and refine**: Decomposition is an iterative process. As you gain more insights and information about the system, revisit your decomposition to refine and improve it as needed. Iterate through multiple levels of decomposition until you achieve a satisfactory level of detail.

- **Document and communicate**: Document your decomposition using diagrams, charts, or other visual aids to clearly illustrate the structure of the system and its components. Communicate your decomposition to stakeholders to ensure a shared understanding of the system architecture.

Establishing communication protocols

Understanding the different components in a system is vital to evaluating how it works, but components do not interact in isolation, and once a functional decomposition has been done, the next step is to look into establishing clear communication protocols that define how each part of a system communicates with each other.

Establishing communication protocols between components is essential for ensuring seamless interaction and interoperability within a system and helps an architect provide the glue that sticks the different parts of a system together.

Here is how an architect can approach establishing communication protocols for a system:

- **Identify communication requirements**: Understand the communication requirements of each component within the system. Determine what information needs to be exchanged, how frequently, and under what conditions.

- **Define interfaces**: Clearly define interfaces between components to specify how they communicate with each other. Interfaces should outline the methods, parameters, and data formats used for communication.

- **Select communication technologies**: Choose appropriate communication technologies and protocols based on the requirements of the system. Consider factors such as speed, reliability, security, scalability, and compatibility with existing infrastructure.

- **Standardize protocols**: Standardize communication protocols across components to ensure consistency and interoperability. Utilize established standards and protocols whenever possible to facilitate integration and compatibility.

- **Implement error handling**: Implement robust error handling mechanisms to manage communication failures and ensure reliable data transmission between components. Include mechanisms for error detection, correction, and recovery as needed.

- **Address security concerns**: Address security concerns by implementing encryption, authentication, and access control mechanisms to protect sensitive data and prevent unauthorized access or tampering.

- **Define message formats**: Define standardized message formats for data exchange between components. Specify the structure, syntax, and semantics of messages to facilitate seamless interpretation and processing.

- **Consider asynchronous communication**: Consider using asynchronous communication patterns to decouple components and improve scalability and resilience. Asynchronous communication allows components to operate independently and handle messages at their own pace.

- **Implement testing and validation**: Test communication protocols thoroughly to ensure compatibility, reliability, and performance. Validate protocols through simulated and real-world scenarios to identify and address any issues or bottlenecks.

- **Document and communicate**: Document communication protocols thoroughly, including interface specifications, message formats, and communication workflows. Communicate these protocols to stakeholders to ensure a shared understanding and facilitate collaboration.

By following these steps, architects can establish effective communication protocols between components, enabling seamless interaction and interoperability within the system. This lays the foundation for building robust and scalable architectures that meet the requirements of modern applications and systems.

Dependency management

Along with having components communicate with each other, they are also dependent on each other. Understanding how these components rely on one another and orchestrating their interactions facilitates seamless development across loosely coupled components, enabling teams to build applications with greater flexibility and efficiency.

Dependency management refers to the process of identifying, controlling, and handling the relationships and connections between various elements or components within a system or project. These elements could include software libraries, modules, packages, frameworks, or external services that are utilized by the system to function effectively.

Dependency management is a critical aspect of software development and system architecture, especially in complex projects with multiple components and dependencies. Effective dependency management practices help ensure that systems are reliable, maintainable, and scalable over time.

Dependency management involves several key aspects:

- **Identification**: This involves identifying the dependencies that exist within a system. Dependencies can be of various types, including direct dependencies (those directly used by the system) and transitive dependencies (dependencies of the direct dependencies). Identifying dependencies is crucial for understanding the components that are required for the system to operate correctly.

- **Versioning**: Dependencies often have different versions available, each with its own set of features, bug fixes, and potentially compatibility issues. Version management ensures that the system uses compatible versions of dependencies to prevent conflicts and maintain stability.

- **Resolution**: Dependency resolution is the process of determining which specific versions of dependencies should be used by the system. This involves considering compatibility requirements, version constraints, and potential conflicts between different dependencies.

- **Lifecycle management**: Dependencies may have their own lifecycle, including initialization, usage, and disposal. Managing the lifecycle of dependencies involves ensuring that they are instantiated, initialized, and disposed of properly to optimize resource usage and prevent memory leaks or other issues.

- **Updating and upgrading**: Dependencies may need to be updated or upgraded over time to incorporate new features, security patches, or bug fixes. Dependency management includes processes for safely updating dependencies while minimizing disruptions to the system.

- **Conflict resolution**: Conflicts can arise when multiple dependencies require different versions of the same library or module. Dependency management involves resolving these conflicts by selecting compatible versions or finding alternative solutions.

- **Documentation and communication**: Effective dependency management requires clear documentation of dependencies, including their purpose, version requirements, and any potential issues or constraints. Communication with stakeholders and development teams is essential to ensure that everyone understands the dependencies and their implications for the system.

Cohesion

Cohesion refers to the degree to which the elements within a module or component are related to each other and work together to achieve a common purpose or functionality. In software engineering and system design, cohesion is a measure of how strongly the internal elements of a module are related to each other. Higher cohesion indicates that the elements within a module are closely related and perform a single, well-defined function, while lower cohesion suggests that the elements are less related and may perform multiple, unrelated functions.

In the context of functional decomposition, cohesion plays a crucial role in determining the effectiveness and quality of the decomposed components. Here is how cohesion influences functional decomposition:

- **Clarity of responsibility**: Functional decomposition aims to break down a system into smaller, more manageable components, each responsible for a specific function or feature. Cohesion helps ensure that each decomposed component has a clear and well-defined responsibility, making it easier to understand and maintain.

- **Modularity and reusability**: Components with high cohesion tend to be more modular and reusable. They encapsulate a coherent set of functionalities, making it easier to reuse them in other parts of the system or in different projects. This promotes code reusability and accelerates development by reducing duplication and promoting consistency.

- **Ease of maintenance**: High cohesion components are typically easier to maintain because they are focused on a specific task or functionality. Changes or updates to the system can be localized to individual components without affecting other parts of the system, reducing the risk of unintended side effects.

- **Reduced complexity**: Components with high cohesion tend to have lower complexity because they have a clear and narrow focus. This simplifies understanding and reasoning about the behavior of the system, making it easier to troubleshoot issues, debug code, and make enhancements.

- **Scalability and flexibility**: Well-decomposed components with high cohesion are inherently more scalable and flexible. They can be easily extended, modified, or replaced to accommodate changing requirements or to support future enhancements without impacting the overall system architecture.

In summary, cohesion is a fundamental principle in functional decomposition that guides the creation of well-structured and maintainable components. By emphasizing high cohesion during the decomposition process, architects and developers can create modular, reusable, and easily maintainable components that contribute to the overall quality and success of the system.

Functional cohesion

Functional cohesion is a type of cohesion in software engineering that refers to the degree to which the elements within a module or component are related and work together to perform a single, well-defined function. In other words, a module or component exhibits functional cohesion when all its elements are focused on achieving a specific task or functionality.

Characteristics of functional cohesion include:

- **Single purpose**: All elements within the module contribute to accomplishing a single, specific function or task. There is a clear and well-defined purpose for the module, and each element within it directly supports that purpose.

- **Minimal interaction**: Elements within the module have minimal interaction with each other beyond what is necessary to accomplish the defined function. The module is designed to be self-contained, with little or no reliance on external components or data.

- **High encapsulation**: The module encapsulates a coherent set of functionalities, with related elements grouped together. This promotes modularity and reusability by allowing the module to be easily incorporated into other parts of the system without introducing dependencies or side effects.

- **Low coupling**: There is minimal coupling between the module and other parts of the system. Dependencies on external components or data are kept to a minimum, reducing the risk of unintended side effects and simplifying maintenance and testing.

Examples of modules exhibiting functional cohesion include utility libraries, mathematical functions, or data processing modules. These modules typically consist of closely related elements that work together to perform a specific computation, calculation, or transformation.

Functional cohesion is considered a desirable attribute in software design because it promotes clarity, maintainability, and reusability. Modules with functional cohesion are easier to understand, maintain, and extend, making them valuable building blocks for creating complex software systems.

Sequential cohesion

Sequential cohesion is a type of cohesion in software engineering that describes the degree to which the elements within a module or component are related by the sequence in which they are executed. In other words, elements within a sequentially cohesive module are arranged in a sequential order, where the output of one element serves as the input to the next.

Characteristics of sequential cohesion include:

- **Linear execution**: Elements within the module are executed in a linear sequence, one after another, without branching or looping structures.

- **Data flow**: Data flows sequentially from one element to the next, with the output of one element becoming the input for the subsequent element.

- **Procedural logic**: The module typically implements a specific procedure or algorithm, with each element performing a distinct step in the overall process.

- **State management**: Elements may share state information, with each element modifying or transforming the state as the sequence progresses.

- **High coupling**: Sequentially cohesive modules often exhibit high coupling between elements, as they rely heavily on the output of preceding elements to perform their tasks.

Examples of modules exhibiting sequential cohesion include procedural algorithms, such as sorting algorithms or data processing pipelines. In these modules, each step in the algorithm or pipeline depends on the output of the preceding step to execute successfully.

Sequential cohesion is commonly found in procedural programming paradigms, where programs are organized around sequences of instructions or steps. While sequential cohesion can lead to straightforward and easy-to-understand code, it can also result in tight coupling between elements, making the module less modular and harder to maintain or extend. As a result, software engineers often strive to balance sequential cohesion with other types of cohesion, such as functional cohesion, to improve the overall quality and maintainability of the software system.

Communication cohesion

Communication cohesion is a type of cohesion in software engineering that describes the degree to which the elements within a module or component are related based on their need to communicate with each other. In other words, elements within a communication-cohesive module are grouped together because they share data or information necessary to perform their respective tasks.

Characteristics of communication cohesion include:

- **Data exchange**: Elements within the module exchange data or information with each other to accomplish their individual functions. This data exchange is a primary reason for the elements to be grouped together.

- **Shared context**: Elements within the module operate within a shared context or domain, with each element relying on the data or context provided by other elements.

- **Message passing**: Communication-cohesive modules often involve message passing or data sharing mechanisms, such as function calls, method invocations, or shared variables.

- **Interdependence**: There is a high degree of interdependence between elements, as changes to one element may affect the behavior or output of other elements within the module.

- **Dependency management**: Effective management of dependencies between elements is crucial in communication-cohesive modules to ensure that data is shared appropriately and that changes are propagated correctly.

Examples of modules exhibiting communication cohesion include collaborative editing tools, real-time systems, or distributed processing frameworks. In these modules, different components or subsystems need to exchange data or messages to coordinate their activities and achieve the overall objectives of the system.

Communication cohesion is essential for promoting modularity, flexibility, and maintainability in software systems, as it helps organize related functionality and facilitates effective data sharing and collaboration between components. However, excessive communication cohesion can lead to tight coupling between elements, making the module less modular and harder to maintain or extend. Therefore, software engineers should strive to achieve a balance between communication cohesion and other types of cohesion to optimize the overall design and architecture of the system.

Procedural cohesion

Procedural cohesion is a type of cohesion in software engineering that describes the degree to which the elements within a module or component are related based on the sequence of actions or steps they perform. In other words, elements within a procedurally cohesive module are grouped together because they are involved in carrying out a specific procedure or algorithm.

Characteristics of procedural cohesion include:

- **Linear execution**: Elements within the module are executed in a sequential order to accomplish a specific procedure or task. Each element represents a step in the procedure, and the module follows a predefined sequence of actions.

- **Procedural logic**: The module typically implements a specific procedure, algorithm, or workflow, with each element performing a distinct step or action in the overall process.

- **Data flow**: Data or control flow moves linearly through the module, with each element consuming inputs from preceding elements and producing outputs for subsequent elements.

- **State management**: Procedurally cohesive modules may share state information, with each element manipulating or transforming the state as the procedure progresses.

- **High coupling**: Procedurally cohesive modules often exhibit high coupling between elements, as they rely heavily on the output of preceding elements to perform their tasks. Changes to one element may affect the behavior or output of other elements within the module.

Examples of modules exhibiting procedural cohesion include sorting algorithms, data processing pipelines, or workflow engines. In these modules, each element represents a step in the procedure or workflow, and the module as a whole follows a predefined sequence of actions to achieve its objectives.

Procedural cohesion can lead to clear and straightforward code that is easy to understand and follow, particularly in procedural programming paradigms. However, it can also result in tight coupling between elements, making the module less modular and harder to maintain or extend. Therefore, software engineers should carefully consider the trade-offs between procedural cohesion and other types of cohesion, such as functional cohesion, to optimize the design and maintainability of the software system.

Temporal cohesion

Temporal cohesion is a type of cohesion in software engineering that describes the degree to which the elements within a module or component are related based on their temporal proximity or timing of execution. In other words, elements within a temporally cohesive module are grouped together because they are executed at the same time or during the same period of the program's execution.

Characteristics of temporal cohesion include:

- **Simultaneous execution**: Elements within the module are executed together as part of the same process, routine, or event. They are temporally related because they are activated or triggered by the same event or condition.

- **Temporal proximity**: Elements within the module have similar or closely related timing requirements, such as being performed in a specific order or within a specific timeframe.

- **Event-driven**: Temporally cohesive modules are often event-driven, meaning that they respond to external events or stimuli by executing a set of actions or operations.

- **Concurrency**: Temporally cohesive modules may involve concurrent execution of elements, where multiple actions or tasks are performed simultaneously or in parallel.

- **Synchronization**: Temporally cohesive modules may require synchronization mechanisms to coordinate the timing and sequencing of actions or tasks within the module.

Examples of modules exhibiting temporal cohesion include event handlers, interrupt service routines, or time-sensitive processing modules. In these modules, elements are grouped together based on their temporal relationship or proximity, such as responding to the same event or being executed concurrently in a multi-threaded environment.

Temporal cohesion is important for ensuring that related actions or tasks are executed together in a coordinated manner, particularly in event-driven or real-time systems. However, excessive temporal cohesion can lead to modules that are tightly coupled and difficult to maintain or extend. Therefore, software engineers should carefully consider the timing and sequencing requirements of elements within a module to achieve an appropriate balance between temporal cohesion and other types of cohesion, such as functional cohesion.

Logical cohesion

Logical cohesion is a type of cohesion in software engineering that describes the degree to which the elements within a module or component are related based on the logical grouping of functionality. In other words, elements within a logically cohesive module are grouped together because they are logically related and contribute to the same overarching purpose or functionality.

Characteristics of logical cohesion include:

- **Related functionality**: Elements within the module perform related tasks or operations that contribute to achieving a common objective or functionality. They are grouped together based on their logical relationship to each other.

- **Single responsibility**: The module encapsulates a single, well-defined responsibility or aspect of the system's functionality. Each element within the module contributes to fulfilling this responsibility, and there is a clear and cohesive purpose for the module as a whole.

- **High abstraction**: Logical cohesion promotes high levels of abstraction by grouping together elements that share similar functionality or behavior. This abstraction simplifies the understanding and maintenance of the module by providing a clear and coherent organization of related functionality.

- **Low coupling**: Logical cohesion encourages loose coupling between modules by organizing related functionality into separate, self-contained units. This reduces interdependencies between modules and promotes modularity, reusability, and maintainability.

- **Domain-driven design**: Logical cohesion aligns with principles of domain-driven design by organizing software components according to the domain concepts and business logic of the problem domain. This helps ensure that the software architecture reflects the underlying structure and requirements of the domain.

Examples of modules exhibiting logical cohesion include user interface components, data access layers, or domain-specific service modules. In these modules, elements are grouped together based on their logical relationship to each other and their shared responsibility for implementing a specific aspect of the system's functionality.

Logical cohesion is considered a desirable attribute in software design because it promotes clarity, modularity, and maintainability by organizing related functionality into cohesive and well-defined modules. By grouping elements based on their logical relationship and shared responsibility, software engineers can create software systems that are easier to understand, maintain, and extend.

Coincidental cohesion

Coincidental cohesion is a type of cohesion in software engineering that describes a situation where the elements within a module or component are grouped together arbitrarily, with no inherent logical or functional relationship between them. In other words, coincidentally cohesive modules contain elements that are unrelated and do not contribute to a common purpose or functionality.

Characteristics of coincidental cohesion include:

- **Heterogeneous elements**: The elements within the module perform unrelated or disparate tasks that do not share a common theme or purpose. They may involve different functionalities or behaviors that have been arbitrarily grouped together.

- **Lack of organization**: Coincidentally cohesive modules lack a clear organizational structure or logical grouping of functionality. The elements within the module may appear to be randomly arranged, with no discernible pattern or rationale.

- **Low abstraction**: Coincidental cohesion results in low levels of abstraction, as the module fails to encapsulate a cohesive set of related functionalities. This makes it difficult to understand the purpose or role of the module within the overall system architecture.

- **High coupling**: Coincidentally cohesive modules often exhibit high coupling between elements, as they may rely on each other for shared resources or data. Changes to one element may inadvertently affect other elements within the module, leading to unintended side effects.

- **Maintenance challenges**: Coincidentally cohesive modules are typically harder to maintain and debug due to their lack of organization and logical structure. Changes to the module may require modifications to unrelated functionality, increasing the risk of introducing errors or inconsistencies.

Examples of modules exhibiting coincidental cohesion include utility classes with unrelated methods, miscellaneous code libraries containing unrelated functions, or legacy modules that have evolved over time without proper refactoring or restructuring.

Coincidental cohesion is generally considered a poor design practice in software engineering, as it leads to code that is difficult to understand, maintain, and extend. Software engineers should strive to refactor coincidentally cohesive modules by identifying and separating unrelated functionality into separate, logically cohesive modules. This helps improve the overall structure, clarity, and maintainability of the software system.

Coupling

We have looked at the different types of cohesion that can play a role in how different software components operate. Now, let us start looking at the idea of component coupling.

Coupling in software architecture refers to the degree of interdependence between different modules, components, or classes within a system. It describes how closely connected or reliant one module is on another. Coupling has a significant impact on software design, maintainability, and scalability.

Here is how coupling applies to software architecture:

- **Types of coupling**: There are different types of coupling, ranging from loose to tight:

  o **Low coupling**: Modules are loosely connected, with minimal dependencies between them. Changes in one module have little impact on others.

  o **High coupling**: Modules are tightly connected, with strong dependencies between them. Changes in one module may require modifications in many other modules.

- **Impact on maintainability**: Low coupling promotes better maintainability by isolating changes. Modules can be modified or replaced with minimal impact on other parts of the system. High coupling, on the other hand, makes it challenging to make changes without affecting other modules, leading to a higher risk of introducing errors.

- **Scalability and flexibility**: Low coupling facilitates system scalability and flexibility. Modules can be easily reused or replaced, and new functionality can be added without disrupting existing components. High coupling restricts scalability and flexibility, as changes in one module may propagate throughout the system, leading to complex dependencies.

- **Testing and debugging**: Low coupling simplifies testing and debugging. Modules can be tested independently, making it easier to isolate and identify issues. High coupling complicates testing and debugging, as changes in one module may impact the behavior of other modules, requiring extensive testing to ensure system integrity.

- **Dependency management**: Coupling affects dependency management. In systems with low coupling, dependencies are minimal and well-defined, making it easier to manage and track them. In systems with high coupling, dependencies may be complex and intertwined, leading to difficulties in managing dependencies and understanding system interactions.

- **Architectural patterns**: Architectural patterns, such as dependency injection, observer, or publish-subscribe, aim to reduce coupling by promoting loose connections between components. These patterns help create modular, maintainable, and scalable architectures by minimizing dependencies and promoting separation of concerns.

Data coupling

Data coupling is a type of coupling in software engineering that describes the degree of dependency between modules based on the passing of data. In data coupling, modules communicate with each other by passing data as parameters or through shared data structures, such as global variables or data buffers.

Characteristics of data coupling include:

- **Data exchange**: Modules communicate by passing data to each other. This can involve passing parameters to function calls, returning values from functions, or accessing shared data structures.

- **Minimal dependency**: Data coupling represents a relatively low level of coupling compared to other types, such as control coupling or stamp coupling. Modules are loosely connected, as they interact primarily through the exchange of data rather than through direct control flow.

- **Encapsulation**: Data coupling promotes encapsulation by allowing modules to operate independently of each other. Modules are self-contained units that rely on input data to perform their tasks, but they do not have direct knowledge of each other's internal implementation details.

- **Flexibility**: Data coupling enhances system flexibility by allowing modules to be easily replaced or modified without affecting other modules. Changes to the data format or data structure can be accommodated without requiring modifications to the interface or implementation of other modules.

- **Simplicity**: Data coupling simplifies system design and understanding by providing a clear and explicit mechanism for communication between modules. Modules are decoupled from each other's internal logic, making it easier to reason about the behavior and interactions of the system.

Examples of data coupling include:

- **Passing parameters to function calls**: Module A calls Module B and passes data as parameters to perform a specific task.

- **Returning values from function calls**: Module A calls Module B, which returns a result or output data back to Module A.

- **Accessing shared data structures**: Modules A and B access the same global variable or data structure to exchange information.

Data coupling is considered a desirable form of coupling in software design because it promotes modularity, flexibility, and maintainability. By minimizing direct dependencies between modules and emphasizing data exchange, data coupling helps create software systems that are easier to understand, extend, and maintain over time.

Control coupling

Control coupling is a type of coupling in software engineering that describes the degree of dependency between modules based on the control flow between them. In control coupling, modules interact with each other by influencing the execution flow, such as by passing control flags or invoking methods that affect the behavior of other modules.

Characteristics of control coupling include:

- **Control flow dependency**: Modules interact by controlling the flow of execution within each other. One module dictates the behavior of another module by passing control information, such as flags, signals, or method invocations.

- **Direct influence**: Control coupling represents a relatively tight form of coupling compared to other types, such as data coupling or message coupling. Modules have direct knowledge of each other's control flow and can affect each other's behavior.

- **Interdependency**: Modules are tightly connected, as changes in one module may require modifications in other modules to accommodate changes in control flow. This can lead to complex dependencies and make the system less modular and more difficult to maintain.

- **Reduced flexibility**: Control coupling can reduce system flexibility by limiting the ability to modify or replace modules independently. Changes to the control flow may have cascading effects on other modules, requiring extensive modifications to maintain system integrity.

- **Increased complexity**: Control coupling can increase system complexity by introducing implicit dependencies and interconnections between modules. Understanding and reasoning about the behavior of the system becomes more challenging due to the intertwined control flow.

Examples of control coupling include:

- **Passing control flags**: Module A calls Module B and passes a flag to control its behavior, such as indicating whether to perform a specific action or skip certain steps.

- **Invoking methods with side effects**: Module A invokes a method in Module B, which has side effects that influence the behavior of Module A, such as modifying global state or altering the execution path.

Control coupling is generally considered a less desirable form of coupling compared to data coupling or message coupling, as it can lead to tight dependencies and reduced modularity. Software engineers should strive to minimize control coupling by designing modules with clear and well-defined interfaces, encapsulating control logic within modules, and promoting loose coupling between components. This helps create software systems that are more modular, flexible, and maintainable over time.

Stamp coupling

Stamp coupling, also known as content coupling, is a type of coupling in software engineering that describes the degree of dependency between modules based on the sharing of complex data structures or composite objects. In stamp coupling, modules interact with each other by passing entire data structures or objects, rather than individual data elements or parameters.

Characteristics of stamp coupling include:

- **Passing complex data structures**: Modules interact by passing complex data structures, composite objects, or records between them. These data structures encapsulate multiple related data elements or attributes.

- **High dependency**: Stamp coupling represents a relatively tight form of coupling, as modules have direct access to and dependence on the internal structure and content of the shared data structures.

- **Complex interactions**: Modules are tightly connected, as changes to the structure or content of the shared data structures may impact the behavior of other modules. This can lead to complex dependencies and make the system more difficult to understand and maintain.

- **Limited encapsulation**: Stamp coupling reduces encapsulation by exposing the internal details of data structures to other modules. Modules have direct access to the internal state of shared data structures, which can lead to unintended side effects and increase coupling.

- **Reduced flexibility**: Stamp coupling can reduce system flexibility by limiting the ability to modify or replace modules independently. Changes to the structure or content of shared data structures may require modifications in multiple modules, leading to cascading changes and increased development effort.

Examples of stamp coupling include:

- **Passing complex data structures**: Module A passes a complex data structure, such as a custom object or record, to Module B, which accesses and manipulates the internal attributes or fields of the object.

- **Sharing global data structures**: Multiple modules access and modify the same global data structures, such as global arrays, lists, or databases, to exchange information or coordinate activities.

Stamp coupling is generally considered a less desirable form of coupling compared to data coupling or message coupling, as it can lead to tight dependencies and reduced modularity. Software engineers should strive to minimize stamp coupling by designing modules with clear and well-defined interfaces, encapsulating data within modules, and promoting loose coupling between components. This helps create software systems that are more modular, flexible, and maintainable over time.

External coupling

External coupling is a type of coupling in software engineering that describes the degree of dependency between a module and external entities, such as other modules, libraries, or systems. In external coupling, a module interacts with external entities by exchanging data, messages, or control signals, but it does not rely on the internal details or implementation of those entities.

Characteristics of external coupling include:

- **Inter-module interaction**: Modules interact with external entities, such as other modules or systems, to exchange data, messages, or control signals. This interaction allows modules to collaborate and coordinate their activities to achieve common goals.

- **Loose dependency**: External coupling represents a relatively loose form of coupling, as modules interact with external entities through well-defined interfaces or protocols. Modules are not directly dependent on the internal implementation details of external entities, which promotes modularity and maintainability.

- **Encapsulation**: External coupling promotes encapsulation by allowing modules to interact with external entities through abstract interfaces or contracts. Modules are shielded from the internal complexities of external entities, which enhances encapsulation and reduces dependency on specific implementations.

- **Flexibility and reusability**: External coupling enhances system flexibility and reusability by allowing modules to be easily replaced or extended with alternative implementations of external entities. Changes to external entities can be accommodated without requiring modifications to dependent modules, which promotes adaptability and scalability.

- **Integration points**: External coupling introduces integration points, where modules interface with external entities. These integration points serve as communication channels or boundaries through which data, messages, or control signals are exchanged, facilitating interoperability and integration between modules and external systems.

Examples of external coupling include:

- **Calling external functions or methods**: A module calls functions or methods defined in external libraries or modules to perform specific tasks, such as mathematical calculations or file operations.

- **Exchanging messages with external systems**: A module communicates with external systems, such as databases, web services, or message queues, by sending and receiving messages over well-defined communication protocols.

External coupling is generally considered a desirable form of coupling in software design, as it promotes modularity, encapsulation, and interoperability. By interacting with external entities through abstract interfaces or contracts, modules can be more easily integrated, maintained, and extended, leading to more robust and scalable software systems.

Common coupling

Common coupling, also known as **global coupling**, is a type of coupling in software engineering that describes the degree of dependency between modules based on shared global data. In common coupling, modules interact by accessing and manipulating shared global variables, data structures, or resources.

Characteristics of common coupling include:

- **Shared global data**: Modules share global variables, data structures, or resources to exchange information or coordinate activities. Changes to the shared data by one module may affect the behavior or state of other modules.

- **High dependency**: Common coupling represents a relatively tight form of coupling, as modules have direct access to and dependence on shared global data. Modules are tightly connected, as changes in one module may propagate throughout the system, affecting other modules that rely on the shared data.

- **Limited encapsulation**: Common coupling reduces encapsulation by exposing the internal state or data of modules to other parts of the system. Modules are not isolated from each other, and changes to the shared data may introduce unintended side effects or dependencies.

- **Global scope**: Shared global data has global scope, meaning it can be accessed and modified from any part of the system. This can lead to difficulties in tracking and managing dependencies, as changes to global data may have unintended consequences across the entire system.

- **Concurrency issues**: Common coupling can introduce concurrency issues in multi-threaded or concurrent systems. Access to shared global data may need to be synchronized to prevent race conditions, deadlocks, or data corruption.

Examples of common coupling include:

- **Global variables**: Modules access and modify global variables to exchange information or share state.

- **Shared data structures**: Modules access and manipulate shared data structures, such as global arrays, lists, or databases, to coordinate activities or collaborate on tasks.

Common coupling is generally considered a less desirable form of coupling compared to other types, such as data coupling or message coupling, as it can lead to tight dependencies, reduced modularity, and increased complexity. Software engineers should strive to minimize common coupling by designing modules with clear and well-defined interfaces, encapsulating data within modules, and promoting loose coupling between components. This helps create software systems that are more modular, flexible, and maintainable over time.

Content coupling

Content coupling, also known as **stamp coupling**, is a type of coupling in software engineering that describes the degree of dependency between modules based on the sharing of complex data structures or composite objects. In content coupling, modules interact with each other by passing entire data structures or objects, rather than individual data elements or parameters.

Characteristics of content coupling include:

- **Complex data exchange**: Modules communicate by passing complex data structures, composite objects, or records between them. These data structures encapsulate multiple related data elements or attributes.

- **High dependency**: Content coupling represents a relatively tight form of coupling, as modules have direct access to and dependence on the internal structure and content of the shared data structures.

- **Direct influence**: Modules are tightly connected, as changes to the content or structure of shared data may impact the behavior of other modules. This can lead to complex dependencies and make the system more difficult to understand and maintain.

- **Reduced encapsulation**: Content coupling reduces encapsulation by exposing the internal details of data structures to other modules. Modules have direct access to the internal state of shared data structures, which can lead to unintended side effects and increase coupling.

- **Limited flexibility**: Content coupling can limit system flexibility by making it challenging to modify or replace modules independently. Changes to the content or structure of shared data may require modifications in multiple modules, leading to cascading changes and increased development effort.

Examples of content coupling include:

- **Passing complex data structures**: Module A passes a complex data structure, such as a custom object or record, to Module B, which accesses and manipulates the internal attributes or fields of the object.

- **Sharing global data structures**: Multiple modules access and modify the same global data structures, such as global arrays, lists, or databases, to exchange information or coordinate activities.

Content coupling is generally considered a less desirable form of coupling compared to data coupling or message coupling, as it can lead to tight dependencies and reduced modularity. Software engineers should strive to minimize content coupling by designing modules with clear and well-defined interfaces, encapsulating data within modules, and promoting loose coupling between components. This helps create software systems that are more modular, flexible, and maintainable over time.

Guidelines for coupling and cohesion

Now, we will focus on some of the guidelines to follow that will help us make the best use of our various cohesion and coupling techniques amongst various components.

Guidelines for coupling and cohesion are essential principles in software engineering that guide the design and architecture of software systems. The following are some guidelines for achieving optimal coupling and cohesion:

- **Guidelines for coupling**:
  - **Minimize coupling**: Aim to reduce coupling between modules as much as possible. Low coupling promotes modularity, flexibility, and maintainability in software systems.

o **Use loose coupling**: Prefer loose coupling over tight coupling. Loose coupling allows modules to interact with each other through well-defined interfaces or contracts, reducing dependencies and promoting independence.

o **Favor message passing**: Use message passing or event-driven architectures to communicate between modules. This promotes loose coupling by decoupling the sender and receiver of messages, allowing them to evolve independently.

o **Encapsulate dependencies**: Encapsulate dependencies within modules to minimize their visibility and impact on other parts of the system. Use abstraction layers or dependency injection to manage and isolate dependencies.

o **Avoid global state**: Minimize the use of global variables or shared global data structures, as they can lead to common coupling and tight dependencies. Use local variables or parameters to pass data between modules whenever possible.

- **Guidelines for cohesion**:

  o **Maximize cohesion**: Strive to maximize cohesion within modules. High cohesion promotes clarity, maintainability, and reusability by grouping related functionality together.

  o **Use functional cohesion**: Aim for functional cohesion, where each module performs a single, well-defined function or task. Functional cohesion ensures that modules have a clear and focused purpose, making them easier to understand and maintain.

  o **Avoid coincidental cohesion**: Minimize coincidental cohesion, where modules contain unrelated or arbitrary functionality. Coincidental cohesion leads to complexity and confusion, making the system harder to maintain and understand.

  o **Promote logical cohesion**: Organize modules based on logical relationships and domain concepts. Logical cohesion ensures that modules are grouped together based on their logical relevance and shared responsibilities.

  o **Strive for sequential cohesion**: Sequential cohesion can be appropriate for certain types of modules, such as procedural algorithms or sequential workflows. However, ensure that the sequence of actions is meaningful and contributes to the overall purpose of the module.

By following these guidelines, software engineers can design software systems that exhibit optimal coupling and cohesion, leading to more maintainable, flexible, and scalable architectures.

High cohesion, low coupling

High cohesion, low coupling is a fundamental principle in software engineering that advocates for designing modules with high cohesion and low coupling. It is often summarized as a guiding principle for creating well-structured, maintainable, and scalable software systems.

Here is what high cohesion means:

- **Definition**: Cohesion refers to the degree to which the elements within a module are related and focused on performing a single, well-defined task or function.

- **Guiding principle**: Modules with high cohesion have elements that are closely related and work together to achieve a specific purpose or functionality.

- **Benefits**: High cohesion promotes clarity, maintainability, and reusability by grouping related functionality together. It simplifies understanding, debugging, and modifying modules since they have a clear and focused purpose.

Here is what low coupling means:

- **Definition**: Coupling refers to the degree of interdependence between modules. It describes how tightly modules are connected to each other.

- **Guiding principle**: Modules with low coupling are loosely connected and have minimal dependencies on each other. They interact through well-defined interfaces or contracts, minimizing direct dependencies.

- **Benefits**: Low coupling enhances modularity, flexibility, and maintainability by isolating changes. Modules can be modified, replaced, or extended without affecting other parts of the system. It facilitates easier testing, debugging, and maintenance since changes are localized.

The key points are as follows:

- **Balance**: High cohesion and low coupling should be balanced to achieve an optimal design. Modules should have a clear, focused purpose (high cohesion) while being loosely connected to other modules (low coupling).

- **Design principle**: High cohesion, low coupling is a design principle that guides the decomposition of software systems into smaller, more manageable units. It helps create modular, flexible, and maintainable architectures.

- **Iterative process**: Achieving high cohesion and low coupling is often an iterative process. It requires continuous refinement and improvement as the software system evolves and requirements change.

In summary, high cohesion, low coupling emphasizes designing modules with a clear purpose and minimal dependencies. By adhering to this principle, software engineers can create systems that are easier to understand, maintain, and extend over time.

Single Responsibility Principle

The **Single Responsibility Principle** (**SRP**) is a fundamental principle in software engineering, often associated with object-oriented programming and design patterns. It states that a class or module should have only one reason to change, meaning it should have only one responsibility or concern.

The key points are as follows:

- **Definition**: The SRP asserts that a class or module should have only one responsibility. It should encapsulate one and only one aspect of the software's functionality.

- **Responsibility**: A responsibility is defined as a reason for a class to change. If a class has more than one responsibility, changes to one aspect may affect other aspects, leading to increased complexity and maintenance challenges.

- **Encapsulation**: SRP promotes encapsulation by ensuring that each class or module focuses on a single concern. This makes the software easier to understand, maintain, and extend, as changes are localized and do not impact unrelated functionality.

- **Modularity**: SRP encourages modularity by breaking down complex systems into smaller, more manageable units. Each module is responsible for a specific aspect of the system's functionality, promoting separation of concerns and reusability.

- **Design guidelines**: SRP guides the design and organization of classes and modules within a software system. It helps developers identify cohesive units of functionality and define clear interfaces between them.

Refer to the following example:

Consider a class that manages both user authentication and user profile management. According to SRP, this class violates the principle because it has two reasons to change: changes to authentication requirements and changes to profile management requirements. Instead, these responsibilities should be separated into distinct classes, each responsible for one aspect (e.g., an **AuthenticationManager** class and a **UserProfileManager** class).

```java
// Violation of SRP
public class UserManagement {
    public boolean authenticateUser(String username, String password) {
        // Authentication logic
    }

    public void updateUserProfile(UserProfile profile) {
        // Profile management logic
    }
}
```

The following are the benefits of SRP:

- **Maintainability**: SRP improves maintainability by reducing the risk of unintended side effects when making changes. Each class or module is focused on a single responsibility, making it easier to understand and modify.

- **Flexibility**: SRP enhances flexibility by enabling components to be reused in different contexts. Modules with single responsibilities are more modular and adaptable to changes in requirements.

- **Testability**: SRP promotes testability by isolating units of functionality. Classes or modules with single responsibilities can be tested independently, leading to more robust and reliable software.

Overall, the SRP is a key guideline in software design that promotes clarity, modularity, and maintainability. By adhering to SRP, developers can create software systems that are easier to understand, extend, and maintain over time.

Encapsulation

Next up is the idea of utilizing encapsulation in your component architecture.

Encapsulation is a fundamental concept in **object-oriented programming** (**OOP**) that refers to the bundling of data and methods (or functions) that operate on the data into a single unit or module. This unit serves as a protective wrapper, hiding the internal state and implementation details of an object from the outside world. Encapsulation enables data hiding, abstraction, and modularity, contributing to the principles of information hiding and separation of concerns.

The key points are as follows:

- **Data hiding**: Encapsulation hides the internal state of an object from external access, allowing access only through well-defined interfaces or methods. This protects the integrity of the data and prevents direct manipulation, reducing the risk of unintended modifications and ensuring data consistency.

- **Abstraction**: Encapsulation provides abstraction by exposing only essential information about an object's behavior, while hiding its implementation details. Clients interact with objects through a set of public methods, abstracting away the complexities of the underlying implementation.

- **Modularity**: Encapsulation promotes modularity by encapsulating related data and behavior into cohesive units known as objects or classes. Each object represents a self-contained entity with its own state and behavior, facilitating code organization, reuse, and maintenance.

- **Information hiding**: Encapsulation facilitates information hiding by allowing objects to control access to their internal data. Objects reveal only what is necessary for their interactions with other objects, concealing unnecessary details and minimizing dependencies.

- **Access control**: Encapsulation enables access control mechanisms to restrict or regulate access to an object's members. By defining public, private, and protected access levels, encapsulation allows developers to enforce encapsulation boundaries and manage the visibility of class members.

Consider the following example:

```
public class Circle {
    private double radius;

    // Constructor
    public Circle(double radius) {
        this.radius = radius;
    }
    // Getter method for radius
    public double getRadius() {
        return radius;
    }
    // Setter method for radius
    public void setRadius(double radius) {
        if (radius > 0) {
            this.radius = radius;
        }
    }
    // Method to calculate area
    public double calculateArea() {
        return Math.PI * radius * radius;
    }
}* radius * radius; } }
```

In this example, the **Circle** class encapsulates the **radius** data member and methods for accessing and manipulating it. The **radius** data member is declared as private, ensuring that it is accessible only within the **Circle** class. Public getter and setter methods provide controlled access to the radius, allowing clients to retrieve and update its value while enforcing validation constraints.

The following are the benefits of encapsulation:

- **Security**: Encapsulation enhances security by protecting sensitive data from unauthorized access and manipulation.

- **Flexibility**: Encapsulation promotes flexibility by allowing changes to the internal implementation of an object without affecting its external interface.

- **Code maintenance**: Encapsulation simplifies code maintenance by localizing changes within the encapsulated units, minimizing the ripple effects of modifications.

- **Code reusability**: Encapsulation facilitates code reusability by encapsulating reusable components into modular units that can be easily integrated into different contexts.

Overall, encapsulation is a fundamental principle in OOP that promotes code organization, abstraction, and maintainability by bundling data and behavior into cohesive units and controlling access to their internal state. It enables the creation of robust, modular, and reusable software components.

Conclusion

Architectural design is not just driven from the top down, but also needs to consider the various components and how they will work together, essentially building it from the bottom up. This balance between finding the right design to achieve your broader organizational goals and the most optimal component interaction is a challenging one, but it leads the architect to ask all the right questions of their design and results in a superior design in the end.

This starts with performing a functional decomposition of what parts of your systems are required to do. Once we have a clear view of how they all work, understanding the different models of cohesion and coupling will help you to refine their operation and find the right communication patterns that will achieve optimal operation.

This can take some time, and there is often no one perfect solution across the many components' interactions, but being aware of these elements can start the journey and lead the architect to further refinement as the software evolves and different usage patterns become preferred.

In the next chapter, we will look at how the design of your architecture can impact overall application performance and the things that architects can look at to better measure and optimize their designs for improved performance.

CHAPTER 8

Architecting for Performance

Introduction

Designing software to meet functional requirements and fulfill specific business needs constitutes the primary focus of software architecture. However, effective software architecture extends beyond mere functionality; architects must also prioritize optimizing performance, ensuring reliability, and being mindful of resource utilization, particularly processing power.

This can be a challenge, as there is no easy way to go about this. You can not just measure performance by looking at ways to solve the solution the quickest or what requires the shortest amount of code. There is significantly more to identifying the most optimal path to a solution, with the following criteria key things for software architects to consider:

- **Efficient algorithms and data structures**: Choosing the right algorithms and data structures can significantly impact performance. Algorithms with lower time complexity and data structures optimized for the task at hand can improve efficiency.

- **Scalability**: Designing software that can handle increased workload without sacrificing performance is crucial. This involves strategies such as horizontal and vertical scaling, load balancing, and efficient resource allocation.

- **Concurrency and parallelism**: Leveraging concurrency and parallelism can enhance performance by allowing tasks to be executed simultaneously. Techniques like multithreading, multiprocessing, and asynchronous programming can help in utilizing system resources effectively.

- **Optimized code**: Writing clean, optimized code can lead to improved performance. Techniques such as code profiling, identifying bottlenecks, and optimizing critical sections can enhance overall efficiency.

- **Caching**: Utilizing caching mechanisms can reduce latency and improve response times. Caching frequently accessed data or computations can significantly enhance performance, especially for repetitive tasks.

- **Minimizing I/O operations**: Minimizing input/output operations, such as disk reads and writes or network requests, can improve performance. Techniques like batching requests, caching data, and optimizing database queries can help reduce I/O overhead.

- **Hardware considerations**: Understanding the underlying hardware architecture and characteristics can aid in designing software that efficiently utilizes available resources. This includes considerations such as CPU architecture, memory management, and disk I/O performance.

- **Testing and profiling**: Thorough testing and profiling are essential for identifying performance bottlenecks and optimizing software. Performance testing tools, profiling software, and benchmarking can help in evaluating and improving the performance of the software.

By considering these key attributes during the design and development phases, software engineers can create highly performant software that meets the demands of users and business requirements effectively.

Thankfully, thinking in an optimal fashion can become a matter of habit the more often it is practice. So, while it will slow you down quite a lot at the start, the more you get used to thinking about efficient coding and design algorithms and putting in the right observability measures to understand how your software preforms under certain conditions, the faster you get at solving these challenges naturally.

Structure

In this chapter, we will discuss the following topics:

- Designing for optimization
- Measuring your existing performance
- Application performance metrics
- Server performance metrics
- Overall performance metrics

- Challenges to code optimization

- Optimizing your design

- Minimizing I/O operation

- Optimizing your code

- Optimizing your code for memory

- Testing for performance

- The right time to run performance tests

Objectives

By the end of this chapter, you will understand the importance of optimal software, how to measure for it, and the different patterns and design principles that can help architects identify the best optimal flow of an application or code.

Designing for optimization

Before getting into things to consider in designing for optimization, it is perhaps worth saying that not everything needs to work ultra-fast. Sometimes you can be working on an API or application that will only get called every few hours or so, is internal facing, and does not impact the dependencies of other code. In cases such as this, often solving the problem as simply as possible is good enough.

However, the majority of systems and code that are being designed will likely have some impact on the overall performance of a system, and so learning how to optimize the design and code for performance is an important skill to master.

Before looking at the attributes of optimal software design, it is important to first focus on observability and how we can measure the optimization of the software we write. Unless we are creating designs for a customer we understand well, we often do not know enough about how users may use our software. This includes both their typical usage patterns that will dictate how information will flow through the system, and various performance considerations, knowing how and when people will be using different parts of the application, and the performance needs thereof.

So, even though we can always design with optimization in mind, we need to get very good at identifying the areas where our software might not be meeting our current performance concerns, and then modify it further from there.

Measuring your existing performance

We will start off by looking at the different aspects to consider in measuring the performance of your applications in a broader software system. Some of these measures may not apply in every scenario, but across an entire system, they can be applied across each individual module and service.

Identify the appropriate metrics

It is easy to gather data on system behavior performance. Just because we have the data, though, does not mean we need it. It does not necessarily mean that we are measuring it in the appropriate way for the performance aspects we are trying to analyze. For example, you can be measuring server response time rather than the time it takes a web page to render, or measuring performance using specific datasets without those datasets necessarily being production-specific. All, great things to measure, but in the provided context, they are not going to derive much value to you and your team.

Measuring the wrong metric can lead to false results and wasted effort that prevent you from making the right performance gains or simply slow down your team because they are starting to optimize areas in your systems that would not make much of an impact. Take the time to ensure you are capturing the correct metrics in your performance results and utilizing the right data and test criteria that will lead you to finding the appropriate performance results for your applications.

Measure right

After identifying those metrics that are important to us and the data needed to understand them, we also need to measure them appropriately and understand how different factors can affect the performance of our application.

To provide another example: You might be a mobile developer with the latest device that has only one program running on it. If your goal is to produce a response in less than 10ms on average, that will be a lot easier on your test device than on your user's four-year-old phone with a low battery and a hundred apps running in the background. The metric we are trying to measure is the correct one. However, there are different ways of measuring this that will provide us with different insights, and again, we need to ensure we measure for and cater to these different scenarios.

It could also cause you to misunderstand your program's characteristics. You might be I/O bound on a test device when on most devices, you are actually CPU bound. So, in this case, measuring I/O usage across our application is an important metric, but missing looking at this in the context of CPU usage is unlikely to help us in understanding the performance constraints of our services.

Knowing the different factors that can affect the performance of an application and system outside of your code will aid in understanding where and how to best optimize the code. Some of these factors are described further in the next section.

Application performance metrics

These are metrics that measure key information in the application itself and help in identifying where the application speed can be optimized:

- **Response time (latency)**
  - o **Definition**: Time taken for a request to be processed and for a response to be returned to the user.
  - o **Importance**: Directly affects user experience. Lower response times are essential for user satisfaction.

- **Throughput (requests per second)**
  - o **Definition**: Number of requests handled by the application per second.
  - o **Importance**: Indicates the capacity of the application to handle load. Higher throughput is desirable.

- **Error rate**
  - o **Definition**: Percentage of requests that result in errors.
  - o **Importance**: Helps identify stability and reliability issues within the application.

- **Apdex (Application Performance Index)**
  - o **Definition**: A standard method to measure user satisfaction based on response times.
  - o **Importance**: Provides a user-centric view of performance and helps prioritize performance improvements.

- **Database query performance**
  - o **Definition**: Time taken for database queries to execute.
  - o **Importance**: Slow queries can significantly impact overall application performance.

- **Cache hit rate**
  - o **Definition**: The percentage of requests that are served from the cache.
  - o **Importance**: High cache hit rates can significantly reduce response times and load on the server.

Server performance metrics

These are metrics that can be tracked from a server or container perspective and reflect how the underlying application host is operating during the operation of an application.

This is useful in identifying areas where your application or specific usage patterns may be affecting these servers or containers, and identifying either areas for further optimization or better scalability. The server performance metrics are listed as follows:

- **CPU utilization**
    - **Definition**: Percentage of CPU capacity being used.
    - **Importance**: High CPU utilization can indicate that the server is under heavy load and may become a bottleneck.

- **Memory usage**
    - **Definition**: The amount of memory being used by the application and server processes.
    - **Importance**: Ensures there is enough memory to handle applications and services without swapping to disk.

- **Disk I/O**
    - **Definition**: Rate at which data is read from and written to disk.
    - **Importance**: High disk I/O can lead to slow performance, especially for database-intensive applications.

- **Network latency and bandwidth**
    - **Definition**: Time taken for data to travel across the network and the amount of data being transmitted.
    - **Importance**: Affects the speed at which data is transferred between users and servers, impacting overall performance.

- **Disk space**
    - **Definition**: The amount of disk space available on the server.
    - **Importance**: Ensures that there is enough space for logs, databases, and other data. Running out of disk space can cause crashes and data loss.

- **Thread and connection pool usage**
    - **Definition**: Number of threads or connections being used by the application.
    - **Importance**: Helps in identifying bottlenecks and ensuring that resources are used efficiently.

Overall performance metrics

These are very important metrics to measure the effectiveness of your app and development processes to adapt, scale, and respond to change. These metrics are best used for identifying future areas for enhancement to help improve the operation and maintainability of the system:

- **Uptime**
    - **Definition**: Percentage of time the application is available and functioning correctly.
    - **Importance**: High uptime is critical for maintaining user trust and service reliability.

- **Scalability**
    - **Definition**: Ability of the application and server infrastructure to handle increasing loads.
    - **Importance**: Ensures that the system can grow to meet demand without performance degradation.

- **Security metrics**
    - **Definition**: Number of vulnerabilities, incidents, and compliance with security policies.
    - **Importance**: Protects the application and data from threats, ensuring secure and reliable operation.

- **Deployment time**
    - **Definition**: Time taken to deploy new features or updates.
    - **Importance**: Affects how quickly new features can be rolled out and issues can be fixed, impacting overall agility.

It can be seen that there are a lot of different measures that can affect software performance. Fortunately, not all of these measures may apply equally depending on the part of an application we are designing. Some focus on the end-to-end behavior of an application across an entire user or functional journey. Some will measure processing across aspects of the backend infrastructure, and others will be applied to the underlying hardware or network nodes running the system. The key is applying the correct measure to the correct part of a system to best measure it effectively.

The biggest challenge in measuring and monitoring these specific factors across an application is that you need to measure them consistently and frequently, so that deviations and patterns can be identified over a long period of time. How long you need to retain information depends on your known usage patterns, data retention policies, and costs, so as an architect, you will need to balance your approach in determining how much information you can track and store.

Measure both prod and test environments

For many businesses, it makes sense to measure how their applications are performing in their production environments so they can respond to any issues affecting client experience immediately. However, teams should also be doing this as part of their general development cycle, as well as in a proper testing environment.

Performance monitoring is underrated in the development and testing space. Often, the reason given is that development and test environment stability is sporadic and not close enough to actual production in terms of configuration. Despite these challenges and the added effort and cost to put monitoring in place across your test environments, the benefits are worth it, and value can quickly be gained by the development teams.

In monitoring test environments, there needs to be an understanding that performance between your production and test environments is likely to be different. So, you need to benchmark based on those differences. And if you have multiple development environments, each one should be benchmarked.

The reason for that is simple. Each environment has a variety of its own environmental variables that affect performance, and you want a standard baseline against which to measure. Some infrastructure as code and containerized systems may reduce these differences, but from a configuration, data, and versioning perspective, differences will still remain. While development environments are less reliable, you can still effectively measure the performance of your code if you measure regularly and often. That way, deviations can be easily picked up, and it will also be a lot easier to determine whether it is code, DB, or environment-related.

Try to integrate performance tests into your pipeline

Additionally, it is important not to leave performance testing for later in the development cycle. Teams should include it as part of their build processes, so that they can catch performance issues early in the process before they affect later environments or production itself.

You should even fail your builds if a commit causes a performance regression, and prevent it from going any further in the pipeline process. If performance is important for your project, consider adding performance as part of your continuous integration. It can help in preventing performance regressions before they get shipped.

The sooner you are aware of performance regressions, the easier they are to fix. In large code bases, small regressions can build up over time unless they are aggressively kept in check. Tests can keep them out of your system. It is difficult to run these tests all the time, and it can slow down the pipeline a little, but the extra few minutes to run the pipeline are much less than the many hours of debugging to find performance issues.

Challenges to code optimization

Before we talk about some design patterns or designs that might help with this efficiency, let us look at some common challenges, so that you can also consider all the aspects of whether you should optimize the code or not. Often, given the challenges, tweaking your code further is just not worth the effort. So, understanding all the different elements to look at should help you and your team to make the right choice.

Understanding the level of gain

You need to know not only how fast (or memory-intensive, etc.) the system is, but also how much marginal gain you will get from improvements. This could mean realizing if improvements are saving the company money or improving user experience by reducing wait times, or recognizing that a script runs only once a week and has minimal impact on anyone. Even savings of an entire minute (basically forever in computer time) might not be worth adding complexity. However, if it is a function that is run a million times per second across a fleet of thousands of servers, savings of microseconds could save a lot of money.

If you understand what your performance goals are before beginning your work, you can make the right call on performance and complexity trade-offs later on. If you are being honest with yourself, you will often see that you should scrap marginal gains and focus on major wins.

Finding the balance

Fast code is not necessarily the most maintainable or easiest to read way of coding. While it makes a lot of sense to always opt for the most optimal route, in a bigger organization, you need to fit into the bigger picture and find the balance between speed and simplicity. A lot of this decision will rest on how important speed is to the piece of code you are working on, or how often you expect the code to be maintained.

Keeping the rest of the system in mind

Often, your code does not sit in isolation and needs to interact with other parts of the system. For back-end API code, for instance, it can often be easy to tweak things for performance, but you also need to keep in mind if there is integration with a UI element or database, and that we are not just testing our code in isolation, but also in conjunction with how it is been designed.

It sounds obvious, but code optimized for the user experience is not necessarily always the fastest solution for throughput, and the overall aim and objective of what you are trying to achieve should be considered.

Third-party integration

For many developers and companies, systems do not sit in isolation and need to interact with a solution that belongs to a third party, where you cannot optimize its code.

In situations like this, you need to factor in the performance of your third-party system and often what is required for it to run optimally, rather than your solutions or preferred methods. This can become tricky in dealing with data or memory management, where it might not fit into the way your own systems may operate.

You may need to make changes to your own software operation to ensure it can operate optimally in the future with your other third-party systems, even if it is less ideal for your own design. The ideal scenario is to always design your own solutions, but in big connected systems, that is just not possible, and so you need to make do with some level of third-party interaction.

Dealing with the data

Often, the biggest performance issues can come from the way our applications handle data. It is not that the code or data scripts are not optimized, but simply that processing the needed data, given the current infrastructure, takes too long. There could be many other solutions to look at, like changing databases, archiving your data, reducing the required data in a database, optimizing DB structure, or even introducing parallelization, where systems can distribute your data and run queries across multiple servers, thereby increasing throughput.

Ultimately, there are a lot of ways to optimize databases and datastores, and these should be explored in detail. We will discuss some solutions later in this chapter.

Understanding how your compiler works

In learning how to optimize code, you will need to learn to understand how the language and its compiler operate and interpret different coding techniques. Sometimes, performance constraints could be a result of the way compilers are interpreting the different methods, functions, and algorithms, and you will need to code in a way that will allow your compiler to optimize most efficiently.

For example, the way Java works is different from Python or C++, and so understanding some of the small nuances of the underlying compiler helps identify ways that your code can work quickly. Some compilers control some of these optimizations for you, while others leave these completely up to the developers.

So, as an architect, be aware of these differences because they will determine how much of the optimization you can control in your designs for the efficiency you require, even if you are using the right programming language. If you want absolute performance, go as low as possible and program in a machine-based language or assembler code, though this would be overkill for many products, and the reality is, with increased processing speeds, the effort made to optimize at this level is simply not necessary.

Optimizing your design

Now that we have looked at the different ways of measuring systems and have become understanding of the different challenges, we are likely to phase in optimization; we can start to look at optimizing the design.

We will look at this by evaluating each of the points we raised earlier in more detail at a design level, before unpacking actual code optimization in more detail, and lastly, ending with some points on performance testing that are critical for all architects to understand, including:

- Algorithms and data structures
- Scalability
- Concurrency and parallelism
- Caching
- Minimizing I/O operation

Designing for algorithms and data structures

Some key points about algorithmic efficiency and data structures are given as follows:

- **Algorithmic efficiency**: Algorithms define the step-by-step procedures for solving specific problems. Efficient algorithms have low time complexity, meaning they execute quickly, and low space complexity, meaning they use minimal memory. Choosing the right algorithm can have a significant impact on the performance of your software.

- **Data structures**: Data structures are essential for organizing and storing data efficiently. Different data structures have different strengths and weaknesses in terms of memory usage and access time. For example:

  o Arrays offer constant-time access to elements but may require resizing and have limitations on insertion and deletion operations.

  o Linked lists allow for dynamic memory allocation and efficient insertion and deletion at the expense of slower access times.

  o Trees and graphs provide hierarchical organization and efficient search operations.

Designing for algorithms and data structures involves the following:

- **Choosing the right data structure**: Selecting the appropriate data structure for your specific use case is critical for performance. Consider factors such as the frequency and type of operations performed on the data, memory constraints, and desired time complexity. For example:

o Use arrays when random access is required and the size of the collection is fixed or can be pre-allocated.

o Choose hash tables for fast lookups and insertions when the keys are known in advance.

o Employ balanced trees like AVL trees or red-black trees for efficient searching, insertion, and deletion operations in ordered data sets.

- **Optimizing operations**: Understanding the characteristics of different data structures and algorithms allows for optimization of operations. For example:

  o When searching in a sorted array, consider using binary search for logarithmic time complexity instead of linear search.

  o Use hashing with appropriate collision resolution techniques to maintain constant-time complexity for insertions and lookups in hash tables.

  o Implement efficient sorting algorithms like quick sort or merge sort for sorting large datasets.

- **Space-time tradeoffs**: There is often a tradeoff between time complexity and space complexity. Choosing a more memory-efficient data structure might result in slower access times, and vice versa. It is essential to strike a balance based on the specific requirements of your application.

- **Profiling and benchmarking**: Use profiling and benchmarking tools to measure the performance of different algorithms and data structures in your application. This helps identify bottlenecks and areas for optimization, ensuring that your software achieves the desired level of performance.

Designing for scalability

Optimizing for scalability involves designing software systems in a way that allows them to handle increasing workloads efficiently without sacrificing performance or reliability. Here are several strategies to optimize for scalability:

- **Decompose into microservices or modules**: Break down your application into smaller, independent services or modules. This allows for better isolation of functionality and scalability of individual components. Microservices can be independently deployed and scaled based on demand.

- **Horizontal scaling**: Design your system to scale horizontally by adding more instances of components or services to distribute the load. This can be achieved through techniques such as load balancing and auto-scaling, where new instances are automatically provisioned or terminated based on workload.

- **Stateless architecture**: Minimize or eliminate server-side state where possible. Stateless architecture makes it easier to scale horizontally since requests can be routed to any available instance without relying on session affinity. State can be managed externally (e.g., in a database or cache) or passed along with the request.

- **Asynchronous processing**: Use asynchronous communication and processing where applicable. This allows your system to handle concurrent requests more efficiently by offloading long-running tasks to background processes or worker queues. Asynchronous patterns such as message queues or event-driven architectures can help decouple components and improve scalability.

- **Cache frequently accessed data**: Employ caching mechanisms to store frequently accessed data closer to the point of use. Caching can reduce the load on backend services and improve response times. Consider using distributed caching solutions for better scalability across multiple nodes.

- **Database scaling strategies**: Choose database solutions that support horizontal scaling, such as NoSQL databases or distributed databases. Sharding, replication, and partitioning can help distribute data across multiple nodes to handle increasing data volumes and transaction throughput.

- **Optimize communication protocols**: Use efficient communication protocols and formats to reduce overhead and latency. For example, consider using binary protocols instead of text-based ones for lower overhead, or compressing data for faster transmission.

- **Monitoring and load testing**: Continuously monitor system performance and conduct load testing to identify bottlenecks and areas for improvement. Load testing helps simulate real-world scenarios and assess how well your system scales under different levels of load.

- **Automated deployment and infrastructure as code**: Implement automated deployment pipelines and use **infrastructure as code (IaC)** tools to provision and manage infrastructure resources. Automation allows for faster scaling and ensures consistency across environments.

- **Design for failure**: Expect and prepare for failures at any level of your system. Implement redundancy, failover mechanisms, and graceful degradation to maintain system availability and performance during outages or unexpected spikes in traffic.

By incorporating these scalability strategies into your software design and architecture, you can build systems that can grow with your business needs and handle increasing loads efficiently.

Concurrency and parallelism

Designing for concurrency and parallelism is crucial for building high-performance and responsive software systems that can efficiently utilize modern hardware resources. Here are some key principles and strategies to consider:

- **Identify concurrent tasks**: Analyze your system to identify tasks that can be executed concurrently. This could include processing multiple requests simultaneously, parallelizing computations, or performing I/O operations concurrently.

- **Choose concurrency models**: Select appropriate concurrency models based on your application requirements and programming language or framework capabilities. Common models include threads, processes, coroutines, actors, and event-driven architectures.

- **Thread safety**: Ensure that your code is thread-safe to avoid race conditions and data corruption when multiple threads access shared resources concurrently. Techniques such as synchronization primitives (e.g., mutexes, semaphores), atomic operations, and thread-safe data structures can help maintain data integrity.

- **Concurrency patterns**: Implement concurrency patterns to manage concurrent tasks effectively. Examples include producer-consumer, worker pools, fork-join, and pipeline patterns. These patterns help orchestrate concurrent operations, manage resource usage, and avoid bottlenecks.

- **Asynchronous programming**: Utilize asynchronous programming paradigms to handle non-blocking I/O operations and improve responsiveness. Asynchronous APIs, event loops, and callback mechanisms allow your application to perform other tasks while waiting for I/O operations to complete.

- **Parallelism and parallel algorithms**: Leverage parallelism to execute computations concurrently across multiple processing units (e.g., CPU cores, GPUs). Parallel algorithms, such as map-reduce, parallel sorting, and parallel search, can significantly improve performance for CPU-bound tasks by distributing workloads across cores.

- **Data partitioning and parallelization**: Partition large datasets or tasks into smaller chunks that can be processed in parallel. Parallelize computations by distributing workloads across multiple threads or processes and aggregating results asynchronously.

- **Avoid lock contention**: Minimize contention for shared resources to prevent performance degradation due to lock contention. Strategies include fine-grained locking, lock-free data structures, optimistic concurrency control, and reducing the duration of critical sections.

- **Scale-out architectures**: Design scalable architectures that can scale horizontally by adding more nodes or instances to handle increasing loads. Distributed systems, microservices, and cloud-native architectures facilitate scalability by distributing workloads across multiple nodes.

- **Performance profiling and tuning**: Profile your concurrent and parallel code to identify performance bottlenecks, contention points, and opportunities for optimization. Techniques such as thread profiling, resource monitoring, and performance analysis tools help fine-tune concurrency settings and maximize throughput.

By adopting these principles and practices, you can design software systems that effectively harness concurrency and parallelism to improve performance, scalability, and responsiveness. However, it is essential to carefully balance concurrency complexity with the added benefits, as overly complex concurrency models can introduce bugs and maintenance challenges.

Caching

Designing for caching involves implementing mechanisms to store and retrieve frequently accessed data in a faster-accessible storage layer, thereby improving the performance and scalability of your software system. Here are some key considerations and strategies for designing effective caching mechanisms:

- **Identify cached data**: Analyze your application's data access patterns to identify data that is frequently accessed or computationally expensive to generate. This could include database queries, computation results, static content, or frequently accessed API responses.

- **Cache invalidation strategy**: Determine how cached data should be invalidated or updated when the underlying data changes. Depending on your application requirements, you can use strategies such as time-based expiration, event-based invalidation, or manual cache clearing.

- **Cache granularity**: Decide the granularity of caching based on the size and access patterns of your data. You can cache individual objects, database query results, partial HTML fragments, or entire pages, depending on the level of granularity required for performance optimization.

- **Cache storage**: Choose appropriate storage solutions for your cache based on performance, scalability, and persistence requirements. Common options include in-memory caches (e.g., Redis, Memcached) for fast access, distributed caches for scalability, and disk-based caches for persistence.

- **Cache eviction policies**: Implement cache eviction policies to manage the size of your cache and prioritize data retention based on access patterns. Popular eviction policies include **least recently used (LRU)**, **least frequently used (LFU)**, **time-to-live (TTL)**, and size-based eviction.

- **Cache key design**: Design cache keys carefully to ensure uniqueness and consistency across cache entries. Consider including relevant identifiers, parameters, or hash values in cache keys to differentiate between different cache entries and avoid key collisions.

- **Cache composition**: Compose multiple caching layers to leverage different caching strategies for different types of data. For example, you can use a combination of in-memory caches for frequently accessed data and disk-based caches for less frequently accessed or larger datasets.

- **Cache replication and distribution**: Replicate or distribute your cache across multiple nodes or servers to improve reliability, fault tolerance, and scalability. Distributed caching solutions provide mechanisms for data partitioning, replication, and consistency to ensure data availability and performance under varying loads.

- **Cache monitoring and management**: Monitor cache usage, hit rates, and performance metrics to identify bottlenecks, optimize cache configuration, and troubleshoot cache-related issues. Use caching libraries or monitoring tools to track cache utilization and performance in real-time.

- **Cache warm-up strategies**: Implement cache warming strategies to prepopulate the cache with frequently accessed data during application startup or deployment. This helps reduce cache miss rates and improve application performance by ensuring that cached data is readily available when needed.

By incorporating these caching strategies into your software design and architecture, you can effectively leverage caching to improve performance, scalability, and reliability across various types of applications and use cases. However, it is essential to carefully consider cache consistency, invalidation strategies, and potential cache-related pitfalls to ensure the correctness and integrity of your cached data.

Minimizing I/O operation

Minimizing I/O operations is crucial for improving the performance and efficiency of software systems, especially when dealing with resource-intensive tasks such as disk reads and writes, network communication, and database access. Here are some strategies to minimize I/O operations:

- **Batching**: Instead of performing multiple individual I/O operations, batch them together to reduce overhead. For example, when reading or writing data from or to disk or a database, batch multiple requests into a single transaction or operation to minimize the number of round trips.

- **Caching**: Cache frequently accessed data in memory to avoid redundant I/O operations. By storing data in a cache, subsequent read requests can be served from memory instead of fetching data from disk or a remote server, reducing latency and improving performance.

- **Optimized database queries**: Write efficient database queries to minimize the number of I/O operations required to retrieve data. Use indexing, query optimization techniques, and appropriate database design principles to minimize unnecessary scans and lookups.

- **Lazy loading and eager loading**: When working with relational databases or **object-relational mapping** (**ORM**) frameworks, consider lazy loading or eager loading strategies to minimize the number of database queries and associated I/O operations. Load only the necessary data when needed to avoid fetching unnecessary data from the database.

- **Asynchronous I/O**: Utilize asynchronous I/O operations to improve concurrency and responsiveness. Asynchronous I/O allows the application to perform other tasks while waiting for I/O operations to complete, reducing idle time and maximizing resource utilization.

- **Streaming**: When reading or writing large amounts of data, consider streaming data instead of loading it all into memory at once. Streaming allows data to be processed incrementally, reducing memory usage and avoiding I/O bottlenecks associated with large datasets.

- **Connection pooling**: Use connection pooling to reuse established connections instead of creating a new connection for each I/O operation. Connection pooling reduces overhead associated with connection establishment and teardown, improving performance and scalability, especially in network-based I/O operations.

- **Compression and encryption**: Compressing and encrypting data before performing I/O operations can reduce the amount of data transmitted over the network or written to disk, minimizing I/O bandwidth usage and improving transfer speeds.

- **Prefetching and prefetch caching**: Anticipate future data access patterns and prefetch data into memory before it is needed. Prefetching can help reduce latency by proactively loading data into cache or memory, avoiding the need for subsequent I/O operations when the data is requested.

- **Optimized file I/O**: When reading or writing files, use optimized file I/O APIs and techniques provided by the operating system or programming language. For example, use memory-mapped files for efficient file access, or use buffered I/O to reduce the number of system calls and improve performance.

By applying these strategies and techniques, you can minimize I/O operations in your software systems, reduce latency, improve performance, and optimize resource utilization. However, it is essential to balance optimization efforts with maintainability, readability, and correctness to ensure the overall quality of the software.

Optimizing your code

Now that we have looked at the ways we can optimize the overall design, let us look at some ways we can refine performance optimization even further by looking at some examples in code. This is by no means an exhaustive list of different ways code can be refined from an optimization perspective, but will hopefully provide you enough understanding of how these aspects of code can affect its overall performance and how you can look at code more closely to identify performance and optimization gains.

Whether designing systems from scratch or trying to improve existing code, optimizing code is a tricky prospect. However, that does not mean that there are not a few tricks to be aware of that could help you make some performance gains in your code. These examples do not apply equally to every solution, language, or compiler, but are important concepts nonetheless that could help to improve the performance of the code.

Not everything is applicable to every situation, language, or compiler, and the intent here is to provide areas to look at and ideas for how to make code more optimized. Additionally, there may be certain considerations and tradeoffs worth looking out for, including the following pointers:

- You could optimize your design for performance using all possible techniques, but this might generate a bigger file with a bigger memory footprint.

- You might have two different optimization goals that might sometimes conflict with each other. For example, optimizing the code for performance might conflict with optimizing the code for a smaller memory footprint and size. You might have to find a balance.

- Performance optimization is a never-ending process. Your code might never be fully optimized. There is always more room for improvement to make your code run faster.

- Sometimes you can use certain programming tricks to make code run faster at the expense of not following best practices, such as coding standards, etc. Try to avoid implementing cheap tricks to make your code run faster.

Calculating true code optimization

Optimizing code involves more than just making it run faster during testing. Various factors influence code performance, and understanding how to evaluate certain aspects of optimization can help pinpoint areas that may negatively impact performance.

Measuring code speed is complex because each line of code does not directly correspond to a CPU operation. Elements such as decision trees, loops, and memory management play significant roles in ensuring code efficiency. Additionally, external factors like hardware (including cache, CPU, or GPU types), operating systems, and web rendering engines also affect how code performs.

Keeping all this in mind, though, these are some big things to consider in the practice of writing optimized code.

Using the appropriate algorithm

Speed is not just about finding the simplest or shortest solution, but also about optimizing CPU processing. When optimizing an algorithm, aim to identify the decision tree or branch logic that requires the fewest options to process, or alternatively, the least CPU time.

Consider this scenario: We have two intervals, one for xxx $[-100,100][-100, 100][-100,100]$ and one for yyy $[-100,100][-100, 100][-100,100]$. We are searching for the maximum value of the function $x2+y2y2+b\backslash frac\{x^2 + y^2\}\{y^2 + b\}y2+bx2+y2$, where bbb is a user-defined constant between 0 and 1000.

Here is a Python example:

```python
# Define the boundaries for x and y
LEFT_MARGIN_FOR_X = -100.0
RIGHT_MARGIN_FOR_X = 100.0
LEFT_MARGIN_FOR_Y = -100.0
RIGHT_MARGIN_FOR_Y = 100.0

# Get the constant value
b = float(input("Enter the constant value b>0: "))
if b <= 0 or b > 1000:
    raise ValueError("Invalid value for b")

# Initialize the maximum value
max_value = (LEFT_MARGIN_FOR_X**2 + LEFT_MARGIN_FOR_Y**2) / (LEFT_MARGIN_
FOR_Y**2 + b)
max_x = LEFT_MARGIN_FOR_X
max_y = LEFT_MARGIN_FOR_Y

# Iterate through all possible values of x and y
for x in range(int(LEFT_MARGIN_FOR_X), int(RIGHT_MARGIN_FOR_X) + 1):
    x_squared = x**2  # Calculate x^2 once
    for y in range(int(LEFT_MARGIN_FOR_Y), int(RIGHT_MARGIN_FOR_Y) + 1):
        y_squared = y**2  # Calculate y^2 once
        current_value = (x_squared + y_squared) / (y_squared + b)
        if current_value > max_value:
            max_value = current_value
            max_x = x
            max_y = y

print(f"Maximum value of the function is = {max_value}")
```

```
print(f"Value for x = {max_x}")
print(f"Value for y = {max_y}")
```

Analyzing this code, we notice that the $x2x^2x2$ and $y2y^2y2$ calculations are optimized by computing them only once per loop iteration, rather than multiple times. This simple optimization reduces unnecessary CPU time usage.

Additional optimizations can be applied to further improve performance, but these are left for the reader to explore.

Optimize your code for memory

Optimizing code for memory means designing and writing code in a way that minimizes memory usage while still achieving the desired functionality. This is important because efficient memory usage can lead to improved performance, reduced resource consumption, and better scalability of software applications. Here are some common strategies for optimizing code for memory:

- **Data structures**: Choosing appropriate data structures can significantly impact memory usage. For example, using arrays instead of linked lists can reduce memory overhead because arrays have a smaller memory footprint per element. Similarly, using compact data structures like bit sets or bitfields can save memory when dealing with Boolean or flag values.

- **Dynamic memory management**: Minimizing unnecessary dynamic memory allocation and deallocation can help reduce memory fragmentation and overhead. Techniques such as object pooling, reuse of memory buffers, and stack allocation instead of heap allocation can be employed to optimize memory usage.

- **Memory layout**: Optimizing the layout of data structures in memory can improve memory locality and cache efficiency. This involves organizing related data together to reduce cache misses and accessing memory in a predictable and efficient manner.

- **Memory alignment**: Aligning data structures and memory allocations to the natural alignment boundaries of the underlying hardware architecture can improve memory access performance. This ensures that data is accessed efficiently and avoids performance penalties associated with unaligned memory access.

- **Memory leak detection**: Detecting and fixing memory leaks, which occur when memory is allocated but not deallocated when it is no longer needed, is crucial for efficient memory usage. Memory leaks can lead to memory exhaustion and degrade the performance of the application over time.

- **Resource sharing**: Sharing resources and reusing memory buffers whenever possible can reduce memory overhead. For example, sharing read-only data among multiple instances instead of duplicating it can save memory.

- **Minimizing copying**: Avoiding unnecessary copying of data can help reduce memory usage. Instead of creating duplicate copies of large data structures, use references or pointers to share data when possible.

- **Memory profiling**: Profiling tools can help identify memory hotspots and areas of high memory usage in the code. By analyzing memory allocation patterns and usage, developers can pinpoint areas for optimization and improvement.

By employing these techniques and considering memory optimization throughout the development process, developers can create software that uses memory efficiently, leading to improved performance, reduced resource consumption, and better overall scalability.

Problems with functions

While using functions makes our code more modular, maintainable, and scalable, improper use can lead to performance bottlenecks.

For example, consider the following loop:

```
for (int i = 1; i <= 10; ++i)
    DoSomething(i);
```

Although this approach simplifies coding, repeatedly calling a function within a loop can unnecessarily consume memory. A better implementation would involve incorporating the loop logic directly within the function, reducing processing overhead.

Next, consider the use of inline functions and macros. Inline functions can replace a function call with the function's code, reducing the overhead associated with function calls. Macros can also be used for small, repetitive tasks, offering speed, better organization, and reusability.

When passing large objects to a function, use pointers or references. References are preferable because they create more readable code. If the object should not be modified, use constant references (**const**). This approach can also save processing time.

Optimizing loops

While recursion is useful in specific scenarios, it generally results in slower code. Avoid using recursion unless it is necessary for your problem.

For example, consider the following loop:

```
for (int i = 0; i < 100; i++) {
    map[i].visited = 0;
}
```

This can be optimized as:

```
int i = 99;
do {
    map[i].visited = 0;
    i--;
} while (i >= 0);
```

Loops have their place, but try to minimize their usage unless multiple operations are needed within them. For iterative tasks like sorting, consider using an efficient sorting algorithm to reduce processing time.

Data structure optimization

Data plays a significant role in code performance, and the way we structure data can greatly enhance the speed of our code.

For example, using a list can often lead to better performance compared to an array. In some cases, organizing data in a tree structure can create a faster program than one using inadequate data structures.

However, be cautious with data structures. Sometimes, a problem can be solved without storing all elements in an array or using any data structure at all.

Binary search or sequential search

A common programming task is searching for a value within a data structure, such as in hash tables or multi-level hash tables.

When searching for a number in an array, you have two strategies:

- **Linear search**: Start at the beginning of the array and look for the value. If you find it, stop the search; if not, continue to the end of the array. There are many ways to improve this simple strategy.

- **Binary search**: This requires a sorted array. If the array is not sorted, this method would not work. With a sorted array, split it into two halves: the first half contains elements smaller than the middle one, and the second half contains elements larger than the middle one. If the markers are not positioned correctly, the value is not present. Although sorting the array takes time, it allows for faster binary searches.

Understanding the specific problem and choosing the best strategy for the situation is crucial for efficient searching.

Optimizing arrays

The array is one of the most basic data structures, occupying space in memory for its elements. To understand optimizations, you need to know the structure of an array. The name of an array is a constant pointer to its first element, allowing the use of pointers and pointer arithmetic.

Instead of using the following:

```
for (int i = 0; i < n; i++)
    nArray[i] = nSomeValue;
```

Use the following:

```
for (int* ptrInt = nArray; ptrInt < nArray + n; ptrInt++)
    *ptrInt = nSomeValue;
```

This approach leverages pointer arithmetic, where the pointer increments by the size of the int data type, resulting in faster code execution. Though harder to read, this method increases program speed due to better syntax that generates more efficient code.

For matrices, access elements row by row. Since a matrix is stored in memory row-wise, this approach aligns with the memory structure, enhancing performance.

Avoid initializing large memory portions with the same value. If unavoidable, consider using **memset** or similar commands for efficiency.

Using operators

Basic operations like **+=**, **-=**, and ***=**, when applied to basic data types, can slow down a program. To optimize effectively, understand how these operations translate into assembly code on your computer.

One interesting optimization is to replace postfix increment and decrement with their prefix versions. For example, use **++i** instead of **i++**.

Sometimes, you can use bitwise operators (**>>** or **<<**) instead of multiplication or division, but be cautious. Incorrect usage can lead to significant errors, and adding range checks to fix these errors can slow down your code more than the original operations.

Bitwise operators and tricks can enhance program speed, but they can result in machine-dependent code, which should be avoided.

Using tables versus recalculating

Tables are often easier to work with and provide simple coding solutions, but they do not scale well. Remember that recalculations offer the potential for parallelism and incremental calculation with the right formulations. Tables that are too large would not fit in your cache, making them slow to access and difficult to optimize. As with other data structures, use tables with caution.

Using smaller data types is faster than larger ones

Originally, the inclusion of **int** in coding languages served to shield programmers from directly handling the fastest data type specific to each platform. However, on contemporary 32 and 64-bit platforms, converting small data types like chars and shorts to and from the default machine word-sized data type can introduce additional overhead. Conversely, one should remain cautious of cache utilization. Employing packed data, including small structure fields, within large data objects may yield greater benefits in terms of global cache coherence compared to addressing local algorithmic optimization concerns.

Use powers of two for multidimensional arrays

Utilizing powers of two for all array sizes except the leftmost one provides a notable advantage during array access. Typically, compiled code would require a multiplication operation to determine the address of an indexed element in a multidimensional array. However, many compilers will optimize a constant multiplication by replacing it with a shift operation whenever possible. Shift operations are generally considerably faster than multiplication operations.

Data type considerations

Frequently, in an attempt to economize on space, there is a temptation to mix integer data types: using chars for small counters, shorts for slightly larger counters, and resorting to longs or int's only when absolutely necessary. Despite the apparent logic in terms of space efficiency, most CPUs end up squandering valuable cycles during data type conversions, particularly when sign preservation is involved.

Before (C code):

```
char x;
int y;
y = x;
```

After:

```
int x, y;
y = x;
```

The aforementioned tips on code optimization are not exhaustive, but they aim to encourage you to contemplate optimization in your code more deeply. Likewise, continue experimenting with different compilers and programming languages to ascertain which ones suit you best and strike that ideal balance between elegance and efficiency. While writing speedy code is crucial, it should not impede your productivity, so ensure your efforts in optimization are worthwhile.

Testing for performance

Understanding the different types of performance testing is crucial for evaluating software performance comprehensively and identifying potential bottlenecks. Here are the key types of performance testing:

- **Load testing**: This assesses the application's ability to handle anticipated user loads. The aim is to identify performance bottlenecks before the software goes live.

- **Stress testing**: Involves subjecting the application to extreme workloads to assess its behavior under high traffic or data processing. The goal is to determine the breaking point of the application.

- **Endurance testing**: Tests the software's ability to sustain the expected load over an extended period, ensuring its stability and reliability over time.

- **Spike testing**: Evaluates the application's response to sudden large spikes in user load, such as during peak usage periods. It helps gauge how the system handles rapid fluctuations in demand.

- **Volume testing**: In this type of testing, a large volume of data is populated in the database to assess the system's performance under varying data loads. It helps identify scalability and efficiency issues related to data handling.

- **Scalability testing**: Determines how effectively the software can scale up to support an increase in user load. It assists in planning for capacity additions and infrastructure scaling to meet growing demands.

Each type of performance testing serves a unique purpose and provides valuable insights into different aspects of software performance and reliability. Integrating these tests into the design process enables a more comprehensive evaluation of the system's performance under various conditions and helps identify and address performance constraints early in the development lifecycle. By considering these testing techniques, developers can ensure that their software meets its performance expectations and delivers optimal user experiences.

Performance testing process

Indeed, the methodology for performance testing can vary significantly, but its overarching objective remains constant. Performance tests aim to achieve several key goals:

- **Demonstrating compliance**: Performance tests can verify whether a software system meets predefined performance criteria. These criteria may include response times, throughput, scalability, and resource utilization benchmarks established during the testing planning phase.

- **Comparative analysis**: Performance testing enables comparisons between different software systems or versions. By assessing performance metrics side by side, testers can determine which solution performs better under specific conditions and identify areas for improvement.

- **Identifying performance degradation**: Performance tests help pinpoint components or functionalities within a software system that degrade its performance. By subjecting the system to varying load levels and stress scenarios, testers can identify bottlenecks, inefficiencies, and areas requiring optimization.

By adopting a structured approach to performance testing, organizations can gain valuable insights into their software systems' capabilities, ensure compliance with performance requirements, and drive continuous improvement to deliver optimal user experiences.

The following sub-sections explore the generic process of performing performance testing.

Identify your testing environment

Before commencing the performance testing process, it is essential to have a comprehensive understanding of the physical test environment, production environment, and available testing tools. This involves gathering detailed information about the hardware, software, and network configurations utilized during testing.

Knowing the specifics of the test environment allows testers to create more efficient tests tailored to the system's capabilities and limitations. Understanding hardware details such as processor specifications, memory capacity, and disk configurations enables testers to optimize test scenarios and anticipate potential performance bottlenecks.

Similarly, being familiar with the software stack, including the operating system, web servers, application servers, and database systems, provides valuable insights into how the system functions under various conditions. Testers can leverage this knowledge to design test cases that accurately reflect real-world usage scenarios and identify areas for optimization.

Furthermore, understanding network configurations, such as bandwidth limitations, latency, and network topology, is essential for simulating realistic user interactions and evaluating system performance in distributed environments.

Lastly, being aware of available testing tools and their capabilities empowers testers to select the most appropriate tools for conducting performance tests effectively. Whether using commercial performance testing suites or open-source tools, having a thorough understanding of their features and functionalities enhances the testing process and enables testers to overcome potential challenges more efficiently.

Identify the performance acceptance criteria

Setting goals and constraints for throughput, response times, and resource allocation is crucial for performance testing. This involves establishing targets for metrics such as the number of transactions processed per unit of time, the maximum acceptable time for a system to respond to a request, and the allocation of resources such as CPU, memory, and disk space.

In addition to these performance benchmarks, it is important to identify project success criteria that extend beyond these goals and constraints. These criteria may include factors such as user satisfaction, system reliability, and overall business impact. Testers should be empowered to set performance criteria and goals, as project specifications may not always encompass a wide enough range of benchmarks, or in some cases, there may be none at all.

When feasible, comparing the application under test to similar applications can be an effective way to establish performance goals. This benchmarking allows testers to gain insights into industry standards and best practices, providing a reference point for setting realistic and meaningful performance targets. Ultimately, by defining clear goals and success criteria, testers can ensure that performance testing efforts align with project objectives and contribute to the overall success of the application.

Plan and design performance tests

To effectively plan performance testing, it is essential to anticipate variations in end-user usage and identify key scenarios to cover all possible use cases. This involves simulating a diverse range of end-users, planning test data that reflects real-world scenarios, and outlining the metrics to be gathered during testing.

Firstly, consider the different types of end-users who will interact with the system and their respective usage patterns. This may include users with varying levels of activity, concurrent usage, and data input/output requirements.

Next, outline key scenarios that represent typical user interactions with the system. These scenarios should encompass common tasks, such as logging in, browsing content, making transactions, and performing searches. Additionally, consider edge cases and potential stress scenarios to ensure the system can handle peak loads and unexpected behavior.

When planning test data, ensure it reflects the diversity and volume of data that end-users will encounter. This may involve creating realistic datasets with varying sizes, complexities, and patterns to accurately simulate real-world usage scenarios.

Finally, define the metrics to be gathered during performance testing. These metrics may include response times, throughput, error rates, resource utilization (CPU, memory, disk I/O), and system stability under load. By collecting comprehensive metrics, you can accurately assess the system's performance, identify bottlenecks, and make informed optimizations to enhance user experience.

Configuring the test environment

Before executing tests, it is critical to prepare the testing environment to closely resemble the production environment. While it may not be feasible to match the speed of production precisely, the test environment should be configured identically to the server setup in order to provide predictable and comparable performance results, even if not exact.

Consistency in benchmarks within the test environment ensures that performance metrics remain consistent in production as well. This approach ensures that any findings or optimizations made in the test environment can be confidently applied to the production environment for consistent performance outcomes.

Implement test design

When creating performance tests based on your test design, it is essential to ensure that they align with actual possible use cases and closely resemble the customer experience. While conducting tests by bombarding every API and UI object with random data might seem comprehensive, it is crucial to acknowledge that user journeys typically entail specific data constraints unique to each scenario. Therefore, your tests should be tailored to accommodate these constraints and accurately reflect real-world usage scenarios. This approach ensures that the performance testing process remains relevant and provides insights into the system's behavior under conditions that mimic actual user interactions.

Run the tests

To effectively conduct performance tests, it is crucial to execute and monitor them meticulously. Ideally, your testing tool should operate on a separate machine from your test environment, preferably one with ample processing power. This separation ensures that the testing process remains unaffected by the performance limitations of the machine and prevents any additional strain on the server's processor, which could skew the analysis.

The true essence of performance testing lies not solely in scripting and executing tests but primarily in monitoring. The insights gleaned from various monitoring tools provide invaluable information, helping to unravel the intricacies of your system's performance and identify underlying issues accurately.

Analyze, tune, and retest

After consolidating and analyzing test results, it is crucial to share them and proceed with fine-tuning the system, followed by subsequent testing to gauge performance improvements or declines. As iterations progress, the magnitude of improvements tends to diminish, prompting a halt when CPU bottlenecking occurs. At this juncture, you may need to explore options such as enhancing CPU power.

Late-stage performance testing can pose significant challenges, especially if optimization has been deferred. In such cases, multiple poorly optimized components within the system may require individual rectification to ascertain their impact on performance accurately.

Example performance test cases

Before closing out this brief section on performance testing, let us look at some examples of brief testing ideas to paint an idea of the things that can be measured through this testing from an architect's perspective.

To do this effectively on any given system takes a significant amount of understanding of the system itself and how it works. The following test ideas should help to get you started in scripting scenarios that should unearth likely performance issues in your system:

- Verify response time is not more than 4 seconds when 1000 users access the website simultaneously.

- Verify that the response time of the application under load is within an acceptable range when the network connectivity is slow.

- Check the maximum number of users that the application can handle before it crashes.

- Check database execution time when 500 records are read or written simultaneously.

- Check CPU and memory usage of the application and the database server under peak load conditions.

- Verify the response time of the application under low, normal, moderate, and heavy load conditions.

During the actual performance test execution, vague terms like acceptable range, heavy load, etc., are replaced by concrete numbers, as you will want to measure against the specific goal that would meet the needs of your software. These numbers should typically form part of the business requirements, and the technical landscape of the application, and be discussed during the planning of a particular part of the system.

The right time to run performance tests

Many developers postpone performance testing until late in the development cycle, once the software is complete and stable. While this approach offers insights into how all components integrate, performance testing should be integrated at every stage. Delaying the identification and resolution of performance issues can be costly and lead to significant project delays, which is unacceptable in today's environment where predictability is paramount.

Every code segment or database modification should undergo performance testing as soon as possible to uncover immediate bottlenecks and optimization shortcomings. While methods for conducting code-level performance testing have been discussed previously, it is crucial to extend this testing to every API and database process, and to perform tests whenever any change, including hardware modifications, is introduced into the system.

The bottom line is that compromising on performance is not an option. Therefore, it is essential to conduct frequent and comprehensive performance testing across all levels and areas of the system. Performance is just as critical to the success of any system or application as its functional quality. Hence, it is imperative to allocate equal emphasis on testing and monitoring performance throughout the development cycle, just as you would with functional testing.

Conclusion

In this chapter, we explored various aspects that aid architects in designing high-performing applications. The initial step in any optimization endeavor is establishing observability, ensuring that we possess the necessary tools to effectively measure the operation of our system components.

Once we have achieved this and comprehended the different trade-offs inherent in the evaluation process, we can proceed to scrutinize our overall design and code, identifying avenues for optimization.

The final step involves implementing a rigorous performance testing approach to accurately assess the application's operation against our predefined expectations.

Designing for optimized performance represents one of the most formidable challenges for a software architect. However, it can significantly enhance the user experience. Software that operates swiftly, responds promptly, scales seamlessly, and imposes minimal processing overhead not only delights users but also facilitates future development endeavors by preserving optimized performance characteristics.

In the next chapter, we look at how to design software to enhance the security of an application.

Join our book's Discord space

Join the book's Discord Workspace for Latest updates, Offers, Tech happenings around the world, New Release and Sessions with the Authors:

https://discord.bpbonline.com

CHAPTER 9

Architecting for Security

Introduction

It should go without saying that with security threats only increasing and becoming more complex on a daily basis in an ever-evolving technological landscape, designing software systems to be secure is a vital responsibility of all software architects.

So, dedicating an entire chapter to the topic is a necessity and, in this chapter, we will look at various ways of identifying different threat operators, be able to identify specific design patterns that might be able to address security threats, along with specific design and coding standards which will provide a good basis for architecting software for security.

The big challenge in addressing a topic like this is that it is difficult to predict what types of security threats may arise in the future, and there is no guarantee that certain design patterns that are effective today may remain effective in the future. For this reason, this chapter is not going to focus on naming all different types of threats and vulnerabilities but rather the steps that architects can follow in identifying and mitigating against them, along with important design principles that form the foundation of keeping software secure.

However, in sticking to most of the principles outlined in this chapter, it is likely that your software design should remain resilient for most purposes and certainly meet the needs of existing application requirements.

Structure

In this chapter, we will discuss the following topics:

- Threat modelling
- Assessing vulnerabilities
- Authentication and authorization
- Secure communication
- Input validation and sanitization
- Secure data storage
- Secure coding
- Secure DevOps
- Security testing
- Incident reporting and forensics

Objectives

By the end of this chapter, you will understand the importance of security in application and software development, how to adequately identify potential threats to an application, and different ways of designing and building software that can best meet the security needs of an ever-increasing threat landscape.

Threat modeling

Knowing how to identify and model potential security threats is an important first step that architects need to keep in their armory if they are to successfully design applications that meet stringent security requirements. This process is called **threat modeling**.

Threat modeling is a systematic approach used to identify and prioritize potential security threats to a system, application, or organization. It is a proactive process that helps in understanding potential vulnerabilities and risks so that appropriate countermeasures can be implemented to mitigate them.

The following are the steps required for architects to effectively identify threats within their application space:

1. **Identify assets**:

    Start by creating an inventory of all the assets within your system or organization that need protection. This includes both tangible assets like hardware and software, as well as intangible assets like sensitive data and intellectual property.

    Categorize assets based on their importance and sensitivity to the organization.

2. **Identify threats**:

   Brainstorm potential threats that could pose a risk to your assets. This could include deliberate attacks from malicious actors, accidental damage, natural disasters, or system failures.

   Consider various threat sources such as internal employees, external hackers, competitors, disgruntled customers, or nation-state actors.

3. **Identify vulnerabilities**:

   Analyze your system, infrastructure, and processes to identify potential weaknesses or vulnerabilities that could be exploited by the threats identified in the previous step.

   Common vulnerabilities include insecure authentication mechanisms, inadequate access controls, unpatched software, weak encryption, and social engineering vulnerabilities.

4. **Assess risks**:

   Assess the likelihood of each threat exploiting the identified vulnerabilities and the potential impact if they were to occur.

   Use risk assessment techniques such as qualitative analysis (e.g., risk matrices), quantitative analysis (e.g., risk scoring), or a combination of both to prioritize risks.

5. **Prioritize threats**:

   Prioritize the identified threats based on their likelihood and impact on your assets and organization.

   Focus on addressing the most critical and high-priority threats first, as these pose the greatest risk to your organization's security and objectives.

6. **Develop countermeasures**:

   Develop and implement countermeasures or security controls to mitigate the identified risks and vulnerabilities.

   Choose appropriate controls based on the nature of the threats and vulnerabilities, such as technical controls (e.g., firewalls, encryption), procedural controls (e.g., security policies, training), or physical controls (e.g., access controls, surveillance).

7. **Review and update**:

   Regularly review and update your threat model to reflect changes in your system, technology, or threat landscape.

   Conduct periodic risk assessments to identify new threats, vulnerabilities, or changes in risk levels, and adjust your security measures accordingly.

8. **Document**:

Document your threat model, including the identified assets, threats, vulnerabilities, risks, and countermeasures.

Maintain comprehensive documentation to ensure consistency, transparency, and accountability in your security efforts and to serve as a reference for stakeholders and future iterations of the threat modeling process.

Assessing vulnerabilities

Alongside performing a threat analysis on a system, it is important to assess the existing vulnerabilities that might exist within your given system. Performing these activities side-by-side can help the architect evaluate the different threats against known vulnerabilities in their systems and better mitigate and adjust the design of the software.

Vulnerability assessment involves identifying, prioritizing, and remediating security weaknesses that could be exploited by attackers to compromise the confidentiality, integrity, or availability of assets.

Here is an overview of the vulnerability assessment process that architects should follow in performing this exercise:

1. **Asset inventory**:

Start by creating an inventory of all assets within the organization, including hardware, software, networks, applications, and data repositories.

Categorize assets based on their criticality, sensitivity, and importance to the organization's operations and objectives.

2. **Vulnerability identification**:

Use automated vulnerability scanning tools to identify known vulnerabilities, misconfigurations, and weaknesses across the organization's IT infrastructure.

Conduct manual vulnerability assessments, penetration testing, and code reviews to uncover complex or undocumented vulnerabilities that automated tools may miss.

Prioritize vulnerabilities based on severity, exploitability, and potential impact on the organization's security posture.

3. **Risk assessment**:

Assess the likelihood and potential impact of each identified vulnerability being exploited by attackers.

Use risk assessment methodologies such as qualitative analysis (e.g., risk matrices), quantitative analysis (e.g., risk scoring), or a combination of both to prioritize vulnerabilities for remediation.

4. **Remediation planning**:

Develop a remediation plan that outlines specific actions and timelines for addressing identified vulnerabilities.

Prioritize remediation efforts based on the risk level, criticality of assets, and available resources.

Involve stakeholders from relevant departments (e.g., IT, security, development) in the remediation planning process to ensure alignment and collaboration.

5. **Patch management**:

Implement a patch management program to regularly update and patch vulnerable software, operating systems, and firmware.

Establish patching priorities based on the severity and exploitability of vulnerabilities, vendor recommendations, and organizational policies.

Automate patch deployment and monitoring processes to streamline and accelerate the patching cycle.

6. **Security controls implementation**:

Implement security controls and mitigations to address vulnerabilities that cannot be patched immediately or are not under direct control (e.g., third-party software).

Use compensating controls, **intrusion detection/prevention systems (IDS/IPS)**, firewalls, and access controls to mitigate risks associated with unpatched vulnerabilities.

7. **Continuous monitoring and improvement**:

Continuously monitor the organization's IT environment for new vulnerabilities, emerging threats, and changes in the threat landscape.

Regularly reassess and update vulnerability assessments, remediation plans, and security controls to adapt to evolving risks and requirements.

Foster a culture of security awareness and proactive risk management across the organization to promote ongoing vigilance and improvement.

By following these steps and adopting a proactive and systematic approach to vulnerability assessment and management, organizations can reduce their exposure to security risks, strengthen their defense against cyber threats, and safeguard their critical assets and information. Regular vulnerability assessments are essential for maintaining an effective security posture and ensuring compliance with regulatory requirements and industry best practices.

Secure design patterns

Now that we have looked at the process for effective threat modeling and vulnerability analysis within an application, it is time to look at ways of designing software in a secure manner to best meet the different threats you are likely to face.

Secure design patterns are reusable solutions to common security problems or challenges encountered during the design and development of software systems, applications, or architectures. These patterns provide best practices and guidelines for incorporating security principles into the design process, helping developers to build more secure and resilient systems from the ground up.

Here are some examples of secure design patterns that architects should consider as part of their application design to help provide security within the design. Some of these patterns we have gone through in more detail in *Chapter 6, Architectural Patterns*, so we will only mention them briefly here, whereas some other patterns we will cover here are more modern design approaches and we will go into these in significantly more detail in how they pertain to providing a secure design:

- **Layered architecture**:

  This pattern divides the application into distinct layers (e.g., presentation, business logic, data access) with each layer having its own specific responsibilities and security controls.

  It helps to enforce separation of concerns and implement security controls at each layer, such as input validation, authentication, and authorization, reducing the impact of security breaches.

- **Input validation and sanitization**:

  This pattern focuses on validating and sanitizing all input data received by the application to prevent common security vulnerabilities such as injection attacks (e.g., SQL injection, XSS).

  It includes techniques such as white-listing input validation, parameterized queries, and escaping user-generated content to mitigate the risk of injection attacks.

- **Secure session management**:

  This pattern provides guidelines for securely managing user sessions to prevent session hijacking, fixation, and other session-related attacks.

  It involves practices such as using secure session identifiers, enforcing HTTPS for secure communication, implementing session timeouts, and regularly rotating session tokens.

- **Data encryption and protection**:

  This pattern focuses on protecting sensitive data both in transit and at rest by encrypting it using strong cryptographic algorithms.

  It includes practices such as encrypting data stored in databases, using SSL/TLS for secure communication over networks, and implementing key management and access controls.

- **Audit logging and monitoring**:

  This pattern involves capturing and logging security-relevant events and activities within the application for auditing, compliance, and forensic purposes.

  It includes practices such as logging security-related events (e.g., authentication failures, access control violations), implementing log integrity and confidentiality, and monitoring logs for suspicious activities.

- **Error handling and exception management**:

  This pattern provides guidelines for handling errors and exceptions in a secure and graceful manner to prevent information disclosure and maintain system integrity.

  It involves practices such as avoiding detailed error messages that leak sensitive information, implementing centralized error handling mechanisms, and logging errors securely.

By incorporating these and other secure design patterns into their software development process, developers can build more robust and resilient systems that are better protected against common security threats and vulnerabilities. These patterns help to promote security by design principles and enable developers to proactively address security concerns throughout the development lifecycle.

API security

With most applications moving towards API communication for their microservices, it is important that we look at API security more closely, and knowing how to secure APIs is a vital aspect of modern application design.

Application programming interface (API) security is crucial for protecting the integrity, confidentiality, and availability of data and resources exposed through APIs. APIs are a great way of breaking down big, complex applications into smaller modular interfaces that can be easily scaled and maintained. However, with more endpoints essentially exposed than an ordinary monolithic system, it does make security more critical.

So, ensuring their security has become paramount to prevent unauthorized access, data breaches, and other security incidents. Here are some key aspects and best practices for API security:

- **Authentication**:

  Implement strong authentication mechanisms to verify the identity of clients accessing the API. This could include using API keys, OAuth tokens, **JSON Web Tokens (JWT)**, or client certificates.

  Consider implementing multi-factor authentication for enhanced security, especially for accessing sensitive APIs or performing critical operations.

- **Authorization**:

  Enforce fine-grained access controls and authorization policies to restrict access to API resources based on the roles, permissions, or attributes of the authenticated users or clients.

  Use **role-based access control (RBAC), attribute-based access control (ABAC)**, or **policy-based access control (PBAC)** to define and enforce access policies.

- **Encryption**:

  Ensure that data transmitted between clients and the API endpoints is encrypted using strong cryptographic protocols such as SSL/TLS (HTTPS).

  Encrypt sensitive data stored in databases or transmitted within API payloads to protect it from unauthorized access or interception.

- **Input validation**:

  Validate and sanitize all input data received by the API to prevent common security vulnerabilities such as injection attacks (e.g., SQL injection, XSS).

  Implement strict input validation and parameterization to mitigate the risk of injection attacks and other forms of input manipulation.

- **Rate limiting and throttling**:

  Implement rate limiting and throttling mechanisms to prevent abuse, **denial-of-service (DoS)**, or brute-force attacks targeting the API.

  Enforce usage quotas, request rate limits, and concurrency limits to control the volume and frequency of API requests from individual clients or IP addresses.

- **Logging and monitoring**:

  Implement comprehensive logging of API requests, responses, and security-related events for auditing, monitoring, and forensic analysis.

  Monitor API usage, traffic patterns, and security events in real-time to detect and respond to suspicious activities, anomalies, or security incidents.

- **API versioning and lifecycle management**:

  Implement versioning and lifecycle management practices to ensure backward compatibility, manage API changes, and deprecate obsolete or vulnerable API versions.

  Communicate changes, updates, and deprecations to API consumers effectively to minimize disruption and ensure a smooth transition to newer versions.

- **Secure coding practices**:

  Follow secure coding practices and guidelines when designing, developing, and testing APIs to mitigate common security risks and vulnerabilities.

  Conduct security reviews, code audits, and penetration testing to identify and address security issues early in the development lifecycle.

By implementing these best practices and adopting a holistic approach to API security, organizations can mitigate risks, protect sensitive data, and ensure the integrity and reliability of their APIs in today's interconnected and distributed software ecosystems.

Container and cloud security

Similar to APIs, container and cloud security are essential aspects of modern IT infrastructure, especially with the widespread adoption of containerization and cloud computing technologies. As a result, we need to focus on specific areas on how we can ensure that we build security into our cloud and container usage in our development ecosystem. Security is not just about the code itself, but also the environments we deploy it on, and so this should remain an important area for all architects to focus on.

We will look at some key considerations and best practices for ensuring the security of containers and cloud environments. This is not an exhaustive list, but represents the main focus areas architects should emphasize. For more detailed security mechanisms, it is important to do the proper certifications in these cloud areas.

Container security

Container security involves securing containerized applications, their environments, and the underlying infrastructure to protect against threats across the container lifecycle. Containers are lightweight, portable, and can be deployed quickly, making them popular for modern software development, but they also introduce unique security challenges. Effective container security includes hardening container images, controlling access to the container registry, managing vulnerabilities, and monitoring runtime behavior. By implementing the following measures, organizations can ensure that their containerized applications remain resilient against attacks, reducing risks to their overall infrastructure:

- **Image security**:
  - When making use of container images, use only trusted container images from reputable sources or build your own images from trusted base images.
  - Regularly scan container images for vulnerabilities using security scanning tools.
  - Implement a secure image registry with access controls and encryption for storing and distributing container images.

- **Runtime security**:
  - Isolate containers using appropriate container runtime isolation mechanisms, such as namespaces and cgroups.
  - Implement network segmentation and firewall rules to restrict network access between containers and external resources.
  - Monitor container runtime activity for suspicious behavior and unauthorized access.

- **Orchestration security (e.g., Kubernetes)**:
  - Harden Kubernetes clusters by applying security configurations, such as network policies, pod security policies, and RBAC.
  - Regularly update Kubernetes and its components to patch known vulnerabilities and ensure the latest security features are enabled.
  - Implement least privilege principles to restrict access to Kubernetes resources and APIs based on the principle of least privilege.

- **Access control**:
  - Use strong authentication mechanisms for accessing containerized environments, such as **multi-factor authentication (MFA)** and identity providers (e.g., LDAP, Active Directory).
  - Implement role-based access control to restrict access to container orchestration platforms, APIs, and resources based on user roles and permissions.

- **Logging and monitoring**:
  - Enable centralized logging and monitoring of containerized environments to detect and respond to security incidents in real-time.
  - Monitor container runtime activity, resource usage, and network traffic for anomalous behavior and security events.
  - Integrate container security logs and alerts with **security information and event management (SIEM)** systems for comprehensive threat detection and response.

Cloud security

Cloud security encompasses the technologies, policies, and practices used to safeguard data, applications, and services hosted in cloud environments. As organizations increasingly rely on cloud computing for its scalability, flexibility, and cost-effectiveness, they face unique security challenges, such as data exposure, identity management, and regulatory compliance. Effective cloud security strategies involve securing access, encrypting data, managing configurations, monitoring threats, and ensuring compliance across public, private, and hybrid cloud infrastructures. By addressing these areas, organizations can protect sensitive information and maintain resilience against cyber threats in the cloud:

- **Identity and access management (IAM)**:
    - Implement robust IAM policies to manage user identities, roles, and permissions for accessing cloud resources.
    - Use least privilege principles to grant only necessary permissions to users, roles, and service accounts.
    - Enable MFA for enhanced security of cloud accounts and resources.

- **Data encryption**:
    - Encrypt data at rest and in transit using strong encryption algorithms and protocols.
    - Implement encryption for sensitive data stored in cloud storage services, databases, and backups.
    - Use **key management services (KMS)** to securely manage encryption keys and access policies.

- **Network security**:
    - Implement network segmentation and firewall rules to control traffic flow between cloud resources and networks.
    - Use **virtual private clouds (VPCs), network access control lists (NACLs)**, and security groups to enforce network security policies.
    - Enable logging and monitoring of network traffic for detecting and responding to security incidents.

- **Compliance and governance**:
    - Ensure compliance with industry regulations and standards (e.g., GDPR, HIPAA, PCI DSS) by implementing appropriate controls and audit trails.
    - Regularly audit and assess cloud configurations, permissions, and security controls to identify and remediate security gaps.

    o   Implement governance frameworks and security policies to enforce security best practices and standards across cloud environments.

- **Incident response and recovery**:

    o   Develop and test incident response plans to quickly detect, respond to, and recover from security incidents in cloud environments.

    o   Implement automated backup and disaster recovery mechanisms to ensure data resilience and business continuity.

    o   Conduct regular security drills and simulations to validate incident response procedures and improve readiness.

By addressing these key considerations and implementing best practices for container and cloud security, organizations can enhance the security posture of their modern IT infrastructure and protect against a wide range of security threats and vulnerabilities.

Blockchain security

Another emerging trend in the software world that we are seeing gain prominence around the world is the concept of blockchain. We will not go into detail here on what blockchain technology is or how it works, as we will cover that in *Chapter 16, Testing in Software Architecture*. So, if you are unfamiliar with how it works, read that chapter before coming back and reading about how we can look at blockchain from a security perspective.

Blockchain security is essentially all about ensuring the integrity, confidentiality, and availability of data and transactions recorded on a blockchain network. While blockchain technology offers several inherent security features such as immutability and cryptographic verification, it is still essential to address various security challenges and vulnerabilities.

Here are key considerations and best practices for ensuring blockchain security:

- **Consensus mechanism**:

    o   Choose a secure and reliable consensus mechanism (e.g., Proof of Work, Proof of Stake) that aligns with the specific requirements and goals of the blockchain network.

    o   Ensure that the consensus mechanism is resistant to attacks, such as 51% attacks, Sybil attacks, and long-range attacks.

- **Cryptographic security:**

    o   Use strong cryptographic algorithms and standards for hashing, digital signatures, and encryption to secure data and transactions on the blockchain.

    o   Regularly update cryptographic libraries and protocols to patch known vulnerabilities and maintain robust security.

- **Access control**:
  - Implement access controls and permissioning mechanisms to restrict access to sensitive blockchain resources and functionalities.
  - Use RBAC, smart contracts, and multi-signature schemes to manage permissions and enforce security policies.

- **Secure smart contracts**:
  - Audit and thoroughly test smart contracts for vulnerabilities and logic errors before deploying them on the blockchain.
  - Implement best practices for secure smart contract development, such as input validation, error handling, and secure storage of sensitive data.
  - Use formal verification techniques and security tools to analyze smart contracts for potential vulnerabilities and security flaws.

- **Network security**:
  - Implement network-level security controls such as firewalls, **intrusion detection systems (IDS)**, and **distributed denial-of-service (DDoS)** protection to protect against network-based attacks.
  - Use secure communication protocols (e.g., TLS/SSL) and encryption to secure communication between nodes and participants in the blockchain network.

- **Immutable audit trail**:
  - Leverage the immutability and transparency of the blockchain to create an immutable audit trail of transactions and data changes.
  - Regularly audit and monitor the blockchain for unauthorized or suspicious activity and take appropriate action to mitigate security incidents.

- **Key management**:
  - Implement robust key management practices to securely generate, store, and use cryptographic keys for signing transactions and accessing blockchain resources.
  - Use **hardware security modules (HSMs)**, secure key vaults, and multi-signature schemes to protect private keys from unauthorized access and theft.

- **Regulatory compliance**:
  - Ensure compliance with applicable regulations and legal requirements (e.g., GDPR, AML or KYC) by implementing appropriate security controls and privacy measures on the blockchain.

- o Work with legal and regulatory experts to navigate the complex regulatory landscape and ensure that blockchain implementations meet compliance requirements.

- **Continuous monitoring and incident response**:

  - o Implement continuous monitoring and real-time alerting mechanisms to detect and respond to security incidents and anomalies on the blockchain.

  - o Develop and test incident response plans to effectively mitigate and recover from security breaches or disruptions in blockchain operations.

By addressing these key considerations and implementing best practices for blockchain security, organizations can enhance the trust, reliability, and resilience of their blockchain-based systems and applications, mitigating risks and vulnerabilities in the process.

Zero Trust Architecture

Now that we have had a look at how to secure some of the emerging trends in software architecture. Let us explore an important principle of architectural design that can help enforce security throughout, the principle of Zero Trust.

Zero Trust Architecture (ZTA) is a security framework and approach that challenges the traditional perimeter-based security model by assuming that threats can exist both inside and outside the network. The core principle of Zero Trust is to never trust, always verify, meaning that access to resources and data is never implicitly trusted based solely on the location of the user or device. Instead, access is continuously authenticated, authorized, and monitored, regardless of whether the user is inside or outside the organizational network perimeter.

Key components and principles of ZTA include:

- **Identity-centric security**:

  - o Verifying the identity of users, devices, and services before granting access to resources. This may involve MFA, device attestation, and strong cryptographic authentication mechanisms.

  - o Implementing fine-grained access controls based on the principle of least privilege, ensuring that users and devices have only the permissions necessary to perform their intended tasks.

  - o Use contextual attributes such as user identity, device status, location, and behavior to make access control decisions dynamically.

- **Micro-segmentation**:

  - o Segmenting the network into smaller, logical segments based on trust levels, applications, or data sensitivity.

- Implementing network segmentation controls at the host level (e.g., using software-defined networking) to isolate and control communication between individual workloads, applications, or services.

- **Continuous monitoring and analytics**:
  - Monitoring network traffic, user behavior, and access patterns in real-time to detect and respond to security threats and anomalies.
  - Using security analytics, machine learning, and behavioral analysis techniques to identify suspicious activities and potential security incidents.

- **Encryption and data protection**:
  - Encrypting data at rest, in transit, and in use to protect it from unauthorized access, interception, and tampering.
  - Using strong encryption algorithms and key management practices to ensure the confidentiality and integrity of sensitive data.

- **Least privilege access**:
  - Applying the principle of least privilege to restrict access to resources and functionalities based on the minimum level of access required to perform specific tasks.
  - Regularly reviewing and updating access permissions to align with business needs and security requirements.

- **Secure access controls**:
  - Implementing secure access controls for remote users, third-party vendors, and external partners, regardless of their location or network environment.
  - Using secure remote access technologies such as **virtual private networks (VPNs)**, **secure sockets layer (SSL)** VPNs, and zero trust access solutions to enforce authentication and authorization for remote users.

- **Zero Trust Network Access (ZTNA)**:
  - Adopting ZTNA solutions that provide secure, identity-based access to applications and resources without exposing them to the internet or relying on traditional VPNs.
  - Use techniques such as application-level proxies, reverse proxies, and secure access brokers to authenticate and authorize user access based on identity and context.

- **Continuous evaluation and remediation**:
  - Continuously assess the security posture of devices, applications, and users to identify vulnerabilities, misconfigurations, and compliance issues.

     ○ Implement automated remediation workflows to address security issues promptly and reduce the attack surface.

By embracing ZTA principles and best practices, organizations can enhance their security posture, protect against evolving threats, and improve resilience in an increasingly dynamic and perimeterless IT environment.

Authentication and authorization

Authentication and authorization are fundamental aspects of ensuring secure access to systems, applications, and resources. As a result, it is important that we focus on these elements in this chapter so that we build security around these areas correctly.

Authentication

Authentication is the process of verifying the identity of a user, device, or service attempting to access a system or resource.

The goal of authentication is to ensure that the entity requesting access is who or what it claims to be.

Common authentication mechanisms include:

- **Password-based authentication**: Users provide a username and password to verify their identity.

- **MFA**: Requires users to provide additional forms of verification, such as a **one-time password (OTP)**, biometric data (fingerprint, facial recognition), or hardware token, in addition to a password.

- **Certificate-based authentication**: Uses digital certificates issued by a trusted authority to verify the identity of users, devices, or services.

- **Single sign-on (SSO)**: Allows users to authenticate once and access multiple applications or resources without re-entering credentials.

Strong authentication mechanisms should be used, especially for accessing sensitive systems or data, to prevent unauthorized access through stolen or compromised credentials.

Authorization

Authorization is the process of granting or denying access to specific resources or functionalities based on the authenticated identity and associated permissions.

After a user or entity has been authenticated, authorization determines what actions they are allowed to perform within the system.

Authorization policies are typically based on:

- **RBAC**: Users are assigned roles, and permissions are granted based on these roles. For example, an administrator role might have full access to all system resources, while a regular user role might have limited access.

- **ABAC**: Access decisions are based on attributes such as user characteristics, environmental conditions, or resource properties. For example, access to a sensitive document might be restricted based on the user's department, location, or security clearance level.

Access controls should be granular and based on least privilege, meaning that users or entities are only granted the minimum level of access necessary to perform their intended tasks. This reduces the risk of unauthorized access or privilege escalation.

Authentication and authorization mechanisms work together to ensure that only authenticated and authorized users or entities can access resources within a system. By implementing strong authentication mechanisms and granular authorization controls, organizations can enforce security policies, protect sensitive data, and mitigate the risk of unauthorized access or data breaches.

Secure communication

Secure communication is essential for protecting the confidentiality, integrity, and authenticity of data transmitted over networks. Whether communicating over the internet, internal networks, or between systems and devices, employing robust security measures helps prevent eavesdropping, tampering, and unauthorized access.

Here are the key components and best practices for ensuring secure communication:

- **Encryption**:
  - Use strong encryption algorithms and protocols to encrypt data in transit, ensuring that it remains confidential even if intercepted by unauthorized parties.
  - **Transport Layer Security** (**TLS**) and its predecessor, **Secure Sockets Layer** (**SSL**), are widely used encryption protocols for securing communication over the Internet. Ensure TLS configurations are up-to-date and properly configured to mitigate known vulnerabilities.
  - **Employ end-to-end encryption** (**E2EE**) for sensitive communications, where data is encrypted on the sender's device and only decrypted on the recipient's device, preventing intermediaries from accessing plaintext data.

- **Secure protocols**:
  - Choose secure communication protocols that have been thoroughly vetted and are resistant to known vulnerabilities and attacks.

- o Avoid using deprecated or insecure protocols such as SSL and older versions of TLS, which may be susceptible to exploits and cryptographic weaknesses.

- o Prefer protocols that provide mutual authentication, ensuring both parties verify each other's identity before establishing a secure connection.

- **Authentication**:

  - o Authenticate both parties involved in the communication to ensure the identity of the sender and receiver.

  - o Use strong authentication mechanisms such as digital certificates, cryptographic keys, and mutual authentication to verify the identity of communicating entities.

  - o Implement **multi-factor authentication (MFA)** where possible to add an extra layer of security and reduce the risk of unauthorized access.

- **Key management**:

  - o Implement robust key management practices to securely generate, store, distribute, and rotate cryptographic keys used for encryption and authentication.

  - o Use **hardware security modules (HSMs)** or secure key management services to protect cryptographic keys from unauthorized access and theft.

  - o Regularly update and rotate encryption keys to mitigate the risk of key compromise or cryptographic attacks.

- **Integrity verification**:

  - o Ensure data integrity by employing cryptographic hashing algorithms or digital signatures to detect unauthorized modifications or tampering during transit.

  - o Include integrity checks (e.g., HMAC) in communication protocols to verify the integrity of transmitted data and protect against data manipulation attacks.

- **Secure configuration**:

  - o Configure communication protocols, encryption algorithms, and security parameters according to best practices and industry standards.

  - o Disable insecure cipher suites, protocols, and features that may weaken the security of communication channels.

  - o Enable security features such as **Perfect Forward Secrecy (PFS)** to ensure that compromised session keys do not compromise past or future communications.

- **Logging and monitoring**:

  - Implement logging and monitoring mechanisms to track and analyze communication activities for anomalies, security events, and potential security incidents.

  - Monitor network traffic for signs of unauthorized access, data exfiltration, or suspicious behavior that may indicate a security breach.

By implementing these best practices and security measures, organizations can establish secure communication channels to protect sensitive data, maintain the confidentiality and integrity of information, and mitigate the risk of unauthorized access or interception by adversaries.

Input validation and sanitization

Input validation and sanitization are essential security measures used to protect against various types of attacks, including injection attacks, **cross-site scripting** (**XSS**), and other forms of input manipulation. These techniques help ensure that data received from users or external sources is safe, trustworthy, and free from malicious payloads or unexpected content. Here's an overview of input validation and sanitization practices:

- **Input validation**:

  - Input validation involves verifying the correctness, format, and structure of data provided by users or external sources before processing or accepting it.

  - Validate input data against expected formats, data types, length constraints, and allowed characters using whitelist-based validation.

  - Reject or sanitize input data that does not adhere to validation rules, preventing potentially malicious or malformed input from being processed.

  - Implement client-side validation to provide immediate feedback to users and reduce the likelihood of submitting invalid data to the server.

  - Validate input data on the server-side as well to enforce security controls and prevent bypassing of client-side validation.

- **Sanitization**:

  - Sanitization involves removing or neutralizing potentially harmful or malicious content from input data, making it safe for processing and rendering.

  - Use input sanitization techniques to remove or escape special characters, HTML tags, JavaScript code, and other potentially dangerous content from user input.

- o   Implement output encoding to convert special characters and symbols into their corresponding HTML entities or escape sequences to prevent XSS attacks.

- o   Use dedicated libraries or frameworks that provide built-in sanitization functions for common input data types and security vulnerabilities.

- **Context-specific validation**:

  - o   Tailor input validation and sanitization rules based on the specific context or purpose of the input data.

  - o   Apply stricter validation rules for sensitive or high-risk input fields, such as authentication credentials, payment information, or SQL queries.

  - o   Consider the intended use of the input data (e.g., display, storage, processing) when determining validation and sanitization requirements.

- **Regular expression validation**:

  - o   Use **regular expressions** (**regex**) to define and enforce complex validation patterns for input data, such as email addresses, phone numbers, URLs, or credit card numbers.

  - o   Validate input data against regex patterns to ensure compliance with expected formats and structures, reducing the risk of injection or manipulation attacks.

- **Parameterized queries**:

  - o   Use parameterized queries or prepared statements when interacting with databases to prevent SQL injection attacks.

  - o   Parameterize input data values in SQL queries to separate them from the query structure, preventing attackers from injecting malicious SQL code into query parameters.

- **Security headers and content security policies**:

  - o   Implement security headers and **content security policies** (**CSP**) to enforce browser-level security controls and mitigate risks associated with XSS attacks.

  - o   Use HTTP headers such as CSP, X-XSS-protection, and X-content-type-options to restrict the execution of scripts, control content types, and prevent XSS vulnerabilities.

By incorporating input validation and sanitization practices into software development processes, organizations can reduce the risk of security vulnerabilities, protect against common attacks, and ensure the integrity and security of their applications and data. These techniques are essential components of a defense-in-depth strategy for web application security.

Secure data storage

Secure data storage is critical for protecting sensitive information from unauthorized access, disclosure, and tampering. Whether storing data in databases, file systems, cloud storage, or other repositories, implementing strong security measures helps ensure the confidentiality, integrity, and availability of stored data. Here are key considerations and best practices for secure data storage:

- **Encryption**:
    - Encrypt sensitive data at rest using strong cryptographic algorithms and encryption keys.
    - Use industry-standard encryption techniques such as **Advanced Encryption Standard** (**AES**) for encrypting data before storing it in databases or file systems.
    - Implement key management practices to securely generate, store, and manage encryption keys, including key rotation and protection against unauthorized access.

- **Access controls**:
    - Implement granular access controls to restrict access to sensitive data based on the principle of least privilege.
    - Use RBAC or ABAC to define and enforce access policies based on user roles, permissions, and attributes.
    - Regularly review and audit access permissions to ensure that only authorized users and applications have access to sensitive data.

- **Secure storage systems**:
    - Choose secure storage systems and platforms that provide built-in security features and compliance certifications.
    - Use data encryption features provided by storage systems, databases, and cloud platforms to protect data from unauthorized access and disclosure.
    - Implement secure configurations, access controls, and monitoring capabilities for storage systems to mitigate risks and vulnerabilities.

- **Data masking and anonymization**:
    - Use data masking and anonymization techniques to protect sensitive information while preserving its utility for legitimate purposes.
    - Replace sensitive data with anonymized or masked values (e.g., using tokenization or pseudonymization) in non-production environments to minimize the risk of data exposure during development, testing, or analysis.

- **Secure backup and recovery**:
    - ○ Implement secure backup and recovery procedures to ensure data resilience and continuity in the event of data loss, corruption, or disaster.
    - ○ Encrypt backup data both in transit and at rest to prevent unauthorized access or interception during backup operations.
    - ○ Regularly test backup and recovery processes to verify their effectiveness and reliability in restoring data to a secure state.

- **Data retention and disposal**:
    - ○ Establish data retention policies and procedures to govern the storage and lifecycle management of sensitive data.
    - ○ Regularly review and dispose of outdated, redundant, or unnecessary data to minimize the risk of data breaches and compliance violations.
    - ○ Implement secure data disposal practices, such as overwriting, degaussing, or physically destroying storage media, to ensure that sensitive data cannot be recovered after disposal.

- **Security monitoring and logging**:
    - ○ Implement logging and monitoring mechanisms to track access to sensitive data, detect unauthorized activities, and respond to security incidents.
    - ○ Monitor storage system logs, access patterns, and data transfer activities for anomalies, suspicious behavior, or potential security breaches.
    - ○ Integrate storage system logs and alerts with centralized SIEM systems for comprehensive threat detection and response.

By following these best practices and implementing robust security measures for data storage, organizations can protect sensitive information, maintain compliance with regulatory requirements, and safeguard the trust and privacy of their customers and stakeholders.

Secure coding

We have looked at a wide variety of different mechanisms that require secure software design, with a lot of good principles that we need to follow. For the rest of this chapter, we will focus on security aspects of the code itself.

Secure coding practices are essential for building robust and resilient software applications that are resistant to security vulnerabilities and attacks. By incorporating security principles and best practices into the software development lifecycle, developers can mitigate risks, protect sensitive data, and ensure the integrity and reliability of their code. Here are key considerations and best practices for secure coding:

- **Input validation and sanitization**:
  - Validate and sanitize all input data received from users, external systems, or untrusted sources to prevent injection attacks (e.g., SQL injection, XSS).
  - Use input validation techniques to enforce strict validation rules and reject or sanitize input that does not conform to expected formats, data types, or length constraints.
  - Implement output encoding and escaping to prevent **cross-site scripting (XSS)** attacks by neutralizing or escaping special characters in output data displayed to users.

- **Authentication and authorization**:
  - Implement strong authentication mechanisms to verify the identity of users and prevent unauthorized access to sensitive functionalities or resources.
  - Use secure password storage techniques (e.g., salted hashing, key stretching) to protect user credentials stored in databases or authentication systems.
  - Enforce fine-grained access controls and authorization policies to restrict access to sensitive data and functionalities based on user roles, permissions, and attributes.

- **Secure communication**:
  - Use secure communication protocols (e.g., HTTPS/TLS) to encrypt data transmitted over networks and protect it from eavesdropping, tampering, or interception.
  - Implement certificate pinning and validation to ensure the authenticity and integrity of SSL/TLS certificates presented by servers during communication.
  - Sanitize and validate input received from network protocols, APIs, or external systems to prevent buffer overflows, injection attacks, or other network-based vulnerabilities.

- **Secure data storage**:
  - Encrypt sensitive data at rest using strong cryptographic algorithms and encryption keys to protect it from unauthorized access or disclosure.
  - Implement secure storage mechanisms and access controls to protect data stored in databases, file systems, or cloud storage platforms from unauthorized access or tampering.
  - Use parameterized queries or prepared statements to prevent SQL injection attacks when interacting with databases, avoiding dynamic SQL queries constructed from user input.

- **Error handling and logging:**

  o Implement secure error handling mechanisms to handle exceptions gracefully and prevent the leakage of sensitive information in error messages or logs.

  o Avoid disclosing detailed error messages or stack traces to users, which may reveal sensitive information about the application's internals.

  o Log security-relevant events, activities, and exceptions to facilitate auditing, monitoring, and forensic analysis of security incidents.

- **Secure configuration:**

  o Configure application components, frameworks, and third-party libraries securely according to best practices and security guidelines.

  o Disable unnecessary features, services, or functionality that could increase the attack surface or introduce security risks.

  o Keep software dependencies up-to-date and apply security patches promptly to mitigate known vulnerabilities and weaknesses.

- **Security testing and code reviews:**

  o Conduct regular security testing, vulnerability assessments, and penetration testing to identify and remediate security vulnerabilities in the codebase.

  o Perform code reviews with a focus on security to identify insecure coding practices, logic flaws, or vulnerabilities introduced during development.

  o Use automated security testing tools and static code analysis tools to identify common security issues and coding errors in the codebase.

By following these secure coding practices and integrating security into the software development lifecycle, developers can build more secure and resilient applications that protect against a wide range of security threats and vulnerabilities. Secure coding is a shared responsibility among developers, architects, testers, and security professionals, and should be prioritized throughout the development process to ensure the security and integrity of software applications.

Secure DevOPs

Secure DevOps, also known as **DevSecOps**, integrates security practices into the DevOps process, ensuring that security considerations are addressed at every stage of the **software development lifecycle (SDLC)**. By embedding security into DevOps workflows, organizations can build and deploy software more securely, detect and remediate vulnerabilities earlier, and improve overall security posture.

Many of the principles here are less technical and more about a shift in development culture within an organization. And as architects, it is important that we advocate for the right development culture in teams to ensure that we produce the right outcomes in our development efforts.

Shift-left security

Shift-left testing is an important concept that we will get into when we talk about testing on software architecture in *Chapter 15, Architecture as Engineering*. However, it is a concept that applies to security as well, with the core idea of ensuring security is not left late in the development cycle but included in implementation from the very beginning.

Shifting security to the left is about integrating security testing tools and techniques into **continuous integration** (**CI**) pipelines to automate security checks and identify vulnerabilities in code early in the development process. Using code analysis tools and **static code analysis** (**SCA**) techniques to identify security vulnerabilities, compliance violations, and coding errors in application code and infrastructure configurations. This allows security issues to be identified early in the development process and can notify developers of security gaps in their code that need to be remediated before they get pushed into any shared environment and, especially, production.

However, shifting security left is not just about the tooling and scanning that is required, but also about changing the culture towards security and the training required to address it. This means that companies should empower developers with security training, tools, and resources to identify and address security issues during code development and testing, as well as allowing them the time to get this right rather than rushing their code and development cycle times.

It also means that aspects of code like security configurations, policies, and controls should be treated as code artifacts that can be version-controlled, automated, and managed alongside application code. This heightens their importance and ensures that the right behaviors are driven in treating security just like any other aspect of code.

It is also important to implement **infrastructure as code** (**IaC**) practices to define and provision secure infrastructure and environments using code templates and configuration files. This help to build the right environment practices into the process and also builds predictability into the deployment process as the environments are guaranteed to have the right security mechanisms throughout.

Continuous security monitoring

DevSecOps is also about observability and ensuring that even though we put in mechanisms to prevent security, that we continue to monitor security threats actively so team can respond to them as soon as possible.

To do this effectively teams should consider the following:

- Implement continuous security monitoring and threat detection mechanisms to monitor application behavior, network traffic, and system activity for signs of security incidents or anomalies.

- Use **security information and event management (SIEM)** systems, **intrusion detection systems (IDS)**, and security analytics tools to analyze security-relevant data and generate actionable insights.

- Leverage log aggregation, monitoring dashboards, and automated alerting to notify security teams of suspicious activities or potential security breaches in real-time.

Secure configuration management

Configuration is another often-overlooked practice in security that architects need to be aware of. The following are good guidelines for all teams to follow:

- Implementing secure configuration management practices to ensure that software components, libraries, and dependencies are up-to-date and configured securely.

- Automating software dependency management, patching, and versioning to minimize the risk of known vulnerabilities and weaknesses in third-party dependencies.

- Enforcing secure configuration baselines for application servers, databases, containers, and cloud environments to mitigate common security risks and compliance gaps.

Collaborative security culture

DevSecOps, at the core, is all about culture. Fostering a collaborative security culture where developers, operations teams, and security professionals work together to address security challenges and prioritize security initiatives.

It is about promoting security awareness and training programs to educate team members about security best practices, threat landscapes, and emerging security trends. It is also about establishing cross-functional security teams or committees to facilitate communication, collaboration, and knowledge sharing across different departments and disciplines.

At the core, any security culture works when everyone works together to ensure security is maintained effectively from all sides. While having a secure architecture and standards is vital, there are still vulnerabilities that can creep into an y system when people leave gaps in their processes around this, so it is important that architects drive this culture through all teams to ensure continued secure operation of the services built.

Continuous improvement and feedback

This culture transcends to learning and constantly improving where security can be improved. Continuously assess and improve security practices, processes, and tooling based on feedback, lessons learned, and evolving security requirements. Also, conduct post-incident reviews, security retrospectives, and root cause analyses to identify areas for improvement and implement corrective actions.

Encourage a culture of learning, experimentation, and innovation, where teams are empowered to experiment with new security tools, techniques, and methodologies to enhance security capabilities.

By embracing secure DevOps principles and practices, organizations can integrate security into the fabric of their DevOps workflows, enabling faster, more secure software delivery and enhancing overall security posture. Secure DevOps emphasizes collaboration, automation, and continuous improvement, enabling organizations to adapt to evolving security threats and challenges in today's dynamic and fast-paced digital landscape.

Security testing

While we will discuss testing in more detail in *Chapter 15, Architecture as Engineering*, it would be remiss if we did not cover the important testing aspects of security in this chapter.

Security testing is a vital component of the **software development lifecycle** (**SDLC**) that focuses on identifying vulnerabilities, weaknesses, and security risks in software applications, systems, and networks. By conducting security testing, organizations can identify and mitigate security issues before they are exploited by attackers, ensuring the confidentiality, integrity, and availability of their systems and data.

Here are key types and approaches to security testing:

- **Static Application Security Testing (SAST):**
    - SAST involves analyzing application source code, bytecode, or binary files to identify security vulnerabilities and coding errors.
    - Automated SAST tools scan code for common security issues such as SQL injection, **cross-site scripting** (**XSS**), buffer overflows, and insecure authentication.
    - SAST helps identify security weaknesses early in the development process, enabling developers to remediate issues before they are deployed to production.
- **Dynamic Application Security Testing (DAST):**
    - DAST involves testing running applications from the outside to identify security vulnerabilities and weaknesses.

- o DAST tools simulate real-world attacks by sending malicious requests and payloads to web applications, APIs, and network services.

- o DAST helps identify vulnerabilities such as injection flaws, broken authentication, **insecure direct object references (IDOR)**, and sensitive data exposure.

- **Interactive Application Security Testing (IAST)**:

  - o IAST combines elements of both SAST and DAST by analyzing application code and runtime behavior to identify security vulnerabilities.

  - o IAST tools instrument the application code or runtime environment to monitor interactions and detect security issues in real-time.

  - o IAST provides deeper insights into application behavior and context, helping identify vulnerabilities missed by traditional SAST or DAST approaches.

- **Penetration testing (Pen testing)**:

  - o Penetration testing involves simulating real-world attacks against systems, applications, or networks to identify security weaknesses and assess overall security posture.

  - o Penetration testers (ethical hackers) attempt to exploit vulnerabilities to gain unauthorized access, escalate privileges, or compromise sensitive data.

  - o Penetration testing can be conducted manually or using automated tools and techniques, such as network scanning, vulnerability exploitation, and social engineering.

- **Vulnerability assessment**:

  - o Vulnerability assessment involves scanning systems, networks, and applications for known security vulnerabilities, misconfigurations, and weaknesses.

  - o Automated vulnerability scanning tools identify **common vulnerabilities and exposures (CVEs)** in software components, operating systems, and network devices.

  - o Vulnerability assessment provides a comprehensive view of the organization's security posture, enabling prioritization and remediation of identified vulnerabilities.

- **Fuzz testing (Fuzzing)**:

  - o Fuzz testing involves sending invalid, unexpected, or random input data to applications, protocols, or file formats to identify potential vulnerabilities and crashes.

- o Fuzzing tools generate large volumes of test cases to systematically explore application inputs and uncover security weaknesses.

- o Fuzz testing helps identify vulnerabilities such as buffer overflows, memory corruption, and input validation errors in software components and network protocols.

- **Code review and security audits**:

  - o Manual code review and security audits involve reviewing application source code, configurations, and architecture to identify security vulnerabilities, design flaws, and compliance gaps.

  - o Security experts analyze code for common security issues, adherence to secure coding practices, and alignment with security policies and standards.

  - o Code review and security audits provide valuable insights into application security, enabling developers to address security issues and improve overall code quality.

- **Compliance testing**:

  - o Compliance testing involves assessing systems, applications, and processes against regulatory requirements, industry standards, and security best practices.

  - o Compliance testing ensures that organizations adhere to legal and regulatory requirements (e.g., GDPR, HIPAA, PCI DSS) and industry-specific security standards.

  - o Compliance testing helps identify gaps in security controls, data protection practices, and governance frameworks, enabling organizations to achieve and maintain compliance.

By incorporating these security testing approaches into the software development lifecycle, organizations can proactively identify and mitigate security risks, improve software quality, and enhance overall security posture. Security testing should be conducted regularly, iteratively, and collaboratively across development, testing, and operations teams to address evolving threats and vulnerabilities effectively.

Incident reporting and forensics

Incident reporting and forensics are crucial aspects of incident response and management, enabling organizations to detect, investigate, and mitigate security incidents effectively. Incident reporting involves promptly documenting and notifying relevant stakeholders about security incidents, while incident forensics involves analyzing and understanding the root causes and impacts of security incidents to prevent recurrence and improve security posture.

As incidents can have a wide organizational impact and often be a direct result of architectural decisions and development processes, architects will often form part of this process to either rectify potential security gaps where they may occur or work with teams in tightening processes and put in place preventative measures against future security threats.

Here is an overview of incident reporting and forensics processes that should form a part of every team's responsibilities:

- **Incident reporting**:
  - o Promptly report security incidents to the appropriate internal stakeholders, such as the IT security team, incident response team, or management, as well as external entities as required by regulatory or contractual obligations.
  - o Establish clear incident reporting procedures and channels for employees, contractors, customers, and partners to report security incidents, breaches, or suspicious activities.
  - o Define incident severity levels and criteria to prioritize response efforts based on the severity, impact, and scope of the incident.
  - o Document incident details, including the date, time, nature of the incident, affected systems or assets, and initial observations, in an incident report or log for tracking and analysis purposes.
  - o Ensure incident reports adhere to regulatory requirements, internal policies, and legal considerations to maintain confidentiality, privacy, and compliance.

- **Incident triage and response**:
  - o Upon receiving an incident report, initiate incident triage to assess the severity and scope of the incident, prioritize response efforts, and allocate resources accordingly.
  - o Activate incident response procedures and teams to contain, mitigate, and remediate the incident, following predefined response playbooks, procedures, and escalation paths.
  - o Communicate with relevant stakeholders, including management, legal counsel, regulatory authorities, and affected parties, to provide updates on the incident response efforts and coordinate response activities.

- **Incident forensics**:
  - o Conduct incident forensics to investigate the root causes, **tactics, techniques, and procedures (TTPs)** employed by attackers, and the extent of the impact on affected systems, networks, and data.

- o Preserve and collect digital evidence, logs, system snapshots, memory dumps, and network captures for forensic analysis and investigation.

- o Analyze digital evidence using forensic tools, techniques, and methodologies to reconstruct the timeline of events, identify **indicators of compromise** (**IOCs**), and determine the attack vectors and attack lifecycle.

- o Document findings, observations, and conclusions in a detailed incident forensic report, including recommendations for remediation, mitigation, and improving security controls and practices.

- **Lessons learned and post-incident analysis**:

  - o Conduct post-incident analysis and lessons learned sessions to review and evaluate the effectiveness of incident response procedures, security controls, and mitigation measures.

  - o Identify gaps, weaknesses, and areas for improvement in incident response capabilities, security posture, and resilience.

  - o Implement corrective actions, enhancements, and preventive measures based on the findings and recommendations from incident forensics and post-incident analysis.

  - o Share insights, best practices, and lessons learned with relevant stakeholders, security teams, and organizational leadership to enhance awareness and preparedness for future incidents.

- **Continuous improvement**:

  - o Continuously refine and improve incident reporting, response, and forensics processes based on emerging threats, evolving attack techniques, and organizational feedback.

  - o Conduct regular tabletop exercises, simulations, and incident response drills to validate incident response procedures, train personnel, and improve readiness for real-world incidents.

  - o Incorporate feedback and lessons learned from incident reporting, response, and forensics activities into security awareness training, policy updates, and security controls to enhance overall security posture and resilience.

By establishing robust incident reporting and forensics processes, organizations can effectively detect, respond to, and recover from security incidents, minimize their impact, and improve overall security posture and resilience. Incident reporting and forensics play a critical role in maintaining trust, compliance, and business continuity in the face of security threats and incidents.

Conclusion

Security is not something that should every be taken for granted. As a results, it is something that architects need to be acutely aware of and look at security through the software architecture and development process. This may not be something that they need to do alone, as it will require extensive collaboration with various security experts and the engineering teams themselves to get right.

And with security threats evolving at such a fast pace, it is also something that requires constant learning and response mechanisms to quickly address security threats when they occur. Building this culture in an organization may not be a direct part of an architect's responsibilities, however, it is vital that architects get involved ensuring the right mechanism are in place.

No architectural design can be considered a success if it does not adequately address security at all levels, so it is imperative time is spent understanding and addressing this in detail. Architects should be one of the biggest security advocates and need to keep themselves constantly informed of new potential threats and processes to continuously enhance and improve security throughout their software design and organization. In the next chapter, we look at the importance of the design and presentation layer in software architecture and how best to design for it.

Join our book's Discord space

Join the book's Discord Workspace for Latest updates, Offers, Tech happenings around the world, New Release and Sessions with the Authors:

https://discord.bpbonline.com

CHAPTER 10
Design and Presentation

Introduction

We looked at a lot of different architectural styles and models that need to be followed, but now let us look a little more closely at some bigger overarching design and presentation principles that are important for architects to be aware of.

While a lot of the foundations of software architecture are structured around important aspects of optimal design, security, performance, and functionality, there is also a human layer that needs to be considered. Our software is used by others, and we need to consider this impact as architects in the way we design it. This requires a fine balance in achieving the best architectural approach for a given system, with the best way for humans to interact with it.

This applies to both the users of the system we are designing for and the people who need to continue maintaining it. We need to ensure that we approach design from an aspect of usability and present our systems in a way that allows others to interact with it across all levels.

A common mistake many architects make is leaving these sorts of design approaches to a UX designer, when the reality is that this has little to do with any form of UX design and should rather be focused on the communication and data flow between different system components to best facilitate the most user-friendly approach. All this, coupled with the considerations of future maintenance.

So, we will start this chapter by looking at this approach to software design called design thinking, before looking at certain design principles that all architects should know and consider before finally looking at the aspects of a presentation layer within the software design, how best to do it and ending off with how all of this will lead to better testability in the software.

Structure

In this chapter, we will discuss the following topics:

- Design thinking
- Single Responsibility Principle
- Open/Closed Principle
- Presentation layer best practices
- Ensuring testability in design

Objectives

By the end of this chapter, you will understand the design principles that create robust and scalable software along with user interfaces that are intuitive, responsive, and user-friendly. All important aspects of how software is used and forming a critical foundation in the design software architects need to consider.

Design thinking

Design thinking in software architecture involves applying the principles and methodologies of design thinking to the process of creating software systems. Design thinking is a human-centered approach to problem-solving that emphasizes empathy, creativity, and iterative prototyping. When applied to software architecture, it helps architects understand the needs and preferences of end-users, identify and define problems, and develop innovative solutions that address those problems effectively.

Here is how design thinking can be applied in software architecture:

- **Empathize**: Understand the needs, goals, and challenges of the users and stakeholders who will interact with the software system. This involves conducting user research, interviews, and observations to gain insights into their behaviors, preferences, and pain points.

- **Define**: Clearly define the problem or opportunity based on the insights gathered during the empathize phase. This involves synthesizing the research findings to identify key user needs and articulate the problem statement that the software system aims to solve or the value it aims to deliver.

- **Ideate**: Generate a wide range of creative ideas and potential solutions to address the defined problem. This is a divergent phase where architects and team members brainstorm and explore different approaches, considering both conventional and innovative solutions.

- **Prototype**: Develop quick, low-fidelity prototypes or mockups of the software system to test and validate the proposed solutions. Prototyping allows architects to gather feedback from users early in the process, iterate on design ideas, and refine the architecture based on user input.

- **Test**: Test the prototypes with real users to gather feedback, insights, and observations. This involves conducting usability tests, user interviews, and other evaluation methods to understand how users interact with the software, identify usability issues, and validate whether the solution meets their needs and expectations.

- **Iterate**: Based on the feedback received during testing, refine and iterate on the design and architecture of the software system. This may involve making adjustments to the user interface, functionality, or underlying architecture to improve usability, performance, and overall user experience.

By incorporating design thinking principles into software architecture, architects can create software systems that are not only functional and technically sound but also user-centered, intuitive, and engaging. This approach helps ensure that the software effectively addresses the needs and preferences of its users, ultimately leading to greater adoption, satisfaction, and success.

Design thinking in software architecture is important for several reasons:

- **User-centered design**: By focusing on the needs, preferences, and behaviors of end-users, design thinking ensures that software systems are developed with the user in mind. This results in products that are intuitive, easy to use, and provide a positive user experience, leading to higher adoption rates and user satisfaction.

- **Innovation and creativity**: Design thinking encourages architects and development teams to think outside the box and explore innovative solutions to complex problems. By embracing creativity and experimentation, software architects can develop unique and novel approaches that differentiate their products in the market.

- **Early validation and feedback**: Through rapid prototyping and testing with real users, design thinking allows architects to gather feedback early in the development process. This helps identify usability issues, validate design decisions, and make necessary adjustments before investing significant time and resources in development.

- **Reduced risk and cost**: By iteratively refining the design based on user feedback, design thinking helps mitigate the risk of developing software that fails to meet user needs or market demands. Early identification and correction of design flaws reduce the likelihood of costly rework or product failures later in the development lifecycle.

- **Alignment with business goals**: Design thinking ensures that software architecture aligns closely with the goals and objectives of the business or organization. By understanding user needs and market trends, architects can design software systems that deliver tangible value and contribute to the overall success of the business.

- **Adaptability and flexibility**: The iterative nature of design thinking allows architects to adapt and respond to changing requirements, technologies, and market conditions. By continuously testing and refining the design, software systems can evolve over time to remain relevant and competitive in dynamic environments.

Overall, design thinking in software architecture fosters a human-centered, iterative approach to design and development that leads to better products, happier users, and greater business success.

Now that we have a good understanding of what design thinking is, let us look at some important design principles that all architects should consider that will aid in both making the software more usable, but more importantly, more maintainable.

Software development principles such as SOLID principles, design patterns, and architectural patterns provide guidelines and best practices for solving common software design problems. Architects can apply design thinking methodologies to identify and define architectural challenges, explore innovative solutions, and apply software development principles to implement robust and scalable architectural solutions.

We will look at different principles that aid the software architect in facilitating a solid design backbone that further aids the enhancement and development of the software to meet the needs of proper user-driven design.

Single Responsibility Principle

The **Single Responsibility Principle (SRP)** is one of the five SOLID principles of object-oriented design, introduced by *Robert C. Martin*. All five of which we will go through in detail in this chapter. SRP states that a class should have only one reason to change, meaning that a class should have only one responsibility or job.

In simpler terms, the SRP advocates for designing classes that have a clear and focused purpose. Each class should encapsulate one and only one aspect of the functionality of the software system. This helps keep the codebase modular, maintainable, and easier to understand, as each class is responsible for a specific task and does not have multiple, unrelated responsibilities.

Here are some key points about the SRP:

- **Clear separation of concerns**: By adhering to the SRP, developers can ensure that each class has a well-defined scope of responsibility. This promotes clear separation of concerns, making it easier to understand, modify, and maintain the code.

- **High cohesion**: Classes that adhere to the SRP tend to exhibit high cohesion, meaning that the methods and properties within the class are closely related and work together to achieve a single purpose. High cohesion is a desirable characteristic of well-designed classes.

- **Low coupling**: Following the SRP can also lead to lower coupling between classes, as each class is responsible for a specific task and does not rely heavily on other classes for unrelated functionality. This improves code maintainability and facilitates code reuse.

- **Easier testing**: Classes with single responsibilities are typically easier to test because their behavior is well-defined and focused. Unit tests can be written to verify the behavior of individual classes without needing to consider complex interactions with other classes.

- **Scalability and extensibility**: Designing classes with a single responsibility makes the codebase more scalable and extensible. When new requirements arise or changes need to be made, developers can modify or extend individual classes without affecting unrelated parts of the system.

- **Improved readability and maintainability**: Code that adheres to the SRP is easier to read, understand, and maintain because each class has a clear purpose and responsibility. This reduces the cognitive load on developers and makes it easier to make changes or debug issues in the codebase.

Overall, the SRP promotes good design practices by encouraging developers to create classes that are focused, cohesive, and loosely coupled. By adhering to this principle, developers can create software systems that are easier to develop, maintain, and evolve over time.

Open/Closed Principle

The **Open/Closed Principle** (**OCP**) is another fundamental principle in object-oriented design, first introduced by *Bertrand Meyer*. It states that software entities (such as classes, modules, functions, etc.) should be open for extension but closed for modification.

In essence, the OCP encourages developers to design software components in a way that allows them to be easily extended with new functionality without modifying their existing code. This promotes code reuse, maintainability, and flexibility, as it minimizes the need for changes to existing code and reduces the risk of introducing bugs or unintended side effects.

Here are some key concepts related to the Open/Closed Principle:

- **Open for extension**: This means that the behavior of a software component should be easily extended to accommodate new requirements or variations in functionality. Developers should be able to add new features or behaviors to the component without modifying its existing code.

- **Closed for modification**: This implies that the existing code of a software component should be stable and resistant to modification. Once a component is implemented and tested, its internal workings should not need to be changed to accommodate new requirements. Instead, new functionality should be added through extension mechanisms.

- **Abstraction and polymorphism**: The OCP is often achieved through the use of abstraction and polymorphism. By defining abstract interfaces and base classes that encapsulate common behavior, developers can create flexible and extensible components that can be easily extended or replaced with alternative implementations.

- **Design patterns**: Many design patterns, such as the Strategy pattern, Template Method pattern, and Decorator pattern, are based on the principles of the OCP. These patterns provide reusable solutions to common design problems and help ensure that software components are open for extension and closed for modification.

- **Benefits**: Adhering to the OCP leads to software systems that are easier to maintain, as changes and new features can be added without impacting existing code. It promotes code reuse, as existing components can be extended and reused in different contexts. Additionally, it encourages the development of loosely coupled and modular systems, which are more flexible and adaptable to change.

Overall, the OCP encourages developers to design software components that are flexible, reusable, and resilient to change.

Liskov Substitution Principle

The **Liskov Substitution Principle** (**LSP**) is another fundamental principle in object-oriented design, formulated by *Barbara Liskov* in 1987. It states that objects of a superclass should be replaceable with objects of a subclass without affecting the correctness of the program.

In simpler terms, the LSP emphasizes the importance of polymorphism and inheritance in object-oriented programming. It ensures that subclasses can be used interchangeably with their base class without altering the desirable properties of the program.

Here are the key points regarding the LSP:

- **Behavioral subtyping**: Subclasses should adhere to the contract established by their superclass. This means that subclasses should provide implementations for all methods defined in the superclass, and these implementations should adhere to the same behavior and semantics as those defined in the superclass.

- **Substitution without surprise**: Clients of a class (i.e., code that uses instances of the class) should be able to substitute objects of subclasses for objects of the superclass without encountering unexpected behavior or errors. This ensures that the behavior of the program remains consistent and predictable.

- **Design by Contract**: The LSP is closely related to the concept of Design by Contract, which involves defining preconditions and postconditions for methods and ensuring that subclasses adhere to these contracts. Subclasses should not weaken the preconditions or strengthen the postconditions of methods defined in the superclass.

- **Violation examples**: Violations of the LSP can lead to unexpected behavior and errors in a program. For example, if a subclass overrides a method from its superclass in a way that changes its behavior or violates its contract, substituting objects of the subclass for objects of the superclass may lead to errors or inconsistencies.

- **Benefits**: Adhering to the LSP promotes code reuse, modularity, and extensibility in object-oriented systems. It allows developers to create hierarchies of classes that can be easily extended and specialized without affecting existing code. It also facilitates polymorphism, allowing code to be written in terms of abstract interfaces and base classes rather than specific implementations.

Overall, the LSP encourages developers to design class hierarchies that are consistent, predictable, and easy to use.

Interface Segregation Principle

The **Interface Segregation Principle (ISP)** is the second of the five SOLID principles of object-oriented design, introduced by *Robert C. Martin*. It states that clients should not be forced to depend on interfaces they do not use.

In simpler terms, the ISP emphasizes the importance of designing interfaces that are specific to the needs of the clients that use them. It suggests breaking large interfaces into smaller, more specific ones so that clients only need to depend on the parts of the interface that are relevant to them.

Here are the key points regarding the ISP:

- **Client-specific interfaces**: Interfaces should be tailored to the specific needs of the clients that use them. This means that interfaces should contain only the methods that are relevant to each client, rather than including a large number of methods that may only be used by a subset of clients.

- **Avoidance of *Fat* interfaces**: Fat interfaces, which contain a large number of methods, can lead to unnecessary dependencies between clients and providers. The ISP suggests breaking these interfaces into smaller, more focused ones to minimize dependencies and improve modularity.

- **Granular interfaces**: Interfaces should be granular and cohesive, containing a small, focused set of methods that are closely related to each other. This makes it easier for clients to understand and use the interface, as they only need to be concerned with the methods that are relevant to their specific requirements.

- **Prevention of interface pollution**: Including unnecessary methods in interfaces can lead to interface pollution, where clients are forced to depend on methods they do not use. This violates the ISP and can make the codebase more difficult to understand and maintain.

- **Benefits**: Adhering to the ISP leads to more modular, maintainable, and flexible code. By designing interfaces that are specific to the needs of each client, developers can minimize dependencies and reduce the impact of changes to the interface on the clients that use it. This promotes code reuse and makes it easier to add new clients or modify existing ones without affecting unrelated parts of the system.

Overall, the ISP encourages developers to design interfaces that are tailored to the specific requirements of clients, rather than imposing unnecessary dependencies or functionality on them.

Dependency Inversion Principle

The **Dependency Inversion Principle (DIP)** is another of the SOLID principles by *Robert C. Martin*. It states that high-level modules should not depend on low-level modules; both should depend on abstractions. Additionally, abstractions should not depend on details; rather, details should depend on abstractions.

In simpler terms, the DIP encourages decoupling between modules by introducing an abstraction layer that both high-level and low-level modules depend on. This abstraction layer represents the contract between modules and allows for greater flexibility and extensibility in the system.

Here are the key points regarding the DIP:

- **Decoupling**: By introducing abstractions between modules, the DIP reduces direct dependencies between them. This promotes loose coupling, making it easier to modify, replace, or extend individual modules without affecting the rest of the system.

- **Abstractions and interfaces**: Abstractions are represented by interfaces or abstract classes that define the contract between modules. High-level modules depend on these abstractions rather than concrete implementations, allowing them to remain independent of specific details or implementations.

- **Inversion of control (IoC)**: The DIP is closely related to the concept of IoC. In IoC, control of the flow of execution is inverted from high-level modules to a framework or container, which manages the creation and lifecycle of objects and resolves dependencies between them.

- **Dependency injection**: Dependency injection is a common technique used to implement the DIP. It involves passing dependencies into a class from the outside rather than creating them internally. This allows dependencies to be easily replaced or modified, promoting flexibility and testability.

- **Benefits**: Adhering to the DIP leads to more modular, flexible, and maintainable code. It allows modules to be developed, tested, and maintained independently of each other, reducing the risk of unintended side effects or breaking changes. It also promotes code reuse and facilitates the development of complex systems by breaking them down into smaller, more manageable components.

Overall, the DIP encourages developers to design systems that are composed of loosely coupled modules that depend on abstractions rather than concrete implementations.

Don't Repeat Yourself

Don't Repeat Yourself (DRY) is a software development principle aimed at reducing duplication of code and promoting code reusability, maintainability, and readability. The DRY principle states that every piece of knowledge or logic within a system should have a single, unambiguous representation.

Here are the key points regarding the DRY principle:

- **Code duplication**: Code duplication occurs when the same or similar code appears in multiple places within a codebase. This can lead to maintenance issues, as changes to duplicated code must be made in multiple locations, increasing the risk of inconsistencies and errors.

- **Abstraction and encapsulation**: The DRY principle encourages developers to identify common patterns or functionality within the codebase and abstract them into reusable components or functions. By encapsulating common logic in a single location, developers can avoid code duplication and promote code reuse.

- **Modularization**: Breaking down the codebase into modular components or modules helps enforce the DRY principle by promoting separation of concerns and modular design. Each module should have a clear and focused responsibility, with minimal duplication of functionality across modules.

- **Reusable libraries and components**: Embracing reusable libraries, frameworks, and components can help reduce duplication of code by leveraging existing solutions for common tasks or functionality. By using well-established libraries and components, developers can avoid reinventing the wheel and focus on solving higher-level problems.

- **Template and pattern usage**: Templates and design patterns provide standardized solutions to common problems in software development. By following established patterns and using templates where applicable, developers can avoid duplicating code and benefit from proven solutions to common problems.

- **Refactoring**: Refactoring is the process of restructuring existing code without changing its external behavior. Refactoring can help eliminate duplication of code by identifying and consolidating duplicated logic into reusable abstractions or components.

- **Code reviews and guidelines**: Establishing code review processes and coding guidelines within a development team can help enforce the DRY principle and identify instances of code duplication. Code reviews provide an opportunity for team members to identify and address duplication issues before they become problematic.

- **Automated tools**: Utilize automated code analysis tools and linting tools to identify instances of code duplication within a codebase. These tools can help highlight areas where the DRY principle is not being followed and suggest ways to refactor or consolidate duplicated code.

By adhering to the DRY principle, developers can create codebases that are more maintainable, reusable, and scalable, leading to improved productivity, reduced development time, and higher-quality software.

Composition over inheritance

Composition over inheritance is a design principle in object-oriented programming that suggests favoring composition (i.e., building classes by combining simpler components) over inheritance (i.e., creating subclasses that inherit behavior and properties from a superclass).

Here are the key points regarding the composition over inheritance principle:

- **Flexibility**: Composition allows for greater flexibility in designing class hierarchies compared to inheritance. With composition, classes can be constructed by assembling different components, each responsible for a specific aspect of functionality. This makes it easier to change or extend the behavior of a class by adding or removing components, without affecting the entire class hierarchy.

- **Reduced coupling**: Composition typically results in lower coupling between classes compared to inheritance. When a class inherits from a superclass, it becomes tightly coupled to the implementation details of the superclass, which can make the codebase more brittle and harder to maintain. Composition, on the other hand, allows classes to interact with each other through well-defined interfaces, reducing dependencies and promoting modularity.

- **Code reuse**: While inheritance can facilitate code reuse by allowing subclasses to inherit behavior from a superclass, it can also lead to the inheritance of irrelevant or unnecessary behavior. Composition, on the other hand, allows for more selective reuse of code components, as classes can be composed of only the components they need.

- **Encapsulation**: Composition promotes encapsulation by allowing classes to hide their internal implementation details behind well-defined interfaces. This makes it easier to reason about the behavior of a class and reduces the risk of unintended side effects caused by changes to its internal implementation.

- **Hierarchy complexity**: Inheritance can lead to complex class hierarchies, especially in large codebases with multiple layers of inheritance. This can make the codebase harder to understand and maintain over time. Composition encourages a flatter class hierarchy by favoring the construction of classes from smaller, more focused components, which can improve code readability and maintainability.

- **Design patterns**: Many design patterns, such as the Strategy pattern, Decorator pattern, and Dependency Injection pattern, promote the use of composition over inheritance. These patterns provide reusable solutions to common design problems and encourage the construction of classes through composition rather than inheritance.

Overall, composition over inheritance encourages developers to build classes by composing them from smaller, more focused components, rather than relying solely on inheritance. By favoring composition, developers can create more flexible, modular, and maintainable code that is easier to understand and extend over time.

Law of Demeter

The **Law of Demeter (LoD)**, also known as the principle of least knowledge or the principle of least coupling, is a design guideline for object-oriented programming. It states that an object should have limited knowledge about other objects and should only interact with objects that are closely related to it.

In simpler terms, the LoD suggests that an object should only talk to its immediate friends, and not reach out to friends of friends. This helps reduce coupling between objects, making the codebase more modular, maintainable, and easier to understand.

Here are the key points regarding the LoD:

- **Minimize object interaction**: According to the LoD, an object should avoid directly accessing the methods and properties of objects that it does not own or directly interact with. Instead, it should delegate such interactions to its immediate collaborators or dependencies.

- **Principle of least knowledge**: The LoD encourages objects to have limited knowledge about other objects in the system. This means that objects should only communicate with their direct dependencies and should not have knowledge about the internal structure or implementation details of other objects.

- **Reduced coupling**: By adhering to the LoD, developers can reduce coupling between objects in the system. This promotes modularity and encapsulation, as objects are less dependent on the internal details of other objects and are more focused on fulfilling their own responsibilities.

- **Improved maintainability**: Objects that follow the LoD are typically easier to understand, modify, and maintain, as they have well-defined boundaries and dependencies. Changes to one part of the system are less likely to have unintended side effects on other parts of the system, making it easier to reason about the behavior of the code.

- **Design guidelines**: The LoD provides guidelines for designing object-oriented systems that are loosely coupled and highly cohesive. It suggests that objects should communicate through well-defined interfaces and that dependencies between objects should be kept to a minimum.

- **Dot counting rule**: The LoD is often expressed in terms of the dot counting rule, which states that a method should only call methods of the following types of objects:

  - Itself
  - Its parameters
  - Objects it creates
  - Objects it aggregates (has as a member)
  - Objects it contains (has a reference to)
  - Global objects

Overall, the LoD encourages developers to design object-oriented systems that are modular, maintainable, and loosely coupled by limiting the interactions between objects and adhering to the principle of least knowledge.

Presentation layer best practices

The presentation layer, also known as the **user interface** (**UI**) layer, is one of the layers in the architecture of a software application. It is responsible for presenting information to the user and capturing user input. The presentation layer acts as a bridge between the user and the underlying business logic and data layers of the application.

Here are the key aspects of the presentation layer:

- **User interface components**: The presentation layer consists of various user interface components such as forms, buttons, menus, dialog boxes, and widgets.

These components are designed to provide an interactive and visually appealing user experience.

- **Visual design**: The presentation layer involves designing the visual layout and appearance of the user interface. This includes aspects such as color schemes, typography, iconography, and layout design, all aimed at creating an intuitive and engaging user experience.

- **User interaction**: The presentation layer handles user interactions such as mouse clicks, keyboard inputs, touch gestures, and screen interactions. It responds to user actions by updating the display, processing input data, and triggering appropriate actions in the application.

- **Feedback mechanisms**: The presentation layer provides feedback to the user in response to their actions. This includes displaying messages, notifications, alerts, and error messages to communicate information, status updates, or validation errors to the user.

- **Client-side processing**: In web applications, the presentation layer often includes client-side scripting languages such as JavaScript, which enable dynamic and interactive behavior without requiring server-side processing. Client-side scripts handle tasks such as form validation, DOM manipulation, and asynchronous communication with the server.

- **Cross-platform compatibility**: With the proliferation of different devices and platforms, the presentation layer must be designed to be compatible across various devices, screen sizes, and browsers. Responsive design techniques and adaptive layouts are commonly used to ensure a consistent user experience across different devices and screen resolutions.

- **Separation of concerns**: In modern software development, there is a focus on separating the presentation layer from the business logic and data access layers. This separation of concerns allows for easier maintenance, testing, and scalability of the application.

Overall, the presentation layer plays a crucial role in delivering a user-friendly and interactive experience to the users of a software application. It involves designing and implementing the visual aspects of the user interface, handling user interactions, and providing feedback to the user, all while maintaining compatibility across different devices and platforms.

Here are some best practices for designing the presentation layer of software applications:

- **Separation of concerns**: Follow the principles of separation of concerns by dividing the presentation layer into distinct components responsible for handling different aspects of the user interface, such as views, controllers, and models. This promotes modularity, maintainability, and testability.

- **Model-View-Controller (MVC) architecture**: Consider using the MVC architectural pattern to organize the presentation layer. In MVC, the model represents the application's data and business logic, the view represents the presentation and user interface components, and the controller acts as an intermediary that handles user input and updates the model and view accordingly.

- **Responsive design**: Design user interfaces that are responsive and adaptable to different screen sizes and devices. Use techniques such as fluid layouts, media queries, and flexible grids to ensure that your application looks and functions well across various devices, including desktops, tablets, and smartphones.

- **Accessibility**: Ensure that your user interface is accessible to users with disabilities by following accessibility best practices. Use semantic HTML markup, provide alternative text for images, ensure keyboard navigation, and test your application with assistive technologies to ensure compliance with accessibility standards such as **Web Content Accessibility Guidelines (WCAG)**.

- **Consistent design**: Maintain consistency in design elements such as layout, color scheme, typography, and navigation across different parts of your application. Consistent design improves user experience, reduces cognitive load, and makes it easier for users to navigate and interact with your application.

- **Performance optimization**: Optimize the performance of your user interface by minimizing the use of heavy assets such as large images, videos, and scripts. Use techniques such as lazy loading, image compression, and script bundling to reduce load times and improve responsiveness.

- **Progressive enhancement**: Adopt a progressive enhancement approach to web development, where you start with a baseline experience that works on all devices and browsers, then progressively enhance the user experience for more capable devices and browsers. This ensures that your application is accessible to all users, regardless of their device or browser capabilities.

- **Cross-browser compatibility**: Test your user interface across multiple web browsers and devices to ensure compatibility and consistent behavior. Use tools such as browser testing suites, polyfills, and feature detection techniques to address compatibility issues and provide a consistent experience to all users.

- **Error handling and validation**: Implement robust error handling and validation mechanisms to provide feedback to users and prevent invalid data from being submitted. Use client-side validation for immediate feedback and server-side validation for security and data integrity.

- **Security**: Implement security best practices to protect your application against common threats such as **cross-site scripting (XSS)**, **cross-site request forgery (CSRF)**, and injection attacks. Use secure communication protocols such as HTTPS, sanitize user input, and implement proper authentication and authorization mechanisms to ensure the security of your application.

Ensuring testability in design

Ensuring testability in design is crucial for developing software that is reliable, maintainable, and easy to test. Here are some guidelines to help ensure testability in software design:

- **Modularity and encapsulation**: Design software components to be modular and encapsulated, with well-defined boundaries and responsibilities. This allows individual components to be tested in isolation, making it easier to identify and isolate defects.

- **Dependency injection**: Use dependency injection to decouple components and their dependencies. Instead of instantiating dependencies within a class, inject them from the outside. This makes it easier to replace dependencies with mocks or stubs during testing, allowing for more controlled and predictable test environments.

- **Interfaces and abstraction**: Define clear interfaces and abstractions for components, rather than relying on concrete implementations. This allows for easier substitution of components with mock or stub implementations during testing. Interfaces also facilitate integration testing by providing clear boundaries between components.

- **Mocking and stubbing**: Use mocking and stubbing frameworks to create test doubles (mocks or stubs) for dependencies that are not under test. Mocks simulate the behavior of real objects, allowing you to isolate the component being tested and verify its interactions with its dependencies.

- **Separation of concerns**: Follow the principles of separation of concerns and single responsibility. Design components to have a clear and focused purpose, making it easier to write focused and targeted tests for each component.

- **Clear and understandable code**: Write clean, readable, and understandable code that is easy to reason about and test. Use meaningful names for variables, methods, and classes, and avoid overly complex or convoluted code structures that are difficult to test.

- **Unit testing**: Write unit tests for individual components to verify their behavior in isolation. Unit tests should be fast, focused, and repeatable, allowing developers to quickly identify and fix defects during development.

- **Test-driven development (TDD)**: Consider adopting TDD practices, where tests are written before implementing the corresponding code. TDD encourages a focus on testability and helps ensure that code is designed to be testable from the outset. A good strategy for architects is to always write tests against their designs first. A design that is not easily testable is often a sign of a bad design and can save a lot of effort if identified early in the development process.

By following these guidelines, you can design software that is easier to test, maintain, and evolve over time. Testable designs lead to higher-quality software with fewer defects and a lower total cost of ownership.

Conclusion

Design thinking is a vital balancing act that architects need to manage. Finding the right designs to provide the best solution for a given functional area, while ensuring they are usable and presentable to the rest of the broader system, is a vital component of good architectural design and one that all architects should endeavor to master to design usable systems.

In the next chapter, we look at the core principles that can be considered when designing software that can be easily adaptable and maintainable, allowing for continued evolution and improvement of software without requiring significant effort.

Join our book's Discord space

Join the book's Discord Workspace for Latest updates, Offers, Tech happenings around the world, New Release and Sessions with the Authors:

https://discord.bpbonline.com

CHAPTER 11
Evolutionary Architecture

Introduction

In most forms of physical architecture, the core design is emphasized for its stability and long-lasting nature, undergoing minimal change over time. In contrast, software architecture operates in a dynamic environment where rapid technological advancements necessitate constant evolution. To remain relevant and effective, software design must adapt quickly, enabling systems to incorporate new technologies and meet changing demands.

Structure

In this chapter, we will discuss the following topics:

- Need for change
- Handling changes in requirements
- Strategies for evolving architectures
- CI for evolving architectures
- Set up proactive monitoring to support change
- Dealing with tech debt and maintenance

Objectives

By the end of this chapter, you will understand the need for rapid growth and change in the software world and why that requires software architects to embrace change in their software designs. You will learn some of the key drivers of change and also some of the core design principles that will make software more responsive to change and evolution.

Need for change

The need for change and evolution in software is rooted in the rapidly shifting landscape of technology, user expectations, business goals, and operational requirements. As software systems grow and technologies advance, the software that once met all demands can quickly become outdated, insufficient, or difficult to maintain. Here are some key factors driving this need for evolution:

Changing business needs

Businesses evolve, introducing new products, services, or features that require modifications to software systems. Software must adapt to these changing needs to support new functionalities, improve user experiences, and enhance operational efficiency.

Competitive pressures demand that software aligns with current market trends, which often means continuous feature updates, enhanced performance, and better scalability. Business needs can change due to the following factors:

- **Advances in technology**

  New technologies, such as cloud computing, AI, and microservices, introduce opportunities to improve software scalability, flexibility, and resilience.

  Legacy systems can struggle to integrate with modern tech stacks, creating a need for architectural modernization. As teams adopt cloud-native, containerized, or serverless technologies, traditional software must evolve to leverage these advancements and stay efficient.

- **Evolving system architectures**

  As software systems scale, the architecture often needs to shift to accommodate growing complexity. For example, monolithic applications might transition to microservices to enable modularity, easier maintenance, and independent scaling.

  This shift in architecture is essential to reduce technical debt, improve flexibility, and enable faster development and deployment cycles, especially for systems integrated into CI/CD pipelines.

- **Increased security and compliance requirements**

  With rising cybersecurity threats and regulatory standards (e.g., GDPR, HIPAA), software systems must continuously evolve to stay secure and compliant.

  Meeting these standards often requires regular updates, patching, and sometimes re-architecting to ensure data protection and risk management in line with current regulations.

- **Enhanced user expectations**

  Users expect more from software: faster response times, more intuitive interfaces, and seamless integration across platforms.

  Software that does not evolve to meet these expectations can quickly lose relevance, as users will opt for more modern, efficient solutions if their needs are not met.

- **Reducing technical debt**

  Software systems accumulate technical debt over time through shortcuts taken to speed delivery. If this debt is not managed, it can become a serious impediment, leading to performance issues, poor code quality, and high maintenance costs.

  Regular refactoring and modernization efforts help address technical debt, improve system maintainability, and allow teams to respond to new requirements more easily.

- **Continuous delivery and Agile methodologies**

  The adoption of Agile and DevOps practices emphasizes rapid iteration and feedback, necessitating adaptable and modular software systems.

  Agile environments drive a culture of continuous improvement, where software is constantly evolving to address new challenges, incorporating feedback, and responding to change without major disruption.

- **Scalability and performance needs**

  As user bases and data volumes grow, software must be optimized for performance and scalability.

  Evolving the software architecture to incorporate load balancing, distributed systems, or cloud-native infrastructure can ensure that systems remain performant even under high demand.

- **Maintenance and longevity**

  Older software can become difficult to maintain as its dependencies become outdated or unsupported. Evolving these systems through modernization efforts allows organizations to keep systems running smoothly.

Without regular updates, legacy software becomes brittle and prone to issues that impact productivity and reliability.

- **Future-proofing**

  Technology and user demands evolve faster than ever, so software that is designed with flexibility and adaptability in mind is better prepared for future needs.

  By building in modularity, automation, and extensibility, software can adapt more easily to unforeseen changes, allowing for longevity and minimizing the need for complete rewrites in the future.

Evolving software is no longer optional; it is a necessity for businesses to stay competitive, meet user expectations, and achieve operational efficiency. The process of continuous improvement enables teams to address new requirements, leverage technological advancements, and manage technical debt, all while maintaining system stability and performance. For software to remain a valuable asset, it must be built to change and evolve, just as the needs of users and businesses inevitably do.

Handling changes in requirements

One of the challenges that this gives architects is balancing designs for planned systems against both current and future needs, while also understanding that requirements are likely to change over time for how the software is expected to perform, and ensure that the software design can cater for that change.

Software architects play a crucial role in designing systems that can accommodate changes in requirements without causing excessive rework or instability.

Here are some effective strategies for managing evolving requirements. Many of these points we have already discussed, but here we will just show how they become applicable in the context of dealing with these within a project space. Some of the following architectural aspects will be covered in the next section on strategies for evolving software architectures:

- **Apply an Agile, iterative development process**
  - **Incremental delivery**: Design the architecture to support incremental development. Deliver small, functional parts of the system iteratively, which allows for gathering feedback early and adjusting to changing requirements.
  - **Continuous feedback**: Build in feedback loops with stakeholders to assess whether requirements are evolving. Regular feedback helps architects adapt designs early, minimizing rework.

- **Implement an abstraction layer**
  - **Abstractions for key dependencies**: Use abstraction layers to shield the core application logic from changes in external dependencies, like third-party

services, databases, or UI frameworks. For instance, using data access layers or facades provides a consistent interface, enabling easier substitution of dependencies.

o **Interface-driven design**: Define interfaces that specify how different components will interact, allowing components to be changed or swapped out without impacting other parts of the system.

- **Utilize domain-driven design (DDD)**

o **Bounded contexts**: Use DDD principles to define bounded contexts, where each part of the system focuses on a specific domain model. This allows architects to manage changes in one area without affecting other domains, reducing complexity.

o **Ubiquitous language**: Develop a shared language between developers and business stakeholders to ensure that everyone has the same understanding of the domain, reducing miscommunication and misalignment in requirements.

- **Use feature toggles and configuration-driven design**

o **Feature toggles**: Use feature toggles to control the rollout of new features or experiments without impacting the entire system. This allows architects to test new changes with limited risk and enable or disable features as needed.

o **Configuration-driven design**: Build configurable components where business logic or rules can be changed through configuration files or settings, reducing the need for code changes when requirements change.

o **Versioning strategy**: Plan for versioning in APIs, enabling backward compatibility when introducing new changes, and minimizing disruptions for clients that rely on older versions.

- **Embrace automated testing and continuous integration and delivery (CI/CD) pipelines**

o **Automated tests**: Ensure comprehensive test coverage, including unit, integration, and regression tests, to detect the impact of changes on the existing system and validate new requirements.

o **CI/CD**: Set up CI/CD pipelines to automate the testing and deployment processes, enabling faster iterations and reducing the risk of defects when making changes to accommodate new requirements.

We cover these sections in more detail later in this chapter.

- **Encourage cross-functional collaboration**

o **Frequent collaboration**: Encourage regular collaboration between architects, developers, testers, and business stakeholders. Frequent discussions can help clarify changing requirements, uncover potential risks, and align technical solutions with business needs.

- o **Feedback loops**: Establish feedback loops with product owners and end-users to gain insight into their evolving needs and ensure that the architectural direction aligns with the product's strategic goals.

Plan for technical debt and refactoring

We will uncover this in more detail at the end of the chapter, but important to highlight this here and how it relates to dealing with ever-changing requirements:

- **Technical debt management**: Allocate time in the project schedule to address technical debt and refactor the codebase. This ensures the architecture remains clean, adaptable, and resilient to requirement changes.

- **Refactoring strategy**: Regularly review the system for areas that could benefit from refactoring, especially when certain parts of the codebase are frequently modified due to evolving requirements.

Strategies for evolving architectures

We have looked at some processes and implementation plans that help architects be prepared for various change needs, but now we will look at specific architectural things that can be done.

A lot of what was discussed in *Chapter 4, The Importance of Modularity*, applies here as well, but we will repeat some concepts at a very high level here to showcase their relevance to this topic.

Designing for independence

Designing for independence is a key architectural approach that enables software components to evolve, scale, and function independently. This not only reduces interdependencies but also allows teams to make changes, test, and deploy parts of the system without affecting the entire application:

- **Adopt microservices or service-oriented architecture (SOA)**

- o **Microservices**: Break down applications into independently deployable services, each responsible for a specific business capability. Microservices enable teams to work on, scale, and deploy services independently without impacting others.

- o **Service boundaries**: Define clear service boundaries and focus each service on a single responsibility, avoiding overlap. Each service should be autonomous and responsible for its own data and logic.

- **Utilize APIs and service contracts**

  o **API-first design**: Design each component with a well-defined API as the main interface for communication, which ensures loose coupling between services.

  o **Service contracts**: Use service contracts to specify how services interact, detailing input, output, and behaviors. This promotes independence, as each component adheres to the contract rather than the specific implementation of the other component.

- **Decouple data ownership and access**

  o **Data ownership**: Assign clear ownership of data to each service or module. This eliminates shared databases, reduces dependencies, and allows each service to manage its own data lifecycle.

  o **Database per service**: Each service should ideally have its own database to avoid tight coupling through shared data. For cases where data sharing is necessary, consider replication or event-driven data synchronization rather than direct access.

- **Leverage event-driven architecture**

  o **Event-based communication**: Use event-driven patterns like publish-subscribe or message queues to allow services to communicate asynchronously. Components can publish or consume events without knowing the details of other components, creating natural independence.

  o **Event sourcing**: Use event sourcing where each change in the system is represented as an event. This allows components to reconstruct their own state independently and minimizes direct dependencies on other components.

- **Implement the Dependency Inversion Principle (DIP)**

  o **Inversion of control (IoC)**: Use IoC principles where high-level modules do not depend on low-level modules but instead depend on abstractions (like interfaces). This allows for changes in specific implementations without affecting the broader system.

  o **Dependency injection**: Use dependency injection frameworks to manage dependencies externally, allowing components to be loosely coupled and easily replaceable. This approach enables components to depend on abstractions rather than specific classes.

- **Design with modularization and separation of concerns (SoC)**

  o **Modularization**: Divide the system into discrete modules where each module is responsible for a distinct function or domain area. Modules should have minimal interdependencies, which allows changes or replacements of modules without affecting the entire application.

- o **Layered architecture**: Use layered architecture to separate concerns (e.g., presentation, business logic, and data access), reducing the risk of cross-layer dependencies and promoting changes within layers independently.

- **Use interface segregation and encapsulation**

  - o **Interface Segregation Principle (ISP)**: Create small, specific interfaces rather than large, general ones. Each component should expose only what is necessary, making it easier to change or extend components without impacting others.

  - o **Encapsulation**: Encapsulate each component's functionality and data, exposing only the necessary parts through APIs or interfaces. This minimizes external dependencies on internal implementation details, reducing the risk of unintended side effects when changes occur.

- **Design for loose coupling and high cohesion**

  - o **Loose coupling**: Minimize the dependencies between components by using design patterns that encourage separation, such as the façade pattern, which provides a simplified interface to a set of subsystems.

  - o **High cohesion**: Organize related functionalities within a single module or service, making it highly cohesive. High cohesion means that a module performs a specific task or function well, reducing the need for it to interact with multiple external components.

- **Enable configuration-driven customization**

  - o **Configuration files**: Store customizable or environment-specific settings in configuration files rather than hard-coding them. This enables changing configurations without modifying code, which allows components to operate independently across different environments.

  - o **Configuration management tools**: Use configuration management tools like *Consul* or *Spring Cloud Config* to centralize and manage configurations for each independent component, allowing easy updates without redeploying components.

- **Plan for independent deployment and versioning**

  - o **Independent deployment pipelines**: Set up separate CI/CD pipelines for each independent component, allowing teams to deploy updates to individual components without needing to redeploy the entire system.

  - o **Versioning strategy**: Implement versioning for APIs and services so that clients and dependent components can continue using older versions while updates are made. This reduces dependency on synchronized releases and allows independent updates.

- **Implement fault isolation and resilience patterns**

    o **Circuit breaker pattern**: Use circuit breakers to prevent cascading failures by isolating failing components and allowing them to recover independently, minimizing their impact on the overall system.

    o **Bulkhead pattern**: Use the bulkhead pattern to isolate critical system resources, preventing failures in one area from impacting others. This creates a buffer around each component, allowing it to operate independently even in degraded conditions.

- **Encourage a culture of continuous refactoring**

    o **Refactoring for independence**: Continuously refactor code to reduce dependencies and promote modularity. For example, remove shared libraries when possible and replace tightly coupled dependencies with abstractions or messaging patterns.

    o **Technical debt management**: Regularly assess and address technical debt that could create dependencies between components, ensuring that the system remains adaptable and components remain independent.

- **Use containers and infrastructure as code (IaC)**

    o **Containerization**: Deploy each component in its own container. Containers encapsulate all dependencies, making each component self-sufficient and portable, reducing dependency on specific infrastructure setups.

    o **IaC**: Use IaC tools (e.g., Terraform, Ansible) to define and provision infrastructure. IaC ensures that infrastructure dependencies are repeatable and independent, allowing each service to have its own environment.

- **Data decoupling and caching strategies**

    o **Data duplication and caching**: Use caching or data duplication techniques to minimize reliance on real-time data from other components. This can improve component independence and performance, as each service can continue operating with its own cached data during temporary outages.

    o **Eventual consistency**: Use eventual consistency rather than immediate consistency for data synchronization across independent components. This approach allows components to function independently while achieving consistency over time.

Designing for independence requires a combination of architectural patterns, modularization, and thoughtful system boundaries. By adopting strategies such as microservices, event-driven architecture, encapsulation, and independent deployment pipelines, architects can build systems that are resilient, adaptable, and maintainable. Independence also enables faster development cycles, easier testing, and simplified deployment, allowing teams to respond more flexibly to evolving requirements.

Isolated testing

Isolated testing is a strategy in software development where individual components, units, or modules are tested independently from the rest of the system. The goal of isolated testing is to verify that each part of the code works correctly in isolation, without interference from dependencies or other parts of the system. This approach provides more precise insights into the behaviour of each component and makes it easier to identify and fix issues.

We discuss testing in more detail in *Chapter 16, Testing in Software Architecture*, but we will at least cover some important ground points here that architects should consider.

Key principles of isolated testing have been listed as follows:

- **Isolation from external dependencies**: Each test should focus solely on the component under test, avoiding reliance on external systems like databases, file systems, or network services. Any external dependencies are usually replaced with mocks or stubs.

- **Deterministic results**: Isolated tests should produce consistent results regardless of external factors, such as system state, network conditions, or time of day. This ensures that test failures are due to issues in the code under test rather than external variables.

- **Repeatability**: Isolated tests can be run repeatedly with predictable results, which makes them suitable for automated testing in CI pipelines. This repeatability ensures stability and reliability in automated testing environments.

- **Focused scope**: An isolated test should cover a small, specific part of the functionality, allowing testers to pinpoint the exact source of failures. By keeping tests focused, debugging becomes much simpler and faster.

- **Fast execution**: Isolated tests are typically faster than integration or system tests because they do not involve complex interactions with other system parts. This makes them ideal for quick feedback in development.

Types of isolated testing have been listed as follows:

- **Unit testing**: The most common form of isolated testing, where individual functions, classes, or methods are tested in isolation. Unit tests typically mock dependencies, allowing each function or method to be tested on its own.

- **Mocking and stubbing**: Mocks and stubs are used to isolate the component being tested. Mocks simulate the behavior of real objects in a controlled way, while stubs provide predetermined responses to calls, reducing reliance on real dependencies.

- **Fakes**: Fakes are lightweight implementations of complex systems or external services, often used in isolated testing. For example, an in-memory database can replace a real database for testing purposes.

Strategies for effective isolated testing have been listed as follows:

- **Use dependency injection**: Dependency injection allows for dependencies (such as services or databases) to be replaced with mocks or stubs during testing, enabling effective isolation.

- **Mock external services and APIs**: When a module depends on an external service, use a mock or stub to simulate the service's behavior. This prevents network latency and unpredictability from affecting the test results.

- **Encapsulate side effects**: Isolate any functions with side effects (like writing to a file, making a network request) and replace them with mocks during tests. This allows you to test core logic without triggering side effects.

- **Use test doubles**: Test doubles (mocks, stubs, spies, and fakes) simulate real objects and help control the behavior of dependencies, providing a controlled environment for testing.

- **Avoid global state and singletons**: Global states or singleton objects can introduce dependencies that are difficult to control in isolated tests. Minimize the use of global states to keep tests self-contained.

- **Automate setup and teardown**: Ensure each test has a setup phase that initializes the test environment and a teardown phase that cleans up afterward. This helps maintain test independence and avoids interference from prior tests.

- **Use a dedicated testing framework**: Many testing frameworks (e.g., JUnit for Java, NUnit for .NET, pytest for Python) provide support for isolated testing with tools for setting up mock objects, assertions, and reporting.

- **Implement test coverage analysis**: Measure test coverage to identify gaps in isolated tests. Code coverage tools help ensure that isolated tests adequately cover all critical paths in the codebase.

- **Establish test naming conventions**: Use descriptive test names and organize tests logically, so it is easy to understand each test's purpose and scope. This makes it easier to maintain and extend the isolated tests over time.

Challenges in isolated testing

Isolated testing goes a long way in helping to make your overall software product more adaptable, but it does not come without its challenges, which are worth mentioning here because of the frequency they often occur in the space:

- **Over-mocking**: Excessive use of mocks and stubs can make tests less representative of actual usage, leading to false confidence. Strive for a balance between isolation and realism.

- **Difficulty in mocking complex dependencies**: When dependencies are highly complex or stateful, mocking can be challenging. Use lightweight fakes or simplified test doubles when possible.

- **Potential overhead in maintenance**: With many isolated tests, maintenance can become challenging, especially if the tests are too granular. Use careful naming and organization to reduce this overhead.

- **Limited insight into integration**: Isolated tests do not reveal how components interact as part of a larger system. Use integration and end-to-end tests alongside isolated tests to cover inter-module dependencies.

Isolated testing is crucial for ensuring software reliability, maintainability, and efficiency. By focusing on individual components, isolated testing enables developers to pinpoint issues quickly and with minimal impact on other parts of the system. When combined with integration and end-to-end tests, isolated testing forms a comprehensive testing strategy that supports robust software development and continuous delivery.

CI for evolving architectures

As software architectures evolve, CI practices must also adapt to handle the unique challenges and complexities each architecture brings. Here is a look at strategies and best practices for implementing effective CI in the context of evolving architectures.

- **Modularization of the CI pipeline**

  o **Microservices and modular architectures**: For applications built on microservices, each service should ideally have its own CI pipeline. This modular approach ensures that changes in one service do not trigger builds in unrelated services, reducing pipeline complexity and speeding up feedback.

  o **Service isolation**: Each microservice pipeline should be isolated, ensuring its tests, dependencies, and resources do not interfere with others. Dependencies between services can be simulated with mocks or stubs for isolated testing.

- **Dependency management**

  o **Version control for dependencies**: Use semantic versioning to manage dependencies among services and libraries, ensuring that changes are backward-compatible. This practice is crucial in microservices to avoid version conflicts and ensure independent deployability.

- **Dependency scanning**: Implement automated dependency scanning tools within CI to identify and update outdated or vulnerable dependencies. This approach is especially important for serverless or cloud-native applications with numerous external dependencies.

- **Containerization and orchestration**

  - **Containers for consistency**: Containers (using Docker, for example) ensure that each component or service runs in a consistent environment across development, testing, and production. This practice minimizes discrepancies that could arise due to environmental differences.

  - **Orchestrated testing in CI**: Use orchestration tools like Kubernetes to simulate production-like environments in the CI pipeline, especially when testing interactions between multiple services. This setup can help identify integration issues before deployment.

- **IaC integration**

  - **Automate infrastructure provisioning**: With IaC tools (like Terraform or AWS CloudFormation), infrastructure changes can be managed and tested in CI pipelines alongside application code. This practice ensures infrastructure consistency and allows for automated testing of infrastructure changes.

  - **Environment parity**: IaC allows different environments (development, staging, production) to have consistent configurations. Regularly testing IaC scripts in CI prevents environment drift and reduces the risk of unexpected behavior due to configuration changes.

- **Shift-left testing for early feedback**

  - **Unit and component testing**: Start with unit and component tests to catch bugs early within individual modules or services. For microservices, test each service in isolation before integrating.

  - **API contract testing**: In loosely coupled architectures, use contract testing (e.g., Pact) to validate communication between services. This approach ensures that changes to one service don't break another, even before they are deployed together.

- **Efficient test orchestration and parallelization**

  - **Parallel testing**: Run tests in parallel whenever possible to reduce build times, especially for larger applications or systems with numerous services. Tools like Jenkins, GitLab CI, and CircleCI support parallel execution to speed up feedback.

  - **Selective testing and smart test execution**: In large systems, only run tests relevant to recent changes. Test-impact analysis can determine which services or modules were affected by a change and trigger only the relevant tests, optimizing CI pipeline performance.

- **Monitoring, observability, and feedback loops**

  o **Continuous monitoring**: Integrate monitoring tools like Prometheus, Grafana, or **Elasticsearch, Logstash, Kibana (ELK)** into CI to track metrics like build duration, test pass or fail rates, and resource usage. Monitoring ensures pipeline health and helps in identifying bottlenecks.

  o **Real-time alerts and reporting**: Set up real-time alerts for critical failures in the CI process, allowing teams to address issues immediately. Detailed reporting dashboards can also provide insights into pipeline stability over time.

- **Managing CI for polyglot environments**

  o **Multi-language pipeline support**: As architectures evolve, teams often use different languages and frameworks across services. Choose CI tools that support polyglot environments, such as Jenkins or GitHub Actions, to handle diverse technology stacks within the same pipeline.

  o **Unified standards and best practices**: Establish standard CI configurations and testing conventions for different languages to maintain consistency across services.

- **Emphasizing security in CI**

  o **Automated security scanning**: Integrate security scanning tools (like Snyk, SonarQube, or OWASP ZAP) to automatically detect vulnerabilities in code and dependencies. Regularly updating these scans in the pipeline ensures compliance with evolving security standards.

  o **Secrets management**: Secure sensitive data (API keys, credentials) with secrets management solutions (like HashiCorp Vault or AWS Secrets Manager). This approach prevents accidental exposure of secrets during CI/ CD processes.

- **Building for scalability and resilience in CI**

  o **Scalable infrastructure**: Use cloud-based CI systems that automatically scale resources based on demand, preventing pipeline bottlenecks as the team grows and projects expand.

  o **Disaster recovery and pipeline redundancy**: Implement backup and failover mechanisms to protect against pipeline outages, ensuring CI reliability. This is particularly important for CI systems supporting critical production deployments.

In the context of evolving architectures, CI becomes a vital tool for maintaining quality, speed, and stability. Each stage of CI must be carefully designed and adapted to fit the specific needs of the architecture, whether it is a monolith, microservices, or serverless application. By implementing modular, flexible, and secure CI pipelines, teams can handle evolving requirements and architectures, ultimately supporting faster releases and more resilient software.

Set up proactive monitoring to support change

Proactive monitoring involves setting up systems and processes that not only react to issues but actively prevent them, giving teams the visibility needed to make data-driven decisions when software or systems are evolving, whether due to changing requirements, architecture upgrades, or increased scale, proactive monitoring supports stability by identifying potential issues before they affect users.

Not just behind changes to their own systems, but in increasingly connected systems within larger organizations, a large part of this monitoring helps to support identifying unanticipated changes in other systems and dependencies. Setting up proactive monitoring involves the following:

- **Define key metrics and establish baselines**

    o **Identify core metrics**: Start by identifying **key performance indicators (KPIs)** aligned with the software's goals and architectural needs. Examples include CPU and memory usage, response times, request rates, error rates, and resource usage.

    o **Establish baselines**: Measure and document baseline values for these metrics in a stable environment to understand what *normal* looks like. Baselines help in setting thresholds for alerts and identifying deviations caused by changes.

- **Implement end-to-end observability**

    o **Distributed tracing**: Use distributed tracing tools (e.g., OpenTelemetry, Zipkin) to monitor requests as they flow through different parts of the system. This helps pinpoint bottlenecks or performance issues within complex architectures like microservices.

    o **Centralized logging**: Implement centralized logging with tools like ELK or Splunk to capture logs from different services in one place. Logs provide context for issues and are critical in troubleshooting and root cause analysis.

    o **Metrics aggregation**: Collect and aggregate metrics across systems to get a holistic view. Prometheus, Grafana, or Datadog are popular choices for gathering metrics and visualizing trends.

- **Set up real-time alerting and automated responses**

  o **Threshold-based alerts**: Define alerts that trigger when metrics exceed predefined thresholds. For example, set alerts for high CPU usage or response time increases beyond the baseline.

  o **Anomaly detection**: Use anomaly detection to catch issues that fall outside typical patterns, even if they do not breach specific thresholds. Many monitoring platforms have built-in anomaly detection for proactive alerting.

  o **Automated incident responses**: Implement automated responses where possible, such as scaling up resources in response to high demand or restarting a service upon repeated failure. Automation minimizes the impact of incidents, especially during off-hours.

- **Conduct regular health checks and synthetic monitoring**

  o **Health checks**: Set up automated health checks to run at intervals, verifying that services and dependencies (e.g., databases, APIs) are accessible and functioning. These checks allow for early detection of connectivity or availability issues.

  o **Synthetic monitoring**: Use synthetic monitoring to simulate user interactions and measure performance from an external perspective. Tools like Pingdom or Uptrends can simulate user workflows, helping you identify issues before real users are impacted.

- **Use CI/CD pipeline monitoring**

  o **Monitor pipeline performance**: Track build times, deployment times, and failure rates within the CI/CD pipeline. This allows for the early identification of bottlenecks in the deployment process.

  o **Automate rollbacks and canary releases**: In case of issues during a release, automated rollbacks and canary releases (gradual rollout to a small subset of users) minimize risk and allow for controlled monitoring of changes in production.

- **Monitor dependencies and external integrations**

  o **Track third-party service health**: Use APIs or third-party monitoring tools to track the health of dependencies like payment gateways, APIs, or cloud services. Many providers offer APIs that provide their system's health status.

  o **Set dependency-specific alerts**: Establish specific alerting and monitoring for critical external dependencies, including rate limits, latency, and availability, to ensure they do not impact overall performance.

- **Correlate metrics across components**

  - **Cross-component correlation**: Establish correlations between metrics (e.g., database latency and response time) to understand the root cause of issues across services. Tools like Grafana can help visualize and correlate data points from different sources.

  - **Root cause analysis**: Set up tools that provide correlation-based root cause analysis (e.g., New Relic or Dynatrace) to quickly identify which component is causing a cascading failure or slowdown, especially important in complex, distributed systems.

- **Use predictive analytics and machine learning**

  - **Predictive analysis for capacity planning**: Leverage predictive analytics to anticipate capacity requirements based on historical data and growth trends, ensuring that infrastructure can handle future load increases without manual adjustments.

  - **Flakiness and stability prediction in tests**: For test automation, ML models can analyze past test data to predict which tests are likely to fail or be flaky. This allows for proactive measures to stabilize those tests and improve CI/CD reliability.

- **Conduct regular monitoring reviews and fine-tuning**

  - **Adjust alert thresholds**: Periodically review and adjust alert thresholds based on changes in baseline metrics or evolving system requirements.

  - **Eliminate noise with alert policies**: Fine-tune alerts to reduce alert fatigue by filtering out low-priority notifications or grouping related alerts. Set up escalation policies for critical incidents that require immediate action.

- **Automate reporting and stakeholder communication**

  - **Automated reports**: Set up automated, periodic reports on system health, performance, and recent incidents. These reports can be useful for stakeholders and ensure that any ongoing issues are visible to the team.

  - **Real-time dashboards**: Build dashboards for real-time monitoring that show critical metrics and alerts, enabling both technical and non-technical stakeholders to stay informed.

By implementing proactive monitoring, organizations can support stable, scalable, and responsive software even as it evolves, minimizing risk and maintaining high levels of performance and reliability. This approach ensures that changes are introduced smoothly, with reduced negative impact on the end user and increased agility for the development team.

Dealing with tech debt and maintenance

The biggest challenge that comes with a lot of change is that technical debt and regular maintenance can often fall aside and be deprioritized in favor of constant functional improvement. Software architects need to manage their space to ensure technical debt and maintenance are properly addressed in their space.

Managing technical debt and maintenance effectively requires strategies that balance ongoing feature development with improvements to code quality and system stability. Here are some practical approaches to deal with technical debt:

- **Prioritize and categorize technical debt**

  - **Categorize debt**: Break down technical debt into types (e.g., code smells, architectural issues, dependencies, outdated libraries). This helps teams focus on the most critical areas first.

  - **Assess and prioritize**: Use a debt matrix to classify debt based on impact and effort required to resolve. Focus first on high-impact, low-effort tasks, and gradually tackle high-impact, high-effort ones.

- **Integrate debt management into development processes**

  - **Technical debt tracking**: Treat technical debt as you would any other requirement by documenting it and tracking it in project management tools. Create specific tickets or user stories for debt work.

  - **Allocate time each sprint**: Reserve a percentage of each sprint or release for tackling technical debt. Even dedicating 10 to 20% of sprint capacity can keep debt manageable over time.

  - **Definition of Done (DoD)**: Include quality requirements in your DoD, such as code review, adequate test coverage, and refactoring. This reduces the chance of new debt being introduced.

- **Refactor continuously**

  - **Continuous refactoring**: Encourage teams to refactor code as part of regular work, especially when making changes in areas that already have debt. Small, incremental refactors are less risky and easier to manage than large overhauls.

  - **Use code review for debt reduction**: During code reviews, focus not just on functionality but also on identifying and reducing potential areas of technical debt.

- **Plan and budget for regular maintenance**

  - **Dedicated maintenance budget**: Advocate for a dedicated budget for technical debt and maintenance work, especially for aging systems. Tie this budget to specific objectives, like reducing incident rates or improving performance.

  - **Establish regular maintenance windows**: Schedule regular maintenance windows where non-critical issues and small refactors can be handled without disrupting development.

- **Focus on documentation and knowledge sharing**

  - **Document technical debt**: Create and maintain a living document of known technical debt areas, providing context on why the debt exists, its risks, and potential solutions.

  - **Knowledge sharing**: Use brown-bag sessions or documentation to share best practices for code quality and maintenance. This helps all team members to avoid practices that could introduce new debt.

- **Make use of technical debt metrics and KPIs**

  - **Code quality metrics**: Track metrics such as code complexity, duplication, test coverage, and maintainability scores. This gives visibility into the state of your codebase and highlights trends over time.

  - **Tech debt ratio**: Track the ratio of tech debt to development time, known as the technical debt ratio, to measure the impact of debt on the team's overall efficiency.

- **Leverage feature toggles and incremental releases**

  - **Feature toggles**: Use feature toggles to manage the release of new features incrementally. This lets you deploy code even if certain parts are not entirely refactored, allowing you to pay down debt gradually.

  - **Incremental releases**: When large refactoring efforts are needed, break them down into smaller releases. This reduces risk, allows for testing in production, and makes it easier to roll back if needed.

- **Plan and execute regular retrospectives on technical debt**

  - **Technical debt retrospectives**: Host regular retrospectives focused solely on technical debt and maintenance. Review past debt reduction efforts, analyze current debt, and plan for future action.

  - **Learn from incidents**: Use post-mortems from production incidents to identify underlying technical debt issues, such as brittle code or lack of tests, and prioritize them accordingly.

- **Communicate the impact of technical debt with stakeholders**

  o **Build a business case**: Articulate the impact of technical debt on customer experience, system reliability, and delivery speed. Show how addressing it can reduce long-term costs and enhance product quality.

  o **Regular updates on debt reduction**: Report on debt reduction metrics or outcomes regularly, showing stakeholders that technical debt reduction is an ongoing investment in quality.

- **Establish a debt prevention culture**

  o **Encourage clean coding standards**: Promote a culture of writing clean, maintainable code by using code reviews and encouraging practices like SOLID principles and **Don't Repeat Yourself (DRY)**.

  o **Training and best practices**: Conduct training sessions on code quality, modular design, and testing practices. Equip team members with the skills needed to prevent technical debt from accumulating.

  o **Lead by example**: Encourage technical leads and architects to model good practices, demonstrating that quality is as important as new features.

Dealing with technical debt requires a balanced approach, where immediate feature needs are met without sacrificing long-term code quality and system stability. By incorporating these strategies, teams can keep technical debt in check, reduce maintenance burdens, and enhance the software's resilience and scalability over time.

Conclusion

Evolutionary architecture is a design approach that emphasizes flexibility and adaptability, enabling a system to evolve in response to changing requirements, technologies, and user needs over time. Unlike traditional architecture, which often aims for a fixed, comprehensive design, evolutionary architecture prioritizes continuous improvement and incremental change, allowing the architecture to grow in manageable steps.

By focusing on adaptability, evolutionary architecture supports long-term agility and resilience, helping teams to manage and optimize for both current needs and future demands. It is particularly valuable in fast-paced environments where technology and business requirements shift frequently, and it aligns closely with agile and DevOps practices that emphasize responsiveness and iterative improvement.

In the next chapter, we will at the critical soft skills that software architects need to master to lead successful development projects.

## CHAPTER 12

Soft Skills for Software Architects

Introduction

This book primarily focuses on the role of the software architect, technical skills, and the ability of a software architect to design software that meets a wide variety of technically diverse goals.

However, this vital leadership role that a software architect plays would not be possible without an equally diverse set of soft skills. An architect's main responsibility might be to build and design systems, but those systems are built by teams of diverse people for an equally diverse user base. Therefore, it is important for us to dedicate a short chapter to some of the softer skills that the architects need to develop to successfully lead the execution of the delivered software product.

Structure

In this chapter, we will discuss the following topics:

- Importance of soft skills
- The role of an architect in leading teams
- Skills for managing stakeholders
- Conducting productive meetings as an architect

- Negotiation skills
- Mentoring skills
- Presentation skills

Objectives

By the end of this chapter, you will understand the importance of soft skills in team leadership and learn how to apply the soft skills needed to help lead software delivery teams to success.

Importance of soft skills

Soft skills are essential for software architects for several reasons:

- **Communication**: Software architects often need to communicate complex technical concepts to various stakeholders, including clients, developers, project managers, and executives. Strong communication skills enable architects to effectively convey their ideas, requirements, and decisions, fostering collaboration and understanding among team members.

- **Team collaboration**: Architects work closely with developers, designers, testers, and other professionals throughout the software development lifecycle. Strong interpersonal skills allow architects to collaborate effectively with diverse teams, fostering a positive and productive work environment.

- **Problem-solving:** Soft skills such as critical thinking, creativity, and adaptability are crucial for architects to solve complex problems that arise during the design and implementation of software systems. Architects must be able to analyze requirements, identify potential issues, and propose innovative solutions to meet project goals.

- **Leadership**: Software architects often take on leadership roles within development teams, guiding and mentoring junior developers, providing technical direction, and making strategic decisions. Strong leadership skills help architects inspire and motivate team members, driving them towards a common vision and ensuring the successful delivery of projects.

- **Client interaction**: Architects frequently interact with clients to understand their requirements, gather feedback, and present proposals. Effective client communication skills enable architects to build strong relationships, manage expectations, and ensure that software solutions align with client needs and objectives.

- **Adaptability and continuous learning**: The field of software development is constantly evolving, with new technologies, methodologies, and best practices emerging regularly. Soft skills such as adaptability and a willingness to learn are essential for architects to stay abreast of industry trends, acquire new knowledge and skills, and adapt to changing project requirements and constraints.

The role of an architect in leading teams

It is clear that people leadership, interaction, and the ability to communicate with a variety of technical stakeholders are all vital to what is required of a software architect. An architect acts as more than just a communication point between different parties, but also needs to be a strong leader themselves, often stepping in to provide direction to the development teams and be able to ensure that teams can be properly structured, led, and empowered to deliver software effectively. The following are some critical aspects where software architects need to fulfill a leadership role in teams:

- **Setting technical direction**: By setting a clear technical direction, architects empower teams to make informed decisions and align their efforts towards common goals. This includes defining their technical vision clearly, establishing guidelines, frameworks, and standards to ensure consistency, scalability, and maintainability across the codebase.

- **Mentoring and coaching**: Architects mentor and coach team members, sharing their expertise, knowledge, and best practices. They provide guidance on software design, development techniques, and problem-solving strategies, helping team members improve their skills and grow professionally. By investing in the development of their team members, architects foster a culture of continuous learning and innovation. We will unpack some important mentoring skills later in this chapter.

- **Facilitating collaboration**: Architects facilitate collaboration among team members by promoting open communication, sharing information, and fostering a collaborative work environment. They encourage cross-functional collaboration between developers, designers, testers, and other stakeholders, breaking down silos and promoting a shared sense of ownership and accountability for project success.

- **Making technical decisions**: Architects do not just set technical direction but also need to be the ones making critical technical decisions throughout the project lifecycle, balancing trade-offs between different architectural options and considering factors such as performance, scalability, security, and maintainability. An architect needs to engage with team members to gather input, evaluate alternatives, and make informed decisions that align with project goals and constraints, and then help motivate, influence, and lead them towards implementing the decisions made.

- **Resolving technical challenges**: When technical challenges arise, architects lead efforts to analyze root causes, identify solutions, and mitigate risks. They collaborate with team members to brainstorm ideas, conduct experiments, and implement changes to address issues effectively. By demonstrating problem-solving skills and resilience in the face of challenges, architects inspire confidence and trust in their teams.

- **Managing stakeholder expectations**: Architects act as liaisons between technical teams and stakeholders, representing the technical perspective while also understanding business requirements and priorities. They communicate project status, risks, and dependencies to stakeholders, manage expectations, and negotiate trade-offs to ensure alignment between technical decisions and business objectives. We will talk further about some additional skills that go into managing these different stakeholders in the next section of this chapter.

- **Risk management**: Architects identify technical risks and dependencies early in the project and develop mitigation strategies to address them effectively. They work closely with project managers and stakeholders to prioritize risks and allocate resources to minimize their impact on project timelines and deliverables. Architects also communicate risks and mitigation plans to the development team and collaborate with them to implement appropriate solutions.

- **Decision making**: Architects make critical technical decisions throughout the project lifecycle, balancing trade-offs between different architectural options and considering factors such as performance, scalability, security, and maintainability. They engage with team members to gather input, evaluate alternatives, and make informed decisions that align with project goals and constraints.

- **Continuous improvement**: Architects promote a culture of continuous improvement within the development team by encouraging feedback, sharing lessons learned, and implementing process enhancements. They foster innovation and creativity by challenging the status quo and exploring new technologies and methodologies that can improve project outcomes.

Overall, the role of an architect in leading teams involves providing technical leadership, mentoring and coaching team members, facilitating collaboration, making technical decisions, resolving challenges, and managing stakeholder expectations. Effective leadership from architects is essential for fostering a high-performing team culture and delivering successful software projects.

Skills for managing stakeholders

We have already established the importance of managing stakeholders for a software architect. It is more than just passing on information, talking in meetings, and sending through documentation.

Managing stakeholders, communicating with development teams, addressing business outcomes, and understanding client needs all require a strong sense of empathy and so rather than focus on technical or practical tips in what an architect needs to supply in communication We will start off by focusing more on the empathy elements first, as these will often have the biggest impact on an architects ability to influence and lead a team, before we tackle other soft skill and leadership aspects.

Empathy skills

Here are some tips to develop empathy in communication:

- **Active listening**: Practice active listening by giving your full attention to the speaker, maintaining eye contact, and avoiding interruptions. Focus on understanding the speaker's perspective, feelings, and underlying concerns.

- **Put yourself in their shoes**: Take the time to empathize with the experiences, challenges, and priorities of your stakeholders, development teams, and clients. Consider how they might be feeling and how their perspectives shape their communication and decision-making.

- **Ask open-ended questions**: Encourage open dialogue and deeper exploration of thoughts and feelings by asking open-ended questions. This allows stakeholders, team members, and clients to express themselves more freely and helps you gain a better understanding of their perspectives.

- **Practice reflective listening**: Reflective listening involves paraphrasing or summarizing what the speaker has said to demonstrate understanding and validate their feelings. This shows that you are actively engaged in the conversation and value their input.

- **Seek feedback**: Actively seek feedback from stakeholders, team members, and clients to understand their satisfaction levels, concerns, and suggestions for improvement. Create a safe and open environment where individuals feel comfortable sharing their thoughts and feelings.

- **Cultivate curiosity**: Approach interactions with curiosity and a genuine interest in understanding others' viewpoints. Ask clarifying questions, explore different perspectives, and remain open to learning from others' experiences and insights.

- **Practice empathetic communication**: Use language and tone that demonstrate empathy and understanding. Acknowledge others' feelings, validate their experiences, and express empathy through your words and actions.

- **Empathy exercises**: Engage in empathy-building exercises and activities to enhance your ability to understand and connect with others emotionally. These may include role-playing scenarios, reading fiction or non-fiction literature, or participating in empathy workshops or training sessions.

- **Self-reflection**: Take time for self-reflection to assess your own thoughts, feelings, and biases that may impact your ability to empathize with others. Identify areas for personal growth and commit to continuous improvement in your communication skills.

- **Practice empathy daily**: Make a conscious effort to practice empathy in your daily interactions with colleagues, stakeholders, clients, and even in your personal relationships. Over time, empathy will become a natural part of your communication style, enhancing your ability to build meaningful connections and foster positive relationships.

Team management tips for software architects

Here are some practical tips for managing software teams effectively as a software architect in helping delivery teams produce the best outcomes:

- **Define clear goals and objectives**: Ensure the team understands the project's architectural vision, goals, and technical objectives. Clearly communicate how their individual contributions align with the broader strategy.

- **Delegate effectively**: Assign tasks based on team members' strengths, skills, and career aspirations. Avoid micromanagement and trust your team to execute their responsibilities while offering guidance when needed.

- **Facilitate cross-functional collaboration**: Act as a bridge between developers, testers, DevOps engineers, and business stakeholders. Promote collaboration by clarifying roles, setting expectations, and encouraging open communication across teams.

- **Foster technical excellence**: Advocate for high coding standards, adherence to architectural principles, and the use of best practices. Provide mentorship and encourage team members to upskill through training or certifications.

- **Enable decision-making autonomy**: Empower team members to make technical decisions within their scope of work. Guide them to align these decisions with the overall architecture, but avoid over-centralizing decision-making.

- **Set realistic timelines**: Work with stakeholders to create achievable timelines that balance technical feasibility with business priorities. Avoid overloading the team with unrealistic deadlines that could lead to burnout or rushed work.

- **Facilitate knowledge sharing**: Organize regular knowledge-sharing sessions such as architecture reviews, lunch-and-learns, or retrospectives. Encourage team members to document technical decisions and learnings to build a knowledge base.

- **Provide constructive feedback**: Offer timely and actionable feedback to help team members improve. Balance criticism with recognition of achievements, ensuring feedback is seen as an opportunity for growth.

- **Encourage innovation**: Give team members room to experiment with new technologies, approaches, or tools. Dedicate time for innovation, such as hackathons or proof-of-concept projects, to spark creativity and boost morale.

- **Resolve conflicts proactively**: Address team conflicts quickly and constructively. Understand all sides of an issue and mediate solutions that prioritize team cohesion and the project's best interests.

- **Monitor progress without micromanaging**: Use tools like standups, dashboards, or project tracking software to stay updated on team progress. Provide support when needed without disrupting workflows.

- **Balance workload**: Keep an eye on workload distribution and adjust assignments to avoid bottlenecks or overburdening specific individuals. Ensure the team has the resources and capacity to meet their commitments.

- **Recognize and reward contributions**: Acknowledge team members' hard work and accomplishments, both publicly and privately. Celebrating successes boosts morale and reinforces a culture of appreciation.

- **Adapt to team dynamics**: Every team is unique. Continuously assess the dynamics and adjust your management style to suit the specific needs, strengths, and challenges of your team.

- **Focus on long-term development**: Support team members' career growth by helping them set professional development goals. Provide opportunities for leadership, challenging projects, and mentorship to keep them engaged and motivated.

By combining these team management practices with your technical expertise, you can create a productive and collaborative environment that drives successful project outcomes and fosters team satisfaction.

Practical communication skills

Empathy is not something that may come naturally to a person, but even while this trait is being developed, the below practical communication guides can be a lot easier to implement in managing the different stakeholders and teams.

Communicating effectively with development teams and stakeholder management is crucial for ensuring clarity, alignment, and productivity throughout the software development process. Here are some tips for communicating with development teams:

- **Clear and concise communication**: Provide clear, concise, and actionable information to the development team. Avoid ambiguity and use simple language to convey complex technical concepts, requirements, and tasks.

- **Set clear expectations**: Clearly define project goals, objectives, and timelines to ensure that everyone on the development team understands their roles and responsibilities. Be transparent about project constraints, such as budget, resources, and technical limitations.

- **Use multiple communication channels**: Utilize a variety of communication channels, such as team meetings, emails, instant messaging, and project management tools, to keep the development team informed and engaged. Choose the appropriate channel based on the urgency and nature of the communication.

- **Encourage two-way communication**: Foster an environment where team members feel comfortable expressing their ideas, concerns, and feedback. Encourage open dialogue, active listening, and constructive criticism to promote collaboration and innovation.

- **Provide regular updates**: Keep the development team updated on project progress, milestones, and any changes in requirements or priorities. Schedule regular status meetings, progress reports, or stand-up meetings to review progress, address issues, and plan next steps.

- **Be accessible and approachable**: Make yourself accessible to the development team for questions, clarifications, and guidance. Be approachable and responsive to team members' inquiries and concerns, whether in person, via email, or through other communication channels.

- **Clarify technical requirements**: Ensure that technical requirements, specifications, and user stories are clearly documented and understood by the development team. Address any ambiguities or gaps in requirements proactively to avoid misunderstandings and rework later in the development process.

- **Provide context and rationale**: When assigning tasks or making decisions, provide context and rationale to help the development team understand the significance and impact of their work. Explain how their contributions align with project goals and customer needs.

- **Celebrate achievements**: Recognize and celebrate the achievements and milestones reached by the development team. Show appreciation for their hard work, dedication, and contributions to the project's success. Celebrating successes boosts morale and fosters a positive team culture.

- **Seek continuous improvement**: Encourage the development team to share lessons learned, identify areas for improvement, and suggest process enhancements. Foster a culture of continuous learning and improvement to drive efficiency, quality, and innovation in software development.

Tips for communicating to business outcomes

Effectively communicating how architectural decisions align with business outcomes is critical for software architects. This ensures that stakeholders understand the value of technical solutions and their impact on organizational goals. Here are some tips for software architects to focus on business outcomes:

- **Understand business goals and priorities**: Take time to learn about the client's strategic objectives, **key performance indicators** (**KPIs**), and long-term vision. Tailor your architectural decisions and recommendations to align with these priorities and drive measurable business value.

- **Ask outcome-driven questions**: Engage stakeholders with open-ended, business-focused questions. For example, *What business challenges are you hoping to solve?* or *What measurable outcomes define success for this initiative?* This approach clarifies the desired results and provides a foundation for aligning technology with business value.

- **Articulate business value**: Clearly demonstrate how architectural choices contribute to business objectives such as increased revenue, cost savings, improved customer satisfaction, or faster time to market. Use specific metrics, case studies, or simulations to highlight the expected **return on investment** (**ROI**).

- **Simplify technical explanations**: Translate complex technical solutions into language that emphasizes their business impact. For example, instead of discussing microservices architecture in technical terms, explain how it enables faster feature delivery and scalability to meet market demands.

- **Align with stakeholder concerns**: Identify the challenges or risks that matter most to business stakeholders, such as budget constraints, time-to-market pressures, or regulatory compliance. Address these directly in your proposals and highlight how your architecture mitigates them.

- **Highlight strategic flexibility**: Emphasize how your proposed solutions future-proof the organization by enabling adaptability to emerging market trends, technological changes, or shifting business requirements.

- **Collaborate on outcome mapping**: Work with stakeholders to map architectural decisions to specific business outcomes. For example, show how adopting a cloud-native approach reduces operational costs or how an API-first strategy drives integration and innovation across teams.

- **Provide actionable insights**: Share data and insights that inform decision-making, such as cost-benefit analyses, benchmarks, or risk assessments. Use these to justify your architectural approach and demonstrate its alignment with business priorities.

- **Set realistic expectations**: Establish clear, achievable goals regarding how and when your architectural solutions will impact the business. Be transparent about limitations or dependencies and provide timelines for realizing outcomes.

- **Maintain continuous feedback loops**: Regularly communicate progress towards business outcomes through reports, dashboards, or presentations. Highlight successes, address challenges, and refine strategies based on evolving business needs.

- **Foster trust through accountability**: Be reliable, transparent, and accountable in all communications. Stakeholders are more likely to support architectural initiatives when they trust the architect's ability to deliver tangible business results.

Tips for communicating with clients

Communicating effectively with clients is essential for software architects to understand and address their needs, expectations, and concerns. Here are some tips for software architects when communicating with clients:

- **Ask open-ended questions**: Encourage clients to share their thoughts, preferences, and priorities by asking open-ended questions. This allows architects to gather comprehensive information about the project requirements and explore various aspects of the client's vision.

- **Clarify expectations**: Clarify the client's expectations regarding project scope, timeline, budget, and deliverables. Ensure that both parties have a shared understanding of the project goals and constraints to avoid misunderstandings later in the development process.

- **Translate technical jargon**: Translate technical terminology and concepts into layman's terms to ensure that clients can understand and make informed decisions about the project. Avoid using overly technical language that may confuse or overwhelm non-technical stakeholders.

- **Educate and empower**: Educate clients about technology trends, best practices, and industry standards relevant to their project. Empower clients to make informed decisions by providing them with relevant information and guidance based on your expertise and experience.

- **Manage expectations**: Set realistic expectations with clients regarding project timelines, milestones, and potential challenges. Be transparent about any risks or limitations that may impact the project and discuss mitigation strategies to address them proactively.

- **Provide regular updates**: Keep clients informed about project progress, accomplishments, and challenges through regular updates and status reports. Schedule periodic meetings or check-ins to review project status, address any concerns, and gather feedback from the client.

- **Demonstrate value**: Clearly communicate the value proposition of your architectural solutions and how they align with the client's business goals and objectives. Highlight the benefits, features, and potential ROI of your proposed architecture to demonstrate its value to the client.

- **Manage changes effectively**: Be prepared to accommodate changes in client requirements or priorities throughout the project lifecycle. Communicate openly with the client about the implications of proposed changes on project scope, timeline, and budget, and work collaboratively to find mutually acceptable solutions.

- **Build trust and rapport**: Build trust and rapport with clients by being responsive, reliable, and transparent in your communication. Foster a positive relationship based on mutual respect, honesty, and integrity, which lays the foundation for successful collaboration and long-term partnerships.

Conducting productive meetings as an architect

Even though software architects are largely seen as a technical role that might sometimes sit in the background as a key leader in the software engineering space, it is important that architects play a key role in both attending meetings and setting up productive meetings that can help to communicate their technical expectations to the teams.

Conducting productive meetings as a software architect involves careful planning, effective facilitation, and clear communication to ensure that meetings are efficient, focused, and achieve their intended objectives. Here are some tips for conducting productive meetings:

- **Set clear objectives**: Define clear objectives and desired outcomes for the meeting. Communicate these objectives to all participants in advance so they understand the purpose of the meeting and what is expected of them.

- **Create an agenda**: Develop a detailed agenda outlining the topics to be discussed, the time allotted for each item, and any pre-meeting preparation required. Share the agenda with participants ahead of time to give them an opportunity to prepare and contribute to the discussion.

- **Invite the right participants**: Invite only essential participants whose presence is necessary to achieve the meeting objectives. Consider the expertise and perspective of each participant and ensure representation from relevant stakeholders.

- **Start and end on time**: Begin the meeting promptly at the scheduled time to respect participants' time and maximize productivity. Adhere to the agenda and allocate time effectively to ensure all agenda items are covered within the designated timeframe. End the meeting on time or even a few minutes early to avoid running over schedule.

- **Encourage participation**: Create a welcoming and inclusive environment where all participants feel comfortable sharing their ideas, opinions, and concerns. Encourage active participation by asking open-ended questions, soliciting input from quieter participants, and facilitating constructive dialogue.

- **Foster collaboration**: Promote collaboration and teamwork by encouraging participants to build on each other's ideas, offer constructive feedback, and work together to solve problems or make decisions. Use collaborative tools and techniques, such as brainstorming, whiteboarding, or breakout sessions, to facilitate engagement and creativity.

- **Manage discussion dynamics**: Maintain control over the meeting by managing discussion dynamics and ensuring that conversations stay focused and productive. Redirect off-topic discussions, address any disruptive behavior or dominance, and facilitate a balanced exchange of ideas among participants.

- **Document action items**: Document key decisions, action items, and follow-up tasks during the meeting. Assign responsibilities and deadlines for each action item and circulate meeting minutes or a summary of outcomes to participants after the meeting to ensure accountability and alignment.

- **Seek feedback**: Solicit feedback from participants to evaluate the effectiveness of the meeting format, agenda, and facilitation. Use this feedback to continuously improve future meetings and ensure that they remain productive and valuable for all participants.

- **Lead by example**: As the meeting facilitator, lead by example, demonstrate active listening, respectful communication, and a commitment to achieving meeting objectives. Set a positive tone and demeanor that encourages collaboration, creativity, and engagement among participants.

By following these tips, software architects can conduct productive meetings that foster collaboration, drive decision-making, and contribute to the success of software development projects.

Negotiation skills

Another vital skill that software architects will need to master is that of negotiation. Negotiating skills are essential for software architects when dealing with various stakeholders, including clients, development teams, project managers, and other decision-makers.

Here are some key negotiating skills for architects, outside of the soft skills like active listening:

- **Preparation**: Prepare thoroughly before entering any negotiation. Understand your goals, priorities, and potential trade-offs. Research the needs and interests of the other party and anticipate their concerns and objections. Having a clear understanding of the negotiation dynamics will empower you to negotiate effectively.

- **Active listening**: We have already mentioned this as a key empathic skill in managing stakeholders, but we are mentioning it here again due to its importance in the negotiation area specifically.

Architects need to listen actively to the other party to understand their perspective, needs, and priorities. Pay attention to both verbal and non-verbal cues and ask clarifying questions to ensure a thorough understanding of their position. Demonstrating empathy and understanding will help build rapport and facilitate productive negotiations. This can be ensured in the following manner:

- **Communication skills**: Communicate your ideas, proposals, and concerns clearly and persuasively. Use language that is concise, confident, and respectful. Articulate the value proposition of your proposals and highlight the benefits for all parties involved. Effective communication can help build trust and credibility during negotiations.

- **Problem-solving**: Approach negotiations as a collaborative problem-solving process rather than a zero-sum game. Focus on identifying common interests and areas of mutual benefit that can lead to win-win outcomes. Brainstorm creative solutions and explore alternative options to address the needs and concerns of both parties.

- **Flexibility**: Be flexible and open to compromise during negotiations. Understand that concessions may be necessary to reach a mutually acceptable agreement. Prioritize your negotiation goals and be willing to adjust your position on less critical issues to achieve overall success.

- **Assertiveness**: Advocate for your interests and objectives assertively while remaining respectful and professional. Clearly articulate your needs and preferences and be willing to assertively defend them if necessary. Assertiveness can help ensure that your concerns are heard and addressed during negotiations.

- **Emotional intelligence**: Develop emotional intelligence to manage your own emotions and navigate the emotions of others during negotiations. Stay calm, composed, and adaptable in the face of conflict or disagreement. Recognize and validate the emotions of the other party and strive to build rapport and trust throughout the negotiation process.

- **Negotiation tactics**: Familiarize yourself with common negotiation tactics and strategies, such as anchoring, framing, and concession trading. Be prepared to counter or respond to these tactics effectively while staying focused on achieving your negotiation goals.

- **Conflict resolution**: Develop conflict resolution skills to manage disagreements and conflicts that may arise during negotiations. Focus on finding common ground, exploring underlying interests, and seeking mutually acceptable solutions that address the root causes of conflict.

- **Follow-up and closure**: Once an agreement is reached, follow up promptly to document the terms and ensure that both parties fulfill their commitments. Celebrate the successful negotiation outcome and maintain open lines of communication to nurture the relationship and address any future concerns or issues.

By honing these negotiating skills, software architects can effectively navigate complex negotiations and drive successful outcomes that benefit all parties involved.

Mentoring skills

Software architects are technical leaders in their firms and so the ability to mentor and develop others vital in raising up teams that can deliver on the architectural plans.

Mentoring skills are vital for software architects to guide and develop the talents of junior developers and other team members. Here are key mentoring skills for architects:

- **Active listening**: Actively listen to mentees to understand their goals, challenges, and aspirations. Pay attention to their concerns and provide empathetic support and guidance.

- **Understand their learning pace**: Put yourself in the mentee's shoes to understand their perspective and experiences. Show empathy towards their struggles and offer encouragement and support as needed. It is important to remember that everyone learns at a different pace and has different strengths and weaknesses and so as an architect, take time to carefully understand where your mentees are and try and help them develop accordingly.

- **Avoid jargon and focus on clarity**: Communicate ideas, feedback, and guidance clearly and effectively. Use simple language and avoid technical jargon that might confuse mentees. Ensure that instructions and advice are easy to understand and actionable.

- **Provide constructive feedback**: Offer constructive feedback to help mentees improve their skills and performance. Focus on specific behaviors or areas for development and provide actionable suggestions for improvement. Balance constructive criticism with praise and encouragement to maintain motivation and confidence.

- **Set goals and expectations**: Collaborate with mentees to set clear, achievable goals and expectations. Establish milestones and timelines to track progress and provide a sense of direction. Adjust goals as needed based on mentees' growth and development.

- **Lead by example**: Demonstrate professionalism, integrity, and a strong work ethic in your own behavior and actions. Serve as a role model for mentees by showcasing best practices, problem-solving skills, and a commitment to continuous learning and improvement.

- **Provide guidance and resources**: Offer guidance and resources to help mentees overcome challenges and achieve their goals. Share relevant articles, books, tutorials, and online resources that can enhance their knowledge and skills. Encourage mentees to explore new technologies and methodologies and support their learning endeavors.

- **Encourage autonomy and independence**: Empower mentees to take ownership of their projects and decisions. Encourage autonomy and independence by giving them opportunities to solve problems, make decisions, and take initiative. Provide guidance and support as needed but allow mentees to learn from their experiences and mistakes.

- **Celebrate achievements**: Acknowledge and celebrate the achievements and milestones reached by mentees. Recognize their hard work, progress, and contributions to foster a sense of accomplishment and motivation. Celebrating successes reinforces positive behavior and encourages continued growth and development.

- **Build trust and rapport**: Build trust and rapport with mentees by establishing a supportive and collaborative relationship. Create a safe and open environment where mentees feel comfortable sharing their thoughts, asking questions, and seeking guidance. Show genuine interest in their personal and professional development and invest time and effort in building a strong mentor-mentee relationship.

By honing these mentoring skills, software architects can make a meaningful impact on the growth and development of their mentees, helping them succeed in their careers and contribute effectively to the team and organization.

Presentation skills

We have already covered a lot of areas where architects need to showcase their soft skills in many ways to various stakeholders. The last big area we will focus on is that on presentation skills. Over and above communicating through meetings with various stakeholders, architects also need to be skilled at talking with a large audience and presenting their approaches clearly.

Presentation skills are crucial for software architects to effectively communicate their ideas, proposals, and technical concepts to various stakeholders, including clients, development teams, executives, and other decision-makers.

Here are some key presentation skills for software architects:

- **Clear communication**: Communicate ideas and information clearly and concisely, using simple language and avoiding technical jargon whenever possible. Structure your presentation logically, with a clear introduction, main points, and conclusion.

- **Know your audience**: Tailor your presentation to the needs, interests, and knowledge level of your audience. Consider their background, roles, and priorities, and adjust your content and delivery style accordingly to ensure relevance and engagement.

- **Engaging delivery**: Deliver your presentation in an engaging and dynamic manner to capture and maintain the audience's attention. Use varied vocal tones, gestures, and facial expressions to convey enthusiasm and confidence. Incorporate storytelling, anecdotes, and real-life examples to make your presentation more relatable and memorable.

- **Visual aids**: Use visual aids such as slides, diagrams, charts, and graphics to enhance your presentation and reinforce key points. Keep visual elements simple, uncluttered, and visually appealing, and use them to illustrate complex concepts or data in a clear and understandable way.

- **Practice and rehearse**: Practice your presentation multiple times before delivering it to ensure smooth delivery and confidence. Rehearse your timing, transitions, and key points, and anticipate potential questions or challenges from the audience. Practicing also helps you become more familiar with your material and reduce nervousness.

- **Handle questions effectively**: Be prepared to answer questions from the audience confidently and knowledgeably. Listen carefully to the question, restate it if necessary for clarity, and provide a concise and relevant response. If you are unsure of the answer, don't hesitate to acknowledge it and offer to follow up later.

- **Stay focused and on track**: Stay focused on your main message and objectives throughout the presentation. Avoid going off on tangents or getting sidetracked by irrelevant details. Keep your presentation within the allotted time frame and be respectful of your audience's time.

- **Adaptability**: Be adaptable and flexible during your presentation, responding to audience feedback, questions, and reactions as they arise. Be prepared to adjust your delivery or content on the fly to better meet the needs and interests of your audience.

- **Confidence and poise**: Project confidence and poise throughout your presentation, even if you are feeling nervous. Stand tall, make eye contact with the audience, and speak with conviction and authority. Confidence in your message and delivery will inspire trust and credibility among your audience.

- **Seek feedback and continuous improvement**: After your presentation, seek feedback from audience members or colleagues to identify strengths and areas for improvement. Use this feedback to refine your presentation skills and enhance future presentations. Continuously strive to improve your presentation skills through practice, feedback, and learning from others.

By honing these presentation skills, software architects can effectively convey their ideas, inspire confidence, and influence decision-making among stakeholders, ultimately contributing to the success of software development projects.

Conclusion

As leaders, architects need to focus on developing their soft skills to better communicate with their respective teams and stakeholders and help grow their development teams through mentoring and showcasing strong empathic traits. Along the way, architects need to also master the art of holding meetings and presenting topics as vital cogs in gaining alignment in their technical vision and achieving delivery.

Software is something that requires collaboration from multiple people to build successfully and an architect is an important person in this process. Soft skills can often be the key difference in the success of an architectural approach coming to successful realization and so hopefully the skills mentioned in this chapter can help architects achieve success.

In the next chapter we will look at the importance of writing skills in the communication of technical requirements.

Join our book's Discord space

Join the book's Discord Workspace for Latest updates, Offers, Tech happenings around the world, New Release and Sessions with the Authors:

https://discord.bpbonline.com

## CHAPTER 13

Writing Technical Requirements

Introduction

Now that we have looked at the soft skills an architect needs, we need to look at another oft-overlooked skill that architects need to possess. That of being able to write technical requirements.

In any project, whether it be architectural, software development, or engineering, requirements serve as the blueprint for success. Among these, technical requirements stand out as a crucial subset, defining the specific functionality, performance, and constraints that shape the project's design and implementation.

So, it is important that a software architect knows how to write technical requirements that can convey their architectural vision in a way that best meets the needs of the various stakeholders and provides the development teams with clear implementation details on how to build and test what is required adequately and effectively.

Structure

In this chapter, we will discuss the following topics:

- A revisit to Codeburg
- Technical requirements
- Stakeholder identification and analysis

- Regulatory and compliance requirements
- Performance requirements
- Design constraints for consideration
- Technical standards and guidelines

Objectives

By the end of this chapter, you will understand the different types of requirements that are needed in designing any new application or feature that provides a team with the full perspective of what to build. You will also learn the different process that are required to help refine and enhance the overall requirements and how to communicate them effectively.

A revisit to Codeburg

To explain the importance of technical requirements, let us take a long overdue visit back to Codeburg and a time when it was governed by a king who did not believe in the importance of requirements and how an architect, Alaric came to save the day:

Back in the bustling realm of Codeburg, where lines of code flowed like rivers and algorithms danced in the air, there was a grand castle, Codekeep, where the greatest minds worked together to create powerful software that kept their world running smoothly.

The kingdom was governed by King Syntax and his council of Code Masters. Among them was a wise and meticulous architect named Alaric. Alaric was known for his insistence on technical requirements. He believed that clearly defined requirements were the cornerstone of any successful project.

One day, the council decided to build a new system, the most ambitious project Codeburg had ever seen. It was designed to automate the kingdom's infrastructure, from the simplest tasks of daily life to the grandest functions of the castle. The Code Masters were excited and quickly set to work, eager to demonstrate their skills.

However, in their eagerness, they overlooked a crucial step: they did not establish clear technical requirements. They assumed that their collective expertise would be enough to guide the project. Alaric, seeing the haste, cautioned them, "We must define our requirements before we proceed. Without them, our work may be for naught."

The other Code Masters brushed off his warnings, confident in their abilities. "We have done this countless times," said Master Loop, a renowned developer. "We do not need such formalities."

Weeks turned into months, and the project progressed haphazardly. Modules were developed independently without coordination, leading to compatibility issues. Some features were redundant, while others were missing altogether. The system, meant to bring efficiency, instead brought chaos.

As problems piled up, Codeburg began to suffer. Tasks that were once simple became complicated, and the citizens grew frustrated. The kingdom's productivity plummeted, and murmurs of discontent echoed through the streets.

Seeing the chaos, King Syntax summoned Alaric. "We have made a grave mistake by ignoring your counsel," the king admitted. "Can you help us save Codeburg?"

Alaric nodded, his eyes gleaming with determination. "It is not too late. We must gather all the developers and start from the beginning. We need to define our technical requirements clearly and ensure everyone understands them."

Under Alaric's guidance, a council was convened. They meticulously documented every requirement, ensuring that all modules would work seamlessly together. Alaric stressed the importance of communication and collaboration, urging the developers to work as a cohesive unit.

With clear requirements in place, the developers returned to their workstations. This time, their progress was swift and efficient. Each line of code was written with purpose, and every module fit together like pieces of a puzzle. Alaric oversaw the integration, ensuring that no detail was overlooked.

Finally, the day came when the new system was ready. With bated breath, the citizens of Codeburg watched as King Syntax activated it. The kingdom sprang back to life. Tasks were automated with precision, and the chaos that had plagued the land was replaced with order and efficiency.

Codeburg flourished once more, and the citizens rejoiced. King Syntax declared a grand celebration in honor of Alaric and his insistence on technical requirements. "Let this be a lesson to us all," the king proclaimed. "Clear requirements are the foundation of success. Without them, even the greatest minds can falter."

Alaric humbly accepted the praise, knowing that his dedication to the fundamentals had saved the day. From that moment on, the importance of technical requirements was etched into the very code of Codeburg, ensuring that the kingdom would never again fall into disarray.

Many software projects may initially be driven by a set of business requirements. These will inform the development teams on what needs to be done from a software perspective to ensure a business can achieve its desired outcome through it. The technical requirements of an application, however, will focus more on how the specific business requirements will be achieved.

Technical requirements

Technical requirements explore the intricacies of a project, outlining the technical specifications and parameters that must be met for successful execution. Unlike general requirements, which may focus on broader goals and objectives, technical requirements provide granular details necessary for architects, engineers, and developers to translate concepts into tangible solutions. Whereas the general requirements will focus primarily on what needs to be built, the technical requirements might focus on broader specifics of how it will be achieved.

Differentiating technical requirements from regular functional requirements in the following:

- **Specificity and detail**: Technical requirements are highly detailed and specific, leaving little room for interpretation or ambiguity. They dive into the nitty-gritty aspects of the project, such as performance benchmarks, design constraints, and compatibility criteria.

- **Focus on implementation**: While regular requirements may outline the *what* and *why* of a project, technical requirements delve into the *how*. They guide the implementation process by specifying the technologies, materials, methodologies, and standards to be utilized.

- **Technical language and terminology**: Technical requirements are often laden with technical jargon and specialized terminology relevant to the field or industry. This ensures clarity and precision among stakeholders with the requisite expertise.

The importance of technical requirements is as follows:

- **Alignment with stakeholder expectations**: Technical requirements serve as a bridge between stakeholder expectations and project outcomes. By clearly articulating the technical specifications, they ensure that the final deliverables meet the desired functionality, performance, and quality standards.

- **Mitigation of risks and uncertainties**: Technical requirements help identify and address potential risks and uncertainties early in the project lifecycle. By outlining constraints, dependencies, and compatibility considerations, they minimize the likelihood of costly rework or project delays down the line.

- **Facilitation of collaboration and communication**: In multidisciplinary projects, technical requirements facilitate effective collaboration and communication among diverse teams. They provide a common language and framework for discussing design decisions, trade-offs, and technical challenges.

- **Guidance for design and implementation**: Architects, engineers, and developers rely on technical requirements as guiding principles during the design and implementation phases. They provide a roadmap for making informed decisions, selecting appropriate technologies, and ensuring compliance with industry standards and regulations.

- **Enhancement of project transparency and accountability**: Transparent and well-documented technical requirements foster accountability among project stakeholders. They serve as a reference point for evaluating progress, resolving conflicts, and justifying design choices throughout the project lifecycle.

Technical requirements play a pivotal role in shaping the success of any project, providing the detailed guidance and specifications necessary for translating vision into reality. By meticulously defining the functional, performance, and design criteria, they lay the groundwork for delivering solutions that meet stakeholder needs, mitigate risks, and uphold quality standards.

Stakeholder identification and analysis

Before writing technical requirements, performing stakeholder identification and analysis is crucial to ensure that the resulting specifications align with the needs, preferences, and priorities of all relevant parties involved in the project. While this might seem like the primary responsibility of an analyst or product owner, a software architect should be involved in this process and understand the stakeholders they need to interact with, especially from a technical and business perspective.

To conduct stakeholder identification and analysis effectively, you will need the following information:

- **Project scope and objectives:**

  o Understanding the overarching goals and objectives of the project.

  o Clarifying the scope of work and the intended outcomes.

- **Project team and key participants:**

  o Identifying individuals and groups directly involved in the project.

  o Determining their roles, responsibilities, and areas of expertise.

  o Recognizing both internal team members (e.g., architects, engineers, developers) and external stakeholders (e.g., clients, end-users, regulatory bodies).

- **Stakeholder categories:**

  o Categorizing stakeholders based on their level of influence, interest, or involvement in the project.

  o Differentiating between primary stakeholders (those directly impacted by the project) and secondary stakeholders (those indirectly affected).

- **Stakeholder needs and expectations:**

  o Gathering information on the needs, expectations, and objectives of each stakeholder group.

  o Conducting interviews, surveys, workshops, or focus groups to elicit stakeholder input.

  o Identifying both explicit requirements (stated directly by stakeholders) and implicit requirements (inferred from stakeholder behavior or context).

- **Stakeholder communication preferences:**

  o Understanding how stakeholders prefer to receive and communicate information.

  o Determining their preferred communication channels (e.g., meetings, emails, reports) and frequency of updates.

  o Recognizing any cultural or organizational factors that may influence communication dynamics.

- **Stakeholder influence and power dynamics:**

  o Assessing the level of influence and power that each stakeholder wields within the project context.

  o Identifying key decision-makers, opinion leaders, and potential sources of resistance or support.

- **Stakeholder relationships and dependencies:**

  o Mapping out the interdependencies and relationships between different stakeholder groups.

  o Recognizing potential conflicts of interest, competing priorities, or dependencies that may impact project outcomes.

Regulatory and compliance requirements

In many different industries, there are various regulatory standards that need to be adhered to, and it is important for the architect to be familiar with the various legal or regulatory requirements that may be required for the application to adhere to and ensure these are spelled out clearly in the technical requirements:

- Identifying regulatory bodies, industry standards, and legal frameworks that govern the project.

- Understanding the compliance requirements and constraints imposed by regulatory agencies or governing bodies.

Application or project risks and constraints are as follows:

- Anticipating potential risks, constraints, or challenges associated with stakeholder involvement.

- Assessing the impact of stakeholder dynamics on project timelines, budgets, and resource allocation.

The stakeholder engagement plan is as follows:

- Developing a stakeholder engagement plan outlining strategies for managing stakeholder relationships, communication, and involvement throughout the project lifecycle.

- Defining roles and responsibilities for stakeholder engagement activities and establishing mechanisms for feedback and stakeholder input.

By gathering and analyzing this information, you can gain valuable insights into the diverse perspectives, interests, and priorities of stakeholders, which will inform the development of technical requirements that are well-aligned with the needs of all parties involved in the project.

Considerations for technical requirements

Once the needs of the application are understood, we are ready to write the requirements for it. As mentioned, functional requirements may be written by an analyst within the different development teams. It is still important for an architect to understand the importance of this, as they will need to shape the technical specifications and requirements against the backdrop of these business needs. Ensuring the technical design can best meet these business requirements.

To write requirements from a technical perspective as architects, you need a comprehensive understanding of the project scope, objectives, and constraints. Here is a detailed list of the information and steps required:

- **Project scope and objectives:**

    o **Define scope**: Clearly outline what the project will entail, including the boundaries and deliverables of the final application and each individual software model.

    o **Set objectives**: Understand the goals and objectives of the project to ensure the functional and technical requirements align with the overall vision.

- **User personas and use cases:**

    o **User personas**: Create detailed profiles of the different types of users who will interact with the software architecture. This can include the users and service providers that will use the software, but also the technical team that needs to support and maintain the application.

    o **Use cases**: Develop scenarios that describe how different personas will interact with the software to achieve specific outcomes. This is different from traditional persona design, as we are not just looking for how the user will engage a system from a usability perspective, but a technical one.

Understanding all the different services they will be interacting with to perform a given action, along with the specific data needs.

- **Regulatory and compliance requirements:**

  o **Industry regulations**: Ensure compliance with the requirements of the specific industry your software falls under. For instance, applications in the banking, payments, or legal spheres need to adhere to certain strict compliance criteria, and as an architect, it is important that you understand these, especially when strict data and security needs have to be considered for the final solution.

  o **Regional regulations**: Different regions or countries globally may have different rules regarding data privacy and security. So these needs have to be factored into the technical requirements of the application.

  o **Industry standards:** Outside of just pure regulatory requirements, architects should also be familiar with specific standards in the industry, especially around accessibility or governance best practices.

  o **Sustainability requirements:** A growing trend in software development is the nature of sustainability, where we design software that is not just functional, but sustainable to operate both from an environmental and financial perspective.

- **Architectural considerations:**

  o **Architecture design compliance**: Overall design of the system, including choice between monolithic, microservices, serverless, or hybrid architectures. All different requirements introduced need to adhere to these chosen patterns and only deviate when it makes architectural sense to do so.

  o **Scalability needs**: Strategies for scaling the system (horizontal vs. vertical scaling, load balancing) to achieve the required operation across expected global usage patterns.

  o **Redundancy and fault tolerance**: Methods to ensure system reliability, such as redundant components and failover mechanisms, need to form part of the software delivered across each team and service.

Performance requirements

Importantly, when addressing the technical requirements of how software should be built, it is important to consider things outside of the immediate functional requirements and also focus on what other performance and security-related requirements need to be addressed. It is also important to provide the relevant details on how these will be archived by the design.

We have already spoken about some specific non-functional requirements in *Chapter 8, Architecting for Performance*, and *Chapter 9, Architecting for Security*, so we will not go into detail here about how they work and just highlight the key measures that need to be considered in the requirements:

- **Response time**: Maximum acceptable response time for various operations.

- **Throughput**: Number of transactions the system must handle per unit of time.

- **Latency**: Acceptable delays in data processing and communication.

- **Concurrency**: Number of simultaneous users or processes the system must support.

Security requirements are as follows:

- **Authentication and authorization**: Methods for verifying user identity and permissions.

- **Data encryption**: Encryption standards for data at rest and in transit.

- **Vulnerability management**: Procedures for identifying, reporting, and mitigating vulnerabilities.

- **Compliance**: Adherence to regulations like GDPR, HIPAA, or PCI-DSS.

Data requirements are listed below:

- **Data models**: Structure and organization of data (relational, NoSQL, graph databases).

- **Data integrity**: Ensuring accuracy and consistency of data through constraints and validation.

- **Data retention and archiving**: Policies for data storage duration and archival methods.

- **Data migration**: Strategies for moving data between systems or formats.

Integration and interoperability

When breaking down requirements into executable stories, it is important to detail how these individual software services will interact with the greater system. It consists of the following:

- **APIs**: Specifications for application programming interfaces, including RESTful or GraphQL APIs.

- **Inter-system communication**: Methods for data exchange between different systems (e.g., SOAP, JSON, XML).

- **Middleware**: Use of middleware solutions for integrating disparate systems.

User interface and user experience

UI and UX depend upon the following factors:

- **UI/UX design**: Design guidelines for user interfaces, focusing on usability and accessibility.

- **Responsive design**: Ensuring interfaces work across different devices and screen sizes.

- **Accessibility**: Compliance with accessibility standards (e.g., WCAG).

Development and deployment

An important aspect of software delivery and the technical requirements includes the process of deployment and how teams will need to deploy and rollback the software. Some of this might be managed by existing processes or tools, but where possible, architects need to ensure all requirements worked on align with certain standards as follows:

- **Development frameworks**: Choice of frameworks and libraries for development.

- **Version control**: Use of version control systems, like Git, and branching strategies.

- **CI/CD pipelines**: Continuous integration and continuous deployment processes.

- **Environment management**: Management of development, testing, staging, and production environments.

Testing

Technical requirements should also consider the important testing criteria that should be covered for each module of work. We will uncover testing in more detail in *Chapter 16, Testing in Software Architecture*.

In general, though, the technical requirements should cover the following:

- **Testing types**: Unit, integration, system, and acceptance testing requirements.

- **Test coverage**: Percentage of code that must be covered by tests.

- **Automated testing**: Use of automated testing tools and frameworks.

- **Performance testing**: Load testing, stress testing, and endurance testing specifications.

Documentation and support

While not part of the system design or build, the documentation to support the application, how it is used and maintained, should be clear. The architect, along with the product experts and professional technical writers in the team, should play a large role in ensuring the appropriate and correct information is provided in the following:

- **Technical documentation**: Requirements for technical documentation, including system architecture, APIs, and deployment guides.

- **User documentation**: Manuals, help files, and online help systems for end-users.

- **Support and maintenance**: Policies for system support, including bug fixes, updates, and maintenance schedules.

Project management

Effective project management is crucial for delivering this project on time and within budget. We will utilize the following project management strategies and tools:

- **Timeline and milestones**: Key project phases, deadlines, and deliverables.

- **Resource allocation**: Allocation of development resources, including team roles and responsibilities.

- **Risk management**: Identification and mitigation of project risks.

- **Quality metrics**: Metrics for assessing the quality of the software, such as defect density and mean time to failure.

Design constraints for consideration

When writing technical requirements for a software engineering project, it is essential to consider various design constraints that can impact the feasibility, performance, and overall success of the project.

Design constraints are limitations or restrictions that the system must operate within, and they can come from different sources, such as technical, business, regulatory, and operational requirements. They differ from the previous section on design considerations in that they represent things that may restrict certain technical choices rather than prescribing a specific approach.

These constraints, while already known at an architectural level, should also be documented clearly to shape the direction of all technical work. The technical requirements should already factor these areas in when defining how work needs to get done, but teams should understand the specifics of these constraints to better understand the decision-making and limitations in which they operate and prioritize accordingly.

Technical constraints

Here are the key technical constraints to consider:

- **Technology stack**:

  - **Predefined technologies**: Limitations on programming languages, frameworks, libraries, databases, and other technologies that must be used.

  - **Legacy systems**: Need to integrate with or maintain compatibility with existing legacy systems and software.

  - **Platform requirements**: Constraints related to operating systems, hardware platforms, or cloud providers.

- **Performance constraints**:

  - **Processing speed**: Minimum processing speed or maximum latency requirements.

  - **Memory usage**: Restrictions on memory usage or memory footprint.

  - **Network bandwidth**: Limitations on network bandwidth or data transfer rates.

Business constraints

The business constraints are as follows:

- **Budget**:

  - **Development costs**: Constraints on the budget allocated for development, testing, and deployment.

  - **Operational costs**: Limitations on ongoing operational costs, including hosting, maintenance, and support.

- **Time**:

  - **Project timeline**: Fixed deadlines or timeframes for project milestones and final delivery.

  - **Time-to-market**: Urgency to release the product or features to the market.

- **Resource availability**:

  - **Team skills**: Availability of team members with specific skills and expertise.

  - **External dependencies**: Dependence on third-party services, vendors, or contractors.

Operational constraints

Here are the operational constraints to consider:

- **Deployment environment**:

    - **Infrastructure**: Constraints related to the infrastructure where the software will be deployed (on-premises, cloud, hybrid).

    - **Compatibility**: Requirements for compatibility with existing systems, software, and hardware.

- **Maintenance and support**:

    - **Maintenance windows**: Constraints on when maintenance activities can be performed.

    - **Support levels**: Required levels of support, including response times and resolution times.

User and UX constraints

Consider the following user and UX constraints:

- **User accessibility**:

    - **Accessibility standards**: Compliance with accessibility standards such as WCAG.

    - **Localization**: Requirements for supporting multiple languages and regional settings.

- **User interaction**:

    - **User interface design**: Constraints on UI design based on branding guidelines or user preferences.

    - **Usability**: Requirements for ease of use, intuitive navigation, and user satisfaction.

Environmental constraints

Architects must take into consideration some environmental constraints, such as:

- **Physical environment**:

    - **Operating conditions**: Constraints related to the physical environment where the software will operate (e.g., temperature, humidity). This is especially true of embedded software that runs on hardware that may operate under very specific conditions.

    - **Device constraints**: Requirements related to device capabilities if the software is to run on mobile or embedded devices.

- **Sustainability**:

  - o **Energy efficiency**: Constraints related to energy consumption and sustainability goals.

Interoperability constraints

Integration with other systems:

- **APIs**: Limitations on how the system can integrate with external APIs or services.

- **Data exchange**: Requirements for data formats, protocols, and standards for data exchange.

By carefully considering these design constraints, architects can ensure that the technical requirements are realistic, achievable, and aligned with the broader context in which the software will operate. This helps in avoiding potential issues during development and deployment, ensuring a smoother project lifecycle and a more successful outcome.

Technical standards and guidelines

We have spent most of this chapter understanding what a technical requirement is, why we need them, and the different things that need to be considered that will form part of your technical requirements. They still need to be written, so we will unpack the different things that should be considered as part of your technical requirements that should live with your software.

Writing technical standards and guidelines for software involves establishing a comprehensive set of rules, best practices, and conventions that guide the development, maintenance, and usage of the software. These standards ensure consistency, quality, and efficiency throughout the software development lifecycle.

It is important to note that, in many modern development approaches, software requirements can be written in the form of user stories. This works well in establishing what needs to be built, but the how that these technical requirements need to cover means that these will likely sit in a document, internal communication platform, or often within the code repositories themselves, where they can be easily referenced and very controlled by the engineering teams.

Here is a structured approach to writing technical standards and guidelines for software:

- **Define the purpose and scope**

  - o **Purpose**: Clearly state the purpose of the specifications, explaining why these standards and guidelines are necessary.

  - o **Scope**: Define the scope, specifying which projects, teams, and technologies the standards apply to.

- **Establish core principles**

  o **Consistency**: Emphasize the importance of consistent coding practices and design patterns.

  o **Quality**: Highlight the need for high-quality code, including readability, maintainability, and performance.

  o **Security**: Stress the importance of secure coding practices to protect against vulnerabilities.

- **Outline the development process**

  o **Development lifecycle**: Describe the stages of the **software development lifecycle (SDLC)** that the standards cover, such as requirements gathering, design, coding, testing, deployment, and maintenance.

  o **Development practices**: If applicable, incorporate agile or other SDLC methodologies, specifying guidelines for sprints, backlogs, and iterative development.

- **Coding standards**

  o **Language-specific guidelines**: Provide detailed guidelines for each programming language used, covering syntax, conventions, and best practices.

  o **Naming conventions**: Standardize naming conventions for variables, functions, classes, and files.

  o **Code formatting**: Set rules for indentation, line length, and spacing to ensure uniform code appearance.

  o **Comments and documentation**: Establish guidelines for commenting code and writing documentation, including what information to include and how to format it.

- **Design and architecture**

  o **Design patterns**: Recommend common design patterns and principles (e.g., SOLID principles, MVC architecture).

  o **Modularity and reusability**: Encourage modular design and code reuse to enhance maintainability and reduce redundancy.

  o **Scalability and performance**: Provide guidelines for designing scalable and high-performance systems, including load balancing and caching strategies.

- **Security standards**

  o **Authentication and authorization**: Define standards for implementing authentication and authorization mechanisms.

- o **Data protection**: Establish guidelines for data encryption, secure storage, and handling sensitive information.

- o **Vulnerability management**: Provide practices for identifying, reporting, and mitigating security vulnerabilities.

- **Testing and quality assurance**

  - o **Testing strategies**: Outline strategies for unit testing, integration testing, system testing, and acceptance testing.

  - o **Automated testing**: Recommend tools and frameworks for automated testing and continuous integration.

  - o **Code reviews**: Define the process for code reviews, including criteria for approval and feedback mechanisms.

- **Version control and configuration management**

  - o **Version control systems**: Specify the use of version control systems (e.g., Git), including branching strategies and commit conventions.

  - o **Configuration management**: Provide guidelines for managing configurations, including environment-specific settings and secrets management.

- **Documentation standards**

  - o **Technical documentation**: Detail requirements for technical documentation, including system architecture, APIs, and deployment guides.

  - o **User documentation**: Establish guidelines for user manuals, help files, and online help systems.

- **Deployment and maintenance**

  - o **Deployment practices**: Standardize deployment processes, including continuous delivery pipelines and rollback procedures.

  - o **Maintenance and support**: Provide guidelines for system maintenance, including patch management and incident response.

- **Compliance and regulatory requirements**

  - o **Legal compliance**: Ensure adherence to relevant legal and regulatory requirements, such as data protection laws and industry standards.

  - o **Audit and monitoring**: Define practices for auditing and monitoring compliance with these standards and guidelines.

- **Continuous improvement**

  - o **Feedback mechanisms**: Establish mechanisms for gathering feedback on the standards and guidelines from the development team.

  o **Regular updates**: Plan for regular review and updates of the standards to incorporate new best practices, technologies, and lessons learned.

Requirements maintenance

The technical requirements have now been written. However, much like the underlying code of the software, it needs to be regularly maintained, and so these next few steps will help us understand how to go about putting processes in place to ensure the technical requirements are correctly maintained.

Maintaining documentation is critical for ensuring that it remains accurate, up-to-date, and useful throughout the software lifecycle. The following sub-sections discuss some tips for effective documentation maintenance.

Establish ownership and responsibility

While architects are documenting the overall software design and the technical requirements around how it should be delivered, they are not alone in creating and maintaining the requirements. So certain rules can be put in place to ensure the requirements are continuously updated as follows:

- **Assign roles**: Designate specific team members or roles responsible for maintaining different parts of the documentation.

- **Documentation leads**: Appoint documentation leads or managers to oversee the entire documentation process.

Implement version control

Like code, the technical requirements should be properly version controlled, with the version of the requirements also changing as they get updated for full traceability of code changes made to specific versions of the requirements. This is implemented as follows:

- **Version control systems**: Use version control systems (e.g., Git) to manage documentation changes, ensuring that all updates are tracked.

- **Branching strategies**: Utilize branching strategies for major updates or changes to documentation, similar to how you manage code.

Schedule regular reviews and updates

It is easy to update and change our requirements when working on specific changes that relate to them. However, we also need to periodically review our technical specifications and ensure they remain relevant in the following manner:

- **Periodic reviews**: Schedule regular intervals (e.g., quarterly or bi-annually) for reviewing and updating your technical documentation and requirements.

- **Review meetings**: Hold review meetings with relevant stakeholders to gather input and feedback on the requirements when clarity needs to be sought on a specific approach.

Automate wherever possible

Requirements writing does not need to be a manual admin task, and certain things can be automated to make it quicker for the teams, such as:

- **Automated checks**: Use tools to automate checks for broken links, outdated information, and compliance with documentation standards.

- **Continuous integration**: Integrate documentation updates into the CI/CD pipeline to ensure they are deployed alongside software changes.

Foster a culture of documentation and requirements

Documenting the technical requirements of an application is often not something that comes natural to development teams who want to focus on the coding and building aspect. So, creating a culture that understands the importance of clear requirements and collaboration in keeping them relevant is helpful in making teams successfully adopt and maintain them as follows:

- **Encourage contributions**: Encourage all team members to contribute to documentation, emphasizing its importance.

- **Recognition and rewards**: Recognize and reward team members who consistently contribute to and maintain documentation.

Use clear and consistent formatting

If your technical requirements are not well structured and horrible to read, it is unlikely they will be read and adhered to. So, put some effort into ensuring certain standards are in place for the requirements.

The following are some things that can help with this:

- **Templates and style guides**: Develop and use templates and style guides to ensure consistency in documentation.

- **Standardization**: Standardize terminology, abbreviations, and formatting across all documentation.

- **Numbering**: Much like your requirements are version controlled, having a clear numbering system that aligns to specific sections helps make things easier to find, updated and adopt. This makes it more traceable when linking requirements to different parts of the code and development process and where it applies.

Ensure accessibility and ease of use

Utilize proper documentation tooling to help make requirements easy to find and meet certain accessibility requirements for all. Include the following:

- **Search functionality**: Implement robust search functionality to help users find the information they need quickly.

- **User-friendly formats**: Use formats and platforms that are easily accessible and user-friendly (e.g., Markdown, HTML).

Link requirements to code

Traceability is critical in understanding the impact specific requirements may have on future code changes, and so having a mechanism where this can be easily seen helps in prioritizing work when technical requirements need to be updated or refined. It can be achieved through:

- **Inline documentation**: Include comments and documentation directly in the code where applicable.

- **Documentation generators**: Use tools like Javadoc, Sphinx, or Doxygen to generate documentation from annotated code automatically.

Solicit feedback and improve

Your technical requirement would not always be comprehensive, and there may be things that need to be refined, improved, or added along the way. Creating a way where this information can flow to the relevant stakeholders and owners to make these changes is vital and can be done through:

- **Feedback mechanisms**: Provide easy ways for users to give feedback on the requirements (e.g., feedback forms, comments) and where certain technical principles need to be reviewed or updated.

- **Iterative improvements**: This helps others to perhaps identify when things are unclear or perhaps obsolete and allows them to be reviewed and updated accordingly.

Archive obsolete requirements

Technical requirements evolve as technology and processes progress, and that means that obsolete requirements need to be properly archived to prevent teams from accidentally following the incorrect standards. Archiving can be done as follows:

- **Version archiving**: Archive old versions of requirements that are no longer relevant but may be needed for historical reference.

- **Deprecation notices**: Clearly mark deprecated or obsolete documentation with notices to prevent confusion.

Integrate with project management tools

There are many tools out there that can help track technical requirements and assist in keeping everything up to date. Some tools are as follows:

- **Documentation tasks**: Track documentation tasks and updates in project management tools like Jira or Trello.

- **Link to requirements**: Link the technical requirements to specific project requirements, tasks, or user stories.

Provide training and resources

Documentation is vital, but do not rely on that alone. Put together additional measures that can add to the implementation of them, that can improve adoption, and help with keeping them relevant:

- **Training sessions**: Conduct regular training sessions on how to write, update, and maintain documentation.

- **Guides and tutorials**: Provide guides, tutorials, and best practice documents for creating and maintaining documentation.

Conclusion

We can put forward the best architectural designs and principles, but if it is not properly documented in a way that provides the right understanding to the development teams, they may not be implemented correctly, and we will not be able to empower them to success.

Documentation may not be the most fun thing that architects do, but it is an important step to get right. The good news is that architects should not need to do this on their own and should leverage skills across the teams to ensure these technical requirements are properly created and maintained across an organization or set of teams.

Do not underestimate the importance that a detailed set of technical requirements will have on a software team in bringing the technical vision to life.

In the next chapter, we look at how different Agile, DevOps, and CI/CD methodologies influence architectural decisions and provide strategies for architects to thrive in this dynamic environment.

CHAPTER 14
Development Practices

Introduction

As we have already explored, software architecture is not just about designing software systems that solve specific needs and requirements, but also about working with the teams that deliver them and aligning the development practices in a way that allows the teams to work on the software effectively.

So, it makes perfect sense to devote a chapter to development practices and, more importantly, the role that architects should play in them. In this chapter, we will look at the value architects bring into the entire development process and common development practices that architects should be familiar with.

Structure

In this chapter, we will discuss the following topics:

- Getting involved early in the design process
- CI/CD process for reliable software delivery
- Ensuring testability in the process
- Determining when software is ready for release
- Monitoring the software for improved delivery

Objectives

By the end of this chapter, you will understand the different development practices that exist, why it is important for an architect to get involved in them as early as possible, and the impact different development, DevOps, and testing practices have on both the architectural design and implementation strategies of a specific solution.

Getting involved early in the design process

Critically, software architects, as key stakeholders of the overall technical vision, should be involved in the software delivery process from very early on in the inception. They should not just be involved in putting together the design but also in implementing the structure of teams and ways of working.

The following are some of the key benefits that architects bring to the development process when introduced early on:

- **Strategic alignment and vision**:

  o **Consistency with business goals**: Software architects ensure that the software design aligns with the overall business objectives and strategies. Their early involvement helps translate business requirements into technical requirements, ensuring that the final product meets stakeholder expectations.

  o **Long-term vision**: Architects have a long-term perspective on the project, considering not just the immediate needs but also future scalability, maintainability, and integration with other systems.

- **Quality and robustness**:

  o **Technical excellence**: Software architects bring a deep understanding of design patterns, best practices, and emerging technologies, which helps in creating a robust, high-quality architecture.

  o **Risk mitigation**: Early involvement allows architects to identify and address potential risks, such as performance bottlenecks, security vulnerabilities, and architectural flaws, before they become costly issues.

- **Efficient resource utilization**:

  o **Optimal design**: By understanding the full scope of the project early on, architects can design systems that make efficient use of resources, avoiding unnecessary complexity and redundancy.

  o **Cost management**: Early architectural decisions can significantly influence the overall cost of the project. Good architectural choices can reduce development time and minimize the need for costly redesigns later.

- **Improved collaboration and communication**:
  - ○ **Cross-functional integration**: Architects facilitate better communication between different teams (e.g., development, operations, quality assurance), ensuring that everyone is on the same page and working towards the same goals.

  - ○ **Clear guidance**: They provide clear guidelines and architectural blueprints that help developers understand the project's direction and constraints, reducing misunderstandings and rework.

- **Foundation for agile development**:
  - ○ **Adaptability**: Even in agile environments, having a solid architectural foundation is essential. Architects ensure that the system can adapt to changing requirements and technologies over time without significant disruptions.

  - ○ **Iterative improvement**: Early architectural involvement allows for iterative refinement, where feedback from initial development cycles can be incorporated into the architecture, leading to continuous improvement.

- **Enhanced decision making**:
  - ○ **Informed decisions**: Architects bring a wealth of experience and technical knowledge, enabling them to make informed decisions about technology stacks, frameworks, and tools that best fit the project's needs.

  - ○ **Trade-off analysis**: Architects are best placed to evaluate trade-offs between different architectural options, balancing factors like performance, security, cost, and time-to-market in order to provide the best business value.

Involving software architects early in the design process ensures that the software system is well-aligned with business goals, technically sound, cost-effective, and capable of adapting to future needs. Their expertise in making strategic decisions, mitigating risks, and fostering effective communication significantly contributes to the overall success of the project.

Aligning development practices to design techniques

Getting software architects involved in the development process is also important because it facilitates the alignment of development practices to the overall design of the software.

As the design of the software affects how it can be deployed, secured, tested, the tooling to be used, and the skillset across the full-stack of technologies required, it is vital that architects help in ensuring a team's process and software delivery can support the required development techniques.

Aligning development practices with design techniques is crucial for ensuring that the software architecture is implemented effectively and that the final product meets its intended goals.

The following are important strategies that can help to bring this alignment between the architectural design to the development practices adopted by a team:

- **Coding standards**: Establish coding standards that align with the architectural vision. This ensures consistency across the development team and adherence to architectural principles.

- **Cross-functional teams**: Promote collaboration between architects, developers, testers, and operations. Regular meetings and workshops can help align the team's understanding of the architecture.

- **Regular reviews and feedback**: Conduct regular code and design reviews to ensure that the development practices adhere to the architectural guidelines. These reviews help catch deviations early and provide a platform for feedback. Architects should also make use of agile practices like sprint planning, daily stand-ups, and retrospectives to keep the development team aligned with the architectural goals. An iterative approach allows for continuous alignment and adaptation of the software in meeting these architectural designs, or oftentimes a revaluation of the architecture as fit for purpose, far earlier in the design process.

- **CI/CD pipeline checks**: Set up **continuous integration/continuous deployment (CI/CD)** pipelines to check certain architectural and testing requirements. This ensures that the software is always in a releasable state and adheres to the architectural standards.

- **Monitoring and metrics**: Use monitoring tools to gather metrics on system performance, reliability, and scalability. Analyze this data to ensure that the architecture meets its **non-functional requirements** (**NFRs**) and to make informed decisions about future enhancements.

- **Knowledge sharing**: Encourage knowledge sharing through documentation, wikis, and internal presentations. This ensures that everyone on the team understands the architectural decisions and their rationale.

- **Prototyping**: Use prototyping to validate architectural decisions early in the development process. This helps in identifying potential issues and aligning the development practices before full-scale implementation.

- **Architectural governance**: Establish an architectural governance framework to oversee the adherence to architectural principles and guidelines. This includes defining roles and responsibilities for architects and setting up governance bodies like architecture review boards.

By implementing these strategies, software architects can ensure that development practices are well-aligned with design techniques, leading to a cohesive, maintainable, and high-quality software system.

Structuring teams for better delivery

Often, companies can structure teams in an ad-hoc manner based on team capabilities or business functionality. However, if these do not align with the overall makeup of the software architecture, it will result in inefficient delivery and likely quality issues.

This is because teams may end up working across multiple connected features and modules to achieve their respective outcomes, which may not allow for seamless and independent delivery. So, to achieve this and increase the delivery time on a software project, it is important to align teams to the way the services are structured and can be best tested, maintained, and deployed.

Structuring teams effectively is crucial for optimizing delivery in software development. The right team structure enhances communication, collaboration, efficiency, and quality of the final product. There is no best option of team structure for delivery, so it is important that architects understand the different team constructs to better know which type of teams can best support their intended design.

Here are several strategies for structuring teams to achieve better delivery:

- **Cross-functional teams**
    - Cross-functional teams include members with diverse skills and expertise, such as developers, testers, designers, product managers, and operations personnel.
    - **Benefits**: This structure promotes collaboration and reduces dependencies between teams, leading to faster decision-making and delivery.

- **Feature teams**
    - Feature teams are organized around specific features or functionalities of the product. Each team is responsible for the end-to-end delivery of a particular feature.
    - **Benefits**: This approach ensures that teams have a clear focus and ownership, which can lead to higher motivation and better quality. It also allows for parallel development, speeding up the delivery process.

- **Component teams**
    - Component teams focus on specific components or subsystems of the architecture, such as the database, backend services, or user interface.

- o **Benefits**: This structure leverages specialized expertise and ensures that each component is built with high-quality. However, it may require strong coordination to integrate components effectively.

- **DevOps teams**

  - o DevOps teams integrate development and operations roles to ensure CI/CD and efficient deployment.

  - o **Benefits**: This structure promotes automation, improves collaboration between development and operations, and enhances the speed and reliability of releases.

- **Agile teams**

  - o Agile teams are small, self-organizing groups that follow Agile methodologies like Scrum or Kanban. They include roles such as Scrum Master, Product Owner, and development team members.

  - o **Benefits**: Agile teams are adaptable, focused on delivering incremental value, and capable of quickly responding to changes. This structure supports iterative development and continuous improvement.

- **Matrix teams**

  - o Matrix teams combine functional and project-based structures. Team members report to both a functional manager and a project manager.

  - o **Benefits**: This structure provides flexibility and resource optimization, allowing for effective use of specialized skills across multiple projects. However, it requires strong communication and conflict resolution mechanisms.

- **Tribe and squad model**

  - o This model involves organizing teams into tribes (larger units) and squads (small, cross-functional teams within tribes). Squads are autonomous and work on specific features or components. Tribes are collections of squads working towards a common goal.

  - o **Benefits**: The model promotes autonomy, alignment, and scaling. It also fosters innovation and a strong sense of ownership among team members.

- **Centers of Excellence/Enablement (CoEs)**

  - o These are specialized teams or groups focused on particular areas of expertise, such as security, performance, or user experience. They provide guidance, best practices, and support to other teams.

  - o **Benefits**: CoEs ensure that critical areas are addressed with a high level of expertise, improving the overall quality and consistency of the product.

As can be seen, there are many different models that should be explored by architects in helping companies to structure their development teams. Often, the decision on which approach to take can be easily identifiable based on the nature of the design itself, but often, as most different software services may follow a variety of different patterns and skillsets, there is no ideal model to follow.

Therefore, it is often best for companies to experiment with different approaches to find out what model works best for them and even once a recipe is decided upon, that does not mean it cannot change over time as companies grow and evolve, software is updated with new features or different systems become outdated and require an introduction of newer technologies and architectures that will require a different team structure.

So, along with understanding these different team constructs, it is also important for architects to understand some different approaches that will help in implementing and evaluating the right team structures in an organization.

Implementing effective team structures

Knowing the different team structures that can be used is helpful, but with often no clear best approach, it is often less about choosing the right team structure in an organization, but allowing for a myriad of hybrid approaches to be used.

What is then often more important is instead providing the right mechanisms for these structures to function effectively, regardless of the chosen structure:

- **Clear roles and responsibilities**:
  - **Define roles**: Clearly define roles and responsibilities for each team member. This avoids confusion and ensures accountability.
  - **Role flexibility**: Encourage role flexibility where team members can take on multiple roles based on project needs.
- **Strong leadership and coordination**:
  - **Leadership roles**: Assign strong leaders such as Scrum Masters, Product Owners, or technical leads to guide and coordinate the teams.
  - **Coordination mechanisms**: Implement coordination mechanisms such as regular stand-ups, sync meetings, and integration reviews to ensure alignment and communication.
- **Effective communication channels**:
  - **Collaboration tools**: Use collaboration tools like Slack, Microsoft Teams, or Jira to facilitate communication and project management.
  - **Regular updates**: Schedule regular updates and check-ins to keep everyone informed about progress, challenges, and changes.

- **Empowerment and autonomy**:

  o **Decision-making power**: Empower teams to make decisions within their scope. This promotes ownership and accountability.

  o **Autonomous teams**: Allow teams to self-organize and manage their workflows. This increases efficiency and adaptability.

- **Continuous learning and improvement**:

  o **Training and development**: Provide ongoing training and development opportunities to enhance skills and knowledge.

  o **Retrospectives**: Conduct regular retrospectives to identify areas for improvement and implement changes.

- **Scalability and flexibility**:

  o **Scalable structures**: Design team structures that can scale as the project grows. This includes having the flexibility to add or reconfigure teams as needed.

  o **Adaptability**: Be prepared to adapt team structures based on project requirements, feedback, and evolving business goals.

By carefully selecting and implementing the right team structures, architects can help organizations enhance collaboration, streamline processes, and ultimately deliver high-quality software more efficiently.

There is no perfect team structure, and often, different designs may be preferred for different teams and supporting different architectures. Most companies, though, will often prefer one approach rolled out across the organization, and this makes it significantly easier to track team delivery consistently and also to scale future teams.

The most critical aspect is consistently measuring the success of different models, and in companies being agile enough to make the necessary changes when inefficiencies are identified.

Assess the effectiveness of software delivery teams

While we have already mentioned the importance of self-organizing and empowered teams earlier in this chapter, that does not mean teams will always operate in an optimal manner, which is why it is important to utilize various measures and metrics to help teams understand how they are actual performing as a team and for a software architect to play a role in helping teams improve on their delivery. This can be done either by evolving the team structure or making design tweaks that resolve identified bottlenecks.

The following is a list of metrics that can be utilized to help identify the effectiveness of the different delivery teams:

- **Productivity and throughput**:

  o **Velocity**: Measure the number of story points or tasks completed in a sprint. Consistent velocity indicates stable performance.

  o **Cycle time**: Assess the time taken to complete a task from start to finish. Shorter cycle times usually mean higher efficiency.

  o **Lead time**: Measure the total time from task creation to completion. This includes waiting times and active work periods.

- **Quality**:

  o **Code quality**: Use metrics like code churn, code complexity, and adherence to coding standards. Automated tools can help analyze these aspects.

  o **Defect rates**: Track the number of bugs found in production versus those caught in development and testing stages.

  o **Automated testing**: Evaluate the coverage and effectiveness of unit tests, integration tests, and end-to-end tests.

- **Collaboration and communication**:

  o **Team dynamics**: Observe interactions during meetings, code reviews, and daily stand-ups. Healthy communication and collaboration are crucial.

  o **User feedback**: Gather feedback from end-users and stakeholders about the product's performance and usability.

  o **Feature delivery**: Track the timeliness and quality of delivered features. Ensure they meet or exceed user expectations.

- **Team morale and well-being**:

  o **Burnout rates**: Monitor for signs of burnout and overwork. High stress levels can negatively impact productivity and quality, but also be a sign that a team is not working effectively, and something needs to change.

  o **Job satisfaction**: Conduct regular surveys to gauge team members' satisfaction with their roles, responsibilities, and work environment.

- **Innovation and improvement**:

  o **Learning and development**: Ensure the team is continually improving their skills through training, workshops, and conferences.

  o **Retrospectives and action items**: Check if retrospectives lead to actionable improvements and if those actions are implemented effectively.

- **Technical debt**:
  - ○ **Management of technical debt**: Assess how well the team identifies, tracks, and addresses technical debt. Ignoring technical debt can slow down development and increase defects over time.

Metrics and indicators to help drive improvement

There is a lot to measure, but when things start to regress, it at least provides teams with measurable areas that can be improved. Rather than enforce change through directives, to keep the teams empowered, it is better to drive that change through the use of **key performance indicators** (**KPIs**) or scorecards that can help teams aim for a better improvement in these different measures:

- **KPIs**: Use **key performance indicators** (**KPIs**) tailored to your team's goals and the nature of your projects.

- **Balanced scorecard**: Employ a balanced scorecard approach to measure performance from multiple perspectives (financial, customer, internal processes, learning, and growth).

By regularly assessing these areas and using both qualitative and quantitative data, you can get a comprehensive understanding of whether your software development team is operating optimally. Continuous monitoring and adaptation are key to maintaining and improving team performance.

CI/CD process for reliable software delivery

One aspect of software delivery that is important is the nature of a CI/CD pipeline. As a development practice, regardless of any team structure or architectural design, it is an important way of ensuring that software can be delivered and deployed in an incremental and quicker way.

CI is a modern software development practice in which incremental code changes are made frequently and reliably. Automated build-and-test steps triggered by a CI process ensure that code changes being merged into the repository meet the relevant quality criteria. This code is then deployed as a part of a CD process which ensures that code is deployed in a safe and secure manner to the required environment. In the software world, the CI/CD pipeline refers to the automation that enables incremental code changes from development through to deployment into production.

CI/CD facilitates an effective process for getting products to market faster, continuously delivering code into production, and ensuring an ongoing flow of new features and bug fixes via the most efficient delivery method.

As a software architect, it is vital that teams institute a mechanism like this to ensure reliable delivery of the software and that you understand how a CI/CD pipeline should be built.

Setup version control system

Let us look at the process of setting up the **version control system (VCS)**:

- **Choose a VCS**: Use a distributed VCS like Git.

- **Repository setup**: Create a repository for your project, ensuring proper branching strategies (e.g., GitFlow, GitHub Flow).

- **Frequent commits**: Encourage developers to commit code frequently to reduce integration problems.

- **Merge requests and code reviews**: Implement a robust code review process to catch issues early. Use tools like GitHub pull requests or GitLab merge requests.

- **Artifact storage**: Use artifact repositories like JFrog Artifactory or Nexus to store build artifacts.

Automate builds

Let us look at the process of automating builds:

- **Build server**: Setup a CI server like Jenkins, CircleCI, Azure DevOps Build Agents or GitHub Actions.

- **Automated build scripts**: Write scripts to automate the build process. These should include compilation, dependency resolution, and packaging.

- **Build triggers**: Configure the CI server to trigger builds automatically on code commits, pull requests, or scheduled intervals.

Automate testing

Let us look at the process of automating testing:

- **Unit tests**: Write unit tests to verify individual components. Use frameworks like JUnit, NUnit, or Mocha.

- **Integration tests**: Develop integration tests to ensure components work together. Tools like Postman, REST Assured, or Selenium can be used.

- **Test automation**: Configure the CI server to run automated tests after each build. Ensure test results are reported, and any failures are flagged.

Static code analysis

Let us look at the process of static code analysis:

- **Code quality tools**: Integrate static code analysis tools like SonarQube, ESLint, or Checkstyle to enforce coding standards and detect issues early.

- **Automated checks**: Configure these tools to run automatically during the build process and provide feedback on code quality.

Continuous deployment setup

Let us look at the process of CD setup:

- **Deployment automation**: Write scripts to automate the deployment process. Use tools like Ansible, Terraform, or Kubernetes.

- **Environment configuration**: Ensure that deployment scripts handle environment-specific configurations. Use environment variables or configuration files.

- **Blue-green deployment**: Implement blue-green deployment strategies to minimize downtime and reduce risks during deployment.

- **Canary releases**: Use canary releases to deploy new features to a subset of users before a full rollout.

CI/CD pipeline creation

Let us look at CI/CD pipeline creation:

- **Pipeline setup**: Create a CI/CD pipeline that automates the entire process from code commit to deployment. This includes build, test, and deployment stages.

- **Pipeline orchestration**: Use CI/CD tools like Jenkins Pipelines, GitLab CI/CD, or Azure Pipelines to orchestrate the pipeline.

- **Approval gates**: Implement approval gates for manual intervention before deploying to production. This adds a layer of security and quality control.

Monitoring and logging

Let us look at monitoring and logging:

- **Application monitoring**: Setup monitoring tools like Prometheus, Grafana, or New Relic to track application performance and health.

- **Log management**: Use centralized logging solutions like **Elasticsearch, Kibana, Beats, and Logstash (ELK Stack)** or Splunk to collect and analyze logs.

- **Alerting**: Configure alerts to notify the team of any issues in the deployment process or application performance.

Security integration

Let us look at security integration:

- **Static application security testing (SAST)**: Integrate SAST tools like SonarQube, Fortify, or Veracode into the CI pipeline to identify security vulnerabilities in the code.

- **Dynamic application security testing (DAST)**: Use DAST tools to perform security testing on the running application.

- **Dependency scanning**: Implement dependency scanning tools like OWASP Dependency-Check or Snyk to identify vulnerabilities in third-party libraries.

By following these steps and leveraging the right tools, you can implement a robust CI/CD process that enhances the reliability and efficiency of your software delivery.

Ensuring testability in the process

Ensuring testability throughout the CI/CD process involves several strategies that span the entire software development lifecycle. The following sub-sections explore how you can ensure testability at each stage of the process.

Building quality gates into the development process

Building quality gates into the CI/CD process is essential for ensuring that code meets predefined quality standards before it progresses through the pipeline. Quality gates act as checkpoints that validate various aspects of the software, such as code quality, security, performance, and functionality. Here's how you can implement quality gates in your CI/CD pipeline:

- **Define quality criteria**:
  - **Code quality**: Establish metrics for code quality, such as code complexity, duplication, and adherence to coding standards.
  - **Test coverage**: Set minimum acceptable thresholds for unit, integration, and end-to-end test coverage.
  - **Security**: Define criteria for security, such as passing SAST and DAST.
  - **Performance**: Set benchmarks for performance metrics, such as response times and resource utilization.

- **Setup CI/CD pipeline**:

    o **Pipeline stages**: Structure your CI/CD pipeline to include stages where quality gates can be applied. Common stages include build, test, static analysis, integration, staging, and production.

Implement quality gates

Let us look at the process of implementing quality gates:

- **Code quality gate**:

    o **Static code analysis**: Use tools like SonarQube, ESLint, or Checkstyle to perform static code analysis. Integrate these tools into your CI pipeline to automatically analyze code for issues such as bugs, code smells, and vulnerabilities.

    o **Thresholds**: Define and enforce thresholds for code quality metrics (e.g., no critical bugs, a maximum of 10% code duplication). An example can be seen in the following YAML code:

```yaml
stages:
  - name: Build
    steps:
      - name: Checkout
        uses: actions/checkout@v2
      - name: Build
        run: mvn clean install

  - name: Static Analysis
    steps:
      - name: Run SonarQube
        run: mvn sonar:sonar
        env:
          SONAR_TOKEN: ${{ secrets.SONAR_TOKEN }}
      - name: Check Quality Gate
        run: curl -u ${{ secrets.SONAR_TOKEN }} 'https://
sonarcloud.io/api/qualitygates/project_status?projectKey=my_
project'
        continue-on-error: false
```

- **Test coverage gate**:

    o **Automated tests**: Ensure that automated tests are run as part of the CI process. Use tools like JUnit, NUnit, or PyTest for unit tests, and Selenium or Cypress for integration/end-to-end tests.

- o **Coverage tools**: Use test coverage tools like JaCoCo, Istanbul, or coverage. py to measure code coverage.

- o **Enforce coverage**: Fail the build if the coverage threshold is not met.

  Following is the sample YAML code for this:

```
- name: Run Tests
  steps:
    - name: Run Unit Tests
      run: mvn test
    - name: Check Coverage
      run: mvn jacoco:report
    - name: Enforce Coverage
      run: |
        coverage=$(mvn jacoco:report | grep -oP 'Instruction
coverage rate: \K[0-9]+')
        if [ $coverage -lt 80 ]; then
          echo "Coverage is below threshold"
          exit 1
        fi
```

- **Security gate**:

  - o **SAST**: Integrate SAST tools like SonarQube, Checkmarx, or Fortify into the pipeline.

  - o **DAST**: Use DAST tools like OWASP ZAP or Burp Suite to scan the running application.

  - o **Dependency scanning**: Use tools like OWASP Dependency-Check or Snyk to check for vulnerabilities in third-party libraries.

    Following is the sample YAML code for this:

```
- name: Security Analysis
  steps:
    - name: Run SAST
      run: mvn verify -P security
    - name: Dependency Check
      run: dependency-check.sh --project my_project
    - name: Enforce Security Gate
      run: |
        issues=$(dependency-check.sh --project my_project |
grep -oP 'Critical: \K[0-9]+')
        if [ $issues -gt 0 ]; then
```

```
    echo "Security vulnerabilities found"
    exit 1
fi
```

- **Performance gate**:

  o **Performance testing**: Use tools like JMeter, Gatling, or Locust to run performance tests on your application.

  o **Benchmarks**: Define acceptable performance benchmarks and fail the build if these benchmarks are not met.

    Following is the sample YAML code for this:

```
- name: Performance Testing
  steps:
    - name: Run Performance Tests
      run: jmeter -n -t test_plan.jmx -l results.jtl
    - name: Check Performance
      run: |
        response_time=$(grep "Response time" results.jtl |
cut -d',' -f2)
        if [ $response_time -gt 2000 ]; then
          echo "Performance benchmark not met"
          exit 1
        fi
```

- **Continuous improvement**:

  o **Review failures**: Regularly review why quality gates fail and address the root causes.

  o **Refine criteria**: Continuously refine quality criteria and thresholds based on project needs and feedback.

  o **Training**: Provide training to the development team on best practices for writing quality, secure, and performant code.

Example CI/CD pipeline with quality gates

Here is another example of a pipeline with quality gates using a YAML script. While these pipelines can be written in many different ways with different programming languages, YAML syntax has been used here, as it is the most widely used pipeline language and compatible with all CI/CD tooling, meaning that you can easily transfer your pipelines from one tool to another, if required:

```
stages:
  - stage: Checkout
    jobs:
      - job: Checkout
        pool:
          vmImage: 'ubuntu-latest'
        steps:
          - checkout: self

  - stage: Build
    jobs:
      - job: Build
        pool:
          vmImage: 'ubuntu-latest'
        steps:
          - script: |
              mvn clean install

  - stage: StaticAnalysis
    jobs:
      - job: StaticAnalysis
        pool:
          vmImage: 'ubuntu-latest'
        steps:
          - script: |
              mvn sonar:sonar

  - stage: Test
    jobs:
      - job: Test
        pool:
          vmImage: 'ubuntu-latest'
        steps:
          - script: |
              mvn test

  - stage: Coverage
    jobs:
      - job: Coverage
        pool:
          vmImage: 'ubuntu-latest'
        steps:
          - script: |
              mvn jacoco:report
```

```
                coverage=$(mvn jacoco:report | grep -oP 'Instruction coverage
rate: \K[0-9]+')
                if [ "$coverage" -lt 80 ]; then
                  echo "Coverage is below threshold: $coverage%"
                  exit 1
                fi

  - stage: Security
    jobs:
      - job: Security
        pool:
          vmImage: 'ubuntu-latest'
        steps:
          - script: |
              dependency-check.sh --project my_project
              issues=$(dependency-check.sh --project my_project | grep -oP
'Critical: \K[0-9]+')
                if [ "$issues" -gt 0 ]; then
                  echo "Security vulnerabilities found: $issues"
                  exit 1
                fi

  - stage: DeployToStaging
    jobs:
      - job: DeployToStaging
        pool:
          vmImage: 'ubuntu-latest'
        steps:
          - script: |
              # Deploy to staging environment

  - stage: PerformanceTesting
    jobs:
      - job: PerformanceTesting
        pool:
          vmImage: 'ubuntu-latest'
        steps:
          - script: |
              jmeter -n -t test_plan.jmx -l results.jtl
              responseTime=$(grep 'Response time' results.jtl | cut -d','
-f2)
                if [ "$responseTime" -gt 2000 ]; then
                  echo "Performance benchmark not met: Response time =
$responseTime ms"
```

```
            exit 1
        fi

  - stage: DeployToProduction
    jobs:
      - job: DeployToProduction
        pool:
          vmImage: 'ubuntu-latest'
        steps:
          - script: |
              # Deploy to production environment
        condition: and(succeeded(), eq(variables['Build.SourceBranch'],
'refs/heads/main'))

jobs:
  - job: PostActions
    pool:
      vmImage: 'ubuntu-latest'
    steps:
      - script: |
          if [ $? -eq 0 ]; then
            echo "Archiving artifacts..."
            # Archive artifacts
            echo "Running junit tests..."
            # Run junit tests
          else
            echo "Sending failure notification..."
            echo "Something is wrong with ${env.JOB_NAME} ${env.
BUILD_NUMBER}. Please check the logs." | mail -s "Pipeline failed:
${currentBuild.fullDisplayName}" team@example.com
```

This YAML script translates the Groovy script into a corresponding YAML structure for an Azure DevOps pipeline or similar CI/CD tool that supports YAML-based configurations. Note that the exact syntax might vary depending on the specific CI/CD tool you are using. Adjustments may be necessary to align with your specific environment and tools.

By following these steps and using the example pipeline, you can implement robust quality gates in your CI/CD process to ensure that only high-quality, secure, and performant code progresses through the pipeline and gets deployed.

Assessing NFRs in the development process

Assessing **non-functional requirements** (**NFRs**) effectively in the development process is crucial for ensuring that the software not only functions correctly but also meet performance, scalability, security, and usability standards.

Here is a detailed approach to assessing NFRs:

- **Identify and define NFRs early**:

  - **Gather requirements**: Work with stakeholders, including business analysts, end-users, and product owners, to identify and define NFRs early in the project lifecycle.

  - **Documentation**: Document NFRs clearly, specifying the criteria for performance, security, reliability, scalability, usability, maintainability, and other relevant aspects.

  - **Prioritization**: Prioritize NFRs based on their importance and impact on the system and user experience.

- **Embed NFRs in the development process**:

  - **Design patterns**: Use design patterns and best practices that align with the NFRs. For example, use caching, load balancing, and microservices for scalability and performance.

  - **Coding standards**: Adopt coding standards that support NFRs, such as secure coding practices to enhance security.

  - **Automation**: Automate repetitive tasks like performance testing, security scanning, and compliance checks to ensure NFRs are consistently assessed.

  - **Quality gates**: As already shared in the pipeline steps setup ahead, implement quality gates in the CI/CD pipeline to enforce NFRs. For example, fail the build if performance benchmarks are not met or if security vulnerabilities are detected.

- **Automated NFR testing**:

  - **Performance testing**: Use tools like JMeter, Gatling, or k6 to simulate load and measure system performance under different conditions.

  - **Security testing**: Integrate SAST tools like SonarQube and DAST tools like OWASP ZAP into the pipeline.

  - **Usability testing**: Use automated tools and scripts to perform usability testing, ensuring that the application is user-friendly.

- **Monitoring and improvement**:

  - **Monitoring**: Implement monitoring solutions like Prometheus, Grafana, or New Relic to continuously monitor performance, security, and other NFRs in production.

- o **NFR reviews**: Conduct regular reviews of NFRs to ensure they are still relevant and being met. This can be done through regular meetings and checkpoints.

- o **Continuous improvement**: Based on the reviews and feedback, continuously refine and improve the processes and tools used for assessing NFRs.

Example of integrating NFR assessments in CI/CD pipeline

Here is an example of how to integrate NFR assessments into pipeline using YAML:

```yaml
stages:
  - stage: Checkout
    jobs:
      - job: Checkout
        pool:
          vmImage: 'ubuntu-latest'
        steps:
          - checkout: self

  - stage: Build
    jobs:
      - job: Build
        pool:
          vmImage: 'ubuntu-latest'
        steps:
          - script: |
              mvn clean install

  - stage: StaticAnalysis
    jobs:
      - job: StaticAnalysis
        pool:
          vmImage: 'ubuntu-latest'
        steps:
          - script: |
              mvn sonar:sonar

  - stage: UnitTests
    jobs:
      - job: UnitTests
        pool:
          vmImage: 'ubuntu-latest'
```

```
            steps:
              - script: |
                  mvn test

      - stage: IntegrationTests
        jobs:
          - job: IntegrationTests
            pool:
              vmImage: 'ubuntu-latest'
            steps:
              - script: |
                  mvn verify

      - stage: PerformanceTesting
        jobs:
          - job: PerformanceTesting
            pool:
              vmImage: 'ubuntu-latest'
            steps:
              - script: |
                  jmeter -n -t test_plan.jmx -l results.jtl
                  responseTime=$(grep 'Average' results.jtl | awk '{print $2}')
                  if [ "$responseTime" -gt 2000 ]; then
                      echo "Performance benchmark not met: Average response time
= $responseTime ms"
                      exit 1
                  fi

      - stage: SecurityTesting
        jobs:
          - job: SecurityTesting
            pool:
              vmImage: 'ubuntu-latest'
            steps:
              - script: |
                  dependency-check.sh --project my_project
                  issues=$(dependency-check.sh --project my_project | grep -oP
'Critical: \K[0-9]+')
                  if [ "$issues" -gt 0 ]; then
                    echo "Security vulnerabilities found: $issues"
                    exit 1
                  fi
```

```
  - stage: DeployToStaging
    jobs:
      - job: DeployToStaging
        pool:
          vmImage: 'ubuntu-latest'
        steps:
          - script: |
              # Deploy to staging environment

  - stage: ManualTesting
    jobs:
      - job: ManualTesting
        pool:
          vmImage: 'ubuntu-latest'
        steps:
          - script: |
              # Perform manual testing and approve deployment to production

  - stage: DeployToProduction
    jobs:
      - job: DeployToProduction
        pool:
          vmImage: 'ubuntu-latest'
        steps:
          - script: |
              # Deploy to production environment
jobs:
  - job: PostActions
    pool:
      vmImage: 'ubuntu-latest'
    steps:
      - script: |
          if [ $? -eq 0 ]; then
            echo "Archiving artifacts..."
            # Archive artifacts
            echo "Running junit tests..."
            # Run junit tests
          else
            echo "Sending failure notification..."
            echo "Something is wrong with ${env.JOB_NAME} ${env.
BUILD_NUMBER}. Please check the logs." | mail -s "Pipeline failed:
${currentBuild.fullDisplayName}" team@example.com
```

This YAML script translates the Groovy script into a corresponding YAML structure for an Azure DevOps pipeline or similar CI/CD tool that supports YAML-based configurations. Note that the exact syntax might vary depending on the specific CI/CD tool you are using. Adjustments may be necessary to align with your specific environment and tools.

By incorporating these strategies and tools into your development process, you can effectively assess and ensure that NFRs are met. This will lead to the delivery of a more robust, secure, performant, and user-friendly application.

Determining when software is ready for release

Determining when software is ready for release involves a comprehensive evaluation of both functional and NFRs, along with thorough testing and validation.

Criteria definition

The distinction between functional and NFRs lies in the type of criteria they define for a software system:

- Functional requirements specify what a system should do. They define the core features, behaviors, and tasks that the system must perform to fulfil its purpose. These requirements are often tied to specific user actions, use cases, or business rules. For example, the system shall allow users to log in using a username and password is a functional requirement.

- NFRs specify how the system should perform its functions and operate under various conditions. They define the quality attributes, constraints, and performance metrics that ensure the system's usability, scalability, and reliability. For example, the system shall handle 10,000 concurrent users with a response time of under two seconds is a NFR.

In summary, functional requirements address functionality and user needs, while NFRs focus on the system's operational qualities and performance. Both are essential for a complete, effective, and high-quality software system.

Functional completeness

Functional completeness refers to the degree to which a software system or application implements all the required features and functionalities specified in its requirements. It ensures that the software performs all intended tasks and meets user expectations without any critical omissions. Functional completeness is evaluated by comparing the implemented features against the defined scope, use cases, and business objectives to confirm that no essential functionality is missing, enabling the software to fulfill its purpose effectively:

- **Requirements coverage**: Ensure all functional requirements are implemented and verified.

- **Acceptance criteria**: Verify that all user stories or features meet their acceptance criteria.

Non-functional requirements

NFRs define the quality attributes, constraints, and performance standards a software system must meet, focusing on how the system operates rather than what it does. These include aspects like performance (e.g., response time, scalability), security, reliability, usability, maintainability, and compliance. Unlike functional requirements, which specify specific tasks or behaviors, NFRs ensure the software delivers a seamless, efficient, and dependable user experience while aligning with business needs and operational environments. These play a crucial role in shaping the system's architecture and overall success:

- **Performance**: Verify that performance benchmarks, such as response times and throughput, are met.

- **Security**: Ensure the software has undergone security testing and that identified vulnerabilities are resolved.

- **Scalability and reliability**: Confirm the software can handle the expected load and has been tested for reliability.

- **Usability and accessibility**: Validate that the software meets usability and accessibility standards.

Quality gates

Quality gates must be implemented to ensure:

- **Code quality**: Ensure code quality metrics (e.g., cyclomatic complexity, duplication) are within acceptable thresholds.

- **Test coverage**: Verify that the codebase has sufficient unit, integration, and end-to-end test coverage.

Testing and validation

Testing is a valuable part of the development process and a key point for validating the effectiveness of what has been built. We will unpack testing in more detail in *Chapter 16, Testing in Software Architecture*, but will explain everything at a high level here so that you understand how it applies to the development process.

Automated testing

Automated testing is the use of software tools and scripts to execute tests, verify results, and compare outcomes against expected behavior, without requiring manual intervention. It is an essential component of modern software development, enabling faster feedback, improved accuracy, and consistency in testing processes. Automated testing supports various types of tests, including unit, integration, functional, and regression testing, ensuring that code changes do not introduce defects or break existing functionality. By automating repetitive and time-consuming tests, teams can focus on higher-value activities, such as exploratory testing and refining test cases. Additionally, automated testing is critical for maintaining quality in fast-paced development environments like Agile and DevOps, as it facilitates continuous integration and delivery pipelines by ensuring that tests are run quickly and frequently. Tests include:

- **Unit tests**: Ensure all unit tests pass consistently.

- **Integration tests**: Confirm that integration tests validate the interaction between components.

- **End-to-end tests**: Verify that end-to-end tests simulate real user scenarios successfully.

Business and manual testing

Business testing, such as **user acceptance testing** (**UAT**) and exploratory testing, focuses on validating that a software application meets business requirements and provides a seamless user experience. UAT is typically conducted by end-users or business stakeholders to ensure the system functions as intended in real-world scenarios, aligning with business goals and expectations. This testing often includes edge cases, workflows, and user-specific requirements that may not have been covered in automated or developer-led testing.

On the other hand, exploratory testing involves testers dynamically interacting with the application to uncover unexpected behaviors, usability issues, or gaps in functionality. Unlike automated testing, these types of testing are often manual, as they require human judgment, creativity, and a deep understanding of business processes and user needs. Together, UAT and exploratory testing are crucial for ensuring that the software delivers value to the business and its users before deployment:

- **UAT**: Conduct UAT sessions with stakeholders to ensure the software meets business needs.

- **Exploratory testing**: Perform exploratory testing to uncover any unexpected issues.

Performance testing

Performance testing evaluates how a software application behaves under various conditions to ensure it meets performance benchmarks, such as speed, scalability, and stability. This type of testing assesses critical metrics like response times, throughput, and resource utilization under normal, peak, and stress conditions. Common forms of performance testing include load testing, which measures the system's behavior under expected user loads; stress testing, which pushes the application beyond its limits to identify breaking points; and endurance testing, which checks the system's stability over prolonged usage. Tools and frameworks are often used to simulate user traffic and measure performance metrics, but real-world scenarios and infrastructure constraints are also considered. The goal is to identify bottlenecks, optimize system performance, and ensure the application provides a smooth user experience even under demanding conditions:

- **Load testing**: Validate that the software performs well under expected load conditions.

- **Stress testing**: Test the software's behavior under extreme conditions to identify its breaking point.

Security testing

Security testing ensures that a software application is protected against threats, vulnerabilities, and unauthorized access. It involves evaluating the system's defenses against potential risks such as data breaches, injection attacks, **cross-site scripting** (**XSS**), and unauthorized access to sensitive information. Key areas of security testing include authentication, authorization, encryption, data privacy, and secure error handling. Techniques like penetration testing, vulnerability scanning, and static and dynamic code analysis are commonly employed. Security testing also ensures compliance with industry standards and regulations, such as GDPR or OWASP guidelines. The primary goal is to identify and fix security flaws before deployment, safeguarding both the application and its users from malicious attacks and ensuring trust in the system:

- **Vulnerability scanning**: Use tools to scan for security vulnerabilities.

- **Penetration testing**: Conduct penetration testing to identify potential security weaknesses.

Compliance and documentation

It is important for software architects to understand the different regulatory and legal requirements they need to comply with and make sure they document this accordingly. Similarly, there are a number of different types of documentation involved in the lifecycle of the software that need to be factored into the engineering process.

Compliance

Compliance requirements in software refer to the set of rules, regulations, standards, and industry guidelines that a software application must adhere to in order to operate legally, ethically, and securely. These requirements ensure the software aligns with legal mandates (e.g., GDPR, HIPAA, or SOX), industry-specific standards (e.g., PCI DSS for payment systems), and organizational policies. Compliance requirements often address data privacy, security, accessibility, financial reporting, and auditability. Meeting these requirements involves implementing features like data encryption, role-based access control, audit trails, and adherence to accessibility guidelines, such as WCAG. Failing to comply can result in legal penalties, reputational damage, and financial losses, making compliance a critical aspect of software development and maintenance. Compliance ncludes:

- **Regulatory compliance**: Ensure the software complies with relevant regulations (e.g., GDPR, HIPAA).

- **Internal standards**: Verify that the software adheres to internal coding and design standards.

Documentation

Documentation requirements in a software project specify the types and scope of documentation needed to support the development, use, maintenance, and management of the software. These requirements ensure that all stakeholders, including developers, testers, end-users, and maintainers, have access to the information they need. Documentation includes:

- **User documentation**: Provide comprehensive user manuals and help guides.

- **Technical documentation**: Ensure technical documentation is complete and up-to-date.

- **Process documentation**: For teams to ensure consistency and quality (e.g., coding standards and workflows).

Deployment and monitoring

Software development is not just about building software, but operating and maintaining it as well, and ensuring it can be deployed successfully. This is why the idea of deployment readiness and monitoring is so important for a software architect to understand.

Deployment readiness

Deployment readiness refers to the state in which a software application is fully prepared for release into the production environment. It involves ensuring that the application has passed all functional, performance, and security tests, meets defined quality standards, and aligns with business requirements. Key aspects of deployment readiness include validated configurations, successful integration with dependent systems, adequate documentation, and thorough stakeholder sign-off. Additionally, a robust deployment plan, rollback strategy, and monitoring setup are essential to minimize risks and ensure a smooth transition to production. Deployment readiness ensures the software is reliable, stable, and aligned with user expectations upon release through the following:

- **Deployment scripts**: Verify that deployment scripts are tested and reliable.
- **Rollback plan**: Prepare a rollback plan in case the release needs to be reverted.

Monitoring

Software monitoring involves the continuous observation and tracking of software systems to ensure their performance, availability, and security. By collecting data on various metrics such as response times, error rates, resource utilization, and system health, monitoring helps identify potential issues before they impact users. Effective software monitoring enables proactive troubleshooting, optimizes system performance, and ensures smooth user experiences, allowing teams to quickly address failures and maintain system reliability. It is a critical component in modern software development, particularly in complex, distributed, or cloud-native environments through:

- **Health monitoring**: Set up monitoring to track the health of the application post-deployment.
- **Error tracking**: Implement error tracking to quickly identify and resolve issues.

By following this structured approach, you can ensure that all aspects of the software have been thoroughly tested and validated, and that it is ready for release. This process helps in minimizing risks and ensuring a smooth deployment, leading to higher-quality software and greater stakeholder satisfaction.

Monitoring the software for improved delivery

Monitoring the development process and identifying areas for process and delivery improvement is essential for maintaining high-quality software delivery and CI. The following sub-sections discuss a structured approach to effectively monitor and improve your development process.

Establish key performance indicators

It is important for any team to measure their performance and effectiveness at any given time to identify areas where they can improve. The following metrics are good ones to measure that give a good idea of the effectiveness of a team's delivery:

- **Cycle time**: Measure the time taken from the start of development to the deployment of a feature or bug fix.

- **Lead time**: Track the total time from feature request to delivery.

- **Deployment frequency**: Measure how often new code is deployed to production.

- **Change failure rate**: Monitor the percentage of deployments that result in a failure requiring immediate remediation.

- **Mean time to restore (MTTR)**: Track the average time to recover from a failure in production.

- **Escaped defects**: The number of defects logged in production that were missed in the development process.

A guide to effective estimation

Estimation is a crucial aspect of project planning and management in software development. Effective estimation helps in setting realistic expectations, allocating resources properly, and delivering projects on time and within budget.

However, estimation is incredibly difficult to get right, and one of the biggest frustrations that many organizations may have with their development teams is the inability to hit expected deadlines or targets. With software complexity often changing as more details of its implementation are figured out or certain technical challenges are unearthed, estimation will always remain a bit of a dark art, but there are things that can be done to improve this within teams.

Choose an estimation technique

Before we get into how to improve estimation, let us look at the different ways we can estimate for delivery and things that need to be considered along the way:

- **Relative estimation (story points)**

  Relative estimation is a technique used in project management where tasks or user stories are estimated based on their complexity or size in relation to one another, rather than assigning absolute values:

  - **Story points**: Assign relative points to tasks or user stories based on their complexity, effort, and risk. Use a standard scale (e.g., Fibonacci sequence) to maintain consistency.

  - **Planning poker**: Use planning poker or similar techniques to facilitate team consensus. Each team member independently assigns story points, followed by a discussion to reach an agreement.

- **Time-based estimation**

  Time-based estimation is a technique where tasks or user stories are estimated based on the amount of time required to complete them, often using hours or days as the unit of measurement:

  o **Use hours or days**: Estimate tasks in hours or days, leveraging historical data or expert judgment. Consider task size and potential challenges.

  o **Consider buffers**: Include buffers for unexpected issues or delays. Typically, add a contingency percentage to the overall estimate to accommodate uncertainties.

- **Expert judgment**

  Expert judgment is a technique where experienced individuals or subject matter experts provide estimates based on their knowledge, expertise, and past experience with similar tasks or projects:

  o **Consult team members**: Leverage the expertise of team members with experience in similar tasks or projects. Conduct brainstorming sessions or individual consultations.

  o **Consult historical data**: Refer to past project data to gain insights into similar tasks or features. Use this data to inform and validate current estimates.

Oftentimes, it is a combination of the above estimation methods that may be applied at once. Teams will need to consolidate a combination of data and experience, while picking a specific measurement that quantifies both the importance and the time it may take for certain features to be fully implemented (which includes development, testing, and successful deployment).

Factors to consider in estimation

To utilize the above techniques effectively, it is also important to consider a range of different factors to ensure you make the right considerations in the estimation process:

- **Complexity**: Evaluate the complexity of tasks or features, considering technical challenges and dependencies. Break down larger tasks into smaller, manageable components.

- **Risk**: Assess risks that could impact the timeline, such as integration issues, third-party dependencies, or unfamiliar technologies. Factor in mitigation strategies for identified risks.

- **Dependencies**: Identify and account for dependencies between tasks or teams. Ensure that dependent tasks are accurately sequenced, and resource availability is considered.

- **Resources**: Consider the availability and skill levels of required resources (developers, designers, testers). Account for any planned time off or other commitments that may affect availability.

Iterative and incremental estimation

Things change, and so should the estimates whenever there is a change. So, even though there may be a bigger deadline that you are hoping to achieve, the actual delivery of smaller tasks should be evolved based on changes in either the team:

- **Refinement sessions**: Schedule regular refinement sessions (e.g., backlog grooming in Agile) to review and adjust estimates based on new information or changes. Engage the entire team in these sessions to ensure alignment and accuracy.

- **Use historical data**: Continuously update and refine estimates based on actuals and lessons learned from previous or similar projects. Maintain a repository of historical data for reference.

- **Validation**: Validate estimates against project constraints, such as budget and timeline requirements. Conduct reviews with stakeholders to ensure estimates align with project goals and constraints.

Tools and techniques

Along with different estimation principles to follow, there are also a lot of tools and models that can be utilized to help with the estimation process:

- **Estimation tools**: Use project management software (e.g., Jira, Trello) or specialized estimation tools (e.g., PERT chart, Monte Carlo simulation) to aid in estimation. These tools can help visualize and track estimates.

- **Estimation models**: Explore different estimation models (e.g., COCOMO, Function Point Analysis) for complex projects. Choose a model that aligns with your project type and complexity.

Monitor and adjust

The last aspect of estimation is monitoring how teams deliver actual results against their expectations and then trying to understand where misalignments occurred and learn to adjust future estimations as a result:

- **Track progress**: Monitor progress against estimated timelines and adjust plans as needed. Use tools like burndown charts to visualize progress.

- **Learn from variances**: Analyze variances between estimated and actuals to improve future estimation accuracy. Conduct retrospectives to identify root causes of variances and implement corrective actions.

Achieving more accurate estimates

Understanding those different aspects to estimation are vital, but estimation is never effective if it cannot be accurate and while this may be difficult to achieve initially, it is something more experienced teams should get better at and there is a lot that can be done to improve the effectiveness and accuracy of estimation in teams.

While some of the preceding steps will help, the following is a process that should help lead to better estimation in a more collaborative and effective way within development teams:

1. **Choose the right technique**: Select an estimation technique that fits the project scope, complexity, and team dynamics. Whether it is story points, time-based estimation, or expert judgment, ensure the chosen method is understood and accepted by the team.

2. **Engage the team**: Involve the entire team in the estimation process to leverage diverse perspectives and expertise. Facilitate discussions and encourage open communication to reach a consensus.

3. **Break down tasks**: Decompose larger tasks into smaller, more manageable pieces. This granular approach reduces ambiguity and improves the accuracy of estimates.

4. **Use historical data**: Refer to historical data from past projects to inform current estimates. Analyze similarities and differences to adjust estimates based on past performance and outcomes.

5. **Incorporate risk management**: Identify potential risks early and include mitigation strategies in your estimates. Allocate time and resources to address uncertainties and reduce their impact.

6. **Regular refinement**: Conduct regular refinement sessions to revisit and adjust estimates. As new information emerges or project conditions change, update estimates to reflect the latest understanding.

7. **Continuous monitoring**: Continuously monitor project progress and compare it against estimates. Use this data to make real-time adjustments and keep the project on track.

8. **Retrospectives and learning**: Conduct retrospectives to review estimation accuracy and identify areas for improvement. Capture lessons learned and apply them to future estimation efforts to enhance precision.

Effective estimation in software development involves a combination of art and science, requiring a deep understanding of project requirements, collaboration within the team, and the use of appropriate techniques and tools. By following these guidelines and continuously refining your estimation process, you can improve accuracy, manage expectations, and deliver successful projects consistently.

Conclusion

A strong grasp of development practices is essential for any software architect. The ability to structure and lead teams to effectively deliver software systems through CI/CD pipelines is a crucial skill that all architects should cultivate. This entails not only a deep understanding of development processes but also a commitment to continuously evaluate and refine these processes. An approach that works well with one team may not be as effective with another, necessitating ongoing adjustments and improvements.

In the next chapter, we explore the invaluable contributions of architecture to the broader field of software engineering. Readers will gain a holistic understanding of architecture's role in shaping software engineering practices in a company and ensuring the success of complex projects.

Join our book's Discord space

Join the book's Discord Workspace for Latest updates, Offers, Tech happenings around the world, New Release and Sessions with the Authors:

https://discord.bpbonline.com

CHAPTER 15
Architecture as Engineering

Introduction

In the software world, software architecture is responsible for the design of software systems, whereas software engineering deals with how that design gets created and maintained. Much like in the construction industry, an architect cannot design a building that cannot be built, and so in the software world, software architects also need to consider software engineering practices so that they can design a system that can make best use of the various engineering methods teams are using.

This is different than what we discussed in *Chapter 14, Development Practices*, which focuses more on things like team structures, team performance, software processes, and team skills, and looks more at the technical practices and engineering techniques that teams will utilize in making software fit for production.

This is why we are dedicating an entire chapter to looking at these different engineering practices and what they entail. As a software architect, it would then be vital to consider these practices in design and ensure that teams can make use of these in delivering on the architecture successfully.

Structure

In this chapter, we will discuss the following topics:

- Assessing engineering maturity
- Ensuring repeatable results
- Emerging engineering practices
- Metrics in software engineering

Objectives

By the end of this chapter, you will understand the different engineering principles and techniques utilized in the software development process and how to capitalize on them as a software architect to ensure your software design is a success. This includes understanding modern software engineering practices, tooling, and how to leverage these to build effective software in a maintainable, efficient, and high-quality way.

Assessing engineering maturity

Often, a good way of looking at the effectiveness of the engineering practices in a team is to look at the existing maturity of the established engineering processes and then use that as a means to design around and assess areas for improvement that need to be considered.

An engineering maturity model is a framework used to assess the maturity of an organization's software engineering practices. It helps teams identify their current capabilities and provides a roadmap for improvement.

There are many different forms of an engineering maturity model, but we will provide an example of the most common one applied in the industry, known as the **Capability Maturity Model Integration** (**CMMI**) index.

CMMI is one of the most widely used maturity models in software engineering. It defines five levels of maturity, each representing a different stage of process maturity within an organization.

Here is a breakdown of how CMMI works:

1. **Level 1: Initial**

    a. **Characteristics**: Processes are typically ad hoc and chaotic. There is little to no process discipline, and success depends heavily on individual effort rather than on proven processes.

    b. **Example**: A team delivers software products with inconsistent quality and often misses deadlines. If a key team member leaves, projects may fail due to a lack of defined processes.

2. **Level 2: Managed**

    a. **Characteristics**: Basic project management practices are established. Projects are planned, executed, and controlled to meet established commitments.

    b. **Example**: The team uses project management tools to track timelines and budgets. Requirements are documented, and progress is monitored. However, processes are often reactive, addressing problems only as they arise.

3. **Level 3: Defined**

    a. **Characteristics**: Processes are well-defined, documented, and standardized across the organization. There is a strong emphasis on process management and improvement.

    b. **Example**: The team follows a standardized **software development lifecycle** (**SDLC**) that includes requirements gathering, design, coding, testing, and deployment. Processes are tailored to the specific needs of the project but are still based on an organizational standard.

4. **Level 4: Quantitatively managed**

    a. **Characteristics**: The organization uses quantitative data to manage and control processes. Statistical techniques are applied to monitor process performance and predict future outcomes.

    b. **Example**: The team collects metrics on code quality, defect rates, and productivity. This data is used to make informed decisions about project timelines and resource allocation. Process performance is predictable, and the team can proactively address potential issues.

5. **Level 5: Optimizing**

    a. **Characteristics**: Continuous process improvement is a key focus. The organization uses feedback from process performance to drive innovation and improvement.

    b. **Example**: The team regularly reviews process metrics and identifies areas for improvement. They implement new tools, techniques, and practices to enhance productivity and quality. For instance, if the data shows that code reviews are a bottleneck, the team might adopt pair programming to streamline the process.

Working of CMMI

To implement CMMI, organizations follow a structured approach involving several key steps:

1. **Assessment**: Organizations assess their current maturity level by evaluating their practices against the criteria for each CMMI level. This can be done through self-assessment, internal audits, or external audits by certified appraisers.

2. **Gap analysis**: After the assessment, organizations perform a gap analysis to identify areas where their practices fall short of the desired maturity level.

3. **Process improvement plan**: Based on the gap analysis, a process improvement plan is developed. This plan outlines specific actions to move from the current maturity level to a higher one. For example, if the organization is at Level 2, the plan might include standardizing processes across all projects to reach Level 3.

4. **Implementation**: The organization implements the process improvement plan, which may involve training, adopting new tools, or revising existing processes.

5. **Monitoring and adjustment**: The organization monitors progress using metrics and feedback. Adjustments are made as needed to ensure continuous improvement and progression through the maturity levels.

6. **Re-assessment**: After a period of implementation, the organization reassesses its maturity level to measure progress and identify new areas for improvement.

Benefits of using CMMI

The following are some of the benefits of using CMMI:

- **Improved process control**: By advancing through the maturity levels, organizations gain better control over their processes, leading to more predictable and reliable outcomes.

- **Increased efficiency**: Standardized and well-managed processes reduce waste, rework, and inefficiencies.

- **Enhanced quality**: A focus on continuous improvement and quantitative management leads to higher-quality products.

- **Better risk management**: Organizations at higher maturity levels are better equipped to identify, assess, and mitigate risks.

CMMI provides a structured approach to improving software engineering practices, helping organizations move from chaotic, ad hoc processes to well-managed, continuously improving ones. By assessing their maturity level and following a clear roadmap for improvement, organizations can systematically enhance their capabilities and achieve higher levels of performance and quality.

Assessing the maturity of a team

Being aware of a model is just one aspect; assessing the real maturity of different teams requires further evaluation. Assessing your software engineering maturity and identifying best practices in your team involves evaluating your processes, tools, and culture against industry standards and established frameworks. Here is how you can go about it:

- **Conduct a best practices audit**

    o **Example**: Perform an internal audit using a checklist of best practices in areas like code quality, testing, deployment, documentation, and collaboration.

    o **How to assess**: Create or use an existing checklist tailored to your organization's needs. Rate each practice as not implemented, partially implemented, or fully implemented. This gives you a clear picture of areas where you excel and where improvement is needed.

- **Benchmark against industry standards**

    o **Example**: Compare your practices with industry standards such as ISO/IEC 12207 (software life cycle processes) or IEEE 730 (software quality assurance plans).

    o **How to assess**: Conduct a gap analysis to identify differences between your current practices and those prescribed by the standards. This can highlight areas for improvement.

- **Use agile maturity assessments**

    o **Example**: If your team follows agile practices, use tools like the Agile maturity model or the Spotify squad health check to evaluate your team's agility.

    o **How to assess**: Conduct regular self-assessments using these tools, focusing on areas like collaboration, transparency, continuous improvement, and technical excellence.

- **Solicit feedback through retrospectives**

    o **Example**: Regularly hold retrospectives at the end of sprints or projects to discuss what went well, what did not, and what can be improved.

    o **How to assess**: Use feedback from these sessions to identify recurring issues and successful practices. Over time, track how improvements are implemented and their impact on the team's performance.

- **Conduct peer reviews and audits**

    o **Example**: Have other teams within the organization review your practices or invite external auditors to assess your processes.

    o **How to assess**: Peer reviews can provide fresh perspectives and highlight blind spots. External audits can give an objective assessment of your practices against industry benchmarks.

- **Evaluate tools and automation**

  - **Example**: Assess the tools you use for version control, CI/CD, testing, and monitoring to verify if they are up-to-date and effective, and if there are manual processes that can be automated.

  - **How to assess**: Create an inventory of your tools and map them to their respective tasks. Identify gaps where automation could improve efficiency or reduce errors.

- **Track technical debt**

  - **Example**: Use tools like SonarQube to measure technical debt (e.g., code smells, duplicated code, etc.). Track it over time to see if it is increasing or decreasing.

  - **How to assess**: Regularly review technical debt metrics to assess whether your team is actively addressing it or if it is accumulating, which can indicate process or quality issues.

- **Assess team collaboration and communication**

  - **Example**: Evaluate how effectively your team collaborates using tools like Slack or Jira, and whether communication flows smoothly during daily stand-ups or code reviews.

  - **How to assess**: Survey your team to gather feedback on collaboration and communication. Look for patterns that indicate strengths or areas where miscommunication or siloed work is causing problems.

- **Measure deployment frequency and lead time**

  - **Example**: Track how often you deploy new features or fixes to production and how long it takes from code commit to deployment.

  - **How to assess**: High deployment frequency with short lead times generally indicates a mature, efficient process. Long lead times may highlight bottlenecks in your pipeline.

- **Assess security practices**

  - **Example**: Evaluate your security practices, such as code scanning for vulnerabilities, regular security reviews, and compliance with data protection regulations.

  - **How to assess**: Use tools like OWASP ZAP for security testing and review compliance with standards like GDPR or HIPAA. Identify gaps in your security posture and address them.

To assess and improve your software engineering maturity, adopt a systematic approach using maturity models, best practices audits, KPIs, and continuous feedback. Regularly review and refine your practices based on these assessments to drive continuous improvement.

Software engineering with architectural principles

Part of the many facets of software engineering is applying systematic, disciplined approaches to software development while adhering to fundamental architectural principles. This approach ensures that software systems are well-structured, maintainable, and scalable, meeting both functional and non-functional requirements effectively.

Key architectural principles

The following are some of the key architectural principles and how engineering practices can help achieve them in the development process:

- **Separation of concerns**:
    - o **Definition**: Dividing a system into distinct sections, each handling a separate concern or responsibility.
    - o **Implementation**: Use modular design, layering, and encapsulation to separate different aspects of the system, such as presentation, business logic, and data access.
    - o **Benefit**: Enhances maintainability and allows teams to work on different components independently without affecting others.

- **Modularity**:
    - o **Definition**: Designing a system as a collection of loosely coupled, interchangeable modules.
    - o **Implementation**: Create modules with well-defined interfaces and responsibilities, allowing them to be developed, tested, and deployed independently.
    - o **Benefit**: Facilitates reuse, simplified testing, and makes it easier to manage and evolve the system over time.

- **Scalability**:
    - o **Definition**: Designing the system to handle increasing loads and accommodate growth effectively.
    - o **Implementation**: Use scalable architecture patterns such as microservices, horizontal scaling, and distributed systems to ensure the system can grow with demand.

- ○ **Benefit**: Ensures the system can handle increasing user traffic and data volume without performance degradation.

- **Fault tolerance and reliability**:

  - ○ **Definition**: Designing the system to continue operating correctly even in the presence of faults or failures.

  - ○ **Implementation**: Implement redundancy, error handling, and recovery mechanisms, and use principles like chaos engineering to test resilience.

  - ○ **Benefit**: Increases the system's availability and reliability, reducing downtime and improving user trust.

- **Security**:

  - ○ **Definition**: Ensuring the system is protected against unauthorized access, breaches, and vulnerabilities.

  - ○ **Implementation**: Apply security principles such as least privilege, secure communication, and regular security assessments.

  - ○ **Benefit**: Protects sensitive data, maintains user trust, and complies with regulatory requirements.

- **Performance**:

  - ○ **Definition**: Designing the system to meet performance requirements such as response time, throughput, and resource utilization.

  - ○ **Implementation**: Use performance optimization techniques like caching, load balancing, and efficient algorithms.

  - ○ **Benefit**: Enhances user experience and ensures the system performs well under various conditions.

- **Maintainability**:

  - ○ **Definition**: Designing the system to be easy to maintain and update over its lifecycle.

  - ○ **Implementation**: Use practices like clear documentation, consistent coding standards, and automated testing to ensure ease of maintenance.

  - ○ **Benefit**: Reduces the cost and effort required to fix issues and implement changes, extending the system's lifespan.

- **Reusability**:

  - ○ **Definition**: Designing components that can be reused in different parts of the system or in other projects.

- o **Implementation**: Create reusable libraries, services, and components with well-defined interfaces and minimal dependencies.

  - o **Benefit**: Reduces duplication of effort and promotes consistency across the system.

- **Design for change**:

  - o **Definition**: Designing the system to accommodate changes and evolving requirements easily.

  - o **Implementation**: Use flexible design patterns, such as dependency injection and service-oriented architecture, to support future changes.

  - o **Benefit**: Ensures the system can adapt to new requirements and technological advancements without major redesigns.

Rigorous software engineering, guided by architectural principles, ensures that software systems are well-designed, maintainable, and capable of meeting both current and future needs. By applying principles such as separation of concerns, modularity, and scalability, teams can build robust, reliable, and adaptable systems that align with project goals and user requirements.

Ensuring repeatable results

Ensuring repeatable results in software engineering is crucial for maintaining quality, consistency, and reliability in your products. So often, the first step of any engineering process is ensuring these various strategies are in place to ensure that whatever software is being delivered, a team can implement and improve them in as fast a way as possible, without compromising on the quality of the software

Here are some practical strategies to achieve this, along with examples:

- **Version control with Git**

  - o **Example**: Use branches for feature development, and ensure every change is tracked with commits. Before merging to the main branch, conduct code reviews and automated tests.

  - o **How it ensures repeatability**: Version control allows you to roll back to previous versions if needed, track changes, and collaborate without conflicts, ensuring that the same codebase produces the same results.

- **Automated testing**

  - o **Example**: Implement unit tests, integration tests, and end-to-end tests using a variety of different approaches, which we will discuss in more detail in *Chapter 16, Testing in Software Architecture*.

- o **How it ensures repeatability**: Automated tests verify that code behaves as expected every time it is run. This ensures that changes or updates do not introduce new bugs, allowing for consistent results.

- **CI/CD**

  - o **Example**: Set up a CI/CD pipeline with Jenkins or GitHub Actions that runs tests, builds the application, and deploys it automatically when code is pushed to a repository.

  - o **How it ensures repeatability**: CI/CD ensures that every change goes through the same process, reducing human error and making sure that the deployment is consistent across environments.

- **Configuration management**

  - o **Example**: Use tools like Ansible, Puppet, or Docker to manage and deploy environments. For instance, containerizing an application with Docker ensures that it runs the same way on any machine.

  - o **How it ensures repeatability**: Configuration management ensures that environments are set up identically every time, reducing discrepancies between development, testing, and production environments.

- **Code reviews and pair programming**

  - o **Example**: Implement mandatory code reviews for all changes, where at least one other developer reviews the code before it is merged.

  - o **How it ensures repeatability**: Code reviews help catch issues early and ensure that best practices are followed, leading to more consistent and reliable code.

- **Use of design patterns**

  - o **Example**: Apply the Singleton pattern for a logging utility to ensure that only one instance of the logger exists throughout the application.

  - o **How it ensures repeatability**: Design patterns provide proven solutions to common problems, ensuring that similar problems are solved in similar ways, leading to predictable and repeatable outcomes.

- **Static code analysis**

  - o **Example**: Integrate tools like SonarQube or ESLint to analyze code for potential bugs, code smells, and security vulnerabilities during development.

  - o **How it ensures repeatability**: Static analysis tools enforce coding standards and catch potential issues before they make it into production, ensuring consistent code quality.

- **Automated build systems**

  - **Example**: Use Maven or Gradle for Java projects to automate the build process. Define dependencies and build scripts in a way that anyone can reproduce the build by running a single command.

  - **How it ensures repeatability**: Automated build systems ensure that the application is built the same way every time, avoiding issues caused by manual build processes.

- **Documentation and knowledge sharing**

  - **Example**: Document the architecture, APIs, and key decision points using tools like Confluence or Markdown in your repository. For example, creating a README with setup instructions ensures that anyone can replicate your development environment.

  - **How it ensures repeatability**: Clear documentation ensures that all team members are on the same page, reducing misunderstandings and ensuring that processes are followed consistently.

- **Environment parity**

  - **Example**: Use Vagrant or Docker Compose to ensure that development, testing, and production environments are as similar as possible.

  - **How it ensures repeatability**: Environment parity ensures that what works in one environment works in all, preventing the **works on my machine** issue.

- **Monitoring and logging**

  - **Example**: Implement centralized logging with ELK Stack to monitor application behavior across different environments.

  - **How it ensures repeatability**: Consistent logging and monitoring help in tracking down issues and understanding the behavior of your application over time, leading to repeatable and predictable operations.

- **Idempotent scripts**

  - **Example**: Write deployment scripts that can be run multiple times without causing different results (e.g., using apt-get install, which would not reinstall a package if it is already installed).

  - **How it ensures repeatability**: Idempotent scripts ensure that repeated executions do not change the result, leading to consistent and repeatable deployments.

Clear success conditions for easier development

Having clear success conditions is essential for guiding your development efforts and ensuring that your team stays focused on delivering value. Clear success conditions help define what *done* looks like, making it easier to measure progress and align everyone's efforts. Here is how you can establish clear success conditions:

- **Define SMART goals**

    o **S: Specific**: Clearly define what you want to achieve.

        ▪ **Example**: Instead of saying *Improve application performance*, specify *Reduce the page load time by 20% within the next quarter.*

    o **M: Measurable**: Ensure that the goal can be quantified or measured.

        ▪ **Example**: Achieve a test coverage of 85% for all new code.

    o **A: Achievable**: Set goals that are realistic and attainable.

        ▪ **Example**: Implement a CI/CD pipeline for automating deployments within three sprints.

    o **R: Relevant**: Align the goal with your team's overall objectives.

        ▪ **Example**: Implement user authentication enhancements to reduce security incidents by 30%.

    o **T: Time-bound**: Set a deadline or time frame for achieving the goal.

        ▪ **Example**: Complete the feature development by the end of Q4.

- **Establish acceptance criteria**

    o **Definition**: Acceptance criteria are specific conditions that a product or feature must meet to be considered complete.

    o **Use case**: Define acceptance criteria for each user story or task. These should include functional requirements, performance benchmarks, and any other relevant conditions.

    o **Example**: For a login feature, acceptance criteria could be: *The system should allow users to log in with their email and password, lock the account after five failed attempts, and redirect to the dashboard upon successful login.*

- **Use Definition of Done**

    o **Definition**: A **Definition of Done (DoD)** is a checklist that defines all the activities that must be completed before a task or feature is considered done.

    o **Use case**: Create a DoD for your team that includes tasks like code review, automated tests, documentation, and deployment.

- o **Example**: A feature is only considered done when it has been peer-reviewed, passed all automated tests, documented in the user manual, and deployed to the staging environment.

- **Implement clear milestones**

  - o **Definition**: Milestones are key points in the project timeline that signify the completion of significant phases or deliverables.

  - o **Use case**: Break down the project into smaller, manageable phases with clear deliverables and set milestones for each.

  - o **Example**: Milestones could include *Prototype completed, Beta version released,* and *Full production launch.*

- **Use testable requirements**

  - o **Definition**: Requirements should be written in a way that makes them easy to test and verify.

  - o **Use case**: When writing requirements, think about how you will test them. Ensure they are clear, unambiguous, and verifiable.

  - o **Example**: The application should support up to 10,000 concurrent users without degradation in performance, which can be tested through load testing.

- **Create a roadmap**

  - o **Definition**: A roadmap is a high-level plan that outlines the key stages of development, along with associated success conditions.

  - o **Use case**: Develop a roadmap that includes timelines, milestones, and key deliverables. Share this with your team and stakeholders.

  - o **Example**: A roadmap might include stages like *MVP development, User feedback collection,* and *Final feature rollout,* each with specific success criteria.

- **Use continuous feedback loops**

  - o **Definition**: Continuous feedback ensures that you are meeting success conditions throughout the development process.

  - o **Use case**: Implement regular feedback loops through sprint reviews, user testing, and stakeholder meetings.

  - o **Example**: After each sprint, review the progress against success conditions with stakeholders and adjust the plan if necessary.

- **Monitor key metrics**

  - o **Definition**: Use **key performance indicators (KPIs)** to track progress toward success conditions.

- o **Use case**: Define KPIs that align with your success conditions and monitor them regularly.

- o **Example**: If a success condition is to improve user engagement, track metrics like daily active users, session length, and feature usage rates.

- **Document and communicate success conditions**

  - o **Definition**: Ensure that success conditions are well-documented and communicated to all team members.

  - o **Use case**: Use tools like Confluence, Jira, or a project management board to document success conditions. Regularly update the team on progress.

  - o **Example**: Create a shared document that outlines all success conditions, including goals, acceptance criteria, and KPIs, and ensure it is accessible to everyone.

By defining and clearly communicating success conditions, you create a shared understanding of what needs to be achieved, making development more focused and measurable. This approach reduces ambiguity, ensures alignment across the team, and increases the likelihood of delivering a successful project.

Designing frameworks that allow for easier execution

Designing frameworks that simplify the software delivery process involves creating structures, guidelines, and tools that standardize and automate key aspects of development, testing, and deployment. These frameworks should be flexible enough to adapt to different projects while providing a consistent and reliable process. Here is how to design such frameworks, with clear examples:

- **Modular architecture**

  - o **Definition**: Designing your software with a modular architecture means breaking down your application into independent, interchangeable modules or services.

  - o **Example**: Implementing microservices architecture, where each service (e.g., user authentication, payment processing, etc.) is developed, tested, and deployed independently.

  - o **How it eases execution**: Modular architecture allows teams to work in parallel, reduces dependencies, and makes it easier to maintain and scale the application.

- **Reusable component libraries**

  - o **Definition**: Creating a library of reusable components or functions that can be used across different projects.

- o **Example**: A React component library for UI elements like buttons, forms, and modals that can be used across multiple web applications.

- o **How it eases execution**: Reusable components reduce the need to write code from scratch, ensure consistency across projects, and speed up development.

- **CI/CD pipeline frameworks**

  - o **Definition**: Setting up CI/CD pipelines to automate the build, test, and deployment processes.

  - o **Example**: Using Jenkins, GitHub Actions, or GitLab CI to automatically run tests, build Docker containers, and deploy to a staging or production environment every time code is pushed to the repository.

  - o **How it eases execution**: CI/CD frameworks ensure that code changes are automatically tested and deployed, reducing manual effort, errors, and time-to-market.

- **Infrastructure as code (IaC)**

  - o **Definition**: Managing and provisioning infrastructure through code rather than manual processes.

  - o **Example**: Using Terraform or AWS CloudFormation to define and manage cloud infrastructure, such as servers, databases, and networking, through code.

  - o **How it eases execution**: IaC allows for consistent and repeatable infrastructure setups, makes it easier to manage and version control infrastructure, and simplifies scaling and replication across environments.

- **Testing frameworks**

  - o **Definition**: Establishing a framework for automated testing, including unit tests, integration tests, and end-to-end tests. We will discuss these in more detail in *Chapter 16, Testing in Software Architecture.*

  - o **Example**: Setting up a testing framework using tools like Jest for JavaScript, JUnit for Java, or pytest for Python, with standardized test structures and reporting.

  - o **How it eases execution**: Automated testing frameworks ensure that code is thoroughly tested before deployment, catching bugs early and ensuring consistent quality.

- **Logging and monitoring frameworks**

  - o **Definition**: Implementing a centralized logging and monitoring system to track application performance and issues.

○ **Example**: Using the ELK Stack or Prometheus and Grafana to collect logs, monitor system metrics, and visualize application performance.

○ **How it eases execution**: Logging and monitoring frameworks provide real-time insights into application behavior, making it easier to detect, diagnose, and resolve issues quickly.

- **Standardized deployment templates**

  ○ **Definition**: Creating templates for deployment processes that can be reused across different environments and projects.

  ○ **Example**: Using Helm charts to define Kubernetes deployments, making it easy to deploy applications across different clusters with consistent configurations.

  ○ **How it eases execution**: Standardized templates reduce the complexity of deployment, ensure consistency across environments, and simplify rollback procedures.

- **Documentation and onboarding frameworks**

  ○ **Definition**: Establishing a framework for documenting code, processes, and onboarding new team members.

  ○ **Example**: Using tools like Confluence or Notion to create and maintain a centralized knowledge base that includes architectural diagrams, coding standards, and onboarding guides.

  ○ **How it eases execution**: Clear documentation ensures that all team members are aligned, reduces onboarding time for new developers, and provides a reference for troubleshooting and best practices.

- **API management frameworks**

  ○ **Definition**: Implementing a framework to design, document, and manage APIs.

  ○ **Example**: Using Swagger or OpenAPI to design and document RESTful APIs, and tools like Kong or Apigee for API management, including rate limiting, authentication, and monitoring.

  ○ **How it eases execution**: API management frameworks standardize how APIs are designed, documented, and consumed, making it easier for teams to integrate and maintain services.

- **Security frameworks**

  ○ **Definition**: Designing a framework that integrates security practices into the software delivery process.

- o **Example**: Implementing a security framework that includes automated code scanning (e.g., with Snyk or OWASP ZAP), secure coding practices, and regular security audits.

- o **How it eases execution**: Security frameworks help in identifying vulnerabilities early, ensuring compliance, and reducing the risk of security breaches, all while integrating seamlessly into the development process.

- **Feedback and iteration frameworks**

  - o **Definition**: Establishing a framework for collecting and acting on feedback during development.

  - o **Example**: Setting up regular sprint reviews and using tools like Jira or Trello to capture user and stakeholder feedback.

  - o **How it eases execution**: A feedback framework ensures continuous improvement and allows teams to iterate quickly, adjusting based on real-world feedback.

- **Version control branching strategies**

  - o **Definition**: Implementing a version control framework with clear branching strategies.

  - o **Example**: Adopting GitFlow, where development, feature, release, and hotfix branches are clearly defined and used consistently.

  - o **How it eases execution**: A well-defined branching strategy ensures that code changes are organized, reducing conflicts and making it easier to manage releases and rollbacks.

Designing frameworks for easier execution in the software delivery process involves creating repeatable, standardized processes and tools that streamline development, testing, deployment, and maintenance. By implementing these frameworks, you reduce complexity, enhance collaboration, and increase efficiency, leading to faster delivery of high-quality software.

Standardized configuration

Standardized configuration refers to the practice of using consistent settings, parameters, and environments across various parts of a software project. Implementing standardized configurations offers numerous benefits that contribute to a more efficient, reliable, and scalable software delivery process. Here are some of the key benefits:

- **Consistency across environments**

  - o **Benefit**: Ensures that development, testing, staging, and production environments are identical or as similar as possible.

- o **Impact**: Reduces the likelihood of **it works on my machine** issues. If the same configuration is used across environments, the behavior of the application is more predictable, leading to fewer environment-specific bugs.

- **Easier troubleshooting and debugging**

  - o **Benefit**: Simplifies the process of identifying and fixing issues.

  - o **Impact**: When configurations are standardized, it is easier to reproduce and diagnose issues because you know the exact setup of the environment. This consistency helps in quickly pinpointing the root cause of problems.

- **Faster onboarding**

  - o **Benefit**: New team members can get up to speed quickly.

  - o **Impact**: With standardized configurations, new developers do not need to spend time figuring out how to set up their environments. They can follow a documented, standardized process, reducing onboarding time and allowing them to contribute sooner.

- **Reduced configuration drift**

  - o **Benefit**: Minimizes the risk of configuration drift, where different environments gradually diverge over time.

  - o **Impact**: Configuration drift can lead to inconsistencies and unexpected behaviors in production. By standardizing configurations, you ensure that environments remain aligned, reducing the risk of deployment issues.

- **Improved collaboration**

  - o **Benefit**: Facilitates better teamwork and communication.

  - o **Impact**: When everyone is working with the same configuration, it is easier for team members to share knowledge, troubleshoot issues collaboratively, and ensure that code works consistently across different setups.

- **Enhanced automation**

  - o **Benefit**: Streamlines automation processes such as CI/CD.

  - o **Impact**: Automated pipelines rely on consistent environments to function correctly. Standardized configurations ensure that builds, tests, and deployments can be automated reliably without manual intervention, leading to faster and more consistent delivery.

- **Scalability and reusability**

  - o **Benefit**: Makes it easier to scale applications and reuse configurations across projects.

    o   **Impact**: Standardized configurations can be easily replicated for new environments or projects, reducing the time and effort needed to scale infrastructure or start new initiatives.

- **Security and compliance**

    o   **Benefit**: Ensures that security policies and compliance requirements are consistently applied.

    o   **Impact**: Security configurations, such as access controls, encryption settings, and firewall rules, should be consistent across all environments to prevent vulnerabilities. Standardized configurations help maintain compliance with security standards and regulations.

- **Cost efficiency**

    o   **Benefit**: Reduces costs associated with maintenance, support, and infrastructure.

    o   **Impact**: When configurations are standardized, less time and resources are spent on troubleshooting, support, and environment setup, leading to cost savings. Additionally, infrastructure can be optimized for cost efficiency when standardized configurations are used.

- **Better documentation and knowledge sharing**

    o   **Benefit**: Improves the quality of documentation and knowledge transfer.

    o   **Impact**: With standardized configurations, documentation becomes more straightforward and easier to maintain. Knowledge sharing within the team is also enhanced, as everyone is familiar with the same setup and configurations.

- **Version control and auditing**

    o   **Benefit**: Enables better version control and auditing of configurations.

    o   **Impact**: When configurations are standardized and version-controlled (e.g., using IaC tools like Terraform or Ansible), it is easier to track changes, roll back to previous versions, and audit configurations for compliance or troubleshooting purposes.

- **Reduced risk of human error**

    o   **Benefit**: Minimizes the chances of mistakes during configuration changes.

    o   **Impact**: Standardized configurations reduce the need for manual configuration changes, which are prone to errors. This leads to more stable environments and fewer issues caused by misconfigurations.

Standardized configurations bring consistency, efficiency, and reliability to the software development process. They enhance collaboration, simplify troubleshooting, and enable faster onboarding and deployment, all while reducing risks associated with configuration drift, security, and human error. Ultimately, adopting standardized configurations leads to higher-quality software and smoother operations.

Deploying code into production

Deploying code into production is a critical phase in the software development lifecycle, and following best practices ensures a smooth, reliable, and secure release. Here are some of the best practices for deploying code into production:

- **Automate deployment with CI/CD pipelines**

    o **Why**: Automation reduces the chances of human error and ensures that deployments are consistent, repeatable, and fast.

    o **How**: Use CI/CD tools like Jenkins, GitLab CI, or GitHub Actions to automate the build, test, and deployment process. Automate the entire pipeline from code commit to production deployment.

- **Version control and branching strategies**

    o **Why**: Clear version control practices ensure that only thoroughly reviewed and tested code reaches production.

    o **How**: Implement branching strategies like GitFlow, where you have dedicated branches for development, testing, and production. Use pull requests to review and approve code changes before merging into the main branch.

- **Use IaC**

    o **Why**: Ensures that your infrastructure is consistent across environments and can be versioned, reviewed, and automated.

    o **How**: Use tools like Terraform, AWS CloudFormation, or Ansible to define your infrastructure. Keep infrastructure code in the same repository as your application code to maintain consistency.

- **Blue-green or canary deployments**

    o **Why**: Reduces downtime and risk during deployments by gradually rolling out new changes and easily rolling back if issues occur.

    o **How**:

        ▪ **Blue-green deployment**: Run two identical environments (blue and green). Deploy the new version to the green environment, test it, and then switch traffic from the blue to the green environment.

- **Canary deployment**: Gradually release the new version to a small subset of users before rolling it out to the entire user base.

- **Automated testing**

  - **Why**: Ensures that the code is stable and free of critical bugs before reaching production.

  - **How**: Implement a robust suite of automated tests, including unit tests, integration tests, and end-to-end tests. Use CI/CD pipelines to automatically run tests before any code is deployed to production.

- **Monitor and log everything**

  - **Why**: Monitoring and logging provide visibility into the application's performance and help quickly identify and resolve issues.

  - **How**: Implement logging and monitoring tools like ELK Stack, Prometheus, or Grafana. Set up alerts for critical issues like high error rates, latency spikes, or resource exhaustion.

- **Feature toggles or flags**

  - **Why**: Allows you to deploy code into production without immediately enabling it for users, reducing risk.

  - **How**: Use feature flagging tools like LaunchDarkly or Feature Toggle to control the visibility of new features. This allows you to deploy features incrementally and easily roll them back if needed.

- **Database migrations**

  - **Why**: Ensures that database changes are managed in sync with application code deployments.

  - **How**: Use tools like Liquibase or Flyway to manage database migrations. Always test migrations in staging environments before applying them in production. Use version-controlled migration scripts to ensure consistency.

- **Rollback strategy**

  - **Why**: Being able to quickly revert to a previous version minimizes downtime and impact in case of a failed deployment.

  - **How**: Implement rollback procedures in your CI/CD pipeline. Maintain previous versions of your application and infrastructure configurations so that they can be quickly redeployed if needed.

- **Security best practices**

  - **Why**: Protects your application and data from potential threats during deployment.

o **How**: Use automated security scanning tools to identify vulnerabilities before deployment.

Secure access controls for deployment pipelines

Encrypt sensitive data and use secrets management tools like HashiCorp Vault to manage credentials securely as follows:

- **Perform deployment during low-traffic periods**

  o **Why**: Minimizes the impact on users in case of issues during the deployment.

  o **How**: Schedule deployments during off-peak hours when user activity is lowest. Consider using maintenance windows to inform users of potential downtime.

- **Perform a post-deployment review**

  o **Why**: Reviewing the deployment process and its outcomes helps identify areas for improvement.

  o **How**: After each deployment, conduct a retrospective meeting to discuss what went well, what did not, and how to improve the process. Use the insights gained to refine your deployment practices.

- **Documentation and communication**

  o **Why**: Clear documentation and communication ensure that all stakeholders are aware of the deployment process and any potential impacts.

  o **How**: Document the deployment process, rollback procedures, and any known risks. Communicate upcoming deployments to the relevant teams and users, including expected changes and impacts.

- **Use immutable infrastructure**

  o **Why**: Ensures that production environments are clean and consistent, reducing the risk of configuration drift.

  o **How**: Implement immutable infrastructure practices, where instead of updating existing servers, you deploy new servers with the updated application. This can be achieved using containerization (e.g., Docker) or by creating new virtual machines with the updated code.

- **Staging environment similar to production**

  o **Why**: Ensures that tests and deployments in staging accurately reflect what will happen in production.

o   **How**: Maintain a staging environment that closely mirrors the production environment in terms of configuration, data, and scale. This allows for more accurate testing and reduces surprises during production deployments.

Deploying code into production requires careful planning, automation, and best practices to ensure a smooth and successful release. By following these best practices, you can minimize risks, reduce downtime, and maintain high-quality software in production.

Have clear abstraction layers

Achieving clear abstraction layers in software engineering processes involves structuring your system in such a way that each layer or component has a distinct responsibility and interacts with other layers through well-defined interfaces. This helps manage complexity, improve maintainability, and promote scalability. Here are strategies for achieving clear abstraction layers:

- **Define clear responsibilities for each layer**

    o   **Strategy**: Clearly delineate the responsibilities of each layer in your system architecture.

    o   **Example**: In a typical three-layer architecture:

        ▪   **Presentation layer**: Handles user interface and user experience.

        ▪   **Business logic layer**: Manages business rules and logic.

        ▪   **Data access layer**: Handles database interactions and data persistence.

- **Use well-defined interfaces**

    o   **Strategy**: Define and use interfaces or APIs to enable communication between layers.

    o   **Example**: In a microservices architecture, services expose RESTful APIs or GraphQL endpoints that other services consume. This ensures loose coupling between services.

- **Encapsulate implementation details**

    o   **Strategy**: Hide implementation details within each layer and expose only necessary information through interfaces.

    o   **Example**: A service class might interact with a database through a repository interface, without exposing the underlying database queries or structure to the rest of the application.

- **Apply design patterns**

    o   **Strategy**: Use design patterns that promote clear abstraction and separation of concerns.

- o **Examples**:

  - **Facade pattern**: Provides a simplified interface to a complex subsystem, hiding its complexity.

  - **Adapter pattern**: Converts one interface to another expected by the client, allowing incompatible interfaces to work together.

  - **Dependency injection**: Injects dependencies into a class, rather than the class creating its own dependencies, to reduce coupling and improve testability.

- **Implement layered architecture**

  - o **Strategy**: Organize your application into distinct layers, each with its own responsibilities.

  - o **Example**: A common approach is to use:

    - **Presentation layer**: For handling user interactions.

    - **Application layer**: For orchestrating business logic.

    - **Domain layer**: For defining core business models and rules.

    - **Infrastructure layer**: For providing technical services (e.g., logging, data access).

- **Use domain-driven design (DDD)**

  - o **Strategy**: Apply DDD principles to organize your system into bounded contexts, each with its own distinct domain model and boundaries.

  - o **Example**: In an e-commerce application, you might have separate bounded contexts for Order Management, Inventory, and Customer Management, each with its own domain model and interfaces.

- **Encapsulate dependencies**

  - o **Strategy**: Minimize direct dependencies between layers to reduce coupling and increase flexibility.

  - o **Example**: Instead of having the business logic layer directly depend on a specific database implementation, abstract the database interactions through a repository interface that the business logic layer depends on.

- **Document abstractions and interfaces**

  - o **Strategy**: Provide clear documentation for each layer's interfaces and responsibilities.

  - o **Example**: Use tools like Swagger or OpenAPI to document RESTful APIs or create clear interface definitions with usage examples and contract details.

- **Adopt API contracts and service agreements**

    - **Strategy**: Define and adhere to API contracts or service agreements that outline the expected inputs, outputs, and behaviors of interactions between layers.

    - **Example**: Implement API contract testing to ensure that changes in one layer or service do not break expected interactions.

- **Implement testing strategies for abstraction layers**

    - **Strategy**: Use different types of tests to validate each layer independently and its interactions with other layers.

    - **Examples**:

        - **Unit tests**: Test individual classes or components in isolation.

        - **Integration tests**: Validate interactions between layers or components.

        - **End-to-end tests**: Test the entire system to ensure that all layers work together as expected.

- **Use dependency management tools**

    - **Strategy**: Manage dependencies between layers using dependency management tools to enforce abstraction boundaries.

    - **Example**: Use tools like Maven or Gradle in Java projects to manage dependencies and enforce boundaries between different modules or layers.

- **Maintain layer boundaries**

    - **Strategy**: Enforce rules that prevent direct access to lower layers from higher layers.

    - **Example**: Ensure that the presentation layer does not directly access the data access layer but instead interacts through the business logic layer.

- **Employ code reviews and architectural governance**

    - **Strategy**: Implement code review processes and architectural governance to ensure adherence to abstraction and separation principles.

    - **Example**: Review pull requests to ensure that new code follows the defined layer boundaries and abstraction principles.

Clear abstraction layers improve the manageability, scalability, and maintainability of software systems by separating concerns and defining clear responsibilities. By following these strategies, you can create a well-structured and modular architecture that simplifies development, testing, and maintenance.

Emerging engineering practices

We have mentioned a lot of different things that we should consider from a software engineering perspective, and the benefits it offers to the overall software delivery and design process. However, it is also important to talk about some modern evolutions in software engineering that have a significant impact on how software is being delivered. Having a deep understanding of these new technologies can greatly help a software architect design systems that make use of these techniques to enable their systems to be better designed to meet future needs.

Infrastructure as code

IaC is the practice of managing and provisioning computing infrastructure through machine-readable configuration files, rather than through physical hardware configuration or interactive configuration tools. IaC enables you to define and manage infrastructure in a way similar to how you manage application code.

The working of IaC is as follows:

- **Declarative vs. imperative approaches**:

    o **Declarative (what to do)**: You specify the desired state of the infrastructure (e.g., *I need 3 web servers, 1 database server*). The IaC tool then ensures that this desired state is achieved and maintained.

    o **Imperative (how to do it)**: You specify the exact steps needed to reach the desired state (e.g., *create a web server, then configure it, then install the application*).

- **Version control**:

    Infrastructure code is stored in version control systems like Git. This allows teams to track changes, collaborate, review, and roll back configurations if necessary, just like application code.

- **Automation and integration**:

    IaC integrates with CI/CD pipelines, allowing automated provisioning, testing, and deployment of infrastructure as part of the overall software delivery process.

Benefits of IaC in engineering processes

The following list illustrates the manner in which IaC improves engineering processes:

- **Consistency and reproducibility**:

    o **Benefit**: IaC ensures that all environments (development, testing, production) are set up in the same way.

- o **Impact**: Reduces **it works on my machine** problems by eliminating discrepancies between environments. Developers and operations teams can work on the same infrastructure definitions, ensuring consistency across the board.

- **Scalability**:

  - o **Benefit**: IaC makes it easy to scale infrastructure up or down by simply modifying configuration files.

  - o **Impact**: For example, during a high-traffic event, you can increase the number of servers by changing a line in the IaC code and re-deploying. This can be automated with policies that scale infrastructure dynamically based on usage.

- **Faster, automated deployments**:

  - o **Benefit**: Provisioning and deploying infrastructure can be done in minutes, not days.

  - o **Impact**: New environments can be spun up quickly, enabling rapid testing and iteration. Changes to infrastructure can be deployed with the same CI/CD pipelines used for application code, speeding up the overall software delivery process.

- **Improved collaboration and transparency**:

  - o **Benefit**: Storing IaC in version control allows teams to collaborate more effectively.

  - o **Impact**: Multiple team members can work on the same infrastructure, review changes, and maintain a history of modifications. This shared visibility reduces the risk of misconfigurations and enhances teamwork.

- **Enhanced security and compliance**:

  - o **Benefit**: Security configurations (e.g., firewalls, access controls) can be defined as code and consistently applied across environments.

  - o **Impact**: IaC ensures that security best practices are enforced consistently, reducing vulnerabilities. Compliance audits become easier because the infrastructure setup is documented and can be reviewed.

- **Disaster recovery and business continuity**:

  - o **Benefit**: IaC allows you to quickly recreate infrastructure in a disaster recovery scenario.

  - o **Impact**: If an environment fails, you can rapidly rebuild it from code, minimizing downtime and ensuring business continuity. This also allows for easier testing of disaster recovery plans.

- **Cost efficiency**:

    - **Benefit**: IaC enables automated infrastructure management, which can lead to more efficient use of resources.

    - **Impact**: Infrastructure can be automatically scaled up or down based on demand, reducing unnecessary costs. Automated de-provisioning of unused resources further optimizes costs.

- **Example tools for IaC**:

    - **Terraform**: A tool for building, changing, and versioning infrastructure safely and efficiently. It uses a declarative configuration language.

    - **AWS CloudFormation**: A service that helps you model and set up your Amazon Web Services resources.

    - **Ansible**: An open-source automation tool that automates software provisioning, configuration management, and application deployment.

IaC transforms infrastructure management into a scalable, repeatable, and automated process. By treating infrastructure like code, you gain consistency, speed, and the ability to easily adapt to changing requirements. This approach ultimately leads to more efficient engineering processes, higher quality software, and reduced operational risk.

Containerization

Containerization is a technology that allows you to package an application and its dependencies together into a single, lightweight, and portable unit called a container. Containers provide a consistent environment for applications across various stages of development and deployment, making them a powerful tool in modern software engineering.

The working of containerization is as follows:

- **Containers vs. virtual machines (VMs)**:

    - **Containers**: Share the host operating system's kernel but run in isolated user spaces. They are lightweight and start quickly because they do not need to boot a full operating system.

    - **VMs**: Include a full operating system along with the application, which can make them heavier and slower to start.

- **Container images**:

    - **Definition**: A container image is a read-only template that contains everything needed to run an application: the code, runtime, libraries, and dependencies.

- o **Creation**: Images are built from a Dockerfile or similar configuration file, which specifies the base image, application code, and dependencies.

- **Container runtime**:

  - o **Definition**: The software that runs and manages containers. Examples include Docker Engine, containerd, and Podman.

  - o **Function**: The runtime uses the container image to create and run instances of containers, ensuring isolation and resource management.

- **Isolation and resource management**:

  - o **Isolation**: Containers are isolated from each other and from the host system using namespaces and cgroups. This ensures that processes within one container do not interfere with processes in another.

  - o **Resource management**: Containers can be limited in terms of CPU, memory, and I/O to ensure fair distribution of resources and prevent any single container from monopolizing system resources.

- **Portability**:

  - o **Definition**: Containers encapsulate all dependencies and configurations, making them portable across different environments (e.g., development, staging, production).

  - o **Implementation**: Containers can run consistently on any system that has a compatible container runtime, regardless of underlying hardware or operating system differences.

Benefits of containerization

Containerization offers the following benefits:

- **Consistency across environments**:

  - o **Benefit**: Containers provide a consistent environment for applications, reducing the **it works on my machine** problem.

  - o **Impact**: Applications behave the same way in development, testing, and production environments, leading to fewer environment-specific issues.

- **Isolation and security**:

  - o **Benefit**: Containers run in isolated environments, minimizing the impact of security vulnerabilities.

  - o **Impact**: Isolation reduces the risk of one application affecting another or the host system. Security practices such as container scanning can further enhance protection.

- **Portability**:
  - **Benefit**: Containers can be easily moved and run across different environments and cloud providers.
  - **Impact**: This flexibility allows for hybrid and multi-cloud deployments and simplifies migration between different infrastructure setups.

- **Resource efficiency**:
  - **Benefit**: Containers are lightweight compared to VMs, using fewer system resources and starting up faster.
  - **Impact**: This efficiency leads to better utilization of server resources and reduced infrastructure costs.

- **Scalability and flexibility**:
  - **Benefit**: Containers can be quickly scaled up or down based on demand.
  - **Impact**: This dynamic scalability allows applications to handle varying loads efficiently and supports modern cloud-native architectures.

- **Rapid deployment and iteration**:
  - **Benefit**: Containers enable rapid deployment and iteration of applications.
  - **Impact**: Developers can build, test, and deploy applications quickly and reliably, enhancing the overall agility of the development process.

- **Simplified dependencies management**:
  - **Benefit**: Containers encapsulate all dependencies required by the application.
  - **Impact**: This reduces the need for complex dependency management on the host system and ensures that the application runs with the exact versions of libraries and tools it needs.

- **DevOps and CI/CD integration**:
  - **Benefit**: Containers integrate well with DevOps practices and CI/CD pipelines.
  - **Impact**: Automated testing, integration, and deployment processes can be streamlined using containers, leading to faster development cycles and more reliable releases.

- **Environment replication**:
  - **Benefit**: Containers can replicate complex environments easily.
  - **Impact**: Developers can replicate production-like environments locally or in staging for more accurate testing and debugging.

- **Microservices architecture support**:

  - **Benefit**: Containers are well-suited for deploying microservices, where each service runs in its own container.

  - **Impact**: This architecture allows for modularity, scalability, and easier management of individual services, contributing to a more flexible and resilient system design.

- **Example use cases**:

  - **Development and testing**: Developers can use containers to create consistent development environments, ensuring that code works as expected across different stages.

  - **Deployment**: Containers simplify the deployment process by providing a consistent runtime environment, making it easier to deploy applications across various infrastructure setups.

  - **Microservices**: Containers can encapsulate individual microservices, allowing them to be independently developed, deployed, and scaled.

Containerization offers significant benefits in terms of consistency, efficiency, and scalability. By encapsulating applications and their dependencies into portable and isolated units, containers enhance the development, deployment, and management of applications, supporting modern software practices and architectures.

GitOps

GitOps is a modern approach to managing and deploying applications and infrastructure using Git as the single source of truth for declarative infrastructure and application configurations. It combines Git workflows with operations practices to automate and streamline the deployment process, providing a more reliable and auditable way to manage your systems.

The working of GitOps is as follows:

- **Declarative configuration**:

  - **Definition**: Infrastructure and application configurations are defined declaratively in code. This means you specify the desired state of your system rather than the steps to achieve that state.

  - **Implementation**: Configuration files, often written in YAML or JSON, describe the desired state of the system, including applications, infrastructure components, and their relationships.

- **Git as a source of truth**:

  o **Definition**: All configuration files and application code are stored in a Git repository. This repository becomes the single source of truth for the system's desired state.

  o **Implementation**: Any changes to the system's state are made by updating the configuration files in the Git repository. The changes are then automatically applied to the system.

- **Continuous deployment**:

  o **Definition**: Changes to the Git repository trigger automated deployment processes.

  o **Implementation**: Tools like Argo CD, Flux, or Jenkins X monitor the Git repository for changes. When a change is detected, the tool automatically applies the updated configuration to the target environment, ensuring that the actual state of the system matches the desired state.

- **Automated syncing**:

  o **Definition**: The actual state of the system is continuously compared with the desired state defined in Git.

  o **Implementation**: GitOps tools continuously monitor the live environment and ensure it matches the state described in Git. If discrepancies are found, they can be automatically corrected or flagged for manual intervention.

- **Rollback and history**:

  o **Definition**: Git provides version control and history for configuration changes.

  o **Implementation**: If an issue occurs, you can roll back to a previous version of the configuration by reverting to an earlier commit in Git. This provides a clear audit trail of changes and simplifies recovery from problematic updates.

Benefits of GitOps

GitOps offers the following benefits:

- **Consistency and reliability**:

  o **Benefit**: GitOps ensures that the desired state of your system is always reflected in the actual state.

  o **Impact**: By using Git as the source of truth, you eliminate configuration drift and ensure that all environments are consistent with the defined configurations.

- **Audibility and version control**:

  o **Benefit**: Git provides a complete history of changes, including who made changes and when.

  o **Impact**: This improves traceability and accountability, making it easier to audit changes and understand the evolution of your infrastructure and application configurations.

- **Automated deployments**:

  o **Benefit**: GitOps automates the deployment process, reducing manual intervention and errors.

  o **Impact**: Changes are automatically applied to the system based on updates to the Git repository, speeding up deployment cycles and ensuring consistency.

- **Simplified rollbacks**:

  o **Benefit**: Rolling back to a previous state is straightforward due to Git's version control.

  o **Impact**: If a deployment causes issues, you can quickly revert to a previous configuration, minimizing downtime and mitigating the impact of problematic changes.

- **Improved collaboration**:

  o **Benefit**: Using Git for configuration management enhances collaboration among team members.

  o **Impact**: Developers, operations, and other stakeholders can work together more effectively by reviewing, commenting on, and merging changes through Git workflows.

- **Enhanced security**:

  o **Benefit**: GitOps promotes security through access control and review processes.

  o **Impact**: Changes to configurations are controlled through Git repository access, and changes must be reviewed and approved before being applied, reducing the risk of unauthorized changes.

- **IaC integration**:

  o **Benefit**: GitOps integrates well with IaC practices.

  o **Impact**: Infrastructure and application configurations defined as code are stored in Git and managed using GitOps practices, ensuring a consistent and automated approach to infrastructure management.

- **Self-healing systems**:

  - **Benefit**: GitOps tools continuously monitor the system to ensure it matches the desired state.

  - **Impact**: Automated syncing and correction of deviations help maintain system health and reduce manual intervention for maintenance tasks.

- **Example GitOps tools**:

  - **Argo CD**: A declarative, GitOps continuous delivery tool for Kubernetes. It synchronizes Kubernetes resources with the state defined in a Git repository.

  - **Flux**: A GitOps operator for Kubernetes that enables continuous deployment by keeping Kubernetes resources in sync with configurations stored in Git.

  - **Jenkins X**: A CI/CD tool that integrates GitOps practices to provide automated deployment and environment management for Kubernetes-based applications.

- **Example workflow**:

  - **Define configuration**: Write declarative configuration files for your application and infrastructure in Git (e.g., YAML files for Kubernetes resources).

  - **Commit changes**: Push the configuration files to a Git repository.

  - **Automated deployment**: A GitOps tool monitors the repository for changes and automatically applies the updated configuration to the target environment.

  - **Continuous monitoring**: The GitOps tool continuously checks the live environment to ensure it matches the desired state in Git.

  - **Rollback if needed**: If issues arise, revert to a previous commit in Git to roll back to a stable configuration.

GitOps provides a modern approach to managing and deploying applications by leveraging Git as the source of truth for configuration. It brings benefits such as consistency, automated deployments, simplified rollbacks, and improved collaboration, making it a powerful practice for modern DevOps and continuous delivery.

Edge computing

Edge computing is a paradigm that involves processing data closer to the source of data generation, rather than relying on a centralized data center or cloud. The goal is to reduce latency, improve performance, and optimize the use of network resources by handling data processing and analysis at the edge of the network, near where the data is generated.

The working of edge computing is as follows:

- **Data generation at the edge:**

    o **Definition**: Data is generated by various IoT devices, sensors, or applications located at the edge of the network (e.g., smart devices, industrial sensors).

    o **Implementation**: Devices collect data in real-time, such as video feeds from cameras, telemetry from machinery, or environmental sensors.

- **Local processing and analysis:**

    o **Definition**: Edge devices or local gateways process and analyze data on-site or close to the data source.

    o **Implementation**: Instead of sending all raw data to a centralized cloud or data center, edge devices perform data filtering, aggregation, and analysis locally. This reduces the volume of data that needs to be transmitted and processed remotely.

- **Reduced latency:**

    o **Definition**: Processing data closer to the source minimizes the time it takes for data to travel to and from a central server.

    o **Implementation**: By handling critical processing tasks locally, edge computing reduces the latency involved in data transmission and improves response times for applications and services.

- **Optimized bandwidth:**

    o **Definition**: Edge computing reduces the amount of data transmitted over the network by processing and filtering data locally.

    o **Implementation**: Only relevant or summarized data is sent to the cloud or central data center, which optimizes network bandwidth and reduces costs associated with data transfer.

- **Integration with centralized systems:**

    o **Definition**: While edge computing focuses on local processing, it often integrates with centralized systems for additional processing, storage, and analytics.

    o **Implementation**: Edge devices can periodically synchronize with the cloud or central systems, providing aggregated or filtered data for further analysis and long-term storage.

Benefits of edge computing

Edge computing offers the following benefits:

- **Reduced latency:**

  o **Benefit**: Local processing of data reduces the time needed for data to travel to and from a central server.

  o **Impact**: This is critical for applications that require real-time processing and immediate responses, such as autonomous vehicles, industrial automation, and real-time video analytics.

- **Improved performance:**

  o **Benefit**: Edge computing enhances the performance of applications by reducing the load on central servers and minimizing network delays.

  o **Impact**: Applications can perform more efficiently and provide better user experiences due to quicker data processing and reduced dependency on centralized systems.

- **Optimized bandwidth and cost savings:**

  o **Benefit**: By processing data locally and transmitting only relevant information, edge computing reduces the amount of data sent over the network.

  o **Impact**: This reduces bandwidth usage and associated costs, especially for applications with large volumes of data, such as IoT deployments and video surveillance.

- **Enhanced privacy and security:**

  o **Benefit**: Sensitive data can be processed and analyzed locally, reducing the risk of data exposure during transmission.

  o **Impact**: Local data handling helps to maintain privacy and security by minimizing the amount of data that needs to be transmitted and stored in centralized systems.

- **Scalability and flexibility:**

  o **Benefit**: Edge computing enables scalable and flexible deployments by distributing computing resources across multiple locations.

  o **Impact**: This allows organizations to scale their infrastructure and deploy applications in diverse environments, from remote locations to urban centers.

- **Resilience and reliability:**
  - o **Benefit**: Edge computing can operate independently of central systems, providing resilience in case of network failures or disruptions.
  - o **Impact**: Applications and services can continue to function locally even if connectivity to centralized systems is temporarily lost.

- **Real-time data processing:**
  - o **Benefit**: Local processing enables real-time or near-real-time data analysis and decision-making.
  - o **Impact**: This is essential for applications that require immediate feedback, such as industrial control systems, smart grids, and autonomous vehicles.

- **Example use cases:**
  - o **Smart cities:** Traffic management systems use edge computing to analyze data from traffic cameras and sensors in real-time, optimizing traffic flow and reducing congestion.
  - o **Industrial IoT (IIoT):** Manufacturing facilities use edge computing to monitor machinery and equipment, perform real-time analytics, and detect anomalies or failures before they impact production.
  - o **Autonomous vehicles:** Self-driving cars use edge computing to process sensor data and make driving decisions in real-time, ensuring safe and efficient operation without relying on distant cloud servers.
  - o **Healthcare:** Wearable health devices process data locally to monitor vital signs and provide immediate alerts for critical conditions, with periodic data uploads to central systems for long-term analysis.
  - o **Retail:** Retail stores use edge computing for inventory management, customer behavior analysis, and personalized marketing by processing data from in-store sensors and cameras.

Edge computing enhances the performance, scalability, and efficiency of applications by processing data closer to the source of generation. It reduces latency, optimizes bandwidth, and provides better privacy and security for sensitive data. By leveraging edge computing, organizations can improve the responsiveness and reliability of their systems, enabling a wide range of applications across various industries.

Chaos engineering

Chaos engineering is a discipline in software engineering that involves deliberately introducing disruptions or failures into a system to test its resilience and robustness. The goal is to identify weaknesses and improve the system's ability to handle unexpected failures, ensuring it remains reliable and operational under various adverse conditions.

Chaos engineering works in the following manner:

- **Define the steady state:**

    o **Definition**: Establish what normal, expected behavior looks like for the system. This includes performance metrics, response times, and operational health indicators.

    o **Implementation**: Identify key metrics and benchmarks that define the system's steady state or normal operation. This baseline helps determine if the system remains functional during and after disruptions.

- **Hypothesize failure scenarios:**

    o **Definition**: Formulate hypotheses about how the system should behave in response to specific disruptions or failures.

    o **Implementation**: Based on the system's architecture and known vulnerabilities, hypothesize how it will react to various failure scenarios (e.g., server crashes, network outages, high traffic loads).

- **Design experiments:**

    o **Definition**: Create controlled experiments to introduce failures or disruptions into the system.

    o **Implementation**: Develop and execute experiments that simulate failure scenarios. This could involve tools and techniques to inject faults or simulate outages in a controlled environment.

- **Run experiments in production:**

    o **Definition**: Implement experiments in the production environment, ensuring minimal impact on users and services.

    o **Implementation**: Use techniques such as canary releases, blue-green deployments, or feature flags to gradually introduce failures and monitor the system's response. Ensure proper monitoring and alerting to detect issues early.

- **Observe and analyze:**

    o **Definition**: Monitor the system's behavior during and after the experiments to evaluate its resilience.

    o **Implementation**: Collect data on how the system responds to disruptions, including performance metrics, error rates, and system logs. Analyze this data to understand how well the system handled the failures and identify areas for improvement.

- **Learn and improve:**

  - **Definition**: Use insights gained from experiments to improve the system's resilience and reliability.

  - **Implementation**: Address identified weaknesses by implementing fixes, improving fault tolerance, or enhancing recovery mechanisms. Repeat experiments as needed to validate improvements and ensure continued resilience.

- **Document and share:**

  - **Definition**: Document the findings and share lessons learned with the team and stakeholders.

  - **Implementation**: Create reports or post-mortems detailing the results of chaos experiments, the impact on the system, and the steps taken to address identified issues. Share this knowledge to foster a culture of continuous improvement.

Benefits of chaos engineering

Chaos engineering has the following benefits:

- **Improved resilience:**

  - **Benefit**: By simulating failures, chaos engineering helps identify and address weaknesses in the system.

  - **Impact**: Systems become more resilient and better able to handle real-world disruptions without significant impact on users or operations.

- **Enhanced understanding of system behavior:**

  - **Benefit**: Chaos engineering provides insights into how systems behave under stress and failure conditions.

  - **Impact**: Teams gain a deeper understanding of system dependencies, failure modes, and recovery processes, leading to more effective design and operational strategies.

- **Reduced downtime and impact:**

  - **Benefit**: Identifying and fixing weaknesses before they cause real outages reduces the likelihood of downtime.

  - **Impact**: Systems are more reliable and less prone to unexpected failures, improving overall user experience and service availability.

- **Faster incident response:**

  - **Benefit**: Regular chaos experiments prepare teams to respond quickly and effectively to real incidents.

  - **Impact**: Improved response times and more effective incident management during actual failures or outages.

- **Increased confidence in system stability:**

  - **Benefit**: Successful experiments build confidence in the system's ability to handle failures.

  - **Impact**: Teams can deploy new features and changes with greater assurance that the system will remain stable and reliable.

- **Continuous improvement:**

  - **Benefit**: Chaos engineering fosters a culture of continuous improvement and learning.

  - **Impact**: Teams regularly challenge and improve the system's resilience, leading to ongoing enhancements in reliability and performance.

- **Example use cases:**

  - **Cloud-native applications:** Testing how a cloud-native application handles the failure of individual microservices or entire availability zones, ensuring that the system can gracefully recover and continue functioning.

  - **Distributed systems:** Introducing network latency or partitioning failures in a distributed database to evaluate its ability to maintain consistency and availability.

  - **E-commerce platforms:** Simulating high traffic loads or service outages to ensure that an e-commerce platform can handle peak traffic periods and maintain transaction integrity.

  - **Financial services:** Testing how a financial services application handles failures in transaction processing or connectivity issues with external payment gateways.

- **Tools for chaos engineering:**

  - **Chaos Monkey:** Part of the *Netflix Simian Army,* Chaos Monkey randomly terminates instances in a production environment to ensure that the system can tolerate instance failures.

  - **Gremlin:** A chaos engineering platform that allows users to inject various types of failures into their systems to test resilience.

- o **Chaos Mesh:** An open-source chaos engineering platform for Kubernetes that enables users to inject faults and simulate failures in a Kubernetes environment.

- o **LitmusChaos**: An open-source project that provides a framework for chaos engineering in Kubernetes, allowing users to define and run chaos experiments.

Chaos engineering is a proactive approach to improving system resilience by intentionally introducing disruptions and testing how well systems handle failures. By identifying and addressing weaknesses through controlled experiments, organizations can build more robust and reliable systems, enhance incident response capabilities, and ensure better overall system stability.

Observability

Observability in software engineering refers to the ability to understand and gain insights into the internal workings of a system by observing its external outputs. It is crucial for diagnosing issues, understanding system behavior, and maintaining system reliability. Observability enables teams to detect, analyze, and resolve issues effectively, leading to improved performance and user experience.

The importance of observability is as follows:

- **Issue detection and diagnosis:**

  - o **Benefit**: Observability helps identify and diagnose issues quickly by providing visibility into system performance and behavior.

  - o **Impact**: Faster detection and resolution of problems reduces downtime and minimizes the impact on users.

- **Performance monitoring:**

  - o **Benefit**: Observability provides metrics and insights into system performance, helping to identify bottlenecks and areas for improvement.

  - o **Impact**: Optimizing performance enhances user experience and ensures efficient use of resources.

- **Understanding system behavior:**

  - o **Benefit**: Observability allows teams to understand how systems behave under different conditions, including normal operations and failure scenarios.

  - o **Impact**: This understanding aids in making informed decisions about system design, scaling, and capacity planning.

- **Proactive issue prevention:**

  - **Benefit**: By continuously monitoring and analyzing system data, observability helps anticipate potential issues before they become critical.

  - **Impact**: Proactive measures prevent outages and improve system reliability.

- **Root cause analysis:**

  - **Benefit**: Observability provides the data needed to perform detailed root cause analysis of incidents and failures.

  - **Impact**: Identifying the root cause of issues leads to more effective solutions and prevents recurrence.

- **User experience improvement:**

  - **Benefit**: Observability provides insights into how users interact with the system, including response times and error rates.

  - **Impact**: Improving user experience by addressing performance issues and errors enhances satisfaction and retention.

- **Compliance and auditing:**

  - **Benefit**: Observability helps ensure compliance with regulatory requirements by providing logs and metrics for auditing purposes.

  - **Impact**: Meeting compliance requirements avoids legal and financial penalties.

- **Collaboration and communication:**

  - **Benefit**: Observability tools facilitate better collaboration among development, operations, and support teams by providing shared visibility into system health and performance.

  - **Impact**: Improved communication leads to more effective troubleshooting and faster resolution of issues.

The following metrics need to be observed:

- **Metrics:**

  - **Definition**: Quantitative data that provides insights into system performance and resource usage.

  - **Examples**: CPU usage, memory consumption, disk I/O, network bandwidth, response times, and request rates.

  - **Importance**: Metrics help monitor system health, performance trends, and resource utilization.

- **Logs:**

  - **Definition**: Records of events, transactions, and system activities.

  - **Examples**: Application logs, error logs, access logs, transaction logs, and system event logs.

  - **Importance**: Logs provide detailed information about system operations, errors, and interactions, useful for debugging and troubleshooting.

- **Traces:**

  - **Definition**: Records of the flow of requests or transactions through a system, capturing timing and context information.

  - **Examples**: Distributed traces showing the path of a request across microservices, including latency and interactions.

  - **Importance**: Traces help understand the performance of individual components and the overall request flow, revealing bottlenecks and performance issues.

- **Events:**

  - **Definition**: Notifications of significant occurrences or changes in the system.

  - **Examples**: Deployment events, system state changes, service failures, and configuration changes.

  - **Importance**: Events provide context for system changes and help correlate them with observed issues.

- **Service health metrics:**

  - **Definition**: Metrics specific to the health and performance of individual services or components.

  - **Examples**: Error rates, availability, latency, and throughput for specific services.

  - **Importance**: Service health metrics help monitor and manage the performance and reliability of individual components within a system.

- **User experience metrics:**

  - **Definition**: Metrics related to user interactions and satisfaction.

  - **Examples**: Page load times, user error rates, and application responsiveness.

  - **Importance**: Monitoring user experience metrics helps ensure that the system meets user expectations and provides a positive experience.

- **Configuration and deployment changes:**
    - ○ **Definition**: Records of changes made to system configurations and deployments.
    - ○ **Examples**: Configuration updates, feature rollouts, and infrastructure changes.
    - ○ **Importance**: Observing configuration and deployment changes helps correlate them with system behavior and identify potential causes of issues.

- **Resource utilization:**
    - ○ **Definition**: Metrics related to the use of system resources.
    - ○ **Examples**: Resource allocation, usage patterns, and limits (e.g., memory limits, CPU quotas).
    - ○ **Importance**: Monitoring resource utilization ensures that systems operate efficiently and can scale appropriately.

Best practices for observability

The following best practices need to be considered:

- **Implement comprehensive monitoring:** Ensure that metrics, logs, traces, and events are collected from all relevant components of the system.

- **Centralize observability data:** Use centralized platforms and tools to aggregate and analyze observability data, making it easier to access and interpret information.

- **Set up alerts and notifications:** Configure alerts for critical metrics and events to proactively address issues before they impact users.

- **Ensure data integrity and security:** Protect observability data to prevent unauthorized access and ensure the integrity of monitoring information.

- **Regularly review and update observability practices:** Continuously refine observability practices based on new insights, system changes, and evolving requirements.

- **Foster a culture of observability:** Encourage teams to leverage observability data for continuous improvement, collaboration, and informed decision-making.

Observability is a critical aspect of modern software engineering, providing the insights needed to maintain, optimize, and troubleshoot systems effectively. By observing metrics, logs, traces, events, and other relevant data, teams can enhance system performance, reliability, and user experience, while also improving their ability to detect and resolve issues promptly. Implementing best practices in observability helps ensure that systems remain healthy and resilient in the face of evolving challenges and demands.

Metrics in software engineering

After looking at observability as a new emerging engineering trend, it is the perfect time to talk about metrics in the software engineering process and how we can utilize certain metrics to track the effectiveness of our software engineering processes through various observability methods.

Metrics are quantitative measures used to assess various aspects of the software development lifecycle, including code quality, performance, productivity, and project management. Metrics provide valuable insights into the effectiveness of engineering practices, the health of the codebase, and the overall success of software projects.

Note that these are not metrics designed to understand the use of software in production or to measure whether the software is achieving its purpose or not, but simply metrics aimed at the software engineering process as a whole.

Types of software engineering metrics

The following are the types of metrics in software engineering:

- **Code quality metrics:** Measures related to the quality and maintainability of code.
  - **Examples:**
    - **Code complexity**: Metrics such as Cyclomatic complexity and Halstead complexity measure the complexity of code, which can impact readability and maintainability.
    - **Code coverage**: The percentage of code covered by automated tests, indicating the extent to which the code is tested.
    - **Defect density**: The number of defects per unit of code (e.g., per thousand lines of code), reflecting the quality of the codebase.
- **Performance metrics:** Metrics that evaluate the performance of software in terms of speed, efficiency, and resource usage.
  - **Examples:**
    - **Response time**: The time taken for the system to respond to a request, reflecting user experience and system efficiency.
    - **Throughput**: The number of transactions or operations the system can handle per unit of time, indicating capacity and performance.
    - **Resource utilization**: Metrics such as CPU usage, memory consumption, and disk I/O, showing how efficiently resources are used.
- **Productivity metrics:** Measures of the efficiency and output of software development activities.

- o **Examples:**

  - **Lines of code (LOC)**: The number of lines of code written, which can be used to estimate productivity, though it should be considered alongside other factors.

  - **Velocity**: In Agile methodologies, velocity measures the amount of work completed in a sprint, indicating team productivity.

  - **Lead time**: The time taken from the initiation of a task to its completion, reflecting the efficiency of the development process.

- **Project management metrics:** Metrics related to project progress, cost, and timelines.

  - o **Examples:**

    - **Burndown chart**: A graphical representation of work remaining versus time, used in Agile projects to track progress.

    - **Earned Value Management (EVM)**: A technique for assessing project performance by comparing planned progress with actual progress and costs.

    - **Schedule Variance (SV)**: The difference between the planned progress and the actual progress, indicating whether the project is ahead or behind schedule.

- **Quality assurance metrics:** Metrics that assess the quality and effectiveness of testing processes.

  - o **Examples:**

    - **Defect resolution time**: The average time taken to resolve defects, reflecting the efficiency of the bug-fixing process.

    - **Test pass rate**: The percentage of test cases that pass, indicating the overall stability and reliability of the software.

    - **Defect escape rate**: The number of defects found in production after release, reflecting the effectiveness of the testing process.

- **Customer satisfaction metrics:** Metrics related to user feedback and satisfaction with the software.

  - o **Examples:**

    - **Net Promoter Score (NPS)**: A measure of customer loyalty and satisfaction based on their likelihood to recommend the software to others.

- **Customer Satisfaction Score (CSAT)**: A measure of customer satisfaction with specific aspects of the software or service.

- **User feedback and ratings**: Direct feedback from users, including ratings and comments on the software's usability and functionality.

- **Maintenance metrics:** Metrics related to the ongoing maintenance and support of the software.

  o **Examples:**

    - **Bug fix rate**: The rate at which reported bugs are fixed, indicating the effectiveness of the maintenance process.

    - **Technical debt**: The cost of addressing issues that arise from taking shortcuts or making trade-offs during development, impacting future maintenance.

    - **Support request volume**: The number of support requests or tickets, reflecting the software's reliability and user experience.

Best practices

The following are the best practices for using software engineering metrics:

- **Align metrics with goals**: Ensure that metrics are aligned with the goals and objectives of the project or organization. Choose metrics that provide meaningful insights and support decision-making.

- **Use a balanced set of metrics**: Combine different types of metrics (e.g., quality, performance, productivity) to get a comprehensive view of the software's health and development process. Avoid relying on a single metric that might provide a skewed perspective.

- **Automate data collection**: Use automated tools to collect and analyze metrics to ensure accuracy and reduce manual effort. Tools for continuous integration, monitoring, and issue tracking can provide valuable data.

- **Regularly review and analyze metrics**: Continuously review and analyze metrics to identify trends, patterns, and areas for improvement. Use data-driven insights to make informed decisions and drive improvements.

- **Avoid metrics overload**: Focus on key metrics that provide actionable insights. Avoid collecting too many metrics, which can lead to analysis paralysis and dilute the focus on critical areas.

- **Communicate metrics effectively**: Present metrics in a clear and understandable manner to stakeholders. Use visualizations, dashboards, and reports to make the data accessible and actionable.

- **Foster a culture of improvement**: Use metrics as a tool for continuous improvement. Encourage teams to use metrics to identify opportunities for enhancement and to drive positive changes in the development process.

Metrics are essential for measuring and improving various aspects of software engineering, including code quality, performance, productivity, and project management. By selecting and analyzing the right metrics, teams can gain valuable insights into their development processes, identify areas for improvement, and ensure the successful delivery and maintenance of high-quality software.

Conclusion

We cannot separate the software architecture and design from the engineering process and how we implement our software systems. Having a good understanding of different engineering processes helps an architect to better understand how their vision may be brought to life and ensures they incorporate the right design techniques that allow the software delivery teams to build and maintain the software in the best way possible.

Much like most aspects of software design, software engineering techniques and processes are also evolving, and so software architects need to stay informed of new development processes, while constantly measuring the effectiveness of the existing delivery processes to evolve and pivot to different methods where needed.

In the next chapter, we will explore software testing techniques and how software architecture plays a critical role in the success of any testing effort in an application.

Join our book's Discord space

Join the book's Discord Workspace for Latest updates, Offers, Tech happenings around the world, New Release and Sessions with the Authors:

https://discord.bpbonline.com

CHAPTER 16
Testing in Software Architecture

Introduction

Verifying that something works as intended and is free from defects is just as critical as the engineering process. So, it is important that all software architects understand how software is tested and design accordingly to ensure the systems they design are testable.

We will begin this chapter by looking at the topic of testability itself before unpacking testing in more detail, looking at different types of testing, different testing techniques, and then focusing on some of the aspects of testing that are critical for all software architects to get involved in.

Structure

In this chapter, we will discuss the following topics:

- Designing for testability
- Designing APIs for testability
- Testability in designing front-ends
- Test-driven development
- Test data management
- Test environments and data privacy

- Performance testing
- Security testing
- Automated testing infrastructure
- Test logging and monitoring

Objectives

By the end of this chapter, you will understand the importance of software testing in the software engineering process, the different levels of testing that are required, and the role of an architect in designing systems with testing in mind.

Designing for testability

Designing software for testability means creating software in such a way that it is easy to test, both manually and automatically. Testability is an essential quality in software engineering because it directly impacts the efficiency and effectiveness of the testing process, which in turn affects the overall quality of the software.

The following sub-sections discuss the key principles of designing software for testability.

Modular design

Modular design in software testing involves breaking frameworks into self-contained, reusable components, each serving a specific purpose. This improves scalability, maintainability, and adaptability, enabling efficient updates and streamlined collaboration as follows:

- **Separation of concerns**: Divide the software into distinct modules or components, each responsible for a specific functionality. This makes it easier to isolate and test individual parts of the system.

- **Loose coupling**: Minimize dependencies between modules. Highly coupled modules can make testing more difficult because changes in one module may affect others.

Clear and simple interfaces

In software testing, clear and simple interfaces refer to well-defined connections between test components, making it easy to understand, use, and integrate them. This ensures that test modules can interact seamlessly, reducing complexity and improving maintainability as follows:

- **Well-defined interfaces**: Ensure that each module or class has a clear and well-defined interface. This makes it easier to mock or stub components during testing.

- **Consistent input/output**: Design interfaces that consistently handle input and output, which helps in predicting and verifying behavior during tests.

Dependency injection

Dependency injection in software testing is a design pattern where test components receive their dependencies externally rather than creating them internally. This allows for greater flexibility, easier mocking or stubbing of dependencies, and more effective testing of individual components in isolation, leading to more reliable and maintainable test automation. This can be achieved as follows:

- **Inversion of Control (IoC)**: Use dependency injection to pass dependencies into a class or module rather than having them hard-coded. This allows testers to inject mock objects or stubs instead of real implementations, facilitating isolated unit tests.

Logging and monitoring

Logging and monitoring in software testing involve capturing and analyzing data about test execution and system behavior. Logging provides detailed records of test steps, errors, and results, aiding in debugging and troubleshooting. Monitoring tracks metrics like test performance, resource usage, and system health during testing, helping identify issues such as bottlenecks or flaky tests. Together, they enhance visibility, improve issue resolution, and ensure the effectiveness of the testing process in the following manner:

- **Comprehensive logging**: Implement detailed logging to capture important events and state changes in the software. This helps testers understand the flow of execution and diagnose issues.

- **Health monitoring**: Include monitoring hooks that allow testers to check the system's health and state at various points during execution.

Deterministic behavior

Deterministic behavior in software testing means that tests consistently produce the same results given the same inputs and conditions. It ensures reliability and repeatability, making it easier to identify actual issues rather than random or environment-dependent failures. Achieving deterministic behavior often involves controlling variables like test data, external dependencies, and execution environments:

- **Avoid randomness**: Ensure that the software's behavior is predictable and consistent, which is crucial for reproducible tests. If randomness is necessary, provide a way to control or seed it during testing.

- **Time handling**: When dealing with time-sensitive code, provide mechanisms to manipulate time for testing purposes, such as using time stubs or mocks.

Error handling and reporting

Error handling and reporting in software testing involve capturing, managing, and communicating issues that arise during test execution. Effective error handling ensures that tests fail gracefully with meaningful messages, helping testers quickly identify the cause of the failure. Reporting summarizes test results, logs errors, and provides insights into test execution, making it easier to track progress, diagnose problems, and communicate findings to stakeholders. Well-implemented error handling and reporting improve test reliability and streamline debugging. This can be achieved as follows:

- **Graceful error handling**: Design the software to handle errors gracefully and report them in a way that is useful for debugging and testing.

- **Clear error messages**: Ensure that error messages are descriptive and provide enough context for understanding the problem.

Automated testing support

These are things that architects need to be aware of to ensure the software design can integrate seamlessly into the respective test automation framework and tooling. Software architects need to ensure that automated testing is supported by a scalable, maintainable framework that integrates seamlessly with the development pipeline and adapts to evolving system requirements:

- **Test hooks**: Provide test-specific hooks or APIs that allow testers to inspect internal states, manipulate conditions, or trigger specific scenarios.

- **Automated test framework integration**: Design the software to integrate seamlessly with automated testing frameworks, including unit testing, integration testing, and end-to-end testing tools.

Configuration for testing

Configuration for testing involves setting up and managing the necessary environment, tools, and parameters to ensure consistent and reliable test execution across different scenarios and systems:

- **Test configuration**: Allow the software to be easily configured for different environments, including test environments. This might include toggling features, simulating failures, or enabling debug modes.

Documentation

Documentation in code and software design for testing involves clearly commenting and describing the purpose, behavior, and structure of test code and components. This helps ensure that tests are understandable, maintainable, and reusable, and provides guidance for developers and testers on how the testing framework is structured and how to extend or modify it:

- **Clear documentation**: Provide thorough documentation that explains the software's architecture, design decisions, and how to interact with it. This helps testers understand what to test and how.

Mocking and simulation

Mocking and simulation in software testing involve creating controlled, simplified versions of real components or systems to isolate and test specific parts of the application. Mocking replaces real dependencies with fake ones that mimic behavior, allowing for unit testing without external dependencies. Simulation, on the other hand, imitates real-world conditions or interactions to test how the system responds in various scenarios, providing insights into performance and behavior without needing the actual environment or services. The following techniques help in testing components in isolation and improve test reliability:

- **Support for mocking**: Design components so that their dependencies can easily be replaced with mock objects during testing.

- **Simulation of external systems**: If the software interacts with external systems (like databases or third-party APIs), provide mechanisms to simulate these systems during tests.

Benefits of designing for testability

The preceding aspects are vital in building software that is suitably testable. And while that does appear like extra effort from an architectural perspective, the following benefits make it worthwhile for any team:

- **Reduced defects**: Easier identification and fixing of bugs.

- **Faster testing cycles**: Tests can be run quickly and frequently, leading to faster feedback.

- **Lower maintenance costs**: Easier to maintain and extend tests as the software evolves.

- **Higher confidence in code changes**: Refactoring or adding new features can be done with higher confidence, knowing that existing functionality is covered by tests.

Designing for testability requires considering testing from the very beginning of the software development process, making it an integral part of software design.

Designing APIs for testability

Along with the above design principles for software, it is important to focus more specifically on different areas from an API perspective. Designing APIs for testability involves structuring the API in a way that makes it easy to test, both in isolation and as part of a larger system. This is vital as APIs are a key aspect of software architecture that play a role in communicating between different systems and if designed correctly, can be easily tested at both an isolated way for independent deployment and in a comprehensive end-to-end manner for larger orchestration.

Design with clear, consistent contracts

Clear, consistent contracts in software testing ensure that test components interact reliably, reducing misunderstandings and making it easier to maintain and extend the testing framework:

- **Use RESTful principles or GraphQL**: If you are designing a REST API, follow REST principles such as using the correct HTTP methods (GET, POST, PUT, DELETE), status codes, and resource naming conventions. If using GraphQL, ensure queries and mutations are well-structured and follow a consistent schema.

- **Consistent naming**: Use consistent naming conventions for endpoints, parameters, and response fields. This predictability makes it easier to write tests.

- **Versioning**: Include versioning in your API URLs (e.g., `/api/v1/resource`) to ensure tests can run against specific versions of the API, even as it evolves.

Idempotent and stateless operations

Refer to the following list for the key concepts related to idempotent and stateless operations:

- **Idempotent endpoints**: Ensure that operations like PUT and DELETE are idempotent, meaning they can be called multiple times without changing the result. This is crucial for testing since tests may run multiple times.

- **Statelessness**: Design APIs to be stateless, where each request is independent and does not rely on a previous request. This makes it easier to test individual endpoints in isolation.

Well-defined input and output

Well-defined input and output in software testing ensure clarity and consistency, enabling accurate test execution, predictable results, and easier validation of system behavior. This can be achieved as follows:

- **Schema validation**: Define and enforce strict schemas for request bodies, query parameters, and responses. Use tools like JSON Schema for validation. This ensures that the API behaves predictably, making it easier to test.

- **Detailed error handling**: Clearly define how errors are handled and what responses (e.g., status codes, error messages) are returned. This predictability allows for thorough testing of error conditions.

Use dependency injection

Dependency injection in software testing is a design pattern where test components receive their dependencies from an external source, rather than creating them internally. This promotes flexibility, makes it easier to swap out dependencies for mock or stub implementations, and enhances test isolation, leading to more effective and maintainable tests:

- **Injectable dependencies**: Design the API so that external dependencies (like databases, third-party services, or configurations) can be injected. This allows you to substitute real dependencies with mocks or stubs during testing.

- **Configuration management**: Use environment variables or configuration files to manage settings that might vary between development, testing, and production environments.

Test hooks and simulated environments

Test hooks and simulated environments are techniques used to control and manage test execution. Test hooks are predefined points in the test lifecycle where custom actions or assertions can be inserted, allowing for greater flexibility and control during testing. Simulated environments replicate real-world conditions, such as databases, APIs, or third-party services, enabling tests to run without relying on the actual external systems, ensuring more reliable, isolated, and repeatable test scenarios. Refer to the following list for the key concepts related to test endpoints and simulated environments:

- **Test endpoints**: Provide hidden or protected endpoints that can be used to manipulate the state of the application for testing purposes (e.g., resetting data, seeding test data).

- **Simulated environments**: Design your API to work in different environments (e.g., development, testing, staging, production). This allows for realistic testing scenarios without affecting production data.

Enable easy mocking and stubbing

Enabling mocking and stubbing for testing allows you to simulate the behavior of external dependencies or complex components in isolation. **Mocking** creates fake objects that mimic the behavior of real components, verifying interactions and ensuring correct function calls. **Stubbing** provides predefined responses from dependencies to control the test environment, focusing on specific behaviors without triggering the full functionality of the real object. Both techniques help isolate the system under test, improve test reliability, and speed up testing by removing dependencies on external systems, shown as follows:

- **External dependencies**: If your API relies on external services, provide interfaces or adapters that can be easily mocked or stubbed during testing.

- **Service layer abstraction**: Use a service layer to encapsulate business logic. This abstraction makes it easier to mock complex operations and test the API's behavior in isolation.

Support for asynchronous operations

Support for asynchronous operations in software testing ensures that tests can handle tasks that run concurrently or independently, such as network requests or background processes. This involves using tools or techniques like promises, callbacks, or async/await patterns to manage and validate the completion of asynchronous tasks, ensuring tests accurately reflect real-world behavior without blocking or waiting for operations to finish. Proper handling of asynchronous operations is crucial for testing the responsiveness and reliability of modern applications:

- **Callbacks or webhooks**: If your API supports asynchronous operations, design it to include mechanisms like callbacks or webhooks. Ensure these can be tested by providing ways to simulate and capture these events.

- **Polling or notification**: If using polling, provide a clear and predictable way to test the API's behavior over time.

Rate limiting and throttling

Rate limiting and throttling in software testing are techniques used to control the number of requests or operations that can be performed in a given time frame, ensuring the system's performance and stability. These concepts are defined as follows:

- **Rate limiting**: It restricts the number of requests a system can handle within a specific period (e.g., 100 requests per minute). It helps prevent overloading and ensures fair use of resources.

- **Throttling**: It controls the rate at which requests are processed, reducing the speed or frequency of operations to maintain system performance, especially under high load conditions.

The following techniques are critical for testing how the system handles load, manages resources, and responds to excessive traffic or requests:

- **Configurable rate limits**: Ensure rate limiting and throttling are configurable so that they can be adjusted or disabled in a testing environment. This prevents tests from being affected by rate limits.

- **Clear documentation**: Document how rate limiting works so testers can design tests that respect these constraints.

Design for failure testing

Designing for failure testing involves intentionally creating test scenarios that simulate potential failures, errors, or unexpected conditions to assess how the system responds. This approach ensures that the system can gracefully handle issues like network outages, invalid inputs, resource limitations, or service unavailability. By testing failure conditions in the following manner, teams can identify weaknesses, improve error handling, and build more resilient systems that perform reliably under adverse conditions:

- **Simulate failures**: Design the API to allow for the simulation of failures, such as network timeouts, service unavailability, or database errors. This helps in testing the API's robustness and error handling.

- **Graceful degradation**: Ensure that the API can gracefully degrade in the event of partial failures and test these scenarios thoroughly.

By following these practices, you can design APIs that are not only functional and reliable but also easy to test. This leads to higher code quality, fewer bugs, and a more maintainable codebase. APIs designed for testability facilitate automated testing, reduce the likelihood of regressions, and improve the overall development and deployment process.

Testability in designing front-ends

Similar to APIS, front-end may also have some additional unique aspects that software architects should consider. Designing a front-end for testability involves creating a UI that is easy to test through automated tests and manual testing. It requires thoughtful structuring of components, separation of concerns, and ensuring that the code is modular and predictable.

Component-based architecture

In a component-based architecture, testability refers to designing components in a way that allows them to be easily tested in isolation. This involves creating clear interfaces, minimizing dependencies, and ensuring components are loosely coupled, making it easier to verify functionality, detect issues early, and maintain high-quality code:

- **Modular components**: Break down the UI into small, reusable, and independent components. Each component should have a single responsibility, making it easier to test in isolation.

- **Props and state management**: Clearly define and manage component inputs (props) and internal state. This ensures that tests can be written to verify the behavior based on different inputs.

Separation of concerns

Separation of concerns in software testing involves dividing a system into distinct sections, each responsible for a specific functionality or task. This approach makes it easier to test individual components independently, ensuring that changes in one area do not negatively affect others, and improving maintainability and scalability of the testing process:

- **Presentation vs. logic**: Separate the UI logic from the business logic. Use container components (smart components) to handle data fetching and state management, and presentational components (dumb components) to render the UI.

- **Services and utilities**: Abstract complex logic and side effects (e.g., API calls, data transformations) into services or utility functions. These can be easily mocked or stubbed during testing.

State management

State management in software testing involves tracking and controlling the state of the system or components during test execution. It ensures that tests are run in a known, consistent state, preventing issues caused by unexpected changes or residual data from previous tests. Proper state management helps isolate tests, improves repeatability, and ensures accurate validation of system behavior under different conditions. State management includes the following:

- **Predictable state**: Use predictable state management libraries (e.g., Redux, Vuex) where state changes are triggered through explicit actions. This predictability makes it easier to test the state transitions.

- **Avoid global state**: Minimize reliance on global state where possible and use context or scoped state management for components. This helps in isolating components during testing.

Testable UI elements

Testable UI elements are user interface components designed to be easily interacted with and validated during automated testing. These elements should have clear, unique identifiers (like IDs or class names) and should be structured in a way that allows for efficient interaction and verification, such as checking visibility, correctness of content, or user actions (clicks, inputs). Designing UI elements with testability in mind ensures that automated tests can reliably verify the UI's functionality and behavior across different scenarios. Some UI elements are listed as follows:

- **Unique identifiers**: Use unique and stable identifiers (e.g., `data-testid` attributes) for critical UI elements. These can be targeted in automated tests without relying on fragile selectors like class names or DOM structure.

- **Accessible design**: Design your UI with accessibility in mind (e.g., using proper ARIA labels, semantic HTML). Accessible UIs are more predictable and easier to test.

Dependency injection

Something which will come up many times in this chapter because of its importance to the topic. Dependency injection allows a component's dependencies to be provided externally, promoting flexibility and easier testing by decoupling components from their dependencies:

- **Mockable dependencies**: Use dependency injection to pass external dependencies (e.g., services, APIs) into components. This allows you to replace real dependencies with mocks or stubs during testing.

- **Configuration via props**: Configure components through props rather than relying on global variables or direct imports. This makes components easier to test with different configurations.

Event handling and asynchronous operations

Event handling and asynchronous operations in software testing involve managing actions triggered by events (like user inputs or system notifications) and ensuring that the system responds correctly without blocking the main execution flow. Tests must verify that events are properly captured and that asynchronous tasks, such as background processes or network calls, complete as expected, without impacting the system's responsiveness or stability:

- **Explicit event handlers**: Define event handlers explicitly rather than inline, making it easier to test the logic triggered by events.

- **Asynchronous testing**: Ensure that asynchronous operations (e.g., API calls, timers) are testable. Use tools like async/await, mocks, and libraries like Sinon to control and verify asynchronous behavior.

CSS and styling

In software testing, CSS and styling are important to ensure that the user interface appears correctly across different browsers and devices. Tests should verify that the right styles are applied, elements are positioned properly, and the layout remains responsive. This can include checking for visual consistency, color schemes, font sizes, and ensuring that dynamic UI changes (like hover effects or animations) function as intended:

- **Avoid inline styles**: Use CSS classes or CSS-in-JS libraries for styling rather than inline styles. This makes it easier to test the rendered output and ensures that styling changes do not break tests.

Accessibility testing

Accessibility testing ensures that a software application is usable by people with disabilities, such as those with visual, auditory, or motor impairments. This involves testing for compliance with accessibility standards (like WCAG), verifying features like screen reader compatibility, keyboard navigation, color contrast, and ensuring that interactive elements are accessible to users with assistive technologies. The goal is to make sure the application is inclusive and provides a good user experience for all users, and can be achieved as follows:

- **Automated accessibility tests**: Integrate tools like axe-core or Lighthouse to automatically test for accessibility issues during development and in CI/CD pipelines.

- **Manual accessibility audits**: Perform manual accessibility testing to catch issues that automated tools might miss, ensuring that the application is usable for all users.

Testability in responsive design

Testability in responsive design involves ensuring that a web application or website behaves correctly across different screen sizes, orientations, and devices. It includes verifying that elements adjust appropriately, such as layouts, navigation, and content, and ensuring that interactive components (buttons, forms, etc.) are functional on various devices. Tests should check for visual consistency, proper scaling, and usability across mobile, tablet, and desktop environments, ensuring the user experience remains seamless regardless of the device used:

- **Responsive testing**: Test your UI across different screen sizes and devices. Tools like BrowserStack or responsive design testing tools can help automate this process.

- **Media query testing**: Ensure that your tests account for different CSS media queries by simulating different viewport sizes and checking the rendered output.

By designing the front-end with testability in mind, you create a more maintainable, reliable, and robust application. The key is to make components modular, predictable, and isolated so they can be tested independently and in combination. With thoughtful architecture, clear interfaces, and proper tooling, you can ensure that your front-end is easy to test, leading to higher quality and more maintainable code.

Understanding where to test

Designing for testability is critical, but it means little without understanding the actual testing processes themselves. Testing software involves various levels and techniques to ensure that the application works as expected, is reliable, and meets user requirements. Each level of testing focuses on different aspects of the software and is typically performed at different stages of the development process. As a software architect, it is imperative to know these different types of testing that are required at different levels.

Levels of testing

The following is the detail of the different levels of testing that you get and some of the common testing techniques associated with these levels to achieve the right quality outcome:

- **Unit testing**
    - **Focus**: Tests individual units or components of the software, such as functions, methods, or classes, in isolation.
    - **Techniques**:
        - **White-box testing**: Testing internal structures or workings of an application, often done by developers who know the internal code structure.
        - **Mocking/Stubbing**: Using mock objects or stubs to simulate external dependencies, allowing the unit under test to be isolated.
        - **Automated testing**: Utilizing testing frameworks (e.g., JUnit, NUnit) to automate unit tests. We will discuss some more specifics of unit tests later in the chapter.

- **Integration testing**
    - **Focus**: Tests the interaction between integrated units or components to ensure they work together as expected.
    - **Techniques**:
        - **Big bang testing**: Testing all components together after all units are developed, though this can make it harder to pinpoint issues.
        - **Top-down testing**: Testing from top modules to lower-level modules, often using stubs for lower modules.
        - **Bottom-up testing**: Testing from lower-level modules to top modules, often using drivers to simulate higher-level modules.
        - **Incremental testing**: Testing components incrementally as they are integrated.

- **Contract testing**: Testing the agreed-upon interactions between services (common in microservices architectures).

- **System testing**

  - **Focus**: Tests the complete and integrated system to verify that it meets the specified requirements.

  - **Techniques**:

    - **Black-box testing**: Testing without knowledge of the internal workings of the system, focusing on inputs and expected outputs.

    - **End-to-end testing**: Testing the entire application flow from start to finish to ensure all components work together.

    - **Load testing**: Testing the system's ability to handle expected load conditions.

    - **Stress testing**: Testing the system under extreme conditions to see how it behaves beyond normal operational capacity.

    - **Security testing**: Ensuring the system is secure from vulnerabilities, threats, and risks.

- **Acceptance testing**

  - **Focus**: Validates the software against business requirements and ensures it meets user expectations.

  - **Techniques**:

    - **User Acceptance Testing (UAT)**: Testing conducted by the end-users or clients to ensure the system meets their needs.

    - **Operational Acceptance Testing (OAT)**: Ensuring the system meets operational requirements, such as maintainability and reliability.

    - **Alpha testing**: Performed by internal staff at the developer's site.

    - **Beta testing**: Performed by a limited number of end-users at their premises to uncover issues in a real-world environment.

- **Regression testing**

  - **Focus**: Ensures that new changes or updates have not adversely affected existing functionality.

  - **Techniques**:

    - **Re-test all**: Re-testing all test cases in the entire test suite, though it is time-consuming and costly.

- **Regression test selection**: Testing a subset of the test suite that is affected by recent changes.

- **Prioritization of test cases**: Prioritizing test cases based on criticality and frequency of use.

- **Performance testing**

  - **Focus**: Evaluates the performance of the software in terms of speed, responsiveness, and stability under a particular workload. We will focus more on performance testing a little later in the chapter.

  - **Techniques**:

    - **Load testing**: Assessing the software's ability to perform under expected user load.

    - **Stress testing**: Determining the software's robustness under extreme load conditions.

    - **Scalability testing**: Testing how the software performs as it scales in terms of users or data volume.

  - **Soak testing**: Evaluating the software's performance over an extended period under normal load conditions.

- **Security testing**

  - **Focus**: Identifies vulnerabilities and ensures that the software is protected against threats. We will focus further on different aspects of security testing later in the chapter.

  - **Techniques**:

    - **Penetration testing**: Simulating attacks to find security weaknesses.

    - **Vulnerability scanning**: Automated scanning for known security vulnerabilities.

    - **Security code review**: Reviewing the source code for security flaws.

    - **Ethical hacking**: Authorized attempts to exploit vulnerabilities in the system.

- **Usability testing**

  - **Focus**: Ensures that the software is user-friendly and provides a good user experience.

  - **Techniques**:

    - **Heuristic evaluation**: Expert-based evaluation against usability principles.

- **User testing**: Observing real users as they interact with the software to identify usability issues.

- **A/B testing**: Comparing two versions of the software to determine which performs better in terms of user experience.

- **Compatibility testing**

  o **Focus**: Ensures that the software works across different devices, browsers, and operating systems.

  o **Techniques**:

    - **Cross-browser testing**: Verifying that the software works correctly across different web browsers.

    - **Cross-platform testing**: Ensuring the software is functional on various operating systems and hardware configurations.

    - **Device testing**: Testing the software on various devices like smartphones, tablets, etc.

- **Smoke testing**

  o **Focus**: A quick check to ensure the basic functionality of the software works after a new build or deployment.

  o **Techniques**:

    - **Build Verification Testing (BVT)**: A subset of tests to verify that a new build is stable enough for further testing.

    - **Sanity testing**: A narrow and deep approach to testing specific functionality after minor changes.

- **Exploratory testing**

  o **Focus**: A simultaneous process of learning, test design, and test execution, where testers explore the software to identify defects.

  o **Techniques**:

    - **Session-based testing**: Time-boxed sessions where testers focus on exploring specific areas of the software.

    - **Ad hoc testing**: Unstructured testing where testers explore the software without predefined test cases.

By leveraging these levels and techniques, testing can comprehensively cover the functionality, performance, security, and usability of the software, ensuring a high-quality product.

Test design techniques

Test design techniques are methods used to create effective test cases that ensure thorough and efficient testing of software. While this might not be the specialization of a software architect and is left largely for the test or quality engineers in a team, it is nonetheless important for software architects to understand these different techniques and how they are applied in software testing.

Black box testing techniques

Black box testing is a software testing technique where the internal workings of the application are not known to the tester. The focus is solely on the functionality of the system, verifying whether it behaves as expected based on the input provided, without concern for the underlying code or structure. Common black box testing techniques include equivalence partitioning (dividing input data into valid and invalid partitions), boundary value analysis (testing values at the boundaries of input ranges), decision table testing (modeling complex logic with decision tables), and state transition testing (examining state changes based on inputs). The following techniques help ensure that the software functions correctly in a variety of scenarios, from a user's perspective:

- **Equivalence partitioning**:
    - **Description**: Divides input data into equivalent partitions where each partition is expected to be processed similarly by the system.
    - **Purpose**: Reduces the number of test cases by covering each partition with one test case.
    - **Example**: For a field that accepts ages between 18 and 60, you might test with ages 17, 18, 30, 60, and 61.

- **Boundary value analysis**:
    - **Description**: Tests the boundaries of input ranges where errors are most likely to occur.
    - **Purpose**: Identifies errors at the boundaries of input ranges.
    - **Example**: For a range of 1 to 100, test with values 0, 1, 2, 99, 100, and 101.

- **Decision table testing**:
    - **Description**: Uses a table to represent combinations of inputs and their expected outcomes.
    - **Purpose**: Ensures that all possible combinations of inputs are tested.
    - **Example**: Testing a login system with different combinations of username and password validity.

- **State transition testing**:

  - o **Description**: Tests the system's response to different state transitions based on inputs.

  - o **Purpose**: Verifies that the system transitions between states correctly.

  - o **Example**: Testing a traffic light system where states change from green to yellow to red.

- **Use case testing**:

  - o **Description**: Focuses on the user's interaction with the system as described in use cases.

  - o **Purpose**: Ensures that the system meets user requirements and use case scenarios.

  - o **Example**: Testing a shopping cart by simulating the user's actions from adding items to completing a purchase.

White box testing techniques

White box testing is a software testing technique where the tester has access to the internal workings of the application and focuses on testing the code's logic and structure. It involves techniques such as statement coverage, branch coverage, path coverage, condition coverage, and loop testing, all aimed at verifying that the internal components work correctly. By examining the code itself, white box testing ensures that all paths, decisions, and conditions are tested, helping identify logical errors, security vulnerabilities, and areas for optimization. This approach is essential for ensuring the robustness and correctness of the software from a code-level perspective. White box testing techniques include:

- **Statement coverage**:

  - o **Description**: Ensures that each statement in the code is executed at least once.

  - o **Purpose**: Provides a measure of code coverage by ensuring all code statements are tested.

  - o **Example**: Testing a function with various inputs to ensure all lines of code are executed.

- **Branch coverage**:

  - o **Description**: Ensures that each branch or decision point in the code is executed.

  - o **Purpose**: Provides better coverage than statement coverage by ensuring all possible branches are tested.

- o **Example**: Testing a function with conditions to ensure both true and false paths are executed.

- **Path coverage**:

  - o **Description**: Ensures that all possible paths through the code are tested.

  - o **Purpose**: Provides comprehensive coverage by testing all possible execution paths.

  - o **Example**: Testing all possible combinations of loops and conditionals in a function.

- **Condition coverage**:

  - o **Description**: Ensures that each condition in decision statements is evaluated as both true and false.

  - o **Purpose**: Provides coverage for individual conditions within decision statements.

  - o **Example**: Testing conditions in an if statement to ensure both true and false conditions are covered.

Experience based testing techniques

Experience based testing techniques rely on the tester's expertise and intuition to identify potential defects. Rather than following predefined test cases, testers use their understanding of the application, domain knowledge, and past experiences to guide their testing efforts. Techniques like exploratory testing allow testers to interact with the system in an unscripted manner, uncovering issues through hands-on exploration. Other techniques, such as error guessing and checklist-based testing, leverage the tester's familiarity with common problems or previous defects. This approach is effective in discovering subtle or complex issues that may not be covered by structured testing methods. The techniques include:

- **Exploratory testing**:

  - o **Description**: Testing without predefined test cases, exploring the application based on the tester's experience and intuition.

  - o **Purpose**: Identifies issues that might not be covered by formal test cases.

  - o **Example**: A tester navigates through a web application and uses various features to find defects.

- **Error guessing**:

  - o **Description**: Uses the tester's experience and intuition to guess where errors might occur.

- o **Purpose**: Identifies potential problem areas based on previous experiences or common issues.

- o **Example**: Testing a form by entering unusual characters or invalid data.

Hybrid testing techniques

Hybrid testing techniques combine elements of both structured and experience-based approaches to create a more flexible and comprehensive testing process. By integrating formal methods, like black box and white box testing, with exploratory testing or error guessing, hybrid techniques allow testers to benefit from systematic test coverage while also leveraging their intuition and domain knowledge. This combination helps address both known and unknown risks, ensuring that tests are thorough and adaptable to different scenarios, often leading to more robust and effective defect detection. Some hybrid testing techniques are outlined as follows:

- **Pairwise testing**:

  - o **Description**: Tests all possible pairs of input values to cover combinations that are likely to cause issues.

  - o **Purpose**: Reduces the number of test cases while still covering important input combinations.

  - o **Example**: Testing a form with different combinations of valid and invalid input pairs.

- **Risk-based testing**:

  - o **Description**: Prioritizes testing based on the risk of failure and impact on the system.

  - o **Purpose**: Focuses testing efforts on high-risk areas to maximize effectiveness.

  - o **Example**: Testing critical features of a financial application more thoroughly than less critical ones.

Choosing the right technique

There are a lot of different testing techniques that can be applied, and often knowing how to apply them in the appropriate way can be the biggest challenge. The following are some things to consider when approaching the use of these different testing techniques:

- **Project requirements**: The choice of technique depends on project requirements, available resources, and the complexity of the system.

- **Test coverage**: Combining techniques often provides better coverage and more effective testing.

- **Test objectives**: Consider the specific objectives of your testing to select the most appropriate technique(s).

Using a mix of these techniques can help you design comprehensive test cases that ensure thorough validation of your software.

Test-driven development

Test-driven development (**TDD**) is a software development practice where tests are written before writing the actual code. It is a cycle that encourages developers to think through their design and functionality before implementation. TDD is closely aligned with the principles of agile development and continuous integration, aiming to produce high-quality, reliable code through an iterative process.

While some of the aforementioned testing techniques were more focused on the work that test engineers will conduct in teams, the TDD process is largely seen as a way of enabling the software engineers themselves to better write their code for testability and contributes to a great unit test coverage.

The TDD process

TDD follows a simple cycle known as **Red-Green-Refactor**:

- **Red**: Write a failing test.

    o **Write the test**: Before any production code is written, a small, specific test is created to define what the code should do. This test will naturally fail because the feature or functionality it is testing has not been implemented yet.

    o **Run the test**: Execute the test to confirm that it fails, which indicates that the test is valid and the feature is not yet implemented.

- **Green**: Write just enough code to pass the test.

    o **Write the code**: Implement the simplest possible code to make the test pass. The goal here is to focus on correctness rather than optimization or completeness.

    o **Run the test again**: Verify that the test now passes with the new code. If it passes, you have achieved the minimal implementation necessary to meet the test's requirements.

- **Refactor**: Improve the code.

    o **Refactor the code**: Once the test passes, clean up the code by removing any duplication, improving the design, and optimizing the implementation. The test ensures that the functionality remains intact during refactoring.

    o **Re-run all tests**: Make sure that all tests (including previous ones) still pass after refactoring. This ensures that the code remains functional and that no regressions have been introduced.

Benefits of TDD

The following are the key benefits software engineers and teams will get from applying a TDD approach before designing and writing their code:

- **Improved code quality**

      o Writing tests first forces developers to think about the requirements and design upfront, leading to cleaner, more modular code.

      o Refactoring is safer because the existing tests act as a safety net, ensuring that the changes do not break the system.

- **Faster feedback**

      o TDD provides immediate feedback on whether the code works as intended, allowing developers to catch bugs early in the development process.

      o Developers can quickly identify when a change introduces a bug because tests are run frequently.

- **Reduced debugging time**

      o TDD encourages small, incremental changes. So, it is easier to identify the cause of bugs, reducing the time spent debugging.

- **Increased confidence in code**

      o With a comprehensive suite of tests, developers can refactor and extend code with greater confidence, knowing that any issues will be quickly identified.

- **Better design and architecture**

      o TDD encourages writing only the necessary code, often leading to simpler and more elegant designs.

      o The focus on testability often results in better-structured, loosely coupled code, which is easier to maintain and extend.

- **Documentation**

      o The tests themselves act as documentation, providing clear examples of how the code is intended to be used and what its expected behavior is.

Challenges of TDD

As effective as TDD is in producing good quality, testable code, it has its challenges that might make it difficult to implement in certain software spaces and often requires a trade-off in managing when a TDD approach should be considered within the development team. The challenges are outlined as follows:

- **Learning curve**

  o TDD requires a shift in mindset and can be challenging for developers who are used to writing code first and testing later.

  o Writing good tests requires experience and understanding of edge cases and potential pitfalls.

- **Initial time investment**

  o Writing tests before coding can feel slower initially, as it requires more upfront work. However, this investment pays off in the long term through higher quality and fewer bugs.

- **Difficulty in testing certain features**

  o Some features, such as user interfaces or complex integrations, can be difficult to test using TDD, requiring additional tools or techniques.

- **Overhead in maintaining tests**

  o As the codebase evolves, tests need to be maintained and updated. Poorly written tests can become brittle and lead to frequent false positives, requiring additional effort to maintain.

TDD best practices

As always, some of those difficulties around TDD can be easily solved with the implementation of best practices. If you are looking to implement TDD practices into your engineering processes, then the following approaches can help:

- **Start small:** Begin with small, simple tests that cover the core functionality. Gradually expand coverage as you gain confidence and understanding of TDD.

- **Write clean, maintainable tests:** Ensure that your tests are easy to read, understand, and maintain. Avoid writing overly complex tests that are difficult to manage.

- **Test behavior, not implementation:** Focus on testing the behavior of the code, rather than its implementation details. This ensures that tests remain relevant even if the underlying implementation changes.

- **Use mocks and stubs appropriately:** Use mock objects and stubs to isolate the unit under test, especially when dealing with external dependencies like databases, APIs, or file systems.

- **Refactor mercilessly:** Do not be afraid to refactor both your production code and tests. TDD provides the safety net to do so with confidence.

- **Integrate with CI:** Use a CI system to run your tests automatically on every commit, ensuring that any issues are caught early.

TDD is a powerful practice that leads to better software design, higher code quality, and more reliable applications. While it requires discipline and a change in mindset, the long-term benefits often outweigh the initial challenges, making it a valuable approach in modern software development.

Unit testing

Unit testing is a fundamental practice in software development that focuses on testing individual components or units of code in isolation. As it is the lowest form of testing and the one closest to the written code, it is the one that should get significant attention from the software architect and engineers to ensure as much as possible is covered. When considering a TDD approach, unit testing is often where you will look to apply the majority of that testing effort, and therefore, it is vital that software architects and engineers know how to write effective unit tests.

You can check the various levels of testing in software development on the following link:

https://toyerm.wordpress.com/2018/10/16/lower-level-automation-and-testing-be-more-precise-the-automation-triangle-revisited-again/comment-page-1/

A stable, high-quality code base that is supported by strong unit testing provides for the highest quality software that can be easily maintained and implemented. While unit testing without other testing forms would not create a high-quality product, a solid base of unit testing removes your reliance on other forms and speeds up delivery considerably.

Here is a detailed look at unit testing, including its purpose, techniques, and key concepts:

- **Definition:** Unit testing involves testing the smallest testable parts of an application, known as **units**, typically at the function or method level. The goal is to ensure that each unit performs as expected independently of other parts of the application.

- **Purpose of unit testing**:

    o **Validate correctness**: Ensure that each unit of code behaves correctly and meets its design specifications.

    o **Catch bugs early**: Identify and fix issues early in the development process, before they propagate to higher levels of testing.

- o **Facilitate changes**: Make it easier to refactor or modify code with confidence that existing functionality remains intact.

- o **Improve design**: Encourage better design and modularity in the codebase by promoting separation of concerns.

- **Key concepts in unit testing:**

  - o **Test cases**: Individual test scenarios that verify the behavior of a unit.

  - o **Input**: Data or parameters provided to the unit.

  - o **Execution**: The action or method call being tested.

  - o **Output**: The expected result or behavior.

  - o **Assertions**: Statements used within test cases to compare the actual output of the unit against the expected result. Assertions help determine if a test has passed or failed.

  - o **Isolation**: Units are tested in isolation from other units to ensure that their behavior is not affected by external factors. This often involves using mock objects or stubs to simulate dependencies.

  - o **Test fixtures**: Set up and tear down code that prepares the test environment before and after each test case.

Unit testing techniques

Along with some of the earlier testing techniques we looked at, a unit test also has some techniques that can be applied to it in a far simpler manner, which are as follows:

- **Positive testing**: Verifies that the unit behaves as expected with valid input data.

  Example: Testing a function that calculates the square of a number with positive integers.

- **Negative testing**: Tests how the unit handles invalid or unexpected input data.

  Example: Testing a function with null or out-of-range values.

- **Boundary testing**: Tests the unit with input values at the edge of acceptable ranges.

  Example: Testing a function that processes a list with zero, one, and the maximum allowed number of elements.

Unit testing tools

There are many different tools that can be used for unit testing. As unit tests are executed at a compiler level along with the code, the tool you use will be dependent on the programming language in which the code is written. The following are some examples of unit testing tools for some popular programming languages, though this is only a small range of testing tools for a small subset of programming languages:

- **Java**:

    o **JUnit**: A widely used framework for writing and running unit tests. Supports annotations like **@Test**, **@Before**, and **@After**.

    o **TestNG**: Another testing framework that provides more advanced features compared to JUnit, such as parallel test execution.

- **Python**:

    o **unittest**: The built-in Python module for unit testing. Provides a test framework with features like test cases, fixtures, and test suites.

    o **pytest**: A popular testing framework that is compatible with **unittest** but offers additional features and a more flexible syntax.

- **JavaScript**:

    o **Jest**: A widely used framework for unit testing in JavaScript, particularly with React. Provides features like snapshot testing and mocking.

    o **Mocha**: A flexible testing framework for JavaScript that can be paired with assertion libraries like Chai.

- **C#**:

    o **NUnit**: A unit testing framework for .NET languages that supports various assertions and test fixtures.

    o **xUnit.net**: A popular testing framework for .NET with a focus on simplicity and extensibility.

Best practices for unit testing

The following are some of the best practices to consider when writing unit tests for your code:

- **Write independent tests**: Ensure that each test case is independent and does not rely on the state or results of other tests.

- **Keep tests small and focused**: Each test should verify a single aspect of the unit's behavior.

- **Use descriptive names**: Name test cases clearly to indicate what aspect of the unit is being tested.

- **Automate testing**: Integrate unit tests into your build process and CI/CD pipelines to run tests automatically.

- **Mock dependencies**: Use mocks or stubs to isolate the unit from external dependencies, such as databases or external services.

- **Test for edge cases**: Include tests for edge cases and boundary conditions to ensure robustness.

- **Maintain test coverage**: Strive for high test coverage but also focus on testing critical paths and business logic.

- **Refactor tests**: Regularly refactor test code to keep it clean and maintainable, just as you do with production code.

Example of a unit test

Here is a simple example of a unit test using Python's unit test framework:

```python
import unittest

def add(a, b):
    return a + b

class TestMathFunctions(unittest.TestCase):
    def test_add_positive_numbers(self):
        self.assertEqual(add(1, 2), 3)

    def test_add_negative_numbers(self):
        self.assertEqual(add(-1, -2), -3)

    def test_add_zero(self):
        self.assertEqual(add(0, 0), 0)

    def test_add_mixed_numbers(self):
        self.assertEqual(add(-1, 1), 0)

if __name__ == '__main__':
    unittest.main()
```

In this example, the add function is tested with various input scenarios to ensure it behaves correctly. Each test case verifies a specific aspect of the function's behavior, and assertions are used to check that the output matches the expected result.

By adhering to best practices and leveraging appropriate tools, unit testing can significantly enhance the quality and reliability of your software.

Test data management

An important aspect of all testing is the need for test data to execute different testing scenarios. While some tests may call for very specific and simple data scenarios, at times, some tests (especially integration and end-to-end tests) may require many different types of test data to be effective.

Test data needs to best represent how data will look in production, though for data privacy and regulatory reasons, actual production data should at no point ever be used for testing. So, test data needs to be generated either uniquely or through a process of sanitization, which will securely read production data and replace confidential information with generic information.

Designing and managing test data effectively is crucial for ensuring that your tests are reliable, repeatable, and meaningful. Test data needs to be carefully planned and organized to cover all possible scenarios while avoiding unnecessary complexity.

Types of test data

Test data refers to the set of input values used during software testing to verify that a system functions as expected. It is essential for assessing the behavior of an application under various conditions. Test data can include both valid inputs, which are expected to be processed correctly, and invalid inputs, which are designed to test the system's ability to handle errors or exceptions. Additionally, test data may include boundary values to check for edge case handling and large datasets to test performance under load. Properly selecting and using test data ensures comprehensive test coverage and helps identify potential defects. The types of test data are as follows:

- **Static test data**: Data that remains constant across different test runs. It is often used for testing fixed scenarios.

- **Dynamic test data**: Data that is generated during the test run, often randomized or based on specific algorithms to cover a wider range of scenarios.

- **Edge case data**: Data designed to test the boundaries of your application, such as maximum and minimum values, empty inputs, or invalid formats.

- **Mock data**: Data that simulates external dependencies (like APIs or databases) to isolate the system under test.

Test data sources

Data comes from many different sources in the application, and similarly, test data can be derived from different sources that should best mimic how the data looks in production. Some test data sources are as follows:

- **Internal data files**: Use files like JSON, CSV, or XML to store test data. These files can be easily read and used by your test scripts.

- **Databases**: For more complex applications, use dedicated test databases. Ensure that the database is seeded with the necessary data before each test run.

- **API stubs**: Use API stubs to return predefined responses during testing, allowing you to test how your application handles different API outputs.

- **In-memory data structures**: For unit tests, you can use in-memory data structures to simulate test data, avoiding the overhead of external dependencies.

Designing test data

The following are some important considerations to ensure that your test data is designed appropriately:

- **Cover a range of scenarios**: Ensure your test data covers normal cases, edge cases, and negative cases (invalid data). This ensures that all aspects of your application are tested.

- **Consistency across tests**: Keep test data consistent to ensure that tests are repeatable and produce the same results every time.

- **Minimal and focused data**: Only include the necessary data required for each test case. Avoid bloating your tests with unnecessary data that can make debugging harder.

Test data management strategies

In addition to the creation of data, teams need to also look at how test data will be managed across the life cycle of the application and kept up to date as test data needs change. The following is a list of approaches that can be taken to manage test data in their respective spaces:

- **Environment-specific data**: Manage different test data sets for different environments (e.g., development, staging, production). This allows you to test under conditions that mimic the environment where the application will run.

- **Test data versioning**: Keep track of changes to your test data, especially if it is stored in files or databases. Versioning helps in rolling back to previous data sets if needed.

- **Centralized data repository**: Store test data in a centralized repository accessible by all tests. This ensures consistency and reduces duplication of data across test suites.

- **Data seeding**: Use scripts or tools to seed your databases with test data before running tests. This ensures that the database is in the correct state for each test case.

Dynamic and randomized data generation

When not utilizing a data sanitization tool, the following approaches can be applied to create unique test data:

- **Randomized data sets:**

  - **Data generators**: Use data generation libraries (e.g., Faker) to create dynamic and randomized test data. This helps in testing how the system handles a wide variety of inputs.

  - **Parameterized tests**: Create tests that accept different sets of data (parameters) to ensure that the same logic works across a range of inputs.

- **Data isolation and independence:**

  - **Test isolation**: Ensure that each test case is independent of others. One test should not depend on the data created or modified by another test.

  - **Data cleanup**: Implement a cleanup process that resets the test environment after each test run, either by rolling back transactions, deleting test data, or resetting databases.

  - **Idempotent test data**: Design your test data in such a way that running the same test multiple times will produce the same result. This often involves resetting the state before each test.

- **Mocking and stubbing for external dependencies:**

  - **Use mocks or stubs**: Replace external dependencies like third-party APIs or services with mocks or stubs that return predefined data. This ensures that your tests are not dependent on external systems, which can be unreliable or slow.

  - **Controlled responses**: Configure mocks and stubs to return different responses, including success, error, and edge case data, to fully test how your application handles different scenarios.

- **Handling sensitive data:**

  - **Data anonymization**: If using real data for testing (e.g., from production), ensure that sensitive information is anonymized or obfuscated to comply with privacy regulations.

  - **Synthetic data**: Where possible, use synthetic data instead of real data to avoid privacy concerns and ensure that your tests are independent of live data.

- **Scaling test data:**

  - **Large-scale testing**: For performance and stress testing, you may need to generate large amounts of test data. Use tools to automate this process, ensuring that the system can handle the expected load.

  - **Data partitioning**: In large test environments, partition data into subsets that can be tested in parallel, reducing test execution time.

- **Data-driven testing:**

  - **Data-driven test cases**: Write tests that iterate over a set of data inputs, using each input to drive the test logic. This allows for broader test coverage with fewer test cases.

  - **Test data as configuration**: Store test data separately from test logic and load it dynamically. This makes it easier to update test data without modifying the tests themselves.

- **Documenting test data:**

  - **Test data documentation**: Clearly document the purpose and structure of your test data. This helps other developers and testers understand what each data set is for and how to use it.

  - **Test case mapping**: Map test data to specific test cases so that it is clear which data is used where. This can help in diagnosing issues when tests fail.

Effective test data management is critical for building reliable and maintainable tests. By designing test data thoughtfully, using automation tools for data generation and management, and ensuring that data is isolated and reusable, you can create a robust testing framework that improves the quality of your software and speeds up the development process.

Test environments and data privacy

Along with test data, tests also require specific environments to execute in, which may in themselves require different types of data.

Types of test environments

The following are some of the important test environments that may be required in the software development process. Not all environment types may be required for different types of applications and architectures, but it is important to understand the purpose they may serve and the characteristics that are normally needed to support effective testing in these areas:

- **Development environment**
    - **Purpose**: Used by developers to build and test new features or bug fixes during the development process.
    - **Characteristics**: Frequent code changes, lower stability, and quick feedback loops.
    - **Data**: Typically uses dummy or synthetic data, as real or sensitive data is not necessary.

- **Integration environment**
    - **Purpose**: Focuses on integrating different modules or components and ensuring they work together as expected.
    - **Characteristics**: Tests are run to validate the interaction between different parts of the application. It may include connected services, APIs, or databases.
    - **Data**: Uses a mix of synthetic and some non-sensitive real data to simulate more realistic scenarios.

- **Testing or QA environment**
    - **Purpose**: Dedicated to functional testing, including unit tests, integration tests, system tests, and user acceptance tests.
    - **Characteristics**: Stable environment where testers can verify that the application meets the required specifications.
    - **Data**: Often uses more representative data, potentially anonymized real data or carefully designed synthetic data.

- **Staging or pre-production environment**
    - **Purpose**: Simulates the production environment as closely as possible. It is the final testing ground before deployment.
    - **Characteristics**: High stability, mirrors production configurations, and is used for performance testing, final bug fixing, and last-minute checks.
    - **Data**: Typically uses anonymized real data or a snapshot of production data, with privacy measures in place.

- **Production environment**
    - **Purpose**: The live environment where the application is used by end-users.
    - **Characteristics**: High availability, performance, and security. Real user data is used.
    - **Data**: Contains real and sensitive data, requiring stringent security and privacy measures.

- **UAT environment**

    o **Purpose**: Allows end-users or stakeholders to validate that the system meets their requirements and is ready for production.

    o **Characteristics**: Very close to production but often more controlled, with specific test cases and scenarios.

    o **Data**: Uses anonymized real data or synthetic data that accurately reflects production scenarios.

- **Sandbox environment**

    o **Purpose**: A safe environment for experimenting, testing new features, or onboarding new users without affecting other environments.

    o **Characteristics**: Isolated, often with fewer restrictions, and designed for exploration.

    o **Data**: Uses synthetic or sanitized data to prevent any potential data leaks or privacy issues.

- **Disaster recovery environment**

    o **Purpose**: Simulates the production environment to test disaster recovery plans and business continuity strategies.

    o **Characteristics**: Should be an exact copy of production or staging, allowing for the testing of recovery procedures.

    o **Data**: Often uses real data, so it requires the same level of security as the production environment.

Considering privacy in the testing space

Ensuring data privacy in the testing environment is crucial, especially with regulations like GDPR, CCPA, and others that govern how personal data is handled. We have briefly mentioned some aspect of data sanitization that looks to help in converting production data into test data, however below we will look at more aspects that might help in ensuring test data is used in a compliant manner and maintains the privacy of user data while providing with suitable production-like test data.

Here is how to consider privacy in the testing space:

- **Data anonymization and masking:**

    o **Data anonymization and masking anonymization**: Remove or obfuscate PII in test data so that it cannot be traced back to an individual. This is irreversible and ensures that data used in tests does not compromise user privacy.

- o **Data masking**: Replace sensitive data elements with fictitious but realistic data. This is reversible but prevents exposure of actual sensitive information during testing.

- **Synthetic data generation:**

  - o **Synthetic data**: Generate entirely artificial data that mimics the structure and distribution of real data but contains no real user information. This allows for robust testing without risking privacy breaches.

  - o **Tools**: Use tools like Faker, Mockaroo, or custom scripts to create synthetic data that meets the needs of your test **cases**.

- **Use of test data management tools:**

  - o **Automated tools**: Use test data management tools that can automate the anonymization, masking, and generation of test data. These tools can also help ensure that data privacy rules are consistently applied across all test environments.

  - o **Audit trails**: Implement audit trails to track who accessed and modified test data, ensuring accountability and compliance with privacy policies.

- **Access control:**

  - o **Restricted access**: Limit access to test environments that use real or sensitive data. Only authorized personnel should be able to access these environments.

  - o **Role-based access**: Implement RBAC to ensure that users only have access to the data they need for their role, minimizing exposure to sensitive information.

- **Encryption:**

  - o **Data encryption**: Encrypt sensitive data both at rest and in transit in test environments. This ensures that even if data is compromised, it remains unreadable without the proper decryption keys.

  - o **Secure storage**: Store test data in secure environments with strong encryption standards, particularly when handling anonymized real data.

- **Legal and regulatory compliance:**

  - o **Compliance checks**: Ensure that your test environments and data management practices comply with relevant data protection regulations (e.g., GDPR, HIPAA). This may involve conducting **privacy impact assessments (PIAs)** and regular audits.

- o **Data residency**: Be aware of data residency requirements, especially if your test data includes information from users in different jurisdictions. Ensure that data is stored and processed in locations that comply with local laws.

- **Regular data purging:**

  - o **Data retention policies**: Implement policies for the regular purging of test data that is no longer needed. This reduces the risk of data breaches and ensures compliance with data minimization principles.

  - o **Automated purging**: Automate the deletion of old test data from environments after a certain period, particularly data that contains any form of sensitive information.

- **Test environment isolation:**

  - o **Isolation from production**: Ensure that test environments are completely isolated from production to prevent accidental data leaks or unauthorized access to real user data.

  - o **Network segmentation**: Use network segmentation to further isolate sensitive environments, reducing the risk of unauthorized access or data breaches.

- **Data minimization:**

  - o **Use minimal data**: Only use the minimal amount of data necessary for testing. Avoid using real or sensitive data unless absolutely necessary and prefer synthetic or anonymized data wherever possible.

  - o **Data subsetting**: Use a subset of data for testing, focusing on relevant parts of the dataset rather than using full-scale production data.

- **Employee training and awareness:**

  - o **Training programs**: Provide regular training for developers, testers, and other personnel on data privacy best practices, emphasizing the importance of handling test data responsibly.

  - o **Privacy policies**: Ensure all team members are familiar with and adhere to company privacy policies and relevant regulations regarding data usage in testing.

By carefully managing test environments and prioritizing privacy, you can create a robust testing strategy that ensures data security and compliance with regulations. Test environments should be designed to mirror production as closely as possible without compromising the privacy and security of sensitive information. Implementing strong data anonymization, access controls, encryption, and compliance measures will help safeguard user data throughout the testing process.

Performance testing

Performance testing is a type of software testing that focuses on evaluating how a system performs under various conditions, such as load, stress, and varying levels of demand. The goal is to identify bottlenecks, measure responsiveness, and ensure that the system meets performance criteria before it goes into production.

Key objectives of performance testing

Key objectives for performance testing are essential to ensure that a software application can handle expected user loads, perform efficiently under stress, and deliver a consistent user experience. By defining clear objectives, such as response times, throughput, and scalability, teams can set performance benchmarks and identify potential bottlenecks or weaknesses in the system. These objectives help ensure that the application meets performance standards, avoids slowdowns or crashes under peak usage, and can scale effectively as user demand increases. Ultimately, establishing these goals helps improve the reliability, efficiency, and overall user satisfaction of the software. The objectives are as follows:

- **Determine speed, scalability, and stability**: Ensure that the application performs well in terms of speed, can scale to meet increasing demands, and remains stable under stress.

- **Identify bottlenecks**: Detect and pinpoint performance issues that could degrade the user experience, such as slow response times, throughput issues, or resource utilization problems.

- **Verify reliability**: Ensure that the application behaves consistently under various conditions without crashing or becoming unresponsive.

- **Benchmarking**: Compare the performance of the application against industry standards or previous versions to measure improvements or regressions.

Types of performance testing

Performance testing includes several types, each focused on different aspects of a system's performance. Load testing measures how the system handles expected user traffic, while stress testing identifies its breaking points under extreme conditions. Scalability testing checks how well the system can handle increased load, and spike testing evaluates its response to sudden traffic surges. Endurance testing assesses the system's stability over prolonged periods of typical usage, while volume testing ensures it can process large amounts of data efficiently. These types of performance testing are essential for ensuring the system can handle varying user demands and maintain reliability under different conditions. The different types of performance testing are shown in more detail as follows:

- **Load testing:**

  o **Purpose**: Simulates expected user loads to see how the system behaves under normal and peak conditions.

  o **Example**: Testing an e-commerce site with the expected number of users during a sale period to ensure that the site remains responsive.

  o **Metrics**: Response time, throughput, resource utilization (CPU, memory, disk I/O).

- **Stress testing:**

  o **Purpose**: Pushes the system beyond its normal operational capacity to determine its breaking point and how it recovers from failure.

  o **Example**: Continuously increasing the number of users on a web application until it crashes to find its maximum capacity.

  o **Metrics**: System stability, error rates, system recovery, failure points.

- **Spike testing:**

  o **Purpose**: Tests the system's ability to handle sudden, extreme increases in load.

  o **Example**: A sudden influx of users during a flash sale or breaking news event.

  o **Metrics**: Response time during spikes, system recovery time, error rates during spikes.

- **Endurance testing (soak testing):**

  o **Purpose**: Evaluates the system's performance over an extended period to identify potential memory leaks or resource depletion.

  o **Example**: Running the application under a normal load for several hours or days to check for degradation in performance.

  o **Metrics**: Memory usage over time, resource utilization trends, system stability.

- **Scalability testing:**

  o **Purpose**: Assesses the system's ability to scale up (handle more users, transactions) or scale out (add more servers) effectively.

  o **Example**: Testing how the system handles adding more users or nodes in a distributed system to ensure it scales as expected.

  o **Metrics**: Performance improvements with scaling, resource utilization efficiency, and cost-effectiveness.

- **Volume testing:**

  - o **Purpose**: Evaluates how the system handles large volumes of data to ensure data processing and storage do not degrade performance.

  - o **Example**: Testing a database with a very large dataset to check for slow queries or system crashes.

  - o **Metrics**: Database query times, data retrieval speeds, storage system performance.

- **Latency testing:**

  - o **Purpose**: Measures the delay between a request and the corresponding response in the system, particularly important for systems requiring real-time processing.

  - o **Example**: Testing a financial trading application to ensure that transaction processing occurs within an acceptable time frame.

  - o **Metrics**: Latency (time delay), jitter (variation in delay), response times.

Performance testing process

The following steps will help teams in approaching their performance testing effectively:

1. **Identify test objectives:**

   - Define what aspects of performance you need to evaluate, such as response time, throughput, or resource utilization.

   - Establish clear goals, such as achieving a specific response time under a given load.

2. **Define performance criteria:**

   - Set benchmarks for acceptable performance, such as maximum response time under peak load, minimum throughput, or maximum acceptable resource utilization.

   - These criteria should be based on business requirements, user expectations, and industry standards.

3. **Plan and design tests:**

   - Design test scenarios that accurately simulate real-world usage, considering user behavior patterns, data volumes, and transaction types.

   - Select tools and scripts that can execute these tests, such as Apache JMeter, Gatling, or LoadRunner.

4. **Prepare the test environment:**

    - Set up an environment that closely mirrors production, including hardware, software, network configurations, and any third-party services.

    - Ensure that the environment is isolated to avoid interference from other processes.

5. **Execute tests**

    - Run the performance tests according to the scenarios designed in the planning phase.

    - Monitor system performance metrics in real-time, using tools like **application performance management (APM)** solutions (e.g., New Relic, Dynatrace).

6. **Analyze results**

    - Analyze the data collected during testing to identify performance bottlenecks, such as slow response times, high resource utilization, or failure points.

    - Compare the results against the performance criteria to determine if the system meets the required standards.

7. **Optimize and re-test:**

    - Based on the analysis, make necessary optimizations, such as improving code efficiency, adjusting database queries, or scaling infrastructure.

    - Re-run the tests to verify that the changes have improved performance without introducing new issues.

8. **Report findings**

    - Document the test results, highlighting any performance issues, bottlenecks, and the steps taken to address them.

    - Provide recommendations for further optimization if necessary.

Common metrics in performance testing

We have already mentioned some of the metrics that are appropriate to different forms of performance testing, which can often seem exhaustive, but the following are some of the key metrics that you would typically look to track in performance testing that can easily provide clear paths for improvement:

- **Response time**: The time it takes for the system to respond to a user request. Lower response times generally indicate better performance.

- **Throughput**: The number of transactions or requests processed by the system in a given time frame. Higher throughput is usually better.

- **Resource utilization**: The percentage of CPU, memory, disk, and network bandwidth used during the test. Optimal performance is often achieved when resources are utilized efficiently without overloading the system.

- **Error rate**: The percentage of requests that result in errors or failures. A low error rate is critical for maintaining system reliability.

- **Concurrency**: The number of simultaneous users or transactions the system can handle. Higher concurrency indicates better scalability.

- **Latency**: The delay before a system starts processing a request. Low latency is important for real-time systems.

Performance testing is essential for ensuring that your application can handle the expected load, scale effectively, and provide a good user experience. By focusing on different types of performance tests and carefully analyzing the results, you can identify and address potential issues before they impact users in production. Performance testing should be an integral part of the development process, especially as systems become more complex and user expectations.

Security testing

Security testing is a crucial aspect of software testing that focuses on identifying vulnerabilities, threats, and risks in a software application to ensure that it is secure from malicious attacks. The goal of security testing is to protect the application, its data, and the infrastructure from potential security breaches, ensuring the confidentiality, integrity, and availability of information.

Objectives of security testing

The primary objectives of performance testing are to ensure that a software application meets its expected speed, stability, and scalability under various conditions. This includes verifying that the system can handle the expected load, perform efficiently during peak traffic, and maintain a smooth user experience without slowdowns or crashes. Performance testing also aims to identify potential bottlenecks, evaluate how the system responds to stress or high traffic volumes, and ensure it can scale appropriately as demand grows. Ultimately, the following objectives help ensure the application is reliable, responsive, and ready for real-world use:

- **Identify vulnerabilities**: Detect weaknesses in the application that could be exploited by attackers, such as coding flaws, configuration issues, or improper access controls.

- **Validate security controls**: Ensure that the implemented security measures (e.g., encryption, authentication, access controls) are effective and functioning as intended.

- **Ensure data protection**: Protect sensitive data from unauthorized access, disclosure, alteration, or destruction.

- **Compliance**: Verify that the application complies with relevant security standards, regulations, and best practices (e.g., GDPR, HIPAA, PCI-DSS).

- **Prevent security breaches**: Reduce the risk of security incidents by proactively identifying and addressing potential security threats.

Types of security testing

Security testing includes several types, each designed to assess different aspects of an application's security posture. Vulnerability scanning identifies potential weaknesses in the system that could be exploited by attackers. Penetration testing simulates real-world cyberattacks to exploit vulnerabilities and assess the system's defenses. Authentication testing ensures that the system properly verifies user identities, while authorization testing verifies that users only have access to the resources they are permitted to. Input validation testing focuses on preventing malicious input that could lead to security breaches, and security auditing involves a comprehensive review of the system's security measures. These types of security testing help identify and address security risks, ensuring the software is protected against unauthorized access and potential attacks. These are detailed in more detail as follows:

- **Vulnerability scanning:**

  o **Purpose**: Automatically scan the application or network for known vulnerabilities.

  o **Tools**: Tools like Nessus, OpenVAS, and QualysGuard are commonly used to identify security flaws such as unpatched software, misconfigurations, and weak passwords.

  o **Outcome**: A list of vulnerabilities ranked by severity, which can then be addressed to strengthen the security posture.

- **Penetration testing (pen testing):**

  o **Purpose**: Simulate real-world attacks on the application to identify security weaknesses that could be exploited by attackers.

  o **Methodology**: Pen testers (ethical hackers) use a combination of automated tools and manual techniques to exploit vulnerabilities and gain unauthorized access.

  o **Tools**: Tools like Metasploit, Burp Suite, and OWASP ZAP are commonly used for penetration testing.

  o **Outcome**: A detailed report highlighting security vulnerabilities, the impact of potential attacks, and recommendations for mitigation.

- **Security auditing:**
  - **Purpose**: Review the application's code, configurations, and processes to ensure they comply with security best practices and standards.
  - **Methodology**: Audits can be manual or automated, involving code reviews, configuration checks, and policy reviews.
  - **Outcome**: A comprehensive assessment of the application's security posture, including gaps in policies, procedures, and technical controls.

- **Ethical hacking:**
  - **Purpose**: A broader approach to security testing, where ethical hackers are hired to use their skills to identify security weaknesses from the perspective of a malicious attacker.
  - **Scope**: Ethical hacking can encompass penetration testing, vulnerability scanning, social engineering, and more.
  - **Outcome**: A report detailing how the application was breached, potential risks, and recommended fixes.

- **Risk assessment:**
  - **Purpose**: Identify and evaluate the risks associated with potential security threats to the application.
  - **Methodology**: Involves identifying assets, threats, and vulnerabilities, and then assessing the likelihood and impact of each risk.
  - **Outcome**: A risk matrix that prioritizes risks based on their severity, helping organizations focus on mitigating the most critical threats.

- **Security posture assessment:**
  - **Purpose**: A holistic evaluation of the overall security posture of an organization, including its policies, procedures, and technical controls.
  - **Scope**: May include penetration testing, vulnerability scanning, risk assessments, and security audits.
  - **Outcome**: An assessment that provides insights into the organization's ability to detect, respond to, and recover from security incidents.

- **Compliance testing:**
  - **Purpose**: Ensure that the application complies with relevant security regulations and industry standards.
  - **Regulations**: Depending on the industry, this could include GDPR, HIPAA, PCI-DSS, SOX, and others.

- o **Outcome**: A compliance report indicating whether the application meets the required security standards, and if not, what steps are needed to achieve compliance.

- **Posture review:**

  - o **Purpose**: Regularly review and update security controls, configurations, and policies to keep them aligned with current threats and best practices.

  - o **Methodology**: Continuous monitoring and periodic reviews of security posture to identify new vulnerabilities or areas for improvement.

  - o **Outcome**: Improved resilience to emerging threats and an up-to-date security posture.

Security testing process

Security testing is a very specialized form of testing, but should not be left too late in the development cycle as you still want to ensure that any key security considerations can be addressed early in the design and development process and do not compromise the system in any way or lead to delays in delivery when trying to address them. Security testing involves the following:

- **Requirement analysis:**

  - o Understand the security requirements for the application, including data protection needs, regulatory requirements, and potential threats.

  - o Identify the key assets that need to be protected, such as sensitive data, intellectual property, and user information.

- **Planning and design:**

  - o Define the scope of the security testing, including which areas of the application will be tested and what types of tests will be performed.

  - o Develop a testing plan that outlines the testing strategy, tools to be used, timelines, and resource requirements.

- **Environment setup:**

  - o Prepare the testing environment, ensuring it closely mirrors the production environment in terms of configurations, data, and security controls.

  - o Ensure that the environment is isolated to avoid impacting production systems during testing.

- **Execution:**

  - o Conduct the security tests according to the plan, using both automated tools and manual techniques to identify vulnerabilities.

- o Perform penetration testing, vulnerability scanning, code reviews, and any other relevant tests.

- **Analysis and reporting:**
  - o Analyze the results of the security tests to identify vulnerabilities, weaknesses, and potential security breaches.
  - o Prioritize the identified issues based on their severity, potential impact, and likelihood of exploitation.
  - o Document the findings in a detailed report that includes recommendations for remediation.

- **Remediation:**
  - o Work with developers, operations teams, and security experts to address the identified vulnerabilities and strengthen security controls.
  - o Implement fixes, such as patching vulnerabilities, hardening configurations, and enhancing access controls.

- **Re-testing:**
  - o After remediation, re-test the application to ensure that the vulnerabilities have been successfully addressed and no new issues have been introduced.
  - o Conduct additional tests if necessary to validate the effectiveness of the security controls.

- **Ongoing monitoring:**
  - o Implement continuous security monitoring to detect and respond to new threats as they emerge.
  - o Regularly update security controls, conduct periodic security reviews, and stay informed about new vulnerabilities and attack vectors.

Best practices for security testing

Security testing best practices focus on proactively identifying and addressing vulnerabilities in software. Key practices include conducting regular penetration testing to simulate attacks, implementing robust authentication and authorization mechanisms to control access, and ensuring secure coding practices to prevent common vulnerabilities like SQL injection or **cross-site scripting** (**XSS**). It is also important to perform thorough input validation to prevent malicious data from compromising the system and to regularly update software and libraries to protect against known exploits. Additionally, adopting a risk-based approach helps prioritize security efforts based on the potential impact and likelihood of threats. The following best practices help create more secure applications and reduce the risk of security breaches:

- **Shift left security**: Integrate security testing early in the development process, making it part of the CI/CD pipeline to catch vulnerabilities as soon as they are introduced.

- **Automate where possible**: Use automated tools for routine security checks, but complement them with manual testing for more nuanced issues.

- **Regular testing**: Conduct security testing regularly, not just before release. Regularly scheduled tests help keep the application secure over time.

- **Educate and train**: Train developers and other stakeholders on security best practices, including secure coding techniques and common vulnerabilities.

- **Collaboration**: Foster collaboration between **development, security, and operations (DevSecOps)** teams to ensure security is a shared responsibility.

- **Comply with standards**: Follow industry standards and frameworks like OWASP Top Ten, CIS Controls, and ISO/IEC 27001 to guide your security testing efforts.

Security testing is essential for identifying and mitigating vulnerabilities in software applications, protecting against potential attacks, and ensuring compliance with security standards. By employing a combination of automated tools and manual techniques, security testing can help ensure that an application is secure, reliable, and trustworthy. Continuous monitoring, regular testing, and ongoing security awareness are key components of a strong security testing strategy.

Automated testing infrastructure

Automated testing infrastructure refers to the systems, tools, and processes put in place to automate the execution of software tests. This infrastructure is designed to support CI/CD pipelines by enabling frequent and reliable testing of software builds. Automated testing infrastructure is crucial for modern software development, especially in Agile and DevOps environments, where rapid and iterative development cycles demand fast and consistent feedback. And again, while oftentimes seen as the domain of quality engineers, it is imperative that architects understand how to build test automation frameworks and systems.

Key components of automated testing infrastructure

The key components of an automated testing infrastructure include the test automation framework, which provides a structured environment for writing and executing automated tests. It typically includes reusable libraries, components, and guidelines to streamline the testing process. Test scripts, which are automated test cases, define the inputs, actions, and expected outcomes needed to validate the system's functionality. The test execution environment encompasses the hardware and software infrastructure required to run the tests, including virtual machines or cloud-based systems. Test data management is essential for creating and maintaining consistent and reliable test data.

Additionally, reporting and logging tools capture detailed logs and generate test reports to provide insights into test results. Version control systems, such as Git, are used to manage changes to test scripts and related components, ensuring consistency across different versions. Finally, integration with CI/CD pipelines ensures that automated tests are triggered as part of the build and deployment process, enabling faster feedback and more efficient software delivery.

Test automation tools

These are the software tools used to create, execute, and manage automated tests. They can be categorized into several types, including:

- **Unit testing tools**: E.g., JUnit, NUnit, xUnit for testing individual units of code.

- **Integration testing tools**: E.g., Postman for API testing, SoapUI for web services.

- **UI testing tools**: E.g., Selenium, Cypress, TestCafe for automating browser-based tests.

- **Performance testing tools**: E.g., Apache JMeter, Gatling for simulating user load.

- **Security testing tools**: E.g., OWASP ZAP, Burp Suite for vulnerability scanning.

- **Mobile testing tools**: E.g., Appium, Espresso for automating mobile app testing.

Test scripts

Automated test scripts are pieces of code written to perform the actual testing tasks. They simulate user actions, make API calls, check outputs, and compare actual results with expected outcomes.

Scripts can be written in various languages depending on the tool and the environment, such as Java, Python, JavaScript, Ruby, or C#.

CI systems

CI systems are platforms that automate the building, testing, and integration of code changes. They run automated tests every time new code is committed, providing immediate feedback to developers.

Test environments

Test environments are isolated setups that replicate the production environment as closely as possible. They include hardware, software, databases, and network configurations.

Multiple environments may be used for different types of testing, such as development, staging, and production environments.

Test data management

Automated tests require test data to run effectively. This data can be static or dynamically generated.

Test data management involves creating, maintaining, and securing test data. This can include using synthetic data, anonymizing real data, or using specific datasets for different test scenarios.

Version control systems

Version control systems (VCS) like Git, Mercurial, or Subversion are integral to automated testing infrastructure as they track changes in the test scripts and codebase.

Test scripts should be version-controlled alongside the application code to ensure that tests are synchronized with the code they are testing.

Reporting and analytics tools

Automated testing infrastructure typically includes tools for reporting test results, analyzing test coverage, and tracking defects.

These tools generate reports that provide insights into test outcomes, pass/fail rates, and areas of the application that may require further testing.

Examples include Allure, TestNG, JUnit reports, and custom dashboards integrated into CI/CD tools.

Test orchestration

Test orchestration involves coordinating the execution of multiple automated tests across different environments and tools.

This can include parallel execution, managing test dependencies, and ensuring tests are run in the correct sequence.

Tools like Jenkins pipelines, GitLab CI/CD, or dedicated test orchestration platforms like TestRail or Zephyr can be used.

Service virtualization

Service virtualization allows testing of components or services that are not yet fully developed, unavailable, or too costly to use in a test environment.

It creates virtual versions of the service with the same behavior, enabling testing without relying on the actual service.

Tools like WireMock, Parasoft, and CA Service Virtualization are commonly used.

Infrastructure as code

IaC tools like Terraform, Ansible, or CloudFormation automate the provisioning and management of test environments.

This allows for consistent and repeatable setup of testing infrastructure, making it easier to spin up environments on demand, especially in cloud environments.

Best practices for automated testing infrastructure

Testing automation systems are still pieces of code that require good architectural design and so it is important to follow certain best practices when building them. The best practices are as follows:

- **Start with the right tests:**

  - Not all tests are suitable for automation. Focus on automating repetitive, time-consuming, and critical-path tests first.

  - Prioritize unit tests, regression tests, and smoke tests for automation.

- **Build modular test scripts:**

  - Write test scripts that are modular, reusable, and maintainable. This makes it easier to update tests when the application changes.

  - Use **page object models** (**POM**) or similar design patterns in UI tests to separate test logic from UI elements.

- **Ensure consistent test environments:**

  - Use automation to provision and configure test environments consistently, reducing the **it works on my machine** problem.

  - Consider using containerization (e.g., Docker) to create portable and consistent environments.

- **Integrate with CI/CD:**

  - Ensure that your automated tests are integrated with your CI/CD pipeline so that they run automatically on each build or deployment.

  - Set up automated triggers to run tests on code commits, merges, or pull requests.

- **Maintain test data:**
    - Regularly refresh and maintain test data to ensure that tests run consistently and reflect real-world scenarios.
    - Use data-driven testing to run tests with different datasets without modifying the test scripts.

- **Monitor and analyze results:**
    - Regularly monitor automated test results to identify trends, flaky tests, or areas where automation may be failing.
    - Use dashboards and reporting tools to keep stakeholders informed about the health of the application and the effectiveness of the test automation.

- **Manage test artifacts:**
    - Store and manage test artifacts such as logs, screenshots, and reports in a centralized location for easy access and review.
    - Use artifacts to troubleshoot and debug failed tests.

- **Keep tests maintainable:**
    - Regularly review and refactor automated tests to keep them maintainable as the application evolves.
    - Remove obsolete tests and update test scripts to reflect changes in the application.

- **Address flaky tests:**
    - Identify and address flaky tests (tests that sometimes pass and sometimes fail for no apparent reason) as they can undermine confidence in the automated testing process.
    - Investigate and fix the root causes of flaky tests or isolate them to prevent them from affecting other tests.

- **Focus on security:**
    - Ensure that your automated testing infrastructure is secure, particularly if it involves sensitive test data or runs in cloud environments.
    - Implement access controls, encryption, and regular security audits.

Automated testing infrastructure challenges

Test automation is important, but there are challenges that need to be addressed that may often stop companies from wanting to invest in them, such as:

- **Initial setup costs**: Building a robust automated testing infrastructure requires an initial investment in tools, time, and expertise.

- **Maintenance overhead**: Automated tests require regular maintenance to keep them in sync with the evolving application, which can be resource intensive.

- **Flaky tests**: Automated tests that fail intermittently can be challenging to diagnose and can erode confidence in the testing process.

- **Tool integration**: Integrating various tools (CI/CD, test management, reporting, etc.) into a cohesive infrastructure can be complex and require custom solutions.

- **Scalability**: As the application grows, the test suite can become large and take longer to execute, requiring infrastructure that can scale accordingly.

- **Skill requirements**: Effective test automation requires a specific skill set, including knowledge of coding, testing frameworks, and CI/CD processes.

Automated testing infrastructure is essential for supporting the fast-paced and iterative development cycles of modern software development. It involves a combination of tools, environments, processes, and best practices designed to automate the execution of tests, integrate testing into CI/CD pipelines, and provide reliable feedback on the quality of the software. While setting up and maintaining this infrastructure can be challenging, the benefits of increased test coverage, faster release cycles, and higher software quality make it a critical component of any software development process.

Designing a test automation framework

While software architects will focus on designing their core systems to achieve the relevant outcome that is needed, they often do not focus much effort on the design of the test automation framework. However, with testing playing such a significant impact on the lifecycle of any set of applications, it is important to design it well and get involvement from an architectural perspective.

One of the critical responsibilities that architects should embrace is the design and oversight of a test automation framework. While many companies may hire a specialized Automation Architect to oftentimes fill this role, regardless of responsibility, it is important all types of software architects to get involved. This involvement is not just beneficial but essential for several reasons.

Firstly, architects possess a holistic understanding of the entire system architecture. This knowledge allows them to design a test automation framework that is tightly integrated with the system's architecture, ensuring that testing is comprehensive and aligned with the system's design principles. By being involved in the framework's design, architects can ensure that it accommodates the complexities and specific needs of the system, resulting in more reliable and efficient testing processes.

Secondly, architects can ensure that the test automation framework aligns with the long-term vision and technical strategy of the project. They are responsible for making architectural decisions that will impact the system's scalability, maintainability, and performance over time. A well-designed test automation framework supports these architectural goals by enabling continuous testing and validation, which is crucial for maintaining system quality as the project evolves. Without an architect's input, the framework might lack the necessary alignment with the system's architectural vision, leading to gaps in testing coverage or inefficiencies in the testing process.

Lastly, involving architects in the design of the test automation framework helps bridge the gap between development and testing teams. Architects can provide guidance on how to structure the framework so that it seamlessly integrates with the development process, fostering collaboration and ensuring that testing is not an afterthought but an integral part of the software delivery lifecycle. This collaboration can lead to a more unified approach to quality, where testing is seen as a shared responsibility rather than a separate, isolated task.

Let us take a more detailed look at the architecture and technical requirements for a test automation framework.

Architecture of the test automation framework

While there is no one way to design a test automation framework, they would typically consist of the following layers:

- **Test layer**: Contains individual test cases or test scenarios.

- **Business logic layer**: Contains reusable methods or functions that interact with the application's business logic.

- **Page object layer**: Encapsulates the details of the web pages or UI elements. This layer is particularly useful in UI automation.

- **Utility layer**: Contains utility classes or functions that provide common functionalities (e.g., data handling, configuration management).

- **Data layer**: Manages test data, including data sources and data-driven testing logic.

Components of the framework

Alongside the different layers, a test automation framework also requires the following components:

- **Test runner**:
  - **Description**: Orchestrates the execution of test cases.
  - **Examples**: TestNG, JUnit, pytest.

- o **Responsibilities**: Initialize framework, execute test cases, manage test execution order, handle test dependencies, and provide test results.

- **Page Object Model (POM)**:

  - o **Description**: Represents UI elements and interactions in a page-specific manner. This can also work for APIs.

  - o **Example**: A class for each web page that contains methods for interacting with elements on that page.

  - o **Responsibilities**: Abstracts the details of the UI and allows tests to interact with the application in a more maintainable way.

- **Test data management**:

  - o **Description**: Handles test input data and expected results.

  - o **Examples**: CSV files, JSON files, databases, or data providers.

  - o **Responsibilities**: Supply data to tests, support data-driven testing, and manage test configurations.

- **Configuration management**:

  - o **Description**: Manages environment-specific settings and configuration parameters.

  - o **Examples**: Configuration files (e.g., `config.json`, `config.properties`), environment variables.

  - o **Responsibilities**: Provide dynamic configuration based on test environments (e.g., development, staging, production).

- **Reporting**:

  - o **Description**: Generates reports based on test execution results.

  - o **Examples**: HTML reports, PDF reports, integrated with CI tools for visualization.

  - o **Responsibilities**: Summarize test results, provide logs, screenshots, and metrics.

- **Logging**:

  - o **Description**: Captures runtime information and errors.

  - o **Examples**: Log4j (Java), logging module (Python).

  - o **Responsibilities**: Record debug information, error messages, and trace logs.

- **Error handling**:

  - o **Description**: Manages errors and exceptions during test execution.

o **Examples**: Custom exception handling mechanisms, retry logic.

o **Responsibilities**: Ensure tests handle failures gracefully and provide meaningful error messages.

Test logging and monitoring

Test logging and monitoring are crucial aspects of a robust test automation framework. They help you track the execution of tests, identify issues, and improve overall test quality. The following sub-sections explore how you can incorporate logging and monitoring into your framework.

Test logging

Test logging is an essential component of automated testing, capturing detailed information about the execution of test cases. It provides a record of each test's execution, including timestamps, test steps, inputs, expected results, actual outcomes, and any errors or failures encountered. Proper test logging helps testers and developers track the progress of tests, identify issues, and understand the root causes of test failures. Additionally, it serves as documentation for audit purposes and provides valuable insights for debugging and improving test reliability. Effective test logging can also be integrated with reporting tools to generate clear, actionable test reports, enhancing overall test management and quality assurance. Test logging includes the following:

1. **Logging mechanisms:**

   o **Log levels**: Use different log levels (e.g., DEBUG, INFO, WARN, ERROR) to categorize messages based on their importance.

   o **Log messages**: Include meaningful log messages that provide context about what the test is doing, any issues encountered, and the state of the application.

2. **Logging frameworks:**

   o **Java**: Use Log4j or SLF4J. Configure loggers in the `log4j.properties` or `logback.xml` files.

   o **Python**: Use the built-in logging module. Configure logging using `logging.basicConfig()` or a configuration file.

   o **JavaScript**: Use libraries like `Winston` or `Bunyan` for Node.js.

3. **Integration:**

   o **Test execution**: Integrate logging into your test scripts and page object methods. Ensure that logs capture key events, including test start, execution details, and test results.

o **Error handling**: Log detailed error messages and stack traces when exceptions occur. This helps in diagnosing issues.

4. **Log management:**

o **File storage**: Store logs in files with timestamps and log rotation to manage log size.

o **Log aggregation**: Use log aggregation tools (e.g., ELK Stack) to collect, store, and analyze logs from multiple sources.

Test monitoring

Test monitoring involves tracking the execution of automated tests in real time to ensure they run as expected and provide immediate feedback on the test results. It helps teams observe the status of tests, identify issues, and ensure the stability of the testing process. Test monitoring typically includes tracking metrics like test execution time, pass/fail rates, and system resource utilization. This data helps detect anomalies, such as failing tests or performance bottlenecks, allowing for prompt investigation and resolution. Additionally, test monitoring tools can integrate with CI systems, alerting teams to failures or performance issues as soon as they occur, ensuring quick response and maintaining the integrity of the testing process. Test monitoring involves the following:

1. **Real-time monitoring:**

o **Execution monitoring**: Track test execution in real-time to get immediate feedback on test runs.

o **Dashboard**: Create dashboards using tools like Grafana or Kibana to visualize test metrics, results, and trends.

2. **Alerts and notifications:**

o **Failure alerts**: Set up notifications for test failures or critical errors. This can be done using email alerts, Slack notifications, or other communication tools.

o **Custom alerts**: Configure alerts for specific conditions (e.g., performance thresholds, execution time).

3. **Integration with CI/CD:**

o **CI/CD monitoring**: Integrate with CI/CD tools (e.g., Jenkins, GitLab CI) to monitor test results and trigger notifications based on test outcomes.

o **Pipeline integration**: Ensure that test results are part of the build pipeline and provide visibility into the overall test status.

4. **Metrics and analytics:**

- o **Performance metrics**: Track performance metrics such as execution time, resource usage, and throughput.

- o **Test coverage**: Monitor test coverage metrics to ensure that all critical parts of the application are being tested.

- o **Trend analysis**: Analyze trends in test results to identify patterns, recurring issues, and areas for improvement.

Example workflow for logging and monitoring

Logging and monitoring are important aspects of test automation systems as they help trace the execution of events that a test executes, which can then be used to understand the root cause of defects. The following are some key steps that should be included in the logging that test automation frameworks capture to best provide engineering teams with the platform for identifying issues through their test automation frameworks:

1. **During test execution:**

- o **Log events**: Log the start and end of each test, significant actions, and any issues encountered.

- o **Capture screenshots**: Include screenshots in logs for visual context in case of test failures.

2. **Post-test execution:**

- o **Aggregate logs**: Collect and aggregate logs from different test runs.

- o **Generate reports**: Use logging and monitoring data to generate test reports that include detailed results and insights.

3. **Monitor in real-time:**

- o **View dashboards**: Monitor test execution and system performance on dashboards.

- o **Receive alerts**: Get notified about test failures or performance issues.

4. **Analyze data:**

- o **Review logs**: Analyze logs for troubleshooting and identifying root causes of failures.

- o **Evaluate metrics**: Assess performance metrics and test coverage to ensure quality and efficiency.

By implementing effective logging and monitoring strategies, you can gain better visibility into your test automation process, quickly identify and address issues, and continuously improve your testing practices.

Conclusion

Software testing, now evolved into quality engineering, is a critical component of software delivery. In today's landscape, more effort is often dedicated to testing software than to developing it, making it essential for architects to prioritize how their systems will be tested. Designing systems with optimized testing in mind is crucial to streamline this process.

Software testing has transformed into a discipline that is as technically rigorous as traditional software engineering. This shift has driven the adoption of automated testing, which is now integrated directly into CI/CD pipelines. Consequently, software architecture must adapt to facilitate automation and support smaller, more iterative development cycles.

As software trends continue to evolve, it is imperative for architects to stay informed about the latest technologies and methodologies. By doing so, they can ensure that their systems are not only testable but also deliver high-quality outcomes to end users.

In the next chapter, we look at current and future trends in software architecture, how they may impact the software industry and what software architects need to know to capitalize and design for these new software trends.

Join our book's Discord space

Join the book's Discord Workspace for Latest updates, Offers, Tech happenings around the world, New Release and Sessions with the Authors:

https://discord.bpbonline.com

## CHAPTER 17

Current and Future Trends in Software

Introduction

One of the challenges of software architecture is that software continues to evolve at a rapid pace. Not only are we seeing rapid transitions in software every five to ten years, but the pace and scale of that innovation, how we consume software, and the architecture designs available to meet these changing needs are growing at an ever-increasing pace. As a software architect, this can be quite a daunting task, but it remains important nonetheless that software architects keep abreast of modern technological evolutions and how software can be built to cater optimally for them.

In this chapter, we will look at some of the trends that are causing the biggest design evolution in the current software landscape, along with some future trends that need to be monitored closely. Predicting the future is an impossible task, so even though we will talk about some key future items, there will continue to be trends and changes that may arise and have a bigger impact on software delivery that we have not realized yet.

Along with that, we will also look at a few things that software architects can implement to help them respond to these changes better and some feedback loops that can help better understand how the software is used and where designs can be changed to better cater to different changes.

Software architects can take solace in the fact that many of the design properties, patterns, structures, and techniques mentioned in this book can be utilized and applied to almost all the different new software. While software designs will evolve, the methods we use may remain the same.

So, as we explore the different software trends, it is important to think about how the different principles may apply to them and how software design may be impacted because of these new trends.

Structure

In this chapter, we will discuss the following topics:

- Emerging technologies in software architecture
- Designing software for a global audience
- AI/ML's impact on architectural decision-making
- Adaptation and building future-fit software
- Building feedback loops

Objectives

By the end of this chapter, you will gain an understanding of key emerging trends in the software industry and how to design software architecture that integrates these advancements. You will also explore strategies for creating adaptable software that seamlessly supports future technologies. Additionally, this chapter will cover approaches to designing software for a global audience while ensuring it remains flexible and easy to modify for future development.

Emerging technologies in software architecture

We will start by looking at some of the major emerging existing technologies constantly affecting software design. This is not an exhaustive list, and it is likely that when you read this, the newer technologies may be even bigger than what has been mentioned. In designing software, it is vital to factor in these emerging trends and ensure your software caters to these technologies as early as possible, otherwise, it will quickly end up becoming legacy.

Cloud computing

Cloud computing is the delivery of computing services, such as storage, processing power, databases, networking, and software, over the internet (the cloud). Instead of owning and maintaining physical servers, organizations can rent access to these resources from cloud providers like AWS, Azure, or Google Cloud. This model offers flexibility, scalability, and cost efficiency, allowing businesses to easily adjust their computing resources based on demand while only paying for what they use.

Cloud computing is continuing to evolve rapidly, driven by new technologies and business needs. As more organizations embrace digital transformation, cloud computing trends are shaping how companies operate, innovate, and grow.

Here is an overview of some of the most significant current and future cloud trends:

- **Multi-cloud and hybrid cloud strategies:** Many organizations are adopting multi-cloud and hybrid cloud approaches, utilizing services from multiple cloud providers or combining private and public clouds. The details are as follows:

  o **Multi-cloud**: Companies use services from multiple cloud providers like AWS, Microsoft Azure, and Google Cloud to avoid vendor lock-in and optimize for cost, performance, and regional availability.

  o **Hybrid cloud**: Combining on-premise infrastructure (private cloud) with public cloud resources, offering greater flexibility, scalability, and control over sensitive data.

  o **Trend drivers**:

    - Flexibility in deployment.

    - Redundancy and disaster recovery.

    - Regulatory requirements for data localization.

    - Avoidance of cloud vendor dependency.

- **Edge computing integration with cloud:** Edge computing (processing data closer to where it is generated) is becoming more integrated with cloud infrastructure. This allows for faster data processing and real-time analytics without relying on centralized cloud servers.

  o **Cloud-edge collaboration**: Edge devices can perform initial data processing, while cloud servers handle more complex tasks like long-term data analysis, storage, and **machine learning (ML)** model training.

  o **Trend drivers**:

    - Growth of IoT devices requires local data processing.

    - Real-time applications like autonomous vehicles and smart cities.

    - Latency-sensitive applications in gaming, video streaming, and healthcare.

Artificial intelligence and ML in the cloud

The integration of **artificial intelligence** (**AI**) and ML into cloud platforms is expanding, making it easier for businesses to leverage advanced analytics without building their own infrastructure, as follows:

- **AI as a service (AIaaS)**: Major cloud providers offer pre-built AI services, such as speech recognition, **natural language processing** (**NLP**), and computer vision, that can be easily integrated into applications.

- **ML as a service (MLaaS)**: Cloud providers offer tools for training, deploying, and managing ML models without needing in-house expertise in AI/ML, making data-driven insights accessible to a broader range of businesses.

- **Trend drivers**:

    o AI-driven automation in sectors like finance, healthcare, and manufacturing.

    o Democratization of AI and ML capabilities for non-tech industries.

    o Cloud-based infrastructure for large-scale AI model training (e.g., GPT models).

Serverless computing

Serverless computing is growing rapidly, as it allows developers to focus on writing code without managing the underlying infrastructure. In this model, cloud providers automatically scale resources up or down based on demand, and users pay only for the compute time they use:

- **Function as a service (FaaS)**: Services like AWS Lambda, Azure Functions, and Google Cloud Functions allow users to execute small pieces of code (functions) in response to events.

- **Trend drivers**:

    The following are some of the key trends that are driving the growth of serverless computing:

    o Increased flexibility and reduced operational costs.

    o Improved scalability and resilience for microservices-based architectures.

    o Faster development cycles, especially for startups and small enterprises.

Cloud-native applications and microservices

Cloud-native development, where applications are designed and optimized to run in cloud environments, is becoming the standard. This is driven by microservices architectures, where applications are composed of loosely coupled, independently deployable services:

- **Kubernetes and containers**: Tools like Kubernetes (for container orchestration) and Docker (for containerization) are essential to building and managing cloud-native applications, enabling flexibility, scalability, and efficient resource utilization.

- **Trend drivers**:
  - Faster and more agile application development.
  - Improved scalability and reliability of cloud-native apps.
  - The shift from monolithic architectures to microservices.

Cloud security and compliance

As businesses increasingly rely on cloud services, the importance of cloud security and regulatory compliance is growing. Cloud providers are focusing on offering more advanced security features, such as:

- **Zero Trust security models**: Moving away from the traditional perimeter-based security model, where every user and device is continuously verified and authenticated before accessing data.

- **Confidential computing**: Cloud providers are introducing confidential computing services, which encrypt data during processing to ensure data security even in multi-tenant environments.

- **Data sovereignty and localization**: Compliance with regulations like GDPR (in *Europe*) and CCPA (in *California*) is prompting companies to ensure that data is stored and processed within specific regions.

- **Trend drivers**:
  - The rise of cyberattacks and data breaches.
  - Increased focus on data privacy regulations across the globe.
  - The need for encryption, secure access, and compliance in industries like finance and healthcare.

Sustainability and green cloud

Environmental impact and sustainability are becoming important considerations for cloud providers and their customers. Cloud providers are focusing on reducing their carbon footprints by:

- **Green cloud computing**: Using renewable energy to power data centers and improving energy efficiency through optimized cooling systems and better hardware management.

- **Sustainability reporting**: Some cloud providers offer transparency on the carbon footprint of their services, enabling companies to make informed decisions to meet their sustainability goals.

- **Trend drivers**:

  o Rising corporate responsibility and regulatory pressure for sustainability.

  o Consumer demand for environmentally conscious businesses.

  o Optimizing data center energy use and carbon reduction strategies.

Industry-specific clouds

To meet the unique needs of different sectors, industry-specific cloud platforms are emerging. These specialized clouds are tailored with tools, regulatory frameworks, and compliance standards for particular industries, such as:

- **Financial services cloud**: Features such as fraud detection, regulatory compliance, and transaction security for banks and financial institutions.

- **Healthcare cloud**: Solutions that ensure HIPAA compliance and enable secure, scalable patient data storage.

- **Retail cloud**: E-commerce platforms with integrated AI/ML tools for customer analytics, personalized marketing, and supply chain optimization.

- **Trend drivers**:

  o The need for industry-tailored solutions that meet specific regulatory and operational requirements.

  o Accelerated digital transformation across sectors like healthcare, finance, and manufacturing.

Quantum computing in the cloud

Quantum computing is still in its early stages, but cloud providers are offering quantum computing as a service to businesses and researchers, giving access to quantum processors without needing specialized hardware:

- **Quantum as a service (QaaS)**: AWS, Google, and IBM are some of the companies offering cloud-based quantum computing platforms, allowing users to experiment with quantum algorithms.

- **Trend drivers**:

  o Advanced research in fields like cryptography, material science, and drug discovery.

- o The potential to solve computational problems that are infeasible for classical computers.

- o Preparing industries for future breakthroughs in quantum computing.

AI-driven cloud management and automation

Cloud management and optimization are increasingly being automated through AI-driven tools that optimize costs, performance, and security across cloud environments:

- **AI cloud monitoring**: Tools that automatically monitor cloud infrastructure and applications, identify performance bottlenecks, and offer predictive scaling recommendations.

- **Automation of DevOps tasks**: AI and machine learning are being used to automate infrastructure management, CI/CD pipelines, and anomaly detection.

- **Trend drivers**:

  - o Increasing complexity in managing multi-cloud and hybrid cloud environments.

  - o The need for real-time monitoring and optimization of cloud resources.

  - o Reducing operational costs through automation.

5G and cloud integration

With the rollout of 5G networks, the combination of high-speed connectivity and cloud services will enable a new generation of applications, particularly in fields like **Internet of Things (IoT)**, autonomous vehicles, and smart cities:

- **5G-edge-cloud integration**: The ultra-low latency of 5G will improve the performance of cloud services, especially in edge computing scenarios where real-time processing is critical.

- **Trend drivers**:

  - o Real-time applications like VR/AR, autonomous vehicles, and healthcare.

  - o Growth in IoT devices requiring constant, high-speed connectivity.

Blockchain

Blockchain technology is a decentralized, distributed ledger system that records transactions across many computers in a way that ensures the data cannot be altered retroactively. The technology was first conceptualized by an anonymous person or group known as *Satoshi Nakamoto*, who implemented it as the backbone of Bitcoin, the first cryptocurrency.

Key features of blockchain:

- **Decentralization:** Unlike traditional databases managed by a central authority, blockchain is maintained by a network of nodes (computers). This reduces reliance on a central entity and increases security and transparency.

- **Immutability:** Once a transaction is recorded on a blockchain, it becomes nearly impossible to alter or delete. Each block contains a cryptographic hash of the previous block, which links them together and secures the entire chain.

- **Transparency:** Every participant in the network has access to the entire blockchain, allowing for greater accountability and traceability.

- **Security:** The use of cryptographic techniques ensures that transactions are secure. Blockchain uses consensus mechanisms, such as Proof of Work (used in Bitcoin) or Proof of Stake (used in Ethereum), to validate transactions.

- **Smart contracts:** Some blockchains, like Ethereum, support programmable contracts, called smart contracts. These are self-executing contracts where the terms of the agreement are written directly into code. They can automatically execute transactions when predefined conditions are met.

Applications of blockchain

While often associated with cryptocurrency blockchain and its unique approach to decentralized and immutable data offers value to a wide number of different applications:

- **Cryptocurrencies**: Bitcoin, Ethereum, and other cryptocurrencies use blockchain to enable secure, peer-to-peer digital payments.

- **Supply chain management**: Blockchain can track the movement of goods across a supply chain, ensuring transparency and reducing fraud.

- **Financial services**: Blockchain can streamline banking processes, reduce fraud, and offer real-time settlement of financial transactions.

- **Identity verification**: Blockchain can be used to create secure digital identities, allowing for safe and tamper-proof identity management.

- **Healthcare**: Securely storing patient records and ensuring privacy while allowing authorized parties to access and verify data.

Virtual reality and the metaverse

Virtual reality (VR) and the concept of the metaverse are closely related, both representing shifts in how we interact with digital environments. Here is a breakdown of each and how they intersect:

- **Virtual reality:** VR is an immersive technology that allows users to experience and interact with a simulated 3D environment using hardware like VR headsets (e.g., Oculus, HTC Vive, PlayStation VR). These headsets track head movements and sometimes hand gestures, creating the sensation of being inside a virtual world. VR environments can be used for gaming, education, training, healthcare, and more.

  The following are the key attributes that make up a basic VR system and application:

  o **Immersion**: VR creates a sense of presence, making users feel as though they are physically inside the virtual space.

  o **Interactivity**: Users can interact with the environment, objects, and other users in real-time.

  o **Hardware**: A VR setup typically includes a headset, hand controllers, and sometimes motion sensors to track body movements.

  The use cases are as follows:

  o **Gaming**: Immersive gaming experiences.

  o **Training**: Simulations for training in fields like healthcare, military, and aviation.

  o **Education**: Virtual classrooms or field trips.

  o **Therapy**: VR is being used for treating conditions like **post-traumatic stress disorder** (**PTSD**) and phobias.

- **Metaverse:** Metaverse is a broader concept that extends beyond VR. It refers to a collective virtual shared space, merging AR and VR, and the internet into a persistent, interconnected, and immersive digital universe. Think of it as a 3D internet where people can socialize, work, shop, play, and learn in digital worlds.

  Key features of the metaverse:

  o **Persistence**: The metaverse continues to exist even when you are not logged in. It is a shared space that is continuously evolving.

  o **Interoperability**: Different virtual environments within the metaverse will eventually be able to connect. Users should be able to move assets, like digital items or avatars, from one world to another.

  o **Economy**: The metaverse will have its own digital economy where users can buy, sell, and trade virtual goods, often using cryptocurrencies or **non-fungible tokens** (**NFTs**).

  o **User-generated content**: In the metaverse, users are active creators, developing virtual spaces, avatars, items, and experiences.

o **Social interaction**: The metaverse fosters real-time interaction between users. It is expected to become a space for virtual socializing, entertainment, work, and even virtual real estate.

Current metaverse examples are as follows:

o **Decentraland and the sandbox**: These are decentralized virtual worlds where users can buy land, create spaces, and trade using cryptocurrency.

o **Meta's horizon worlds**: *Facebook* (*Meta*) is heavily invested in building a metaverse where users can interact through VR.

o **Roblox and Fortnite**: These gaming platforms have started incorporating metaverse-like experiences, where users create and participate in virtual worlds.

VR's role in the metaverse

VR is a crucial technology for fully immersive experiences within the metaverse. With VR headsets, users can enter virtual worlds, interact with 3D spaces, attend virtual concerts or meetings, and explore digital landscapes in a more engaging way. However, the metaverse would not be limited to VR, people can also access it via regular computers, smartphones, and AR devices.

Edge computing

Edge computing is a distributed computing model where data processing and computation occur closer to the source of data, rather than relying solely on a centralized cloud or data center. In this model, devices and infrastructure at the edge of the network (e.g., IoT devices, sensors, and local servers) handle much of the data processing. This reduces the need to send data back and forth to the cloud, improving speed and efficiency.

Key features of edge computing

The following are the key features that provide the main drivers to the benefits of edge computing:

- **Low latency**: Since data is processed near the source, edge computing reduces the delay (latency) that occurs when sending data to distant servers. This is critical for real-time applications like autonomous vehicles, industrial automation, and VR/AR experiences.

- **Bandwidth optimization**: Instead of transmitting massive amounts of data to the cloud, edge computing processes much of the data locally, reducing the strain on network bandwidth. This is particularly important for applications with large volumes of data, such as video streaming or smart cities.

- **Data privacy and security**: By processing data locally, edge computing reduces the risk of data breaches during transmission to remote servers. This is crucial in sensitive industries like healthcare and finance, where data privacy is a major concern.

- **Scalability**: Edge computing enables efficient scalability by distributing computing resources across various locations, reducing the need for massive central data centers and enabling better performance as the number of devices increases.

- **Autonomous systems**: In scenarios where continuous connectivity to the cloud is not guaranteed, edge devices can process data and make decisions independently, ensuring uninterrupted operation. Examples include self-driving cars, drones, and remote healthcare systems.

Working of edge computing

In a traditional cloud model, data is generated by devices, sent to a centralized server for processing, and then results are returned. In edge computing, much of that data processing happens closer to the data source (e.g., on a device or nearby edge server), minimizing the back-and-forth communication with the cloud. Cloud infrastructure is still involved, but it plays a secondary role, handling less time-sensitive tasks or long-term data storage.

Example use cases for edge computing

The following are some use cases of edge computing technology:

- **Autonomous vehicles**: Self-driving cars rely on edge computing to process vast amounts of sensor data (e.g., from cameras, radar, and lidar) in real-time. They need to make split-second decisions without relying on cloud-based servers.

- **Smart cities**: In a smart city, IoT devices like cameras, traffic sensors, and utility meters generate large amounts of data. Processing this data locally at the edge allows for real-time monitoring and decision-making, such as adjusting traffic lights based on vehicle flow or optimizing energy usage in buildings.

- **Healthcare**: Wearable devices and smart medical equipment can process patient data at the edge to monitor vital signs and detect abnormalities without needing constant connection to a centralized server. This ensures faster response times and can be crucial in emergencies.

- **Retail**: Edge computing can power advanced analytics in retail environments. For instance, stores can use edge devices to track customer movement and behavior in real-time, adjusting in-store displays and marketing based on customer preferences.

- **Manufacturing**: Edge computing in factories enables real-time monitoring and predictive maintenance of equipment. Machines equipped with sensors can process data locally to predict failures and improve operational efficiency.

Edge vs. cloud computing

While cloud computing centralizes processing power and storage in data centers, edge computing brings these resources closer to the devices generating the data. Edge computing does not replace cloud computing but complements it by handling real-time tasks locally while offloading more extensive data analysis, storage, and less time-sensitive tasks to the cloud.

The benefits and challenges are as follows:

- **Benefits**: Improved response time, reduced network costs, enhanced security, and real-time processing.

- **Challenges**: Managing distributed devices can be complex, and there are challenges around infrastructure, maintenance, and ensuring consistent security protocols.

Edge computing, combined with technologies like 5G, AI, and IoT, is helping drive the future of industries requiring real-time data processing, like smart cities, healthcare, and finance.

Machine learning and artificial intelligence

AI and ML are two closely related fields, often overlapping in their applications. While AI refers to the broader concept of machines that can mimic human intelligence, ML is a specific subset of AI that enables systems to learn and improve from experience without being explicitly programmed.

Artificial intelligence

AI refers to the simulation of human intelligence in machines designed to think and act like humans. AI encompasses various tasks, including problem-solving, decision-making, perception, and language understanding. AI can be classified into two types:

- **Narrow AI (weak AI)**: Systems designed to perform a specific task. Examples include voice assistants like *Siri* or *Alexa*, recommendation algorithms on *Netflix*, and autonomous vehicles.

- **General AI (strong AI)**: A more theoretical concept where machines possess human-like cognitive abilities and can solve any intellectual task that a human can do. General AI does not exist yet.

Machine learning

ML is a subset of AI where algorithms learn patterns from data and improve their performance over time without needing explicit programming. Instead of following predefined rules, ML models make predictions or decisions based on patterns in the data they are trained on.

ML can be broadly categorized into the following types, depending on the nature of the learning process and the availability of labeled data:

- **Supervised learning:** In supervised learning, the algorithm is trained on a labeled dataset, where the input data (features) comes with corresponding outputs (labels or targets). The model learns to map inputs to the correct output and then makes predictions on new, unseen data.

  o **Use case:** Predicting house prices based on features like location, size, and number of rooms (inputs), where the actual prices (labels) are known.

  o **Examples of algorithms:** While there many different types of ML algorithms, below are some of the basic ones that architects should be aware of:

    ▪ **Linear regression:** Predicting continuous outcomes.

    ▪ **Logistic regression:** Used for classification tasks (e.g., spam detection).

    ▪ **Support vector machines (SVM):** Used for classification and regression.

    ▪ **Decision trees:** Classifies data by splitting it into subsets based on feature values.

    ▪ **Neural networks:** Mimics human brain function to learn complex patterns in data.

- **Unsupervised learning:** In unsupervised learning, the model is trained on data without labeled outcomes. It tries to identify patterns, structures, or groupings in the data without prior knowledge of what the outputs should be.

  o **Use case:** Customer segmentation, where the system groups customers based on behavior without predefined labels.

  o **Examples of algorithms:** The following are some examples of unsupervised learning algorithms:

    ▪ **Clustering (e.g., K-means):** Grouping similar data points together based on similarities.

    ▪ **Principal component analysis (PCA):** Reducing the dimensionality of the data while retaining the most important patterns.

    ▪ **Anomaly detection:** Detecting unusual data points that do not conform to the general pattern of the dataset.

- **Reinforcement learning:** In reinforcement learning, the algorithm learns by interacting with an environment and receiving feedback in the form of rewards or penalties. The system tries to maximize cumulative reward by taking actions that lead to better outcomes.

- o **Use case**: Self-driving cars, where the system learns to make driving decisions by receiving rewards (e.g., staying in the lane) or penalties (e.g., hitting obstacles).

- o **Examples of algorithms:** The following are some examples of reinforcement learning algorithms:

  - ▪ **Q-learning**: A value-based approach where the agent learns to maximize the total reward over time.

  - ▪ **Deep reinforcement learning**: Combines neural networks with reinforcement learning, used for complex decision-making tasks (e.g., AlphaGo, game-playing agents).

- **Semi-supervised learning:** In semi-supervised learning (hybrid approach), the model is trained on a combination of a small amount of labeled data and a large amount of unlabeled data. This approach is useful when acquiring labeled data is expensive or time-consuming.

  - o **Use case**: Document classification, where only a few documents are labeled, but the algorithm uses the unlabeled data to improve its performance.

  - o **Example of algorithm:** The following is an example of a semi-supervised algorithm:

    - ▪ **Self-training algorithms**: Initially trained on labeled data, then used to label some of the unlabeled data to improve learning.

- **Self-supervised learning:** Self-supervised learning is a recent approach where the model generates its own labels from the input data, rather than relying on external labels. It is particularly useful in areas like NLP and computer vision, where manually labeling data is hard. Models like GPT (for text) or SimCLR (for images) are examples of self-supervised learning.

Machine learning pipeline

ML itself is built on solid data engineering principles, and as such, it is important to understand how the typical software and data pipeline will work to produce the right ML outcomes for an organization. The pipeline includes:

- **Data collection**: Collecting relevant data that will be used to train the model.

- **Data preprocessing**: Cleaning and transforming raw data into a usable format (e.g., handling missing values, scaling features).

- **Feature engineering**: Selecting or creating relevant features (inputs) that will help the model make accurate predictions.

- **Model selection**: Choosing the appropriate algorithm based on the task (classification, regression, clustering, etc.).

- **Training**: Feeding the data to the model so it can learn patterns and relationships.

- **Evaluation**: Testing the model on unseen data to assess its accuracy and performance.

- **Deployment**: Integrating the trained model into a real-world application for making predictions or decisions.

AI and ML challenges

AI and ML might be radically changing the way we use and build software. However, utilizing these is not without challenges, and it is important that software architects carefully think about how to address them when looking to employ AI or ML into their existing software strategies. The challenges are as follows:

- **Data quality**: ML models are only as good as the data they are trained on. Poor quality or biased data can lead to inaccurate predictions or unfair outcomes.

- **Explainability**: Complex models like deep neural networks can act as black boxes, making it hard to explain how decisions are made, which is an issue in highly regulated industries like finance.

- **Ethical concerns**: Ensuring that AI is used responsibly and fairly is critical, especially when models are used for decision-making that affects people's lives (e.g., loan approvals or insurance claims).

Designing software for a global market

In addition to keeping up with emerging trends, one of the most crucial responsibilities for software architects is designing software for a global audience. The evolution of technologies such as the internet and cloud computing has transformed the software landscape, enabling simultaneous global releases. As a result, software must be adaptable and responsive to the diverse needs of users from various regions around the world.

Designing software for a global audience involves building applications that can adapt to various cultural, linguistic, legal, and technical environments across different regions of the world. To ensure that your software meets the needs of diverse users, you need to consider multiple factors related to **internationalization (i18n)**, **localization (l10n)**, performance, usability, and compliance.

Best practices

The following are some best practices to be aware of when designing software for a global market:

- **i18n**: i18n is the process of designing your software so that it can easily be adapted to various languages and regions without requiring major changes to the underlying code.

- **Separation of code and content**: Keep language strings, date formats, time zones, and other locale-specific elements separate from the core code. This enables easier localization later.

- **Unicode support**: Use **Unicode** (**utf-8**) encoding to handle multiple character sets, ensuring that the software can display any language, including complex scripts like Chinese, Arabic, and Cyrillic.

- **Right-to-left support**: Design for both **left-to-right** (**LTR**) and **right-to-left** (**RTL**) languages like Arabic and Hebrew. Ensure UI elements, such as menus, align correctly for RTL users.

- **Flexible UI layouts**: Ensure that UI elements like buttons, text fields, and menus can expand or contract to accommodate different languages. For example, some languages may take more space to display the same text.

- **l10n**: l10n is the process of adapting your software for specific regions, languages, and cultural norms. This includes translating text and adjusting the UI for local preferences.

- **Language translation**: Translate all user-facing content, including error messages, prompts, and tooltips. Use professional translators or localization platforms (e.g., Transifex, Phrase) rather than machine translation for accurate results.

- **Cultural sensitivity**: Adapt images, icons, and symbols to align with cultural norms. For example, hand gestures and colors may have different meanings in various cultures.

- **Local formats**: Adapt to local standards for:

  o **Date and time**: Use appropriate date formats (e.g., DD/MM/YYYY in Europe vs. MM/DD/YYYY in the US) and time zones.

  o **Currency**: Display local currency and adapt numeric formats (e.g., commas vs. decimal points in numbers).

  o **Units of measurement**: Switch between metric and imperial units based on the region.

  o **Local regulations**: Ensure compliance with local legal requirements, such as GDPR in Europe, CCPA in California, or other data privacy and security laws.

Performance optimization for global access

Global users often face diverse technical challenges, such as varying internet speeds, data costs, and device capabilities. Optimizing your software for performance across different regions is critical.

Best practices

The following are some best practices in achieving performance optimization with global access systems:

- **Content delivery network (CDN)**: Use a CDN to distribute content from servers located closer to users worldwide, reducing latency and improving load times.

- **Offline functionality**: Design the app to work offline or in low-connectivity environments. Use techniques like caching and local storage for uninterrupted user experience.

- **Adaptive loading**: Implement adaptive strategies for loading content based on users' network speeds (e.g., providing low-resolution images for users on slower networks).

- **Minimal data usage**: Design with data constraints in mind, especially for mobile-first markets where data is expensive. Offer lightweight versions of your app or website (e.g., lite versions).

- **Cross-platform compatibility**: Ensure the software works well across different devices and platforms, especially mobile. Consider browser differences and varying mobile operating systems (Android, iOS).

User experience and usability

Creating a universally accessible and intuitive interface for users from different cultures is crucial for global adoption. Pay attention to cultural and language differences that may affect how users interact with your software.

Best practices

The following are some best practices to follow in ensuring your user experience works for a global market:

- **User research across regions**: Conduct user research with participants from different countries and regions to understand their unique needs, behaviors, and preferences.

- **Simplified navigation**: Use intuitive and universal icons, buttons, and navigation patterns to ensure ease of use across cultures. Avoid relying on language-specific elements for key functions.

- **User testing**: Test your software with users from different regions to identify usability issues related to cultural or linguistic barriers.

- **Inclusive design**: Consider accessibility for all users, including those with disabilities. Use large, readable fonts, provide text alternatives for non-text content (e.g., images, videos), and ensure compatibility with screen readers.

Legal and compliance considerations

When expanding to a global audience, you must be aware of and comply with various local regulations and standards.

Best practices

The following are some best practices to follow:

- **Data privacy regulations**: Comply with data privacy laws such as the **General Data Protection Regulation** (**GDPR**) in the EU, **California Consumer Privacy Act** (**CCPA**), and other region-specific privacy laws.

- **Age restrictions**: In some regions, there are laws governing age-appropriate content (e.g., **Children's Online Privacy Protection Act** (**COPPA**) in the US, which regulates online services for children).

- **Accessibility standards**: Ensure your software meets local accessibility laws, such as the **Web Content Accessibility Guidelines** (**WCAG**), which ensure inclusivity for users with disabilities.

Scalable infrastructure

As your user base grows globally, your software infrastructure needs to scale to meet demand from different regions.

Best practices

The following are some best practices in creating scalable infrastructure can reach people around the world:

- **Cloud deployment**: Use cloud platforms (e.g., AWS, Azure, Google Cloud) that offer global data centers and services, allowing for geographically distributed infrastructure to serve users with low latency.

- **Auto-scaling**: Implement auto-scaling mechanisms to adjust server resources based on the number of active users from different regions, ensuring smooth performance during peak usage times.

- **Globalization of payments**: Support multiple currencies, payment methods (e.g., credit cards, PayPal, local e-wallets), and localized tax calculations to cater to global markets.

Documentation and support

For a global audience, providing comprehensive and localized documentation and support is essential.

Best practices

The following are some best practices that can be followed to ensure your software is correctly documented to support a wider global audience:

- **Multilingual documentation**: Offer user guides, FAQs, and tutorials in multiple languages to cater to different regions. This helps users easily understand and troubleshoot issues.

- **24/7 support**: If possible, offer customer support across different time zones. Automated chatbots can provide initial support, with escalations to human agents if needed.

- **Community forums**: Build global community forums where users from different countries can share tips, ask questions, and provide support to each other.

Continuous localization updates

As your software evolves, continuous localization and cultural adaptation will be necessary. Stay flexible and responsive to new markets, languages, and regional changes.

Best practices

The following are some best practices that help make continuous localization of software significantly easier:

- **Automated localization workflows**: Set up automated localization pipelines to ensure that updates, new features, or content are localized quickly.

- **Monitor regional trends**: Stay aware of cultural trends, political changes, and local news that could affect user preferences, regulations, or behaviors.

Designing software for a global audience requires a thoughtful approach that encompasses internationalization, localization, performance optimization, and cultural sensitivity. By adhering to these principles, you can create an inclusive, scalable product that resonates with users worldwide.

AI/ML's impact on architectural decision-making

The impact of AI and ML on architectural decision-making in software development is transformative. AI/ML technologies not only shape how systems are built but also influence the choices architects make across multiple dimensions: from design patterns and infrastructure decisions to security, performance optimization, and scalability.

The following sub-sections talk about how AI and ML affect architectural decision-making.

Data-driven architecture design

Traditionally, architectural decisions are based on best practices, human experience, and industry standards. With AI and ML, decisions can now be driven by data and real-time insights rather than assumptions or past experiences.

Impact

The following are some key impacts that can be gained by using AI/ML for architectural design:

- **Predictive analytics for system behavior:** ML models can predict system behavior, performance bottlenecks, or failures by analyzing historical data. This insight helps architects proactively design for scalability, availability, and performance.

- **Feedback loop for continuous improvement:** AI/ML systems can provide real-time feedback on how software is used, enabling architects to adapt or evolve the architecture over time to meet changing user needs or operational demands.

For example, an ML-driven system can analyze usage patterns in a cloud-based application and recommend scaling strategies, helping architects make more accurate decisions about infrastructure sizing and resource allocation.

AI-driven design patterns

AI is influencing the creation and adoption of new design patterns. Some architectural patterns are emerging specifically to support AI/ML applications, which introduce different requirements for data processing, computation, and scaling.

Impact

The following are some design patterns that can have an impact on AI/ML systems:

- **Microservices architecture for AI/ML workloads**: AI applications often rely on modular, loosely coupled microservices for flexibility, parallelism, and scalability. Architects increasingly design AI solutions using microservices to compartmentalize data processing, model training, and inference.

- **Event-driven architectures**: ML models benefit from event-driven architectures, where real-time data streams can trigger specific actions or predictions. This design is suitable for AI systems that need to make decisions in real time, such as fraud detection or autonomous vehicles.

- **Serverless computing**: AI/ML applications often leverage serverless design patterns, where inference tasks can scale up automatically based on demand, reducing the need for dedicated infrastructure management.

For example, in fraud detection systems, event-driven architectures can trigger ML models to analyze transactional data in real time, making instantaneous decisions to flag or approve transactions.

Infrastructure and resource allocation decisions

The infrastructure needed to support AI/ML workloads can differ significantly from traditional software applications. Decisions around compute power, storage, and networking need to be made with the specific demands of AI/ML models in mind.

Impact

The following are some of the infrastructure considerations that need to be factored in when approaching designing your AI/ML models:

- **Specialized hardware (GPUs, TPUs)**: AI/ML workloads often require specialized hardware like GPUs or TPUs, which have optimized capabilities for parallel computations required for training deep learning models. Architects must decide when and where to integrate these resources.

- **Hybrid cloud and edge computing**: AI/ML architectures often use hybrid setups that combine cloud services for large-scale data processing and edge computing for real-time inference closer to where the data is generated (e.g., IoT or autonomous systems).

- **Cost optimization**: Architecting for AI means balancing between computational needs and cost. Efficient scheduling and allocation of resources like cloud compute instances, storage for large datasets, and high-speed networking are critical considerations.

For example, an AI-based video surveillance system may need edge computing resources for real-time image processing on-site (at the edge) while sending data to the cloud for more intensive analytics, requiring a hybrid cloud/edge architecture.

Security and privacy considerations

AI/ML introduces unique security and privacy challenges that architects must address. The handling of sensitive data, the potential for model exploitation, and the need for privacy-preserving ML techniques require specific architectural decisions.

Impact

The following are some of the security and privacy considerations that need to be factored into AI/ML model design:

- **Data privacy**: AI models often rely on large datasets, some of which may include sensitive or **personally identifiable information** (**PII**). Architects must ensure compliance with data protection regulations like GDPR by integrating privacy-preserving techniques such as differential privacy and federated learning.

- **Model security**: ML models can be vulnerable to attacks like adversarial attacks, where malicious inputs are crafted to deceive the model. Architects must design architectures that include robust security measures to detect and mitigate such attacks.

- **Encryption and secure access**: Data at rest and in transit must be encrypted, and only authorized users should have access to sensitive AI models and data pipelines. Access control mechanisms need to be built into the architecture.

For example, in healthcare, privacy-preserving techniques like federated learning allow AI models to be trained across multiple healthcare institutions without sharing sensitive patient data, maintaining data privacy while still benefiting from large-scale learning.

Model lifecycle management

Managing the lifecycle of ML models introduces new challenges that influence architectural decisions. From model training and deployment to monitoring and retraining, AI/ML requires specific architectural components to handle the end-to-end workflow.

Impact

The following are some considerations for model lifecycle management:

- **Model versioning**: Just like software versioning, ML models require version control to manage different iterations. Architects need to ensure that their system supports easy versioning, rollback, and updates of models without disrupting operations.

- **Monitoring and drift detection**: Once deployed, models may degrade in accuracy over time due to data drift (where the data distribution changes). The architecture must include continuous monitoring and automated alerts to detect when a model needs retraining or replacement.

- **Model deployment pipelines (MLOps)**: AI/ML introduces the concept of MLOps, an extension of DevOps that deals with the automation of the model lifecycle, from development to deployment and maintenance. Architecture must integrate tools and platforms to support these workflows (e.g., Kubeflow, MLflow).

For example, an ML model used for predictive maintenance in industrial machines might require automated pipelines to retrain and redeploy the model when sensor data changes over time, ensuring consistent accuracy in predictions.

Ethical AI considerations in architecture

Ethical concerns around bias, transparency, and fairness in AI systems are becoming more prominent. Architects must design systems that mitigate bias and ensure that the AI models' decisions can be explained and audited.

Impact

The following are some ethical considerations when building AI systems:

- **Explainability and interpretability**: Many AI/ML models, especially deep learning models, are often considered black boxes, making it difficult to explain their decisions. Architects must incorporate techniques like XAI to ensure that the system's decisions are transparent and can be justified, especially in regulated industries like finance and healthcare.

- **Bias mitigation**: AI models can reflect or amplify biases present in the data. Architects must design the system to include bias detection and mitigation mechanisms, ensuring fairness and equality in decision-making.

- **Auditability**: The architecture should support audit trails and logs that track model decisions, inputs, and outputs, ensuring that decisions can be traced and reviewed for compliance or regulatory purposes.

For example, in a loan approval system, AI might be used to assess credit risk. The architecture must ensure that bias is minimized and that decisions are explainable, allowing regulators to review how and why a particular applicant was approved or denied.

Scalability and high availability

AI workloads, especially those involving real-time inference or massive datasets, can put a significant strain on systems. Architects need to design for scalability and high availability to ensure that AI systems perform efficiently under load.

Impact

The following are some design considerations for achieving scalability and high availability in AI systems:

- **Horizontal scalability**: AI/ML models, particularly in real-time applications like recommendation engines or fraud detection systems, must be able to scale horizontally to handle increasing volumes of data and users.

- **High availability for AI services**: For mission-critical AI services, architects must design for high availability with failover mechanisms, redundancy, and load balancing to ensure that AI models remain accessible, even during peak usage.

For example, a real-time recommendation engine for a global e-commerce platform needs to be able to scale dynamically to handle fluctuating user traffic, especially during peak shopping seasons.

The rise of AI/ML is profoundly changing the way architects make decisions when designing systems. From new architectural patterns like microservices and event-driven architectures to advanced infrastructure choices, privacy considerations, and ethical frameworks, AI/ML is redefining traditional approaches. Architects must now consider the entire AI/ML lifecycle, data handling, model deployment, and the challenges of scaling and securing intelligent systems as they build the next generation of software solutions.

Adaptation and building future-fit software

To ensure that software is future-fit and aligned with modern industry trends, software architects need to adopt strategies that incorporate flexibility, innovation, and proactive planning. Here are some key approaches that architects can follow to adapt to emerging trends like AI/ML, cloud computing, microservices, and edge computing, among others, and ensure that their software solutions are scalable, secure, and adaptable to future needs.

Embrace continuous learning and skill development

Modern software architecture is constantly evolving, so staying updated with the latest technologies, patterns, and best practices is critical.

Stay current with emerging technologies: Continuously follow advancements in AI/ML, cloud platforms, DevOps, IoT, and edge computing. Participate in industry conferences, online courses, and certifications as follows:

- **Cross-disciplinary skills**: Learn concepts from related fields such as data science, machine learning, cybersecurity, and blockchain to understand how these disciplines impact architecture decisions.

- **Collaborate with teams**: Work closely with data scientists, DevOps engineers, security experts, and business stakeholders to gain a holistic view of technology integration and its impact on the software lifecycle.

For example, an architect may need to gain a deeper understanding of MLOps (the AI equivalent of DevOps) to ensure that the deployment and maintenance of machine learning models integrate smoothly with software systems.

Design for scalability and flexibility

Modern systems must be built to handle rapid growth, changing requirements, and diverse workloads. Flexible, scalable systems are more adaptable to future trends and technologies. Consider the following to design for scalability and flexibility:

- **Adopt microservices architecture**: Design systems using microservices and event-driven architectures to decouple services and allow independent scaling. This approach also supports continuous deployment and easier updates.

- **Use cloud-native design patterns**: Leverage cloud-native technologies like containers (Docker), orchestration tools (Kubernetes), and serverless computing to build scalable, flexible, and fault-tolerant systems.

- **Architect for edge and hybrid clouds**: Design systems that can operate in hybrid cloud environments or edge computing scenarios to handle data closer to the source, improving performance and reducing latency.

For example, by building cloud-native microservices, an e-commerce platform can handle seasonal spikes in user traffic and easily scale across regions, ensuring consistent performance worldwide.

Leverage automation and AI-driven decision-making

Automation and AI are integral in optimizing modern software systems. Architects must integrate these tools to reduce manual intervention, optimize performance, and facilitate real-time decision-making:

- **MLOps and automation**: Implement MLOps practices to automate the deployment, monitoring, and retraining of machine learning models. Integrate CI/CD pipelines to ensure continuous delivery and updates.

- **AI-Driven monitoring and optimization**: Use AI/ML tools for predictive analytics, monitoring, and performance optimization to detect system bottlenecks and preemptively scale or adjust resources.

- **Infrastructure as code (IaC)**: Automate infrastructure deployment using IaC tools like Terraform and AWS CloudFormation to ensure consistent, replicable environments that can be scaled or modified as needed.

For example, AI-driven monitoring tools in a cloud environment can predict when servers need to scale up or down based on user behavior, reducing costs and improving performance without manual intervention.

Adopt security-first architecture

With the increasing complexity of systems and the rising risk of cyberattacks, security must be a fundamental consideration from the outset:

- **Zero Trust Architecture**: Implement Zero Trust principles where every user and device is continuously authenticated, authorized, and validated, regardless of their location in the network.

- **Privacy-preserving AI**: Ensure that AI/ML systems are built with privacy in mind, using techniques like differential privacy, federated learning, and data anonymization to protect sensitive user data.

- **Automated security testing**: Integrate security checks into your CI/CD pipelines with DevSecOps practices, ensuring continuous vulnerability scanning, threat detection, and compliance audits.

For example, for a financial services platform, employing a Zero Trust Architecture combined with real-time fraud detection via AI ensures that both internal and external threats are mitigated effectively.

Focus on cloud and edge integration

Cloud computing is evolving, and the need to balance centralized and decentralized computing with edge computing is becoming crucial. Architects must design systems that seamlessly interact with both cloud and edge environments as follows:

- **Hybrid cloud and multi-cloud**: Architect systems to leverage hybrid cloud setups where some components are on-premises, some in the public cloud, and some in edge environments for latency-sensitive applications.

- **Edge-optimized applications**: Design applications that can perform critical processing at the edge (near the data source), while non-time-sensitive tasks can be handled in the cloud.

- **Global load balancing**: Use global load balancers and CDNs to improve performance for globally distributed users, particularly for applications with heavy multimedia content or real-time requirements.

For example, an IoT system monitoring smart cities can use edge devices for real-time data processing (e.g., traffic management) while sending aggregated data to the cloud for long-term analytics and forecasting.

Architect for future technology integration

Emerging technologies like quantum computing, blockchain, and 5G are on the horizon. Architects should be prepared for future technological integrations by building adaptable and modular systems:

- **Modular architecture**: Build modular, loosely coupled systems that can easily integrate with future technologies or services as they become mainstream, reducing the need for extensive rewrites.

- **Quantum computing readiness**: Although quantum computing is still nascent, architects can design systems that allow for integration with quantum services in the future, particularly for complex optimization tasks, cryptography, and large-scale simulations.

- **Blockchain and distributed ledger integration**: Explore how blockchain can be used for securing transactions, data integrity, and decentralization. Be prepared to integrate blockchain-based systems where applicable (e.g., in financial services, supply chain, or identity verification).

For example, a global payment gateway could design its architecture to integrate blockchain for secure and transparent cross-border transactions in the future while maintaining compatibility with current systems.

Foster collaboration across teams

Modern software architecture is a collaborative effort that involves developers, operations, data scientists, security teams, and business stakeholders. It is a collaboration across teams of DevOps and MLOps:

- **DevOps and MLOps integration**: Implement a culture of collaboration through DevOps and MLOps, ensuring that development, operations, and machine learning teams work together seamlessly. Use integrated tools for continuous development, deployment, and monitoring.

- **Cross-functional teams**: Encourage cross-functional teams that include architects, developers, data scientists, and security professionals to collaborate from the initial design phase, ensuring all aspects of the system are considered holistically.

- **Shared responsibility for success**: Foster a culture of shared responsibility, where all teams are invested in the success of the architecture, from scalability and security to performance and user experience.

For example, an organization adopting MLOps ensures that data scientists and developers collaborate effectively to deploy machine learning models into production environments, with continuous monitoring and updates, streamlining the model lifecycle.

Prioritize user-centric and inclusive design

A future-fit system must consider the end-user experience, ensuring that software is intuitive, inclusive, and adaptable to diverse global audiences as follows:

- **User-centric design**: Ensure that the architecture supports features that enhance user experience, such as low-latency interactions, personalization through AI, and mobile-first designs for global audiences.

- **Inclusive design**: Design systems that are accessible to a diverse user base, considering factors like language localization, RTL support, cultural sensitivities, and accessibility standards for users with disabilities (e.g., WCAG compliance).

- **Real-time personalization**: Architect AI-driven systems that can deliver personalized experiences (e.g., personalized recommendations, localized content) based on user behavior and preferences.

For example, an international e-commerce platform can leverage AI-driven recommendation engines to provide personalized product suggestions while also offering multi-language support and adapting to local payment methods and cultural nuances.

To build future-fit software, architects must proactively embrace emerging trends, foster collaboration across teams, and remain adaptable to new technologies and methodologies. By leveraging cloud-native architectures, AI-driven automation, modular systems, and inclusive design principles, software architects can ensure that their solutions remain scalable, secure, and ready to integrate with future advancements.

Building feedback loops

Building feedback loops into software is essential for continuous improvement, real-time decision-making, and adaptive functionality. Feedback loops help gather insights about system performance, user behavior, and operational efficiency, allowing software to evolve based on real-world data. There are various types of feedback loops, such as those for user behavior, system health, and business metrics, each serving different purposes.

The following sub-sections discuss how to build effective feedback loops into software.

User feedback loops

User feedback is vital for improving usability, identifying pain points, and refining the user experience. These loops provide direct insights into how users interact with the software and include the following:

- **In-app feedback mechanisms**: Integrate feedback forms, rating systems, or surveys directly into the software. For example, after specific actions (e.g., completing a task or making a purchase), prompt users to provide feedback.

- **Usage analytics**: Implement tools like Google Analytics, Mixpanel, or Hotjar to track user behavior, such as click patterns, page views, session duration, and feature usage. This indirect feedback can help identify trends and areas for improvement.

- **User testing and A/B testing**: Conduct A/B testing to compare different versions of a feature, collecting user behavior data to understand what works best. Regular user testing can provide qualitative feedback on the software experience.

- **Net Promoter Score (NPS)**: Measure customer satisfaction by integrating an NPS survey into your software. This provides direct feedback on how likely users are to recommend your product.

For example, in a mobile banking app, users could be prompted to rate their experience after completing a transaction. Usage data could reveal that users abandon certain workflows, highlighting opportunities to streamline the UI.

System and performance monitoring feedback loops

Feedback loops that monitor system performance are critical for identifying issues like slow response times, outages, or resource bottlenecks. This can be done by as follows:

- **Application performance monitoring (APM)**: Use APM tools like New Relic, Datadog, or Prometheus to continuously monitor key system metrics, such as response times, error rates, and resource usage (CPU, memory, database queries). Alerts can be triggered if thresholds are crossed.

- **Real-time alerts**: Set up real-time alert systems to notify development and operations teams of critical performance issues. This can be done through integrations with Slack, PagerDuty, or Opsgenie.

- **Health checks and self-healing systems**: Implement automated health checks to ensure system components are functioning properly. If a failure is detected, the system can trigger automatic remediation actions (e.g., restarting services, re-routing traffic).

- **Log aggregation and analysis**: Collect and aggregate logs from all parts of the system using tools like ELK Stack or Splunk. Analyzing logs provides valuable feedback on errors, crashes, or security threats.

For example, a SaaS platform could automatically scale cloud resources based on feedback from performance monitoring tools that detect CPU spikes during peak usage hours, ensuring smooth performance for users.

AI and ML feedback loops

For systems that use AI/ML, feedback loops are essential for model training, adaptation, and continuous improvement. AI/ML feedback loops include:

- **Data feedback for model retraining**: ML models need to be updated with fresh data to maintain accuracy. Set up a feedback loop where user interactions and new data are continually fed back into the system to improve the model. For example, a recommendation engine could learn from user preferences to refine its suggestions.

- **Performance monitoring for ML models**: Use tools like MLflow or Kubeflow to monitor model performance in production. This ensures that the model is performing as expected and identifies when retraining or model adjustments are needed (e.g., detecting model drift).

- **Human-in-the-loop**: For critical decisions (e.g., in healthcare or finance), a human-in-the-loop approach can be used, where human feedback helps refine AI predictions, allowing the model to learn from human expertise over time.

For example, an e-commerce platform could use a machine learning model to recommend products. A feedback loop where users click-through rates and purchases are analyzed could help the model improve its recommendations over time.

Business metrics and analytics feedback loops

Measuring business outcomes through software is essential for understanding whether the product is meeting its goals, such as driving user engagement or increasing revenue. This can be done as follows:

- **Business analytics integration**: Integrate business intelligence tools like Power BI, Tableau, or Looker to track KPIs, such as conversion rates, customer acquisition costs, and retention rates.

- **Custom dashboards**: Build real-time dashboards that provide an overview of critical business metrics, such as user growth, sales performance, or operational costs. Use this feedback to make data-driven decisions about feature prioritization, marketing strategies, or product updates.

- **Experimentation frameworks**: Use experimentation frameworks to test new features or pricing models. A feedback loop based on real-time business metrics will allow you to optimize based on what drives the best outcomes.

For example, a subscription-based service might use feedback from churn rate analytics to identify when users are most likely to cancel their subscriptions and implement retention strategies, such as special offers or personalized communication, to address this.

Developer and team feedback loops

Feedback loops are not just for users and system monitoring, they are also essential for internal teams, ensuring that development processes are continuously improving. These include:

- **CI/CD pipeline feedback**: Integrate CI/CD tools like Jenkins, CircleCI, or GitLab to provide immediate feedback to developers on the success or failure of code changes. Automated tests provide continuous feedback on code quality.

- **Code review and peer feedback**: Implement peer code review processes, using tools like GitHub or GitLab for pull requests, to ensure that code quality is continuously reviewed and improved through developer feedback.

- **Agile retrospectives**: Regularly hold agile retrospectives at the end of each sprint to gather feedback from development teams on what went well, what did not, and how processes can be improved.

- **Error tracking and debugging**: Use tools like Sentry or BugSnag to gather developer feedback on bugs and errors in real-time. These tools help identify recurring issues and areas for refactoring.

For example, by implementing a CI/CD pipeline with automated tests, a development team receives instant feedback on whether new code changes have introduced bugs or passed quality checks, leading to faster and more reliable releases.

Customer support feedback loops

Customer support is a crucial feedback loop for addressing real-time user issues, improving satisfaction, and identifying potential feature improvements or bugs. These loops can be set up as follows:

- **Integrate customer support platforms**: Use platforms like Zendesk, Intercom, or Freshdesk to gather and track user issues. Analyze support tickets for patterns or frequently occurring issues to prioritize fixes or new features.

- **Chatbots with feedback mechanisms**: Deploy chatbots for real-time support, ensuring that interactions are logged and analyzed for insights. After each interaction, ask users to rate the service, and use this feedback to improve chatbot performance.

- **User communities and forums**: Foster a community where users can provide feedback and help each other solve common problems. Actively monitor these forums for feedback and feature requests.

For example, a SaaS company can monitor customer support tickets for feedback on a new feature, identifying user pain points and adjusting the design based on recurring feedback from customers.

Security feedback loops

Security is an ongoing concern, and incorporating feedback loops to detect, respond, and adapt to potential threats is essential, and can be done as follows:

- **Real-time security monitoring**: Use SIEM tools like Splunk, QRadar, or ArcSight to monitor for security threats in real-time. Set up automated alerts and feedback loops for immediate response to potential breaches.

- **Penetration testing and ethical hacking**: Continuously perform penetration testing to identify vulnerabilities in your system. Implement a feedback loop where the findings are used to fix issues and improve security practices.

- **Automated security updates**: Ensure that security patches and updates are automatically deployed through feedback-driven mechanisms. Automate vulnerability scanning and ensure that systems are constantly up to date.

For example, an e-commerce platform can use a real-time security feedback loop where SIEM tools detect suspicious login patterns, triggering immediate alerts and potential blocking of accounts to prevent unauthorized access.

Integrating feedback loops into software development is crucial for continuous improvement, adaptation, and long-term success. Whether through user behavior analytics, system performance monitoring, or AI model retraining, feedback loops ensure that the software evolves in response to real-world usage and needs. By carefully designing these loops, you can make informed decisions, optimize operations, and provide better user experiences.

Conclusion

Software is evolving at a rapid pace and as software architect, it is important to keep up to date with the latest software trend. However, it is more than simply catering for these latest trends in your software design but also looking at how you can make your software future fit and adaptable to change. While also opening your software to regular feedback, so that you can adapt to change and innovation quicker.

In the next chapter, we will close out the book and provide a brief summary of points we learnt in this book, along with defining what makes a great architect and why software architecture plays such a critical role in software development.

Join our book's Discord space

Join the book's Discord Workspace for Latest updates, Offers, Tech happenings around the world, New Release and Sessions with the Authors:

https://discord.bpbonline.com

CHAPTER 18
Synthesizing Architectural Principles

Introduction

We hope you have enjoyed your journey into software architecture. In this concluding chapter, we will briefly look at some key highlights of the book and the importance of a software architect.

However, this book would not be complete if we did not go and visit the fantasy of Codeburg and see the last impact software architects have made to the kingdom.

A last return to Codeburg

As the last bug was vanquished and the great firewall of Codeburg stood tall and unbreached, the citizens of the kingdom rejoiced. Order had been restored, and chaos, the great scourge born from poor planning and hastily written code, was no longer a threat. Thanks to the wise architects who had woven the kingdom's future in the fabric of clean, scalable design, Codeburg flourished once more.

The architects' teachings became the foundation of the kingdom's prosperity, where code was not written in haste but with the care of a craftsman. The kingdom had learned a valuable lesson: without structure, even the grandest of castles would crumble, but with the right architecture, anything could be built to last.

In time, the wisdom of these architects became legend, passed down from one generation of developers to the next. The kingdom had been saved not by swords or spells, but by a deeper understanding of balance, foresight, and the enduring principles of good software design.

And so, as Codeburg continued to grow, the architects knew their work was never truly done, for in every new line of code, there was a spark of creativity, a chance to build something even greater. And in this ever-evolving world, the architects stood as the guardians of order, ensuring that Codeburg would forever thrive in the code they shaped.

The kingdom was saved, not just for today, but for all time.

Structure

This chapter will cover:

- Overview of the book
- What makes a great software architect?
- The importance of software architecture

Overview of the book

In this book, we have explored software architecture from a wide number of angles. We started off by defining the concept of software architecture, before looking at the crucial role the software architect plays in a team.

We then looked at some of the important foundation elements of software architecture by describing the different architectural properties, styles, patterns, and components in detail, and trying to provide some examples of how they are used in software today.

We then looked at how to architect software for performance and security, which are critical in our modern digital world, where the speed and security of our software are critical to its success.

We then looked at the design and presentation layer of software and the crucial role this plays in different software components working together. We also looked at the evolutionary nature of software architecture and how software needs to be adaptable to a rapidly evolving technology landscape.

We then focused on some of the other important non-technical skills that all architects need to possess, like soft skills that can help them become great leaders in their spaces and writing skills to ensure all technical requirements are properly communicated and implemented.

Lastly, we looked at a variety of practices in development, engineering, and testing space and how software architecture plays a role across all these disciplines, before closing out with a look at some of the emerging trends in the software world.

Hopefully, all these different topics have helped you develop a strong understanding of software architecture and how to look at it holistically across the software development landscape. Finding the balance between sufficiently explaining concepts in an easy manner, while still trying to provide a level of technical understanding has not been an easy one, but hopefully you have been able to master most of these concepts and where more information is needed, you have been able to research and dig even further on these topics.

Making a great software architect

In summary, a great software architect is a balanced individual who combines technical expertise with leadership, foresight, and a deep understanding of both people and business needs. Their ability to think strategically, communicate effectively, and continuously learn makes them invaluable to any engineering team.

The skills of a software architect:

- **Strong technical expertise**: A software architect must have deep technical knowledge across multiple domains, including software design patterns, system architecture, and various development frameworks. They should be proficient in coding and experienced in designing scalable, secure, and maintainable systems. This technical foundation enables them to make informed decisions and provide guidance to engineering teams.

- **Visionary and strategic thinker**: A great architect does not just focus on the present; they must be able to envision how the software will evolve and scale over time. They understand both the short-term and long-term needs of the business and design systems that align with the broader strategic goals. Their ability to anticipate future challenges, such as scaling or integrating new technologies, ensures the architecture remains relevant as the system grows.

- **Problem-solving and analytical skills**: Software architects often face complex challenges that require creative and thoughtful solutions. They need to analyze requirements, constraints, and trade-offs to design systems that meet business objectives. Being able to break down complex problems and provide clear, actionable solutions is key to their role.

- **Excellent communication skills**: One of the key responsibilities of an architect is to communicate complex technical concepts to both technical and non-technical stakeholders. They must explain the rationale behind architectural decisions in a way that resonates with engineers, product managers, and executives alike. This ensures that everyone is aligned and understands the technical direction.

- **Leadership and mentorship**: A great architect leads by example, guiding engineering teams not just by making decisions, but also by mentoring and fostering a collaborative environment. They help team members grow, encourage the adoption of best practices, and promote a culture of continuous improvement. Their leadership is often informal, inspiring teams through their expertise and actions rather than through formal authority.

- **Adaptability and lifelong learning**: The software landscape evolves rapidly, and a great architect is always learning. They stay updated with emerging trends, new tools, and evolving best practices. Adaptability is key, as the ability to pivot and incorporate new ideas keeps their designs future-proof and relevant in a fast-changing industry.

- **Empathy and collaboration**: Understanding the human side of software development is crucial. Architects must be empathetic toward the needs of end users, the challenges faced by developers, and the goals of the business. By collaborating effectively with cross-functional teams, including UX designers, product owners, and operations, they ensure that the architecture serves all stakeholders.

- **Attention to detail**: While software architects operate at a high level of abstraction, they also need to have a keen eye for detail. The smallest architectural decisions can have significant long-term effects, and understanding how individual components integrate within the larger system is essential.

- **Passion for quality**: Great architects are advocates for high standards and best practices. They champion the importance of testing, code quality, and security, ensuring that the systems they design are robust and reliable. They have a passion for delivering systems that not only meet business needs but also adhere to best practices for performance, maintainability, and reliability.

- **Business acumen**: A great software architect has a deep understanding of the business domain they are working in. They align technical decisions with business objectives, ensuring that their designs not only solve technical challenges but also contribute to the overall success and profitability of the organization.

The software architect forms one of the key roles of any software development effort and requires a person with a very diverse skillset.

The importance of software architecture

Software architecture forms the backbone of any application or system. It provides the foundational structure and high-level design that dictates how the system will perform, scale, and evolve. A well-crafted architecture ensures maintainability, scalability, security, and flexibility, allowing the system to grow alongside business needs. It also mitigates risks by identifying potential bottlenecks and inefficiencies early in the development process. Without solid architecture, systems become fragile and harder to adapt as requirements change.

Software architects bring value to engineering teams as they play a pivotal role in bridging the gap between business objectives and technical execution. They guide engineering teams by making strategic design decisions, ensuring alignment with both current and future business goals. Architects also foster collaboration, ensuring that teams are unified in their approach to system design. By offering a broad view of the system's architecture and its implications, they help engineering teams avoid technical debt and future-proof their work. Their experience and vision enable teams to navigate complex problems and deliver high-quality solutions efficiently.

The consequence of poor design

Poor software design leads to a host of problems, from decreased system performance to increased costs for maintenance and development. Over time, systems built on weak architectures become difficult to modify, riddled with bugs, and fragile in the face of change. This can result in frequent outages, security vulnerabilities, and technical debt that erodes team productivity and customer trust. The cost of fixing poor design after the fact far outweighs the investment in getting it right from the start. It is not just about the short-term gains but ensuring that the software remains viable and sustainable over the long haul.

Embracing lifelong learning

The field of software architecture is constantly evolving, and architects must embrace lifelong learning to stay relevant. New tools, paradigms, and methodologies emerge regularly, and an architect's ability to adapt and continuously improve their skills is crucial. Beyond technical knowledge, understanding evolving business needs, user expectations, and market trends allows architects to stay ahead. This commitment to learning ensures that architectural designs remain forward-looking, innovative, and aligned with industry's best practices.

Driving software delivery growth and innovation

Software architects are key drivers of innovation and growth within development teams. By setting a clear architectural vision, they enable teams to experiment with new technologies, methodologies, and approaches, fostering an environment where innovation thrives. Moreover, a well-thought-out architecture supports faster, more efficient software delivery, empowering teams to deliver features and updates at a rapid pace. Architects ensure that systems are designed with flexibility and scalability in mind, facilitating the organization's ability to meet growing demands and remain competitive in a fast-changing digital landscape.

Conclusion

Software architecture is not just about designing systems; it is about solving problems, enabling teams, and shaping the future of technology. As you continue on your journey, remember that architecture is a craft, one that requires continuous learning, adaptability, and a deep understanding of both technical and business needs.

You will face challenges, uncertainty, evolving requirements, and the pressure to balance scalability, performance, and maintainability. However, each challenge is an opportunity to grow. Embrace experimentation, seek feedback, and refine your designs iteratively. Great architects are not those who have all the answers, but those who know how to ask the right questions.

Surround yourself with a community of practitioners. Learn from the successes and failures of others, mentor those who come after you, and stay humble in your pursuit of knowledge. Technology will change, but the principles of good architecture, modularity, simplicity, and resilience will always hold true.

Most importantly, enjoy the journey. Software architecture is as much about creativity as it is about structure. Every system you design, every problem you solve, and every lesson you learn contributes to a larger vision. Keep building, keep improving, and never stop exploring the possibilities ahead.

Join our book's Discord space

Join the book's Discord Workspace for Latest updates, Offers, Tech happenings around the world, New Release and Sessions with the Authors:

https://discord.bpbonline.com

Appendix

The following are some additional resources that we formed a lot of the foundation of what you read in this book, and we would recommend reading if you want to learn more:

Books

The following are some important foundational books on the topic of software architecture that are worth reading, and many of the concepts in this book are influenced by.

Foundational books

Software Architecture in Practice

- **Authors**: *Len Bass, Paul Clements*, and *Rick Kazman*
- **Publisher**: *Addison-Wesley Professional*
- **Published**: 2012 (3rd Edition)
- This book covers the essential principles and practices of software architecture with a focus on real-world examples.

The Software Architect Elevator: Redefining the Architect's Role in the Digital Enterprise

- **Author**: *Gregor Hohpe*

- **Publisher**: *O'Reilly Media*

- **Published**: 2020

- *Gregor Hohpe* explores the evolving role of software architects, focusing on digital transformation and strategic influence within enterprises.

Designing Software Architectures: A Practical Approach

- **Authors**: *Humberto Cervantes* and *Rick Kazman*

- **Publisher**: *Addison-Wesley Professional*

- **Published**: 2016

- A practical, hands-on guide to designing software architectures using a systematic approach.

Modern architecture and best practices

Building Evolutionary Architectures: Support Constant Change

- **Authors**: *Neal Ford, Rebecca Parsons,* and *Patrick Kua*

- **Publisher**: *O'Reilly Media*

- **Published**: 2017

- This book explains how to create architectures that can evolve alongside changing business and technical needs.

Clean Architecture: A Craftsman's Guide to Software Structure and Design

- **Author**: *Robert C. Martin (Uncle Bob)*

- **Publisher**: *Prentice Hall*

- **Published**: 2017

- A pragmatic guide to designing flexible and maintainable software architectures, drawing from SOLID principles.

Software Architecture: The Hard Parts

- **Authors**: *Neal Ford, Mark Richards, Pramod Sadalage,* and *Zhamak Dehghani*

- **Publisher**: *O'Reilly Media*

- **Published**: 2021

- This book addresses tough architectural decisions and trade-offs, especially in the context of modern architectures like microservices and distributed systems.

Patterns and styles

Pattern-Oriented Software Architecture: A System of Patterns

- **Authors**: *Frank Buschmann, Regine Meunier, Hans Rohnert, Peter Sommerlad,* and *Michael Stal*

- **Publisher**: *Wiley*

- **Published**: 1996

- A deep dive into software design patterns, offering a catalog of patterns for recurring architectural challenges.

Enterprise Integration Patterns: Designing, Building, and Deploying Messaging Solutions

- **Authors**: *Gregor Hohpe* and *Bobby Woolf*

- **Publisher**: *Addison-Wesley Professional*

- **Published**: 2003

- Essential for architects working with integration and messaging systems, this book covers reusable patterns for enterprise systems.

Domain-specific and specialized

Microservices Patterns: With Examples in Java

- **Author**: *Chris Richardson*

- **Publisher**: *Manning Publications*

- **Published**: 2018

- Focused on microservices architecture, this book explores practical patterns for building and deploying microservices systems.

Domain-Driven Design: Tackling Complexity in the Heart of Software

- **Author**: *Eric Evans*

- **Publisher**: *Addison-Wesley Professional*

- **Published**: 2003

- A foundational work on modeling complex business domains in software, offering a comprehensive approach to **domain-driven design** (**DDD**).

Practical and case studies

The Art of Scalability: Scalable Web Architecture, Processes, and Organizations for the Modern Enterprise

- **Authors**: *Martin L. Abbott* and *Michael T. Fisher*
- **Publisher**: *Addison-Wesley Professional*
- **Published**: 2015 (2nd Edition)
- A practical guide to scaling software systems and organizations, with a focus on processes and patterns for large-scale solutions.

Architecting for Scale: High Availability for Your Growing Applications

- **Author**: *Lee Atchison*
- **Publisher**: *O'Reilly Media*
- **Published**: 2020 (2nd Edition)
- This book covers how to design systems that scale while maintaining high availability, reliability, and operational resilience.

Agile and architecture in context

Continuous Delivery: Reliable Software Releases through Build, Test, and Deployment Automation

- **Authors**: *Jez Humble* and *David Farley*
- **Publisher**: *Addison-Wesley Professional*
- **Published**: 2010
- A crucial book for architects designing systems with continuous delivery in mind, focusing on automation and rapid feedback loops.

Fundamentals of Software Architecture: An Engineering Approach

- **Authors**: *Mark Richards* and *Neal Ford*
- **Publisher**: *O'Reilly Media*
- **Published**: 2020
- A comprehensive guide that covers architecture patterns, trade-offs, and real-world issues, offering practical guidance for making informed architectural decisions.

Bonus

Refactoring: Improving the Design of Existing Code

- **Author**: *Martin Fowler*
- **Publisher**: *Addison-Wesley Professional*
- **Published**: 2018 (2nd Edition)

- While not exclusively about architecture, this book is invaluable for improving the structure of existing codebases and ensuring they are adaptable and maintainable.

Important blogs and websites

Here is a list of popular blogs that cover software architecture, providing a mix of deep technical insights, best practices, and industry trends:

Martin Fowler's Blog

- **Author**: *Martin Fowler*

- **URL**: **https://martinfowler.com/**

- **Overview**: *Martin Fowler*, a renowned software architect and author, covers topics related to software architecture, refactoring, microservices, and continuous delivery. His blog is a valuable resource for practical advice on architecture patterns, design principles, and clean code practices.

ThoughtWorks Technology Radar

- **Authors**: *ThoughtWorks Technology Advisory Board*

- **URL**: **https://www.thoughtworks.com/radar**

- **Overview**: Published quarterly, this blog highlights emerging technology trends and architectural patterns. *ThoughtWorks* is known for its work on microservices, evolutionary architectures, and continuous delivery, making it a key resource for architects staying up-to-date with modern practices.

InfoQ Architecture

- **Authors**: Various contributors (industry experts)

- **URL**: **https://www.infoq.com/architecture/**

- **Overview**: *InfoQ* offers in-depth articles, interviews, and case studies on software architecture topics, including microservices, event-driven systems, DevOps, and cloud architecture. The content is often written by industry thought leaders and experienced practitioners.

High Scalability

- **Author**: *Todd Hoff*

- **URL**: **https://highscalability.com/**

- **Overview**: Focuses on building systems that scale, covering real-world architecture patterns and case studies from companies like *Netflix*, *Amazon*, and *Google*. It is a valuable resource for learning how large-scale systems are designed and operated.

Architect Elevator Blog

- **Author**: *Gregor Hohpe*

- **URL**: **https://architectelevator.com/**

- **Overview**: *Gregor Hohpe* writes about the evolving role of software architects in large organizations, especially in the context of digital transformation and cloud computing. He focuses on strategic thinking, system architecture, and leadership in architecture roles.

The Practical Dev (DEV.to)

- **Authors**: Community of developers and architects

- **URL**: **https://dev.to/t/softwarearchitecture**

- **Overview**: *DEV.to* is a community-driven platform where architects and developers share their experiences, insights, and best practices. It offers a wide range of articles on various aspects of software architecture, from cloud-native design to architectural patterns.

Herbert's Dev Blog

- **Author**: *Udi Dahan*

- **URL**: **https://udidahan.com/**

- **Overview**: *Udi Dahan* is a thought leader in **service-oriented architecture (SOA)** and the founder of NServiceBus. His blog focuses on distributed systems, event-driven architectures, and best practices for building scalable systems.

The Netflix Tech Blog

- **Authors**: Netflix engineering team

- **URL**: **https://netflixtechblog.com/**

- **Overview**: *Netflix* is known for its cutting-edge architectural innovations, especially in microservices, resilience engineering, and cloud-native systems. Their tech blog offers deep dives into the architectural patterns, tools, and approaches they use to scale their platform.

Simon Brown's Coding the Architecture

- **Author**: *Simon Brown*

- **URL**: **https://simonbrown.je/**

- **Overview**: *Simon Brown* is the creator of the C4 model for software architecture visualization. His blog focuses on architectural modeling, design techniques, and bridging the gap between developers and architects.

Microsoft Architecture Blog

- **Authors**: Microsoft architects and developers

- **URL**: **https://devblogs.microsoft.com/architecture**

- **Overview**: This blog provides guidance on cloud architecture, distributed systems, and best practices for building applications on the Azure platform. It covers architectural patterns, real-world implementations, and cloud-native design principles.

The Rabid Application Developer Blog (Vagif Abilov)

- **Author**: *Vagif Abilov*

- **URL**: **https://rabdullin.com/**

- **Overview**: *Vagif* writes about real-world architecture challenges, particularly in distributed systems, event sourcing, and functional programming. His blog is a practical resource for architects working with complex systems.

IBM Developer Blog: Architecture

- **Authors**: *IBM* developers and architects

- **URL**: **https://developer.ibm.com/architecture**

- **Overview**: IBM blog covers enterprise-level architecture patterns, cloud-native solutions, AI integration, and blockchain. It is a useful resource for architects working in enterprise environments with complex, legacy, or hybrid systems.

NGINX Blog

- **Authors**: *NGINX* engineering team and contributors

- **URL**: **https://www.f5.com/company/blog**

- **Overview**: While focused on web performance, security, and scaling, the NGINX blog offers valuable content on software architecture topics like microservices, service mesh, and load balancing strategies, with practical guides for architects working with distributed systems.

Adrian Colyer's Blog: The Morning Paper

- **Author**: *Adrian Colyer*

- **URL**: **http://www.acolyer.org/**

- **Overview**: *Adrian Colyer* summarizes academic papers on software engineering, systems architecture, and distributed systems. It's a great resource for architects looking to stay up-to-date with cutting-edge research and innovations in software architecture.

These blogs provide a wealth of knowledge, from foundational architectural principles to the latest trends in software engineering. They are an excellent way to stay informed and continuously learn about software architecture.

Tools and frameworks

There are several tools and frameworks that are incredibly useful for software architects, helping with design, documentation, collaboration, decision-making, and system management. Here is a categorized list:

Design and modeling tools

These tools help architects visualize and model the system architecture, making it easier to communicate design decisions to stakeholders.

- **Enterprise Architect (by Sparx Systems)**
  - **Purpose**: UML modeling, business process modeling, and system design.
  - **Why it is useful**: Provides comprehensive support for UML, SysML, BPMN, and other notations. Helps architects model, design, and manage complex systems.

- **Lucidchart**
  - **Purpose**: Online diagramming tool for architecture visualization.
  - **Why it is useful**: Great for creating flowcharts, UML diagrams, network architecture, and other system models. Collaborative and easy to use with real-time editing.

- **Draw.io (diagrams.net)**
  - **Purpose**: Open-source diagramming tool for system and architecture diagrams.
  - **Why it is useful**: Free and easy to use for creating flowcharts, network diagrams, and system architecture blueprints.

- **C4 Model**
  - **Purpose**: A lightweight approach to visualizing software architecture.
  - **Why it is useful**: Helps architects create clear, hierarchical diagrams using context, containers, components, and code diagrams. Promotes simplicity and readability.

- **ArchiMate (by Open Group)**
  - **Purpose**: An open standard for enterprise architecture modeling.

    o **Why it is useful**: It provides a high-level, conceptual view of enterprise architectures, helping architects model, analyze, and document complex systems.

Documentation tools

Documentation is critical for communicating architectural decisions and maintaining system understanding over time.

- **Confluence**

  o **Purpose**: Wiki-based collaboration platform.

  o **Why it is useful**: Widely used for documenting architecture decisions, specifications, and design rationales. Allows teams to collaborate and access documentation easily.

- **Architecture Decision Records (ADR)**

  o **Purpose**: A lightweight framework for documenting architecture decisions.

  o **Why it is useful**: Encourages clear and concise documentation of key architectural decisions, helping architects track reasoning and design choices.

- **Markdown**

  o **Purpose**: Lightweight markup language for formatting text.

  o **Why it is useful**: Popular for writing ADRs and technical documentation due to its simplicity and integration with many documentation platforms like GitHub and GitLab.

Architecture decision tools

These tools help software architects make, manage, and document decisions in an organized way.

- **Structurizr**

  o **Purpose**: Web-based architecture modeling tool based on the C4 model.

  o **Why it is useful**: Allows architects to create architecture diagrams as code, using various programming languages. It integrates with existing documentation systems.

- **ADR Tools**

  o **Purpose**: Command-line tools for managing ADRs.

  o **Why it is useful**: Helps software architects record, manage, and retrieve key architectural decisions efficiently.

Prototyping and design validation

These tools help architects validate design decisions through prototyping, simulation, or analysis of different scenarios.

- **AWS Well-Architected Tool**

    o **Purpose**: Helps architects review and improve cloud-based architecture.

    o **Why it is useful**: Provides guidance on best practices for building secure, high-performing, and cost-effective applications on AWS.

- **Terraform**

    o **Purpose: Infrastructure as code (IaC)** tool.

    o **Why it is useful**: Enables architects to define cloud infrastructure in code, which helps in testing, automating, and versioning architecture setups.

- **Azure Architecture Center**

    o **Purpose**: Best practices, guidelines, and reference architectures for cloud solutions on Microsoft Azure.

    o **Why it is useful**: Offers templates, reference architectures, and decision guides for building cloud-native architectures on Azure.

- **Puppet, Chef, and Ansible**

    o **Purpose**: Configuration management and automation tools.

    o **Why it is useful**: Useful for architects designing automated, repeatable infrastructure setups, especially for DevOps and cloud-based systems.

Cloud and infrastructure tools

Architects working on cloud solutions need tools that can manage and optimize infrastructure.

- **Kubernetes**

    o **Purpose**: Container orchestration platform.

    o **Why it is useful**: Helps architects design scalable, fault-tolerant microservices architectures, automating deployment, scaling, and operations of application containers.

- **Docker**

    o **Purpose**: Platform for developing, shipping, and running containerized applications.

- o **Why it is useful**: Allows architects to create reproducible environments and define software components in containers, streamlining testing and deployment.

- **CloudFormation (AWS)**

  - o **Purpose**: IaC tool for AWS.

  - o **Why it is useful**: Allows architects to define AWS resources in code, ensuring consistent deployment and management of infrastructure.

- **Prometheus and Grafana**

  - o **Purpose**: Monitoring and alerting toolkit (Prometheus), visualization dashboard (Grafana).

  - o **Why it is useful**: These tools are essential for monitoring distributed systems and microservices architectures, providing insights into system health and performance.

Collaboration tools

Collaboration is vital for software architects to communicate effectively with engineering teams and stakeholders.

- **Miro**

  - o **Purpose**: Online whiteboarding tool for collaboration.

  - o **Why it is useful**: Helps software architects brainstorm, plan system architectures, and collaborate with teams in real time on visual designs.

- **Slack**

  - o **Purpose**: Messaging and collaboration platform.

  - o **Why it is useful**: Allows architects to collaborate with engineers, product managers, and other stakeholders through integrated communication, documentation, and code-sharing.

- **Jira**

  - o **Purpose**: Project management tool, commonly used with Agile development teams.

  - o **Why it is useful**: Helps architects track the progress of system implementation and manage technical debt, ensuring alignment with the architectural vision.

Performance and reliability tools

Architects need to ensure that their systems are performant, scalable, and reliable.

- **Blazemeter**

    o **Purpose**: Continuous testing and performance monitoring platform.

    o **Why it is useful**: Allows architects to simulate load testing and ensure that their architecture can scale to meet demand.

- **New Relic and Datadog**

    o **Purpose**: Monitoring and observability platforms.

    o **Why it is useful**: These tools give architects deep insights into the performance of their applications and infrastructure, helping them identify bottlenecks and optimize system performance.

- **Chaos Monkey (Netflix)**

    o **Purpose**: Tool for testing system resilience by randomly terminating instances in production.

    o **Why it is useful**: Helps architects ensure that their systems are resilient to failure by proactively testing robustness under real-world conditions.

Code analysis and quality tools

Ensuring the quality of the code and the architectural integrity is a crucial aspect of software architecture.

- **SonarQube**

    o **Purpose**: Continuous code quality inspection tool.

    o **Why it is useful**: Helps architects enforce coding standards, spot bugs, and identify technical debt early in the development cycle.

- **ESLint and TSLint**

    o **Purpose**: Static code analysis tools for JavaScript or TypeScript.

    o **Why it is useful**: Ensures that coding best practices are adhered to, which contributes to maintainability and consistency in system architecture.

Architectural frameworks

- **The Open Group Architecture Framework (TOGAF)**

    o **Purpose**: A high-level framework for enterprise architecture.

o **Why it is useful**: Provides a structured approach for designing, planning, implementing, and governing enterprise architecture.

- **Scaled Agile Framework (SAFe)**

    o **Purpose**: Framework for scaling Agile across large organizations.

    o **Why it is useful**: Guides architects in scaling architecture practices across large teams in Agile environments, ensuring alignment between technical and business goals.

These tools and frameworks provide software architects with a comprehensive toolkit to design, document, collaborate, and manage software systems effectively. They enable modern practices like cloud architecture, DevOps, automation, and Agile methodologies, ensuring that systems are scalable, maintainable, and aligned with business objectives.

Glossary

Here is a comprehensive glossary of essential terms and acronyms that every software architect should be familiar with. This glossary covers architectural patterns, methodologies, and technologies that are vital to the role of a software architect.

A

- **Application programming interface (API)**: A set of rules that allow different software entities to communicate with each other, typically over the web.

- **Agile**: A software development methodology focused on iterative progress, collaboration, and flexibility in responding to change.

- **Amazon Web Services (AWS)**: A cloud computing platform provided by Amazon that offers infrastructure services like storage, computing power, and databases.

- **Architecture Decision Record (ADR)**: A lightweight method for recording key architectural decisions in a format that is easy to understand and maintain.

B

- **Business Process Model and Notation (BPMN)**: A graphical representation for specifying business processes in a business process model.

- **Blueprint**: A high-level design of a system's architecture, providing a visual or conceptual framework that guides implementation.

- **Bounded context**: A concept in **domain-driven design** (DDD) that refers to the boundaries within which a particular model applies. It helps separate parts of a system into distinct areas with well-defined interfaces.

C

- **CAP (consistency, availability, partition tolerance) Theorem**: A principle that states it is impossible for a distributed data store to simultaneously provide all three guarantees.

- **Continuous integration/continuous deployment (CI/CD)**: Practices that automate software testing, integration, and deployment to enable rapid releases of code.

- **Cloud-native**: An approach to building and running applications that leverage cloud services and infrastructure, designed to scale and adapt dynamically.

- **Command Query Responsibility Segregation (CQRS)**: A design pattern that separates reading data (query) and writing data (command) operations into distinct models to optimize performance, scalability, and security.

- **C4 model**: A visual framework for software architecture that organizes system diagrams into four layers: context, container, component, and code.

D

- **Domain-driven design (DDD)**: A methodology that emphasizes aligning software design with the core business domain. It advocates breaking systems into bounded contexts with rich domain models.

- **DevOps**: A set of practices that integrate software **development (Dev)** and IT **operations (Ops)** to improve efficiency, shorten the system development life cycle, and deliver high-quality software continuously.

- **Docker**: A platform for developing, shipping, and running applications in containers, making it easier to manage dependencies and improve portability across environments.

E

- **Event-driven architecture (EDA)**: A software architecture pattern that uses events to trigger actions or communicate between decoupled services.

- **Enterprise Architect (EA)**: A role or a tool focusing on the strategic design of an organization's technology infrastructure and the alignment of IT assets with business goals.

- **Event sourcing**: A design pattern in which state changes are stored as a sequence of events rather than current state snapshots.

F

- **Fault tolerance**: The ability of a system to continue operating properly in the event of the failure of one or more of its components.

- **Function as a service (FaaS)**: A cloud computing model that allows developers to deploy individual functions (small units of work) in the cloud. It is the foundation of serverless architectures.

G

- **Garbage collection (GC)**: An automatic memory management feature in programming languages like Java and C#, which reclaims memory that is no longer in use by the program.

- **GraphQL**: A query language for APIs that allows clients to request only the data they need, improving efficiency in data communication.

H

- **High Availability (HA)**: A system design pattern that ensures a system is continuously operational and minimizes downtime.

- **Horizontal scaling**: The process of adding more machines or nodes to a system to handle increased load, commonly used in distributed architectures.

I

- **Infrastructure as a service (IaaS)**: A cloud computing service that provides virtualized computing resources over the internet, such as AWS, Azure, and **Google Cloud Platform (GCP)**.

- **Idempotence**: A property of an operation in which executing it multiple times produces the same result as executing it once, crucial for ensuring reliable system behavior.

K

- **Kubernetes (K8s)**: An open-source platform for automating deployment, scaling, and management of containerized applications.

- **Kafka**: A distributed event streaming platform used for high-throughput, low-latency message-driven architectures.

L

- **Load balancing**: The process of distributing network or application traffic across multiple servers to improve reliability, availability, and performance.

M

- **Microservices**: A software architectural style in which applications are structured as loosely coupled services that are independently deployable and scalable.

- **Monolith**: A traditional software architecture where the entire application is built as a single, unified codebase.

- **Message queue (MQ)**: A communication method that allows decoupled systems to exchange messages asynchronously.

N

- **NoSQL**: A class of database management systems that does not adhere strictly to relational database models, allowing for more flexible data storage and retrieval.

- **Non-functional requirements (NFR)**: Requirements that define the performance, security, usability, reliability, and other non-functional aspects of a system.

O

- **OAuth**: An open-standard authorization framework that allows third-party services to access user data without exposing credentials.

- **OpenAPI**: A specification for building and documenting RESTful APIs, formerly known as Swagger.

P

- **Platform as a service (PaaS)**: A cloud computing service that provides a platform allowing customers to develop, run, and manage applications without dealing with the underlying infrastructure.

- **Polyglot persistence**: The use of different types of databases (relational, NoSQL, etc.) for different parts of an application, depending on the specific requirements of each component.

- **Publish-Subscribe (Pub/Sub)**: A messaging pattern where messages are broadcast by a publisher and received by subscribers, useful in decoupled architectures.

R

- **Representational State Transfer (REST)**: An architectural style for designing networked applications. REST APIs are stateless and communicate over HTTP using standard methods (GET, POST, PUT, DELETE).

- **Resilience**: The ability of a system to handle and recover from faults, disruptions, and unexpected conditions.

S

- **Service-oriented architecture (SOA)**: An architectural pattern where services provide reusable, business-focused functionality through well-defined interfaces.

- **Service level agreement (SLA)**: A contract that defines the expected performance and availability levels of a system or service.

- **Software as a service (SaaS)**: A cloud computing model where software applications are delivered over the internet and accessed via a web browser.

- **Scalability**: The ability of a system to handle increased load by expanding its capacity (horizontally or vertically).

T

- **The Open Group Architecture Framework (TOGAF)**: A widely used framework for enterprise architecture that provides methods and tools for designing and managing a broad range of systems.

- **Test-driven development (TDD)**: A development process where tests are written before the code itself, ensuring that the code is designed to meet specific requirements.

U

- **Unified Modeling Language (UML)**: A standardized modeling language used to specify, visualize, and document the components and behavior of a system.

- **Usability**: A non-functional requirement that ensures software is easy to use and intuitive for end users.

V

- **Vertical scaling**: Increasing the capacity of a single machine (e.g., adding more CPU or memory) to handle a greater load, typically used in monolithic systems.

- **Version control**: A system that manages changes to source code over time, commonly used in software development to track changes and enable collaboration (e.g., Git).

W

- **Waterfall**: A traditional software development methodology where each phase (e.g., requirements, design, implementation) must be completed before moving on to the next.

Y

- **YAML Ain't Markup Language (YAML)**: A human-readable data serialization format, often used in configuration files for tools like Kubernetes and Ansible.

Z

- **Zero downtime**: The ability to deploy or update a system without interrupting its availability or service.

This glossary includes a mix of architectural concepts, development practices, cloud terminology, and more. It provides software architects with a strong foundation to communicate effectively, design robust systems, and manage the complexity of modern software environments.

Join our book's Discord space

Join the book's Discord Workspace for Latest updates, Offers, Tech happenings around the world, New Release and Sessions with the Authors:

https://discord.bpbonline.com

Index